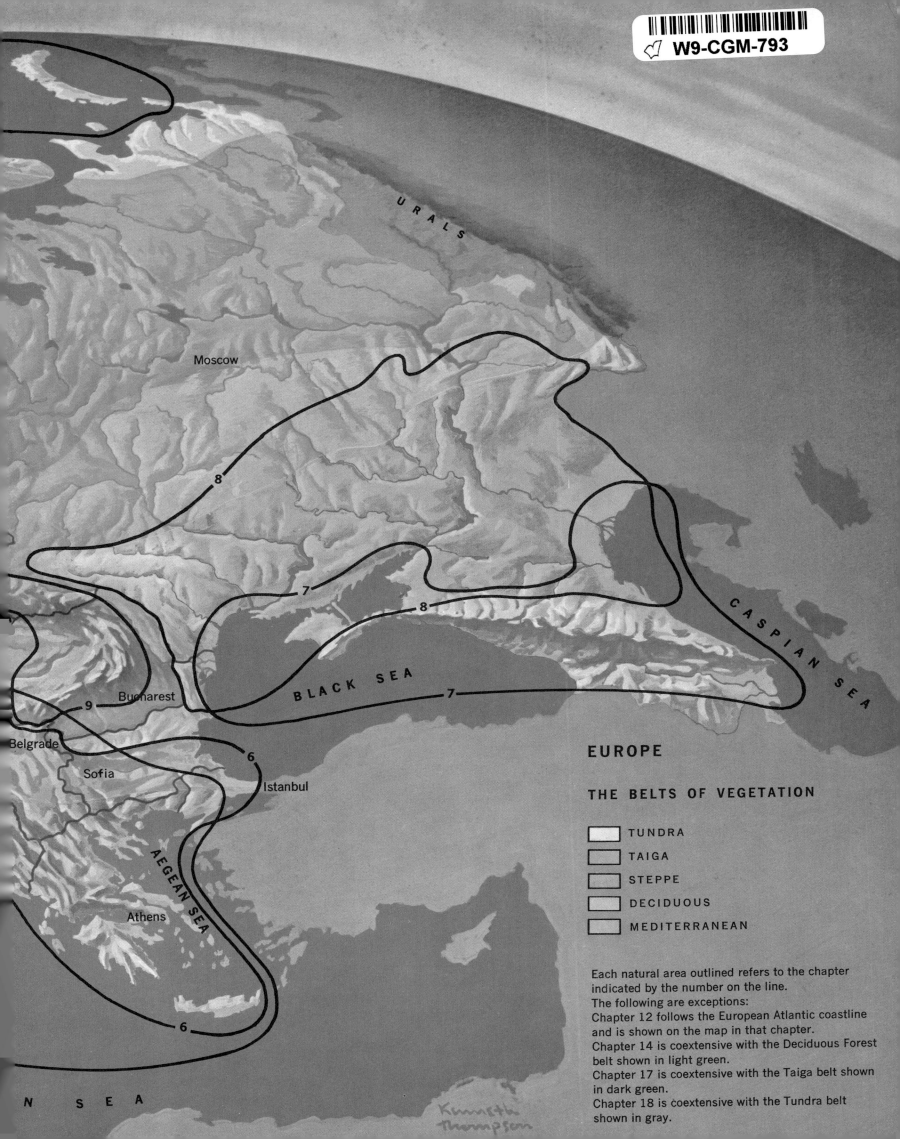

URALS

Moscow

CASPIAN SEA

BLACK SEA

8

7

8

7

9

Bucharest

Belgrade

Sofia

6

Istanbul

AEGEAN SEA

Athens

6

N SEA

EUROPE

THE BELTS OF VEGETATION

TUNDRA

TAIGA

STEPPE

DECIDUOUS

MEDITERRANEAN

Each natural area outlined refers to the chapter
indicated by the number on the line.
The following are exceptions:
Chapter 12 follows the European Atlantic coastline
and is shown on the map in that chapter.
Chapter 14 is coextensive with the Deciduous Forest
belt shown in light green.
Chapter 17 is coextensive with the Taiga belt shown
in dark green.
Chapter 18 is coextensive with the Tundra belt
shown in gray.

Kenneth
Thompson

EUROPE

Photographs by

Julius Behnke, Germany

René Pierre Bille, Switzerland

Sven Gillsater, Sweden

B. Gippenreiter, U.S.S.R.

Ingmar Holmåsen, Sweden

Jaroslav Holoček, Czechoslovakia

Eric Hosking, England

Gerhard Klammet, Germany

Pepi Merisio, Italy

Josef Muench, U.S.A.

Erich Sochurek, Austria

Teuvo Suominen, Finland

Michel Terrasse, France

Z. Z. Vinogradov, U.S.S.R.

and others

Maps drawn by Kenneth Thompson

EU

A Chanticleer Press Edition

The Continents We Live On

ROPE

A NATURAL HISTORY

Kai Curry-Lindahl

Random House · New York

Planned and produced by Chanticleer Press, New York

Manufactured by Conzett & Huber in Zurich, Switzerland

Library of Congress Catalog Card Number 64:20042

Contents

Foreword

Over millions of years the landscape of Europe has changed constantly. Mountain chains were formed, vast sheets of ice imprisoned the earth, rivers wore their way to the sea, immense deltas were built up, steppes and forests waxed and waned. A continent has been created by inconceivably gigantic natural forces. Compared to the long life of Europe, man has been in existence for only a very short time. But in that time he has shaped not only the continent of Europe but the whole earth—an incredible achievement.

During the last century in particular the landscape of Europe has been altered most violently. A book on the natural history of Europe today cannot help noting the havoc wrought by man on this continent. Nevertheless, an astonishing amount of free and wild nature still remains. What is tragic is that these enclaves of living nature are almost all threatened by man and are becoming more and more scarce. It is necessary to preserve such areas as marshes, lakes and rivers, shores, steppes and forests because they are of inestimable esthetic, recreational, educational, economic and scientific importance to mankind.

During recent years several international organizations have fought for the conservation of such areas and a better understanding of ecological principles. They include UNESCO, the International Union for Conservation of Nature and Natural Resources (IUCN), the World Wildlife Fund (WWF), the International Council for Bird Preservation (ICBP), the International Wildfowl Research Bureau (IWRB), and the Council of Europe's Committee of Experts for Conservation of Nature and Landscape. Among organizations acting on a national level, Great Britain's Nature Conservancy deserves special mention because it has been an inspiration to conservationists all over Europe.

This book tries in pictures and text to describe the nature of Europe as it is today. Special attention has been paid to areas particularly interesting for their wealth of plants and animals, but of course other regions have not been neglected. A popular book on the natural history of a continent cannot, of course, be thorough; for that we should need a shelf of volumes. Many groups of plants and animals, as well as geological formations, have had to be omitted or mentioned only in passing. Among animals, the emphasis has been on verte-brates, whereas, for instance, the insects and other invertebrates—despite their abundance and the great role they play in biocommunities—are mentioned more or less incidentally. The seas surrounding the continent have also not been dealt with, though marine life comes into the picture in connection with coasts and islands.

There is some controversy as to where in the Caucasus the boundary between Europe and Asia lies (see Chapter 7). This was of more than theoretical interest for me, for I had to know the limits of the region I was describing. I finally decided to include the whole of the Caucasus down to the river Kura in Georgia.

Europe exhibits many climates and vegetation regions, ranging from the subtropical Mediterranean to the Arctic islands. This book is arranged according to biogeographic and ecological areas, beginning in the south, which never underwent glaciation and where animals and man have been active longer than elsewhere on the continent. From the Mediterranean we move northward, through forests, steppes and tundras to Europe's Arctic outposts. Such a division ignores the political boundaries of the various European countries.

The scientific (Latin) name of a species has, in general, been given only the first time a plant or an animal is mentioned. For the convenience of the reader, however, such a name has sometimes been repeated in a later chapter.

Many voyages, journeys and expeditions in various parts of Europe had given me numerous firsthand impressions of the continent. There were however still some areas that I wished to visit, or revisit, because there is no substitute for personal experience of living nature. Journeys especially for this book were therefore made to Great Britain, Ireland, Germany, Switzerland, France, Spain, Rumania and the U.S.S.R.

A generous invitation from the Academy of Sciences of the U.S.S.R. to be its guest for a month enabled me to make excursions through vast areas of the Soviet Union. I wish to express my gratitude to Academician, Professor I. P. Guerassimov, Director of the Institute of Geography of the Academy of Sciences in Moscow, and his associates, who arranged to have all doors to Russian nature reserves and research stations opened to me. I am indebted to Dr. L. Serebryanny, my companion and interpreter, for his great patience during our daily excursions. It is also my pleasure to acknowledge the assistance of the following scientists: Professor A. G. Bannikov, Moscow; Professor G. P. Dementiev, Moscow; Dr. N. Dzibuti, Batumi; Dr. V. I. Eliseeva, Selichovy Dvory, Kursk; Professor A. N. Formozov, Moscow; Dr. O. O. Guerassimova, Moscow; Professor N. A. Gladkov, Moscow; Professor W. G. Heptner, Moscow; Dr. K. S. Gogishvile, Tiflis; Professor J. A. Isakov, Moscow; Dr. R. G. Jordania, Tiflis; Dr. M. E. Kutubidse, Tiflis; Professor L. A. Portenko, Leningrad, and Professor D. Ryabchikov, Moscow.

In Rumania, the government, the Academy of Science of Rumania and the universities of Bucharest and Iasi gave me invaluable assistance, procuring a vessel and a crew for an expedition into the Danube delta and an automobile for an excursion into the Carpathians. Several scientists spared no effort to enable me to visit regions and nature reserves otherwise closed to visitors. I am especially indebted to Professor M. Ionescu Varo, Director of the Museum of Natural History, Bucharest, Professor Valer Puscariu, Secretary of the Committee for Conservation of Nature of the Academy of Sciences, Bucharest, and Professor Stefan Vancea, University of Iasi.

Other participants in the Danube delta expedition were Professor B. Banarescu, Iasi; Mr. N. Constantiu, Bucharest; Dr. I. Fuhn, Bucharest; Dr. M. Talpeanu, Bucharest and Dr. W. B. Ziemiankowski, Maliuc. I also wish to acknowledge the help of Professor C. Motas, Bucharest, and Professor L. Rudescu, Bucharest.

My gratitude goes to Dr. L. Hoffmann, Director of the Station Biologique de la Tour du Valat in the Camargue, France, and to Dr. J. A. Valverde, Consejo Superior de Investigaciones Cientificas, Madrid, for their cooperation during my visits to the Camargue in France and to the Coto Doñana and Las Marismas in Spain. Scientists of the Nature Conservancy, Aberdeen University and the Scottish Centre for Ornithology, were most helpful during my travels in Scotland. I want to thank particularly Dr. D. Jenkins of Blackhall, Dr. E. Dunnet of Newburgh, Mr. G. Waterston of Edinburgh, and Professor V. C. Wynne-Edwards of Aberdeen.

The immense task of mobilizing the top nature photographers of Europe as well as organizing the pictures for this book was carried out by Mrs. Jean I. Tennant of Chanticleer Press. I cannot satisfactorily express my thanks to Mrs. Tennant for assembling such a wealth of photographs for our selection. The collaboration with her was always a pleasure to me.

I am also deeply grateful for having had the privilege of working with Dr. Milton Rugoff of Chanticleer Press. He had the arduous task of editing the manuscript and revising it in terms of language and expression. He showed the greatest patience and was an inspiring help to me.

For helping me with the translation and with linguistic problems I am indebted to Mr. Lorimer Moe of the U.S. Embassy in Stockholm and Mr. Albert Read, also of Stockholm.

My deep gratitude is also due to the following experts, who were kind enough to read drafts of various chapters or subchapters: Professor P. Banarescu, Rumania; Professor N. Botnariuc, Rumania; Professor S. Caransu, Rumania; Dr. A. W. Colling, Great Britain; Dr. J. Dorst, France; Professor G. E. Du Rietz, Sweden; Dr. B. Ferens, Poland; Dr. I. Fuhn, Rumania; Dr. F. Gudmundsson, Iceland; Professor J.-P. Harroy, Belgium; Dr. L. Hoffmann, France; Director H. Holgersen. Norway; Professor J. A. Isakov, U.S.S.R.; Professor T. Jaczewski, Poland; Dr. D. Jenkins, Great Britain; Dr. A. Keve, Hungary; Professor S. V. Kirikov, U.S.S.R.; Professor J. Kratochvil, Czechoslovakia; Professor K. Krysiak, Poland; Dr. A. Kuster, Switzerland; Professor L. Machura, Austria; Professor A. A. Nasimovich, U.S.S.R.; Dr. A. Noirfalise, Belgium; Dr. H. Offner, Germany; Dr. J. C. Ondrias, Greece; Professor M. Pavan, Italy; Professor V. Puscariu, Rumania; Dr. F. Roux, France; Major J. B. Ruttledge, Ireland; Dr. F. Salomonsen, Denmark; Dr. L. Serebryanny, U.S.S.R.; Professor H. Sjors, Sweden; Dr. M. Talpeanu, Rumania; Professor A. Toschi, Italy; Dr. J. A. Valverde, Spain; Professor S. Vancea, Rumania; Professor K. H. Voous, Holland, and Dr. E. B. Worthington, Great Britain.

Finally, I would like to express my indebtedness to a great number of naturalists for their good companionship during my travels in Europe during the past twenty-five years. They are too numerous to be named here. I look back with great pleasure on time spent in the field with these people, who shared with me so much of their knowledge and experience.

If this book can contribute to an increased appreciation of the natural treasures of Europe and the need to preserve them for mankind I shall be very happy.

KAI CURRY-LINDAHL

What is Europe?

1 Surprising as it may at first seem, Europe is a peninsula attached to the largest continent in the world, the enormous land mass of Asia. Considered as a peninsula, it is huge, stretching westward to the Atlantic and bounded in the south by the Mediterranean and in the north by the Arctic Ocean.

But Europe has other distinctive features that are not so easily recognized. Its shoreline contrasts with the relatively unbroken coast of neighboring Africa, since it is marked by seas alternating with narrow fjords, by wide bays that penetrate deep into the land, and by vast archipelagos. The peninsula is itself rich in peninsulas. Indeed, about half of it consists of such extensions: the Kola peninsula and the Scandinavian peninsula in the north, Brittany in the west, and the Iberian, Italian and Balkan peninsulas in the south. These give Europe, in proportion to its area, a longer coastline than any other continent.

The most striking fact about Europe as a continent is its small size—about 3,900,000 square miles, which is only slightly more than Canada's 3,851,800 square miles and only a small fraction of the Soviet Union's 8,599,000 square miles. The only continent that is smaller is Australia. Yet Europe does not seem small when its size is expressed in linear distances. It is over 3000 miles, as the crow flies, from Ireland to the Urals, and almost 4800 from Spitsbergen to Malta. This raises the perplexing question of the eastern boundaries of Europe: in the east the Ural Mountains and the Ural River, and in the southeast the Caucasus Mountains. But these have not always been considered as its boundaries. In ancient times all land east of the Black Sea and the Sea of Azov was assigned to Asiatica, and as late as the eighteenth century the Don River was regarded as the boundary. In the U.S.S.R., Georgia, which is south of the Caucasus, is often regarded as European. During recent years, moreover, the significance of the Urals as a boundary has been reduced by Russian activity in Siberia. From a purely natural or geographic aspect, of course, Europe is not a continent at all, but rather a geopolitical or cultural geographic region. The true geographic unit is Eurasia.

Adding greatly to the extent of Europe are various large islands, such as Novaya Zemlya, Spitsbergen, Jan Mayen, Iceland, Malta and Crete, that fringe it on the north, west, and south.

Europe is the only continent, except for the Antarctic, without territory in the tropics. Thus its climatic and vegetation zones are much narrower than those of Asia, Africa, and the two Americas, and it has none of the immense diversity of habitats and plant and animal species found on the other continents. In fact, Europe is biologically a poor continent. Very few wild areas remain except in northern Scandinavia and Russia. Nowhere can Europe show the kind of spectacular natural scenery found in the tropical areas of Asia, Africa, and America.

The tight little continent of Europe has been the home of human beings for a very long time, and nature has suffered grave damage at their hands, especially in the Mediterranean countries. Yet, Europe has been able, after thousands of years, to retain much of what we are justified in calling unspoiled and beautiful country.

Man's reshaping of the scenery of a region is not always an esthetically negative process, but it generally does imply an impoverishment of the flora and fauna. Cultivation of the soil does create new habitats that become filled with plants and animals. Many cultivated parts of northern Europe have in recent times probably harbored more species of animals than did the coniferous forests that formerly covered the land. Since World War II, the indiscriminate use of toxic chemical pesticides has, however, been fatal to many vertebrates—particularly birds—living in cultivated habitats. The use of this blind weapon in the war on insect pests has become part of the daily routine of almost every farmer, and consequently many agricultural regions of Europe are now almost devoid of wildlife.

PREHISTORIC EUROPE

To understand the nature of Europe today we must first look very far back into the past. In the last million years—just a moment in the history of the earth—Europe has been partly covered by enormous sheets of ice during at least four periods. These Ice Ages were interrupted by interglacial periods during which many animals and plants attained a wide distribution, and during which human beings reached Europe.

The next-to-last glaciation was the most extensive one. The southern limit of the ice reached to about 50 degrees latitude, that is on a line south of where Prague now lies—although Prague itself was just south of the edge of the ice. Local ice fields occurred in the mountain regions, the one in the Alps being especially extensive. This was also true during the last period of glaciation, though the continuous sheet of ice (shown on map overleaf) did not extend so far south. At that time northern Europe and the Alps were imprisoned for the fourth time under a mighty sheet of ice for nearly one hundred thousand years. Possibly mountain peaks, called nunataks, covered with a scant vegetation, jutted above the ice. Northern Europe of the Ice Age, barren, and showing few signs of life, must have resembled the desolate

On Europe's southernmost Atlantic coast, near Portimao, Portugal, the sedimentary rocks show strikingly the shaping effect of the sea. (Julius Behnke)

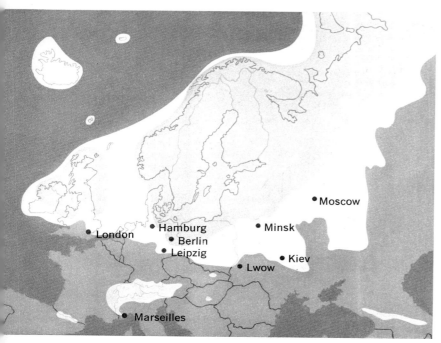

Maximum extent of the last European glaciations, the Riss and the Würm. The icecap of the next-to-the-last glaciation, the Riss, reached farther south than the Würm. The zone south of the ice sheet was permafrost tundra; still farther south came loess tundra, steppe and forest. (Adapted from "Sveriges geologi" by N. H. Magnusson, G. Lundqvist and E. Granlund, 1957)

interior of Greenland today. Perhaps a flock of long-tailed ducks now and again flew over the white waste on a migration along the open waters of the Atlantic, or a cormorant, gannet, puffin, or other sea bird passed by, driven by storms over the wilderness of ice. In spring an arctic tern may have ventured to lay her eggs by the glistening edge of the snowy blanket somewhere in what is now Denmark. And perhaps the nunataks, if such existed, were a haven for a few kinds of insects or spiders. Otherwise, windborne insects were probably the only sign of life.

But in parts of Scandinavia life was not so scant. It is believed that during the last glaciation there were ice-free areas along the coast of Norway, where the Gulf Stream to some extent counteracted the ice and cold. Relatively large areas of this kind served as refuges. These coastal strips were the Noah's Ark of the Ice Age. Many species of plants and probably of animals survived there, though there is no reliable fossil evidence of this. This theory of Ice Age refuges in Scandinavia is supported mainly by the present distribution of several species of plants and animals; but geologists are not convinced of its validity.

Europe south of the land ice was covered by belts of tundra, coniferous forest, steppe, and, finally, in the Mediterranean area, mixed and deciduous broad-leaved woodland.

When, more than twenty-five thousand years ago, the great inland icecap began to retreat—that is, when summer gains of ice-free earth were not canceled by winter losses—Cro-Magnon man in Spain and France had already executed his celebrated paintings of large mammals. The ice receded slowly at first—two or three paces backward in summer and one pace forward in winter—at an average rate of about

fifty yards a year. The slow, many-thousand-year retreat of the ice left behind very fertile virgin soils and countless marshes and lakes. Many of our present-day wetlands represent, in their various stages of vegetational colonization, the residual lakes and vegetable or animal remains of the Ice Age of Europe. Those parts of Europe never covered with ice are today different indeed—relatively poor in lakes and marshes and in deposits from the Quaternary Period.

THE MAKING OF THE MOUNTAINS

The story of the European mountain ranges belongs to an even more distant past than that of the great glaciations. The mountains of present-day Europe are the result of extensive folding in Archean or later geological times. The most ancient mountain regions have been worn away by erosion and frost, whereas the more recent ones are still relatively intact; the highest mountains are therefore the youngest.

The oldest of Europe's mountain formations, the Caledonian, is found in the British Isles and Scandinavia. This chain was formed during the Silurian period, about 450 million years ago, so that irresistible natural forces have had a chance to reduce it to currently rather modest proportions. Other mountain ranges worn down by the ravages of time are to be found in the Cornish highlands, in eastern Russia, and here and there in Central Europe. These are the remains of mountains thrown up about two hundred to three hundred million years ago during the Carboniferous and Permian periods, and later modified by erosion and by faults and other movements in the earth's crust.

Youngest are the alpine formations, formed more than fifty million years ago during the Tertiary period. The alpine mountain ranges of Europe are found only in the central and southern parts of the continent, where the Pyrenees, Alps, Apennines, Carpathians, and Caucasus stretch in an almost unbroken chain. These include the highest mountains in Europe, with Mount Elbrus in the Caucasus and Mont Blanc in the Alps raising their icy heads 18,481 and 15,781 feet above sea level, respectively. There are still a few active volcanoes in southern Europe, the most famous being Vesuvius, Stromboli, and Etna. These indicate that the crust of the earth has not yet become stabilized in their regions. Also unstable are arctic Iceland, which has both hot springs and active volcanoes, and Georgia, where hot springs and quite frequent earthquakes represent the traces of former volcanic activities.

THE RANGE OF CLIMATE

Since glacial times, the climate of Europe has fluctuated enormously. Climatic zones from north to south have therefore changed continuously, and are still doing so, though what we now experience as annual changes are merely tiny irregularities in a great curve covering centuries. The present

Northernmost Europe: The Arctic Tundra and glaciers of Spitsbergen constitute a true permafrost area and almost without vegetation, but during the brief summer, flowers and grass lend color to the landscape around bogs and meandering rivers. (Sven Gillsater: Tio)

climatic belts of Europe include a Frigid Zone, comprising the islands in the Arctic Ocean and North Atlantic; the tundra in the northernmost parts of the mainland; a subtropical region along the Mediterranean; and a Temperate Zone, covering the immense area between the other two.

Characteristic of the tundra climate is permafrost, where the surface of the soil thaws in summer but the subsoil remains eternally frozen.

The Temperate Zone is so wide that it contains several varieties of climate. In general, two strikingly different types can be distinguished here, the oceanic climate of western Europe and the continental climate of eastern Europe; between these extends a broad transitional zone with unsettled climatic conditions. The oceanic type is characterized by high humidity and precipitation, mild winters, and rainy, relatively cool summers, whereas the climate of the interior is marked by a dry atmosphere, cold winters, and very warm summers.

The subtropical zone has what is termed a Mediterranean climate—usually mild, rainy winters; early springs; hot, dry summers; and long, warm autumns.

THE BELTS OF VEGETATION

The distribution of vegetation in Europe has varied with the climatic changes since the last glaciation. The vegetation regions of Europe today may be divided very roughly into five main belts. Beginning from the south, these are: the Mediterranean area, with so-called macchia vegetation (that is, various species of evergreen shrubs) and forests where many of the trees are evergreen; the steppes north of the Caspian Sea, around the Black Sea, in the Ukraine, and in part of Hungary; the central deciduous forest region; the coniferous forest region, or taiga, (north of the deciduous forests and steppes), and finally the tundra (north of the timberline).

All these zones may be naturally divided into subzones; in addition, each belt is interrupted by many mountain ranges (with their vertical zonation of vegetation) and by land cultivated by man. Thus the European deciduous forest region now consists largely of a cultivated steppe, or plain, and the Mediterranean region of barren mountains; but if they had

been left untouched by man they would be covered with deciduous forest, the type of plant community natural to them.

As we shall see, the types of vegetation on high mountains differ from those roughly outlined above. It suffices to observe that in the mountains of Europe coniferous forest usually constitutes the timberline, but in large parts of the northern regions of the continent as well as in the Apennines deciduous trees climb higher up the hills than do conifers.

ANIMAL LIFE

From the zoogeographic aspect (that is, the geographical distribution of animal life) Europe lies in the Holarctic region, which also includes North America, North Africa, and most of Asia. The Old World part of this region is called the Palaearctic subregion and may be further divided into two areas, the boreal (below, or south of, the timberline) and the arctic (above, or north of, the timberline).

Animal distribution is determined largely by such environmental factors as climate, topography, vegetation, supply of food, and competition, as well as by the physiological and structural characteristics of the animals. Historical and geographical factors also play their part. The zoogeography of Europe is partly a matter of immigration routes and distribution patterns, seen against the background of the last glaciation and the climate during and after that long period. Climatic changes occurring during the recent postglacial period (the last twenty-five thousand years) have also much affected both the immigration timetable of various species and animal movements generally. Man's recent transformations of the landscape are another significant element.

Another fact worth noting is that immigration of animal species into Europe after the last glaciation came mainly from the east, and that Europe itself served as a kind of animal storehouse during the glaciation. Populations living south of the ice sheet reoccupied areas liberated as the ice receded.

Though the fauna of Europe may be considered impoverished in species in comparison with that of Asia, Africa, and America, its animal life is nonetheless amazingly rich and fascinating.

Created about fifty million years ago, the Alps are relatively young mountains. Here one of their most famous peaks, the Matterhorn (14,678 feet), in Switzerland, raises bare slopes far above the upper coniferous forests. (Josef Muench)

Eden in a Ruined Landscape

The Mediterranean Lands

2

The Mediterranean region is Europe's jewel, but also the most betrayed area on the Continent. It has an atmosphere of sun, life, and richness, which is genuine, yet there death and destruction rule. Every year people from all over the world flock to the Mediterranean beaches to enjoy their warmth and beauty. The countries of this region have been, so to speak, a trysting place of Europe for at least three thousand years.

It is somewhat amazing that the countries around the Mediterranean still have vital energy, still are highly productive, and still support large populations. These bear witness to how great the natural wealth of the region, based on a favorable climate and fertile soils, once was. During the past three thousand years the soils have been dissipated, and although the climate has hardly changed, its effects are no longer what they were when the land was rich in forest. Today the Mediterranean countries are living on a rapidly diminishing capital, with fertile soil being washed into the sea or blown away; unless a radical change occurs soon, all the land is doomed to exhaustion.

The Mediterranean countries were the cradle of Western civilization, and no place on earth has witnessed so many historic events in the last three millennia. The chronicles of these events reflect the natural environment of each period; they help us reconstruct the slow but dramatic changes that have turned fertile, flowering coasts, plains, and mountains into a ruined landscape. It is an utterly depressing record of biological and economic misuse, for which man alone is responsible. The history vividly demonstrates how profoundly the rise and fall of culture depends on natural conditions. The Hellenic epoch and the greatness of Greece were based on natural resources, and persisted as long as the forests

The Apennines near Atri in Abruzzi, Italy, illustrate erosion in mountains in the Mediterranean area. If the vegetation cover is gone, limestone and sandstone slopes are particularly vulnerable to the devastating effect of wind and rain. (Pepi Merisio)

produced timber and the equilibrium of nature was preserved. When this balance was disturbed by ruthless exploitation of the forests and overproduction of cattle and goats, the power of Greece declined.

The same destructive course followed in the Roman Empire, though it took longer—nearly a thousand years. As the soil of Italy lost its fertility and could no longer support the people of Rome and other towns, the empire reached out to include all the Mediterranean countries and many others. The Mediterranean became the *Mare Nostrum* of the Romans, and the whole of this mighty empire became the larder of Rome. This golden age, the *Pax Romana,* was the longest period of peace in the history of the world. When at last the Roman Empire fell, the productivity of the Mediterranean area had sunk tremendously, and the causes were the same as those that had led to the decline of Greece.

Man has not allowed nature in the Mediterranean region to recuperate. There has been an uninterrupted decline in arable lands and a permanent misuse of the living resources. The result has been tremendous erosion, with the soil left bare and dead.

A FLOWERING EDEN

The average tourist to the Mediterranean certainly does not realize the extent of the destruction. And very few even of its inhabitants seem to understand that they live literally on the verge of disaster. They still continue to abuse the soil, to let their goats graze on the poor foliage, and to cut down the last remaining forests. The inevitable consequence will be starvation, not only of cattle and goats, but also of human beings. The aridity of the area is increasing at an accelerated rate. What was previously a paradise may become a desert.

Despite the toll of the last three thousand years, the Mediterranean countries still possess so much charm and so many natural wonders that we will devote no fewer than four more chapters to them. Almost every part of the Mediterranean area—Spain, southern France, Italy, and the Balkan peninsula—has been reshaped by man. Only small segments, such as delta regions, strips of coast, and the highest mountains, may be characterized as untouched. Luckily, a few patches of virgin forest also remain. Perhaps they are not purely virgin, but they surely approximate the type of the deciduous forests of ancient times.

It has often been debated whether it was a change in climate or the action of man that caused the impoverishment of the Mediterranean region. Most of the evidence supports the view that the desolation is man's work. For six or seven thousand years, the climate of the Mediterranean area has been largely constant; though there was a somewhat higher precipitation during the last century before Christ, such fluctuations do not deserve the name of climatic changes. The conclusion we are justified in drawing is a very important one: if no clear, long-term climatic change has taken place in the thousands of years during which the natural wealth of the Mediterranean countries has been squandered by man, the present development toward a sterile, desert-like condition can be halted. We may even dare to hope that this dead landscape can be revived, the dying soils saved and the vanished forests restored. The climate clearly would not prevent a return to former natural conditions.

Such a development would, however, certainly seem to require several thousand years. Possibly, technological aids could shorten the time needed to restore this landscape to its former glory, but at best a thousand-year reconstruction program would be necessary. The trees planted on the mountain slopes must produce a carpet of debris as thick as that on which the forests once grew; until that has been done erosion of low-lying land cannot be effectively prevented.

It is not so difficult to imagine what the Mediterranean landscape was like when it had the most luxuriant forests in Europe and a rich animal life. Its vegetation was always unlike that of the rest of Europe. Generally, the land was covered with light open-canopy woods of deciduous trees with a dense undergrowth as a response to the rich light. On sandy soils grew various conifers—umbrella pines, stone pines, cypresses, cedars, and so on. Undoubtedly there already existed in ancient times coastal strips with the macchia, or maquis, vegetation (shrubs and low evergreen trees) that today is so characteristic of the Mediterranean region. Nowadays the macchia has spread to areas where deciduous forests have been cut down. In the past, the woods and forests climbed high up the mountain slopes along the coasts as well as in the interior, reaching an altitude of about four thousand feet. Another type of dense mountain woods extended even higher; at that level, pines and other montane conifers took over, forming a zone up to the timberline. Today it seems almost impossible to believe that the whole Mediterranean basin was once covered with such full-grown, climax forests.

As the vegetation was being destroyed, the animal life was decimated and changed. Not only did the altered environment make life more difficult for the animals, but man also deliberately hunted them down and thus gradually eliminated them. Very few species of large mammals remain of the great variety of Mediterranean fauna in ancient times.

ACACIAS AND MIMOSA

It is in spring that the vegetation of the Mediterranean countries is most glorious, with cascades of color and a riot of forms. Only the artist's paintbrush or color photography can do justice to the dazzling variety of flowers. Most of the wild species bloom at the same time, when winter rains have given way to the warm spring sun. Then the yellows of the broom *(Genista)* and the acacias dominate. The former is native to the Mediterranean area, with representative species found along the coast of Europe northward to southwestern Scandinavia, whereas the Mediterranean "mimosa" *(Acacia dealbata)* came originally from Australia.

For many people the "mimosa" is the best known species of plant in the Mediterranean region. But this so-called mimosa does not belong to the Mimosas at all; it is an *Acacia,* a thorn tree. This genus, of which there are nearly seven hundred species, is also well represented in Africa, and there, too, it is called mimosa. The true genus *Mimosa* is related to the acacias, but is found mainly in the tropical and subtropical parts of America. The Mediterranean area has become

The Mediterranean coast exhibits an immense variety of formations from rocky coves (as shown in this view of the Isle of Corfu) to smooth beaches. (Josef Muench)

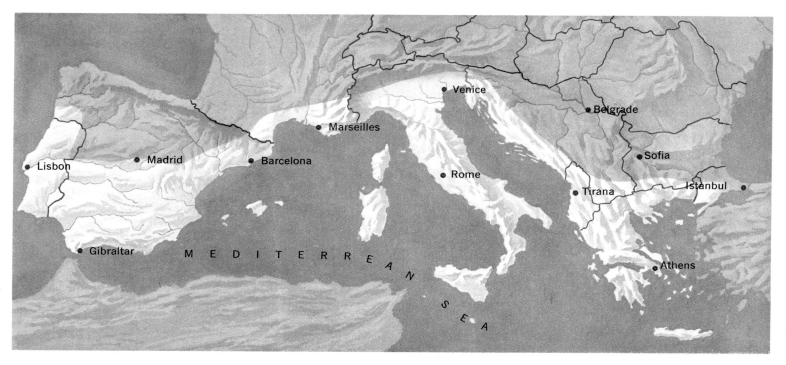

The Mediterranean region is subtropical, consists chiefly of large peninsulas, and includes all the countries of southernmost Europe—Portugal, Spain, France, Italy and the Balkans. The vegetation is evergreen shrubs and trees; not much is left of the extensive deciduous forests that once covered this mountainous area.

a floral mosaic of native and introduced species. The numerous flower gardens lining these shores are wonderful to behold. They help disperse many exotic plant species to habitats in which they then grow in a wild state. Many of these floral intruders thrive and successfully compete with the native vegetation and may even, unfortunately I feel, displace them completely.

One of the trees that has been driven from its wild habitats is *Abies nebrodensis,* a spruce. But it has fortunately been preserved as a cultivated tree. Now this spruce, originally a native of Sicily, could be used to restore the forests of that island, since a native species has a better chance of spreading than have alien trees.

Although most species of plants and trees from the Mediterranean still exist here and there inside or outside their old distribution ranges, the reduction of forest land has meant radical changes in animal life. Some species have adapted themselves to the new conditions, while others have been driven away or exterminated. Many are now engaged in their final struggle for existence.

THE ADAPTATIONS OF A LIZARD

If we take a long-term view of the Mediterranean fauna, we will find a large number of animal species with many different origins. By his introductions man has influenced the composition of the animal life as well as the plant life of the Mediterranean region, but not at all to the same extent. The great diversity and different origins of the animals of the region can be explained simply by natural phenomena. Through the ages, the Mediterranean has been an area of passage and refuge for animals driven there by climatic

changes between and during the glacial periods. Such animals came chiefly from the north, but many African and Asiatic forms may also be distinguished in the fauna living on the European side of the Mediterranean Sea. Inaccessible mountain ranges in most countries of southern Europe have made it possible for some species to survive, since, until very recent times, these areas have been too difficult for man to penetrate. Such patches preserve remnants of what biologists call "relics" of ancient Mediterranean vertebrate fauna and are, therefore, of great scientific value. Together with fossils and, of course, the cultural history of the region, they help us understand the natural environment of the classical Mediterranean area.

Since the Mediterranean countries have never been glaciated except by local glaciers in the highest mountains, the flora and fauna have been able to evolve without interruption for very long periods. In addition, isolation on numerous islands, especially in the archipelagos of the Aegean Sea, have favored the multiplication of species. There are, for instance, no fewer than eighteen species of the lizard genus *Lacerta,* all peculiar to the Mediterranean region. Many of these are divided into subspecies occurring only on islands. In many cases, moreover, each island is inhabited by distinct races. Thus, due to insular isolation, the species *L. sicula* is divided into thirty-nine subspecies, *L. pityuensis* into thirty-two, *L. erhardi* into thirty-one, and so forth. All these forms are restricted to the Mediterranean.

How did the lizards reach the various islands of the Mediterranean? Subspeciation is a rather slow process, and apparently many of these lizards colonized the islands long ago, some of them perhaps before the islands were broken up and reduced to their present size. On the other hand, human beings are also an old species in the Mediterranean, and it is possible that man, intentionally or otherwise, spread lizards (as well as other reptiles) across several Mediterranean islands. The present distribution of some lizards, especially *L. sicula* and *L. perspicillata*—the latter apparently introduced onto the Balearic island of Minorca—can hardly be explained in any other way. A dispersal of lizards from the Mediterranean area to other parts of the world has also occurred; for example, the Turkish gecko *(Hemidactylus turcicus turcicus)* has been transported by man from its original haunts in the Mediterranean to America, and is now found in North and Central America and in Cuba.

Mediterranean lizards living on isolated islands in the sea have evolved not only morphologically, that is, in form, but also ecologically, that is, in relation to environment. If the environmental conditions on an island differ too much from those in the original habitats of a species to allow an attempt at colonization, the reptile just dies out. But if the animal is sufficiently adaptable, it will gradually make itself at home under the local conditions, and this process may lead to a peculiar specialization of the animal. For example, on some rocky islands in the Adriatic, where food is scarce, certain races of the lizard *Lacerta melisellensis* are very common where sea gulls breed in colonies. It seemed strange that these lizards should congregate among the gulls—which may, in fact, prey on small reptiles—until it was found that the lizards fed on the lice *(Mallophaga)* and mites that live as parasites on gulls. Here the food specialization of the insular races of a lizard has turned to a true symbiosis between a reptile and a bird—a relationship advantageous to both of them. It may be added that such a symbiosis is paralleled on the famous guano islands off Peru, where a certain lizard has the same feeding habits as the Mediterranean one; but there its partner is a cormorant—a striking example of parallel reptilian adaptation.

There are, of course, other causes of the various lines of development of animal life, such as the fact that the region is a transitional area not only between different climates but also between three continents. Europe, Asia, and Africa form the coasts of the Mediterranean, and this greatly·affects the vegetable and animal life of the region. The location of the Mediterranean between the deciduous forest region of Central Europe and the great African desert also proves important. We will see later how these contrasting conditions affect the flora and fauna of the region.

LIONS AND WILD GOATS

Many large mammals of species no longer found in Europe once inhabited the Mediterranean countries. Some are no longer found anywhere. As late as historic times, for example, the lion was a spectacular part of Mediterranean fauna. There are unfortunately no remains of this lion, and it is not known whether it was identical with the species that today roams the savannas of tropical Africa or the Gir forest in Asia.

Wild goat (Capra ibex cretensis) *shown in an unusual photograph taken in the White Mountains of western Crete. These are considered pure wild ibexes, which are very rare in the Mediterranean. On Crete they are known as far back as the Minoan period, about 3800 years ago. (Dimitrios Harissiadis)*

Herodotus reported 2400 years ago that there were many lions in Thrace, and declares that during the march of the Persian king Xerxes through Macedonia (480 B.C.), some of the baggage camels were killed by lions. Later on, Aristotle (384–322 B.C.) assigns the same range to the lion, but refers to it as rare. By A.D. 80–100 the lion was considered entirely exterminated in Europe, having gradually retreated before man and his civilization.

It cannòt be taken for granted that the lion of ancient Greece was identical with *Panthera leo,* the species we know today, although the latter certainly had a much wider range in the past. Formerly the cave lion *(P. spelaeus)* was distributed over large parts of Europe and it still existed in the postglacial period; it retreated gradually from Europe and is thought to have become extinct as late as the third century B.C. If the Greek lions were of the species *P. spelaeus,* they did not become extinct until about four hundred years later.

The reason for the disappearance of the lion from the European scene must be traced to the unceasing warfare man has carried on against this animal. Neither the climate nor

Right: On western Corsica, at the Calanches of Piana, eroded porphyry cliffs crowd to the edge of the sea, 1300 feet below. (Josef Muench) Below: On some of the plateaus around Granada a few green patches contrast sharply with dreadfully eroded surroundings. In the foreground is meagre farmland shadowed by olive trees, on the opposite slope is the evergreen shrub vegetation called macchia, and beyond are the snowy ridges of the Sierra Nevada. (J. Blauel: Bavaria Verlag)

the food supply could have been important factors in the elimination of the lion at that time. Remains of cave lions have been found in the ancient dwelling places of postglacial man in Aurignac and La Madeleine in France. Other large mammals disappeared from the European Mediterranean regions during the postglacial period. We will consider them in connection with Central Europe, because their main distribution ranges were in the temperate zone.

Typical but very rare mammals of the Mediterranean are the ibexes, or wild goats *(Capra ibex)*. The nomenclature of this Mediterranean group is rather confusing; some students consider the many isolated populations of European ibexes as distinct species, others as subspecies. Interbreeding in zoological gardens has shown that they originally belonged to the same species: both sexes of the hybrids are usually fertile. We have therefore considered these ibexes as belonging to the same species, with the different populations distinguished as races.

These wild goats are now found in scattered areas from the Pyrenean sierras in the west to some of the Greek islands in the east, and they also occur in the Alps.

The ibex was probably one of the ancestors of the European domestic goat, which man carried to many islands in the Mediterranean Sea thousands of years ago. As domestic goats easily become feral and also often interbreed with true wild goats, it is difficult to determine to what extent the insular populations are pure ibexes. Probably most wild goats now living on islands in the Mediterranean have a domestic past;

otherwise their dispersal throughout such areas would be difficult to explain. Such "wild goats" are today found on the following European islands of the Mediterranean: Tavolara, northeast of Sardinia; Monte Cristo, between Italy and Corsica; Samothrace, in the northern part of the Aegean Sea; Yioura, in the Cyclades; and Crete, as well as three smaller islands north of Crete. The only island inhabited by pure wild ibexes is Andimilos, also in the Cyclades. In addition, there are several islands, especially in the Greek archipelagos, that have wild goats that are definitely of domestic origin.

The ibexes and wild goats of the Mediterranean show us, as do the lizards, that human influence on the distribution of animals is unavoidable in an area that has long been occupied by man. But man was not the only factor in changing the character of the Mediterranean region; he controlled a most important agent in this huge task of soil destruction—the goats themselves. Thus the goat, represented in schoolbooks all over the world as a useful animal, is in the Mediterranean area man's greatest enemy. This also holds true, in the long run, in many other parts of the world, above all in Africa and Asia.

WILD SHEEP AND MONK SEALS

Another ungulate of Mediterranean origin is the mouflon, or wild sheep *(Ovis musimon),* whose real home is Sardinia and Corsica. From the large islands it has been introduced into several European countries. Also native to the Mediterranean region is the fallow deer *(Dama dama).* Today this beautiful animal is commoner in the northern part of its European range than in its original habitats. In the Mediterranean region it occurs locally in Spain, France, and Italy, but has been almost exterminated in the Balkan area. There are probably not more than six limited areas on the Iberian peninsula where wild populations are still living. In the Mediterranean part of France, only two regions, in the vicinity of the Rhone valley, harbor this deer, and in Italy seven areas. Sardinia also seems still to have a considerable number.

Europe has only three members of the cat family, two species of which, the wildcat *(Felis silvestris)* and the pardel lynx *(Lynx pardellus),* belong to the Mediterranean, and the third one, the lynx *(Lynx lynx),* did so in the past. Most pardel lynx populations are in Spain, and we will return to this interesting animal when dealing with that area. The wildcat is today mainly an inhabitant of Mediterranean countries, although it was formerly found as far north as Scandinavia.

The crested porcupine *(Hystrix cristata)* is a large, well armed rodent living in Italy and the Balkan peninsula. It is an African animal and its occurrence in Europe is puzzling. It may have been introduced during ancient times.

One of the rarest Mediterranean animals is the monk seal *(Monachus monachus),* formerly abundant along the coasts of this region, but today limited to a few places on some Medi-

Left: The high plateaus of central Spain are situated in arid country, which emphasizes their vegetation. This land near Segovia in the Sierra de Guadarrama was abandoned after having been exhausted. (Julius Behnke)   Right: When goats, which can even climb trees—and kill them—are brought into an area, vegetation cover is rapidly destroyed. (UNESCO)

terranean islands. In fact, a report in 1962 (to the International Union for the Conservation of Nature and Natural Resources) declared that only five areas in the Mediterranean were known to have monk seals. One colony is on the coast of Africa, one on Corsica, one in the Adriatic off the coast of Yugoslavia, and an unknown number lives around the Ionian Islands west of Greece and in the Cyclades. A few of these seals have in recent times been noted elsewhere in the Mediterranean Sea, but it is doubtful whether these indicate the existence of colonies.

Although man has not yet conquered the depths of the Mediterranean Sea, he has definitely occupied all the beaches. Therefore a marine animal such as the monk seal, which needs an undisturbed stretch of beach for breeding purposes, is very vulnerable to disturbance by man. The reason for the marked decline of the only seal living in the Mediterranean is, however, primarily direct destruction by man. Although the monk seal is protected by law in most parts of its range, this does not prevent its slaughter by fishermen, who regard it as a competitor and as a danger to their livelihood. In order to save the monk seal from extinction it must be given greater protection and have strictly maintained sanctuaries on the breeding islands.

The Mediterranean nations are eager to preserve ancient monuments and buildings as a cultural heritage and as memorials of bygone glories, but they do not seem to realize that plants and animals are also part of our heritage, a marvelous monument created by nature itself through the long process of evolution, and thus much older than man's antiquities. Once a species is gone, it can never be replaced.

THE MARCH OF THE DESERTS

As one flies eastward over the Mediterranean countries from the Iberian peninsula, one sees everywhere—on the large islands in the sea, the ancient lands of Italy, the mountains and archipelagos of Greece—eroded areas like open wounds in the earth, and one realizes with a shock the incredible extent to which man has destroyed his environment. As one passes above Portugal and Spain it is already evident that vast expanses have become a desert—dead ground. As this reality sinks home, one is reminded that the Iberian soil has almost the same ancient history as that of Greece and Italy. Phoenicians, Carthaginians, Romans came and vanished, all exploiting the natural resources in ruthless and uneconomic ways, exhausting the forests and fertile soils, leaving the earth unprotected from winds and winter rains. Later, the Moorish occupation of Iberia made its contribution to the impoverishment of arable lands. The result is that Portugal and Spain are perhaps even more eroded than Italy and Greece.

Flying over Spain leaves an indelible impression of a mountainous desert in which erosion has made ravines like great

Left: In the Mediterranean area sheep, here shown on Sardinia, are not so injurious as goats, but they, too, influence the vegetation and shape the landscape. (Giuseppe Palazzi) Right: A few thousand years ago, the Mediterranean mountains were covered by luxuriant forests that kept the area in biological balance. Today they are denuded and exposed to erosion, as seen here in southern Italy. (Pal-Nils Nilsson: Tio)

gashes in the reddish-brown earth. Here is a literally murdered landscape, where rivers on their way down from the mountains have torn up the defenseless earth, and wind has blown away the soil. Now the river beds are dry and bare, for even during the sudden floods of spring and autumn the waters do not bring them to life but only eat still further toward sterile bedrock. Not even lichens are given an opportunity to conceal the jagged rocks.

Over the centuries, most of the topsoil has been washed away, and what was left on the mountains has been blown down into the valleys; there, for the time being, it has taken the place of the original soil—which has also been washed away because of the destruction of the vegetation. This flight of soil is still going on, but the reserves in the highlands will soon be exhausted, and the valleys will then no longer be replenished from the heights. This will mean the end of agriculture in the valleys and on the plains of the lowlands unless there is radical reforestation.

The same depressing scene confronts one over the large Mediterranean islands and over Italy and Greece. Of course there are still some green oases, either vestiges from earlier times or the results of persevering toil in the face of adverse conditions. Here and there certain valleys even seem rich in flourishing vegetation. They inspire hope, but unfortunately they must all too often be regarded as the last manifestations of life before death sets in. It is these green patches that will be considered in the following chapters, for they represent the natural life of the Mediterranean today.

A warning of what may happen on the European side of the Mediterranean is provided by neighboring Africa, where the Sahara Desert reigns. The desert is now spreading over larger and larger areas of Mediterranean Europe.

A plane flight over the blue waters of the Mediterranean reminds one of other flying travelers—birds of passage. Immense numbers of such birds cross the sea twice a year. A large proportion of the insect-eating birds that breed in Europe and Western Asia winter in Africa south of the Sahara. Many of them migrate on a wide front over the Mediterranean and then over the great desert, which is even larger than the sea. R. E. Moreau, a British ornithologist, has calculated that on an average one bird for every five acres in Europe leaves its breeding grounds to winter either in the Mediterranean basin or in Africa south of the Sahara. He estimates the autumn flood of birds crossing the Mediterranean between the Straits of Gibraltar in the west and Palestine in the east at no less than six hundred million. The autumn movement of the trans-Mediterranean-Saharan migrants occurs mostly within the two months from the end of August to the end of October.

Even though there naturally will be rather fewer birds on the return flight, the spring migration over the Mediterranean is also a remarkable spectacle. Only a few places along the European coast of the Mediterranean are constantly used as routes by the migrating birds. Capri, just off Naples, is one of these and has become famous for its birds of passage. On the other hand, Sicily, though long considered a natural resting place for any migration over one of the narrowest parts of the Mediterranean, attracts only a certain few species.

Devastating erosion, caused by continuous misuse of the land, changes fertile soil into barren ground. (Pal-Nils Nilsson: Tio)

Marshes, Valleys and Sierras

Spain

3 It always seems surprising that the southernmost parts of Europe, located in Spain, are farther south than such areas of North Africa as Algiers and Tunisia. At one point, in fact—the Straits of Gibraltar—the two continents almost meet. Thus, Spain may be considered a transitional zone between Europe and Africa. The fauna and flora of southern Spain also provide evidence of the proximity of Africa. Many of the animals and plants that occur in Spain, moreover, have their main distribution in Africa.

Of the many types of European landscapes none has been so altered by man during the past 150 years as have marshes and bogs. So many of them have been drained that the total area of permanent marshland and of land that is flooded annually has now shrunk to only a fraction of its former size. This drainage has not always been economically sound.

Right: Behind the coastal dunes of the Coto Doñana of south-western Spain a wood of stone pines and scrub has partially stabilized the sand. (P. Straw) Below: Griffon vultures at their nests on a mountain ledge, their most common habitat. (Michel Terrasse)

Spain is a land of sierras and high plateaus. Saw-toothed ridges of faulted and folded mountains form mighty chains around the plateaus and lowland plains.

Instead, there has sometimes been a loss; besides this, it has destroyed valuable natural assets.

Southern Europe is not so rich in marshes as the northern, previously glaciated parts of the Continent. The icecap and the prolonged period of melting left thousands of marshes and shallow lakes in northern Europe. Thus, southern Europe has suffered proportionately more from this obsession with drainage than the northern countries. The marshes of southern Europe are usually rich in organic life. The biological productivity of such areas is great, not only during summer growth but also in winter, when they act as nutritional reservoirs for the flocks of migratory geese and ducks of northern Eurasia. In addition, the few marshes in such southern European latitudes are often the only remaining wild areas— except for the highest peaks and submarine environments. So there are not only economic but also social and scientific reasons why these marshes should be preserved.

There are only seven large marshlands left in southern Europe, all of them in river deltas: those of the Guadalquivir River in Spain, of the Rhone in France, of three regions along the Adriatic coast of Italy, of the Danube in Rumania, and of the Volga in Russia. Rich inland swamps are also found at La Dombes, west of Jura, at Neusiedlersee in Austria, at Lake Balaton in Hungary, and in a few places in the Balkans, but they are less important than the coastal regions mentioned above, and none of them exceeds in beauty or wealth of species the Coto Doñana and Las Marismas near the Atlantic coast not far from the Gulf of Cadiz.

The location of the Coto Doñana below the mountains of Andalusia, with the Atlantic to the west, the great delta of the Guadalquivir to the east, and Africa to the south, has, as a consequence of the varying terrain; given rise to a fauna unique in Europe. Most of the Coto Doñana consists of vast fields of sand drift and marshland, *marismas,* along the Guadalquivir.

Despite the fact that the score or so of biologists and naturalists who have studied Las Marismas are agreed that it is one of the richest natural areas in Europe, it is not well known. Since the late 1950's the threat of exploitation has hung over it, and several international conservation organizations have been struggling to preserve the region. Their efforts have met with a measure of success: the Spanish Government has dedicated Las Nuevas, a large area in the center of Las Marismas, as a reserve, and a scientific research station is to be established there. A part of the Coto Doñana, an ecological complement to Las Nuevas, has been bought in order to extend the reserve westward. It is hoped that still more land can be acquired so that the greater part of Las Marismas west of the lower reaches of the Guadalquivir, the last wild region of southern Europe, covering about 385 square miles, will be protected. It is a prehistoric landscape, a living museum of a period long before the dawn of culture in the Mediterranean.

AUTUMN AND WINTER IN LAS MARISMAS

Las Marismas is fascinating the year round: in autumn and winter the ground is flooded; spring brings rebirth; and summer is marked by drought and stabilization. The wealth of animals and habitats exceeds that found anywhere else in Europe. Such extravagance of forms of life seems almost paradoxical when it is remembered that, apart from the sand dunes, the country is perfectly flat. Nowhere else in Europe have I seen such enormous flocks of ducks and geese as on the marshes of Las Marismas. And that was in November, at a time when nature lies dormant in most of Europe.

Once, for a week at the end of November we traveled through Las Marismas on horseback, the only way to get about at that time, for the autumn rains flood great parts of the region. The first thirteen-hour ride through the delta was an exciting lesson, for I had never ridden before, and my five companions were excellent horsemen. When their horses set off at a trot or gallop, mine followed, for I could not curb it with the piece of rope tied to the primitive halter that served as bridle. Reins and bits were not used. I clung desperately to my horse during these rides, for a fall would have meant at least a cold bath. It was especially exciting when we vaulted over channels, of whose depth I remained in blissful ignorance. But I somehow survived all our excursions without mishap. Or perhaps the good sherry our host, Don Mauricio Gonzales Diaz (whose family has owned the Coto Doñana for centuries), served every time we rested had a stimulating effect on my horsemanship.

Wherever we rode, we found birds. The swamps had been turned into lakes by the autumn rains, and they were completely covered with ducks—mostly widgeons *(Anas penelope).* Flocks of up to ten thousand birds rose with an almost deafening clatter of wings. At the same time an equally large flock might fly up from an adjacent lake; there must have been hundreds of thousands of ducks. It was a stunning sight, reminiscent only of the massing of swallows and locusts in Africa. The enormous flocks of geese were made up of graylags *(Anser anser)*. We estimated that there were about eight thousand of them. Where, one wondered, did they come from? José A. Valverde, the Spanish zoologist who knows Las Marismas best, thought they were of Scandinavian origin, but that many graylags hardly exist in all of Scandinavia.

In winter a waterlogged region, in summer Las Marismas is largely a dry heath. To the west of the mighty marsh is the region called the Coto Doñana, consisting of a heath grazed by semiwild cattle and a few introduced dromedaries, succeeded by a savanna-like belt of cork oaks *(Quercus suber)*, a ground cover of *Halimium halimifolium* and a scattering of macchia vegetation, with tree heaths *(Erica arborea)* as a prominent element. The savanna eventually becomes a treeless steppe and then an umbrella pine forest *(Pinus pinea)*. Nearer the coast the pine forest is characterized by wandering sand dunes until it gives way to completely desert-like features—including some of the highest sand dunes in Europe—and at last meets the sea.

Our sketch of the habitats of the Coto Doñana gives only a faint idea of the abundance of plants and animals there. Even during the winter months, the number of species is remarkable. Red deer *(Cervus elaphus)*, fallow deer *(Dama dama)* and wild boars *(Sus scrofa)* are common sights. They showed no fear when I approached within thirty or forty yards of them. We even saw traces of that extremely rare cat, the pardel lynx *(Lynx pardellus)*. Several of the mammals that live here have their greatest distribution in Africa; in fact, from the point of view of natural history, Africa and Europe meet in the delta of the Guadalquivir. In addition to the maneuvers of imperial eagles *(Aquila heliaca)*, a few species of vultures, black kites *(Milvus migrans)* and short-toed eagles *(Circaëtus gallicus)*, and flocks of pin-tailed sand grouse *(Pterocles alchata)* with white bellies flashing in the sun, gave as impressive an exhibition of aerobatics as one could wish to see. Cranes *(Grus grus)*, black-tailed godwits *(Limosa limosa)*, glossy ibises *(Plegadis falcinellus)*, short-eared owls *(Asio flammeus)*, bluethroats *(Luscinia svecica)*, and red-throated pipits *(Anthus cervinus)* were other, sometimes unexpected, winter visitors to the region. In the shrubs European robins *(Erithacus rubecula)* sang the silvery notes so well known in the woods of north and central Europe in spring. The most common bird of the macchia was undoubtedly the long-tailed and decorative Dartford warbler *(Sylvia undata)*, with its dark, reddish-brown underparts. One of the rarest birds in the world, the extremely beautiful azure-winged magpie *(Cyanopica azurea)*, which has a very puzzling distribution—it is found only in the Iberian peninsula and in eastern Asia—flocked in the pine woods and uttered sounds like a nutcracker. We sighted as many as eighty-two azure-winged magpies at one time.

A visit to Las Marismas in November, the month when it rains most there, reveals how very important the marshes and lakes on the Guadalquivir delta are as wintering grounds for the migratory geese and ducks of northern Europe. This is also true of the Camargue, the delta of the Rhone on the Mediterranean coast of France. The Camargue and Las Marismas are clearly the principal winter quarters of many species. It would be a catastrophe for large sections

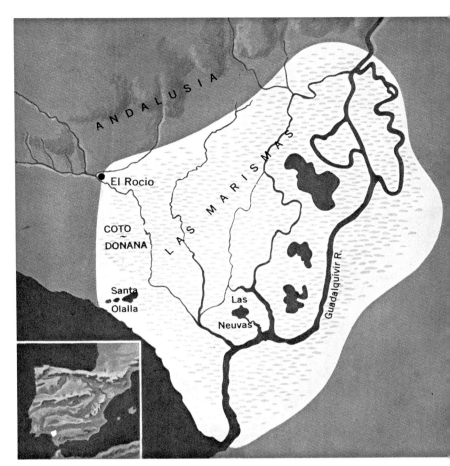

The delta of the Guadalquivir, together with the Coto Doñana, Las Marismas and Las Nuevas, is one of Europe's largest marshlands; it has a wealth of wildlife and unique habitats.

of the bird populations if these marshes were to disappear.

Ecologically, the Camargue and Las Marismas are as important for geese and ducks as are the breeding grounds of the birds in northern Europe. These birds, representing a potential source of protein-rich food in a starving world, are economically important. Everyone knows, moreover, what they mean as recreation both for lovers of nature and, whether we approve of them or not, hunters. Nor should the other values of marshes be forgotten: they produce organisms and links in nutritional chains profitable to human beings, and they are significant to science as natural environments. Surface and subsoil waters are, moreover, essential factors for agriculture, water supply, irrigation, and the biological functioning of our environment. Finally, marshes are precious exceptions to the devastating regimentation that man is imposing on nature in his unrelenting effort to make what he considers profitable use of all land.

ANIMALS WITHOUT FEAR

It is a day's journey from Seville to the Coto Doñana, the first part of it through the orange groves of Andalusia and through extensive forest belts with a dense ground vegetation mainly of halimium. The road ends at the village of El Rocio; there Las Marismas begins. The white houses of El Rocio lie just above the marsh, but near the village is a cluster of hovels, the like of which I have rarely seen in

Europe. They look very African, but I have seldom seen such rudimentary dwelling places even in Africa. They are perhaps well adapted to the climate but are hardly suitable for people living so close to a marsh full of mosquitoes.

The Coto Doñana and Las Marismas begin where man's domain ends, but this vast expanse of wild country in the delta of the Guadalquivir has not completely escaped the attention of man and his cattle. The most northerly part of the sandy area of the Coto Doñana was planted with eucalyptus during the early 1940's in the hope that it would form forest land. This project does not seem to have been entirely successful, for the normally fast-growing eucalyptus trees are in many places still not more than about six to nine feet tall. The richness of wildlife in these sparse eucalyptus woods is, moreover, not very great and is often greatly exceeded by that of the original natural habitats.

The northern part of the vast Las Marismas, around the meandering delta arms of the Guadiamar and the Guadalquivir rivers, is better adapted to exploitation by man. The very northernmost sections have already been converted into Spain's most fertile rice fields. But for the time being the greater part of these magnificent marshes is being allowed to develop in its own natural way.

One of the many phenomena that astonish visitors to the Coto Doñana is the lack of fear manifested by the large mammals. The visitor daily comes across red deer, fallow deer and wild boars, and can approach quite close to them, whether he is on foot or on horseback. I formed the habit of taking walks in the November twilight to study animal life at the beginning of evening. Even in November the sun sets as late as 7 P.M. in this corner of Europe, for it is not only far to the south, but also a long way to the west. Even earlier than this, the wild boars are out rooting for food in the wet ground and in the soft mud at the base of the tussocks. I could get within ten or fifteen yards of them without attracting their attention; they just continued to grub energetically. Even in the woods they appeared not to notice me, but I am sure they knew they had company.

One evening in the semidarkness, an old male happened to approach quite close to my observation post. His white-red tusks flashed as he worked on roots and other parts of plants. Eventually it got so dark that he was visible only as a dark shadow against the blackness of the night. When at last I left my hiding place, I purposely made a noise, yet he barely glanced at me and then went on eating. He had known all the time that I was there.

The deer, too, are more timid in the daytime than at night or at dawn or twilight. One evening, as the setting sun illuminated autumn vegetation with a warm, rosy tint, I met twenty-two fallow deer moving along in Indian file; they all stopped, and so did I. While I remained perfectly still, harts and hinds moved past me in calm procession. The sun tinted them a golden red, so that they stood out from the dark-green winter vegetation and the shadows of the cork oaks. Beyond the deer a short-eared owl flew low, hunting over open country—another sign of winter.

The large mammals of the Coto show the same lack of fear in the presence of human beings as do those in the great national parks of Africa and North America, where they are never hunted. The remarkable thing, however, is that hunting parties are organized in the Coto Doñana two or three times a year. Such hunting is necessary, for otherwise the deer

population would increase so quickly that in the long run the animals would die of hunger; very few of Andalusia's original carnivores remain, and thus no natural predators control the deer population. These hunts evidently do not seriously disturb the peaceful existence of the animals.

THE KINGDOM OF THE BIRDS

The rich bird life of Las Marismas during autumn and winter is most remarkable. Ducks and geese, whose main haunts are lakes and flooded meadows, are the most numerous. Wading birds are less common, because most of them migrate in winter to tropical Africa, only a few remaining along the river banks and around lakes and lagoons. Graceful avocets, with elegant black-and-white plumage, wade in the shallow water on steel-blue legs. They crouch when feeding, and with a rapid side-to-side movement of their heads use their up-curved bills to sift small animals from the surface water and the muddy bottoms. These birds swallow their prey with a quick jerk of the head. Unlike most waders, avocets possess well developed webbed feet, which make it easy for them to walk over soft mudflats in search of such small organisms as mollusks, crustaceans, and insect larvae. In Las Marismas avocets usually spend the winter on the gently sloping sandy or muddy beaches, which are similar to their summer habitats. Here and there they are found in the company of a few black-winged stilts (Himantopus himantopus); these have even longer legs than the avocets. Both species breed in Las Marismas, but it is uncertain whether the summer populations remain there in the winter.

Small plovers—ringed plovers (Charadrius hiaticula), little ringed plovers (C. dubius) and Kentish plovers (C. alexandrinus)—often winter on the same beaches as the avocets, but they get their food in a quite different way. Tripping along the edge of the water, they halt suddenly, stand perfectly still for a moment, then rush forward and with a rapid dip of the head seize some small organisms from the water. Unlike sandpipers, plovers usually do not stab the mud or bore in it with their bills. Rather, they stand still, as though concentrating on the sound of small animals moving in the sand.

The Kentish plover around the coasts of Europe has a predilection for saltwater. It is rarely found near freshwater, although two related species are at home in such habitats. It is not surprising that the species winters around the Guadalquivir—and at some distance indeed from the Atlantic coast, for the low-lying ground of Las Marismas has a very high salt content.

The widespread, flooded salicornia heaths provide excellent autumn and winter quarters for snipe (Gallinago gallinago). When flushed, these birds fly up quickly with a sharp, hoarse cry, and then rise in erratic, zigzag flight. Snipe nearly always seek their food on flooded ground or in shallow water

Facing page, above left: The European pond tortoise shares one of the Coto Doñana's freshwater lagoons with the Spanish terrapin. (Weber and Hafner) Right: A squacco heron, partly nocturnal in its habits, perches in the reeds. (Walter Fendrich) Below: The Guadalquivir, main river of the vast marsh of Las Marismas, near where it empties into the Atlantic Ocean. (Julius Behnke)

along shores. Their long bills, with organs of touch at the point, are perfectly adapted to the task. The birds advance into the water and drive their bills deep into the mud, sometimes straight down, sometimes diagonally or almost horizontally. If the bottom is very soft, a snipe may simply move forward, its bill in the mud, instead of making new holes. Clearly, snipe search for food through their sense of touch.

Curlews *(Numenius arquata)* winter in Las Marismas, haunting the waterlogged meadowland. Their beautiful song, a long series of bubbling trills, is a most charming specimen of the winter music of the region.

The most abundant species of wader in Las Marismas, in November at least, is the wood sandpiper *(Tringa glareola),* as it also is in tropical Africa during the same season. In winter this bird is distributed over vast areas, just as it is in Europe and Asia during its breeding season. In Las Marismas its cries are occasionally mixed with the melodious triad, "tew-tew-tew," of greenshanks *(T. nebularia)* and the short "tchuit" of the spotted redshanks *(T. erythropus).* Both the greenshank and the spotted redshank are found in the northern parts of Europe and Asia, making Las Marismas a trysting place for birds from northern tundras and marshes as well as from southern lakes and beaches.

Various species of larks and pipits tripping about the dry heaths include crested larks *(Galerida cristata),* thekla larks *(G. theklae),* and calandra larks *(Melanocorypha calandra).* This last species can easily be distinguished by a bold black patch on its throat. Skylarks *(Alauda arvensis)* are also common here; now and again their clear, charming call sounds over the heath. Their brown plumage precisely blends with the color of the vegetation, an example of the fact that a bird's protective coloring is often adapted to its winter habitat rather than to its breeding ground. This is natural for some species, since they spend most of their time in winter quarters.

Where the heaths have been colonized by occasional shrubs, great gray shrikes *(Lanius excubitor)* may often be seen sitting in their favorite trees, ready in a flash to swoop down upon a small rodent, shrew, lizard or large insect. There is much evidence that these shrikes possess winter territories like those of their American relative, the loggerhead shrike *(L. ludovicianus).* The winter territories of great gray shrikes, however, seem to be important only in the daytime, when the birds are searching for food, for at night several birds may share a bush.

Short-toed tree creepers *(Certhia brachydactyla)* climb up tree trunks in the groves of the Coto Doñana searching for pupae and hibernating insects, while the tiny wren *(Troglodytes troglodytes)* boldly sings its surprisingly loud song throughout the winter. Quite a number of thrushes winter in the Coto Doñana—the mistle thrush *(Turdus viscivorus),* the song thrush *(T. philomelos),* and the redwing *(T. musicus)*—revealing their presence by their calls as they pass from one thicket to another or fly high overhead.

One of the most common winter birds in the Coto Doñana is the stonechat *(Saxicola torquata),* which finds the extensive heaths overgrown with shrubs a favorable habitat. Its song is heard on all sides, and with field glasses, one can count half a score or so nearby.

In winter, lagoons form in the macchia areas of the Coto Doñana, and thus tree heaths often grow in, or very close to, water—a curious combination. The Cetti's warbler *(Cettia cetti),* which prefers an environment very close to water, takes over the heath, and its loud but brief song rings out abruptly. The mustached warbler *(Lusciniola melanopogon),* another southern European bird, may sometimes occupy such temporarily wet habitats, and the fan-tailed warbler *(Cisticola juncidis),* the only European representative of various species of this African genus, may also be observed.

Still other southern birds inhabit the cork oak and olive woods, among them the Sardinian warbler *(Sylvia melanocophala)* which, like some other species, does not seem to leave Andalusia in winter. It may be seen hunting for food in shrubs, and can be recognized by its black head and blood-red eye ring. The chiffchaff *(Phylloscopus collybita)* is common in winter, but it is difficult to recognize in November, because it never sings then, and its song and call are the easiest way to identify it.

Another interesting bird of the Coto Doñana is the spotless starling *(Sturnus unicolor).* In November there was a large flock of them in the acacia and eucalyptus trees around El Palacio—one of the few buildings in the region, except for some Moorish lookout towers inhabited by birds. At sunrise and sunset the starlings sang in unison in a shrill, whistling tone, very beautifully and from a distance astonishingly like the redwing chorus during the spring migration. Among

other songbirds are the brightly colored goldfinch *(Carduelis carduelis)*, standing out brilliantly against a background of pine woods and bushes. Small flocks of linnets *(C. cannabina)* also visit the edges of the woods from haunts on the heaths.

HERONS, FLAMINGOS AND DUCKS

Las Marismas has a number of heron species in summer, and some stay on in winter, occupying chiefly the shores of lagoons and lakes. The most common is the gray heron *(Ardea cinerea)*. Occasionally little egrets *(Egretta garzetta)* may be seen, snow-white against the reeds around which they search for food. Hidden in the reeds are bitterns *(Botaurus stellaris)*; they can be seen only when they stretch their great wings in slow flight between their fishing grounds. This species also visits the flooded glasswort heaths in November.

During my autumn visit to Las Marismas, one of the rarest birds in Europe was there—the glossy ibis *(Plegadis falcinellus)*. Its annual breeding haunts are in southeastern Europe and Italy; otherwise it is found mainly in Asia. Its presence in Las Marismas was certainly unexpected. The species has been found there in summer since 1909, but never nesting. If these ibises live in Las Marismas the year round, they probably breed there, too; if not, we must conclude that this extreme southwestern corner of Europe is visited regularly in summer and winter by birds from the southeastern corner of the Continent. This would involve an almost directly western migration. But the mystery of the presence of the glossy ibis in Las Marismas is yet to be solved.

Another exotic apparition at Las Marismas is the flamingo *(Phoenicopterus ruber)*. Its arrival in, and departure from, southern Spain is another mystery. We know that the species is found at Las Marismas, particularly in Las Nuevas, now in summer, now in winter. But its breeding has not been observed since 1941. Probably these flamingos should be considered together with the great colony that breeds in the Camargue area of southern France. We do know that when in the summer of 1963 a colony of flamingos breeding in the Camargue was disturbed and left the area, a colony of 3600 nests was, according to Dr. Valverde, established in Spain soon afterward.

In Africa, where the same species of flamingo occurs, the flocks move about very freely, migrating between lakes. Las Marismas may well be a halfway house for flamingos in the years when they migrate from the Camargue—perhaps on their way to Africa. Or the flamingo population of the Camargue may move only between this region and Las Marismas. The flamingos occurring at Las Marismas may also be the last remnants of a population that finds breeding conditions no longer good enough there. Or did the flamingos of the Camargue settle there after abandoning Las Marismas as a breeding place? How many unanswered questions there are about these flamingos!

The magnificent imperial eagle, not uncommon around Las Marismas, is shown with its young in a nest in the crown of a stone pine in the Coto Doñana. (Eric Hosking)

As we have said, vast flocks of duck attract most attention at Las Marismas during the winter months. Every species of duck in Europe and northwestern Asia is found there. The main reason for this is that the flooded plain with its lakes and lagoons is a larder from which each species can obtain the food suitable to its needs. Las Marismas is thus a highly productive region. For at least half of the year hundreds of thousands of geese and ducks graze on the vegetation without damaging the habitat; then, well fed and in good condition, the birds spread over the greater part of Europe—their breeding grounds.

Equally important to geese and ducks in waterlogged Las Marismas is the fact that it is genuine wilderness. Although the region, like all low-lying land in Southern Europe, has been subjected to some cultivation, it is still essentially wild country, virtually uninhabited, and without roads. A few cowherds tend half-wild, free-roaming cattle, and live in huts many miles from each other. A handful of gamekeepers patrol the huge domain, moving about the marshlands on horseback, on foot, or in flatbottomed boats. Around the Guadalquivir the land is flat as far as the eye can see. There is water everywhere, but it is shallow, and the bottom, with its plants, is within reach of a duck's bill. This is a veritable kingdom of aquatic birds, one of the rare places where man leaves them in peace. The few days of winter shooting do not disrupt the essential serenity of Las Marismas.

The climate also attracts the birds. This southern outpost of Europe has very mild winters. Even when the rest of Europe is stricken with cold, as happened, for example, in 1962-1963—when ice and snow for months on end turned even freshwater or brackish lakes and lagoons of the Mediterranean coast into deathtraps for ducks and waders—Las Marismas remains unaffected. Only occasionally, at most for a few early morning hours, does the water freeze. Such favorable climatic conditions must necessarily have led to a higher rate of survival among birds wintering there than among those wintering elsewhere in Europe. This in turn means that, through centuries of selection, an increasing proportion of Europe's duck population is wintering at Las Marismas. The faithfulness usually shown by birds to their breeding grounds and winter quarters justifies this assumption.

Since it is mainly grazing ducks that are favored by the food situation in Las Marismas, the region is dominated in winter by surface-feeding ducks, while diving ducks, which usually live on animal organisms, constitute a minority. Mallards *(Anas platyrhynchos)*, Europe's most common duck, are naturally very numerous, but they are outnumbered—in November, at least—by the widgeons, which are sometimes present in extraordinary numbers. Bobbing up and down everywhere on the lakes and lagoons, they are readily identifiable by their characteristic colors and by the small, finely shaped head of the female.

When widgeons rose in flight, darkening the sky and clashing their wings, we could truly appreciate how numerous they were. And in the evenings sweet music floated over the meadows and the water: thousands of widgeons whistled their shrill "whee-oo" while countless mallards, teals *(A. crecca)*, gadwalls *(A. strepera)*, pintails *(A. acuta)* and shovelers *(A. clypeata)* murmured an accompaniment.

Like the deer and the wild boar, the great flocks of ducks must have felt secure, for they were not especially timid, allowing us to approach much nearer than birds resting on water usually do.

BIRDS OF PREY

Las Marismas, like the Coto Doñana, has a large population of birds of prey—indeed the largest in Europe, not only in spring and summer, but in winter. The presence of birds of prey the year round in the Guadalquivir delta and westward to the Atlantic is a token of the wealth of wildlife that once existed in southern Europe and elsewhere on the Continent.

The Coto Doñana and Las Marismas provide conclusive proof that predators cannot be regarded as altogether destructive. On the contrary, they plainly contribute to maintaining the balance of nature and healthy animal communities. Here we have one of the most productive regions of Europe and also the largest population of birds of prey on the Continent. How can these facts be reconciled with the popular notion that predatory birds and beasts are harmful and should be exterminated? Many people have come to realize in the last twenty years that eliminating predators in order to encourage other wildlife has seldom brought the result man has hoped for.

Three species of vultures live around the Guadalquivir throughout the year. The very presence of these birds implies an abundance of prey as well as of predators, since vultures feed on carrion, generally the remains of animals that have been killed by other creatures. Griffon vultures *(Gyps fulvus)*, black vultures *(Aegypius monachus)* and Egyptian vultures *(Neophron percnopterus)*—although the latter are rare in winter—are seen daily in November over the Coto Doñana and Las Marismas. They soar for hours over the heaths, or sit in solitary trees or on the ground. The black vultures seem to have a predilection for taking siestas on sand dunes, where their silhouettes form the only break in the expanse of sand.

Other large birds take advantage of the rising currents of

warm air to sail about on broad wings. One of these is the imperial eagle, which breeds on the Coto Doñana and is relatively common in November. The race that breeds in Spain is easily recognized by large white patches that contrast sharply with its otherwise brownish-black plumage. The golden eagle *(Aquila chrysaëtos)* is a winter visitor, along with Bonelli's eagle *(Hieraëtus fasciatus)*, buzzards *(Buteo buteo)*, kites *(Milvus milvus)*, black kites and short-toed eagles. In November an impressive flock of kites and black kites soared around in a kind of living spiral, as buzzards and kites often do on migration. The purpose of such a flight pattern when it occurs in winter quarters is a puzzling one. Can it be interpreted as the beginning or end of the migration urge? During migration, gyration flight is clearly part of the take-off procedure. Perhaps kites in winter quarters fly in spirals simply because they enjoy doing so. It can hardly be part of their hunting behavior; none broke out of the formation to catch prey on the ground. Nor does it seem practical for thirty or forty kites to hunt simultaneously over the same limited area. Moreover, neither eagles nor vultures indulged in such gyration flights in the Coto Doñana in November. Whatever the reason for this flocking of kites here, their social aerial exhibitions are a common winter sight.

The marsh harrier *(Circus aeruginosus)* is likewise an integral part of the winter scene at Las Marismas. All day long it flies to and fro or sits in a tree shrub near the reeds. One or two ospreys *(Pandion haliaëtus)* may visit the flooded meadows in November, but the water is so full of twigs and the fish so scarce that such a bird can hardly find satisfactory fishing there. Peregrine falcons *(Falco peregrinus)* are also frequent visitors, since their favorite food—duck—abounds. Kestrels *(F. tinnunculus)* are common although their hunting grounds are greatly reduced by floods that drive away their prey, mostly small rodents and insects.

The fate of terrestrial animal life when the widespread salicornia heaths are flooded in winter is one of the most fascinating problems in the ecology of Las Marismas. Throughout their whole life cycle many insects can survive great changes in environment, but this seems impossible for small rodents, shrews, and reptiles. Perhaps the parts of Las Marismas that are flooded in winter do not harbor mammals and reptiles either underground or on the surface simply because these animals do not have time to colonize such areas during the dry season. But nature usually fills all empty spaces, even seasonally, so here we are probably facing a situation in which small mammals and reptiles migrate annually between two habitats. Otherwise, there would not be much food in these vast areas for the many birds of prey that hunt there in summer. I have learned from Dr. Valverde that hares, wild boars and fallow deer migrate in autumn from Las Marismas to the Coto, while colonies of lizards, established in summer, perish when the area becomes flooded.

The Coto Doñana and Las Marismas are, for Europe, immensely rich in wildlife in winter, but the area then is only a pale image of its magnificence in spring and summer.

THE WATERS OF LAS MARISMAS

The autumn rains that flood the great delta area, beginning in October or November, have hardly had a chance to dry out in some parts of the marshes before the sun begins to melt

In the Coto Doñana, two Egyptian vultures and a raven look on as a black kite feeds on a dead lamb. (Eric Hosking)

the snow in the mighty Sierra Morena Mountains; the water rushes past Seville and, augmented by spring rains from February to April, reaches the flat country of Las Marismas. There, drawn into innumerable meandering branches, it overflows its banks and inundates a land just waking from winter sleep. Las Marismas again becomes one vast sheet of water where the hidden arms of the delta can be discerned only by studying the surface flow.

The Guadalquivir delta covers an area of about 740 square miles, of which Las Marismas occupies about 620 square miles. It is the largest marsh on the Iberian peninsula. Like all living deltas, Las Marismas is constantly being changed by the action of the river. Usually the sediment deposited by rivers consists of fertile, sandy soils, which are gradually colonized by plants and trees, or become productive cultivated land. This does not happen at Las Marismas; the Guadalquivir spreads a layer of mud over the whole of the delta land and the summer drought turns this into a dry caked surface. The result is very sparse vegetation. The region nevertheless has a rich animal life.

From descriptions by the Romans we know that in ancient times the delta was even larger than it is now. *Lacus lagustinus*, the name the Romans gave to Las Marismas, was then a lagoon stretching all the way from Seville to about the present Coto Doñana. The lagoon gradually silted up to form a marsh or partly dry land. Now only about half of the former marsh is true marshland, but this still covers an immense area.

A significant and unique feature of Las Marismas is the fact that, unlike most deltas, it lies inside the point where its waters flow into the ocean. After leaving the principal beds of the Guadalquivir and the Guadiamar and meandering around over the marshy plain, the innumerable channels flow into the Guadalquivir before it reaches the sea. This unusual circumstance, which is only a few centuries old, is due to the great barrier of sand dunes raised by the Atlantic winds between the sea and Las Marismas. These dunes, among the highest in Europe, now form a mighty barrier, from one to nine miles wide, blocking the network of rivers that once ran straight from Las Marismas into the sea. Now the lesser rivers have been forced into the Guadalquivir, and it alone drains the whole delta. But much water remains in Las Marismas and gives the region its character.

The isolation of Las Marismas behind the barrier of dunes causes great masses of fresh water to be dammed up during the annual floods. On the other hand, salt water from the sea pours into the Guadalquivir with the high tides of winter and spring, overflows the river banks, and spreads over Las Marismas, making it largely a brackish-water delta. The salinity of the subsoil water is high, with an average of about one-third more salt than in the very saline Mediterranean. This is one reason why flamingos are found here. Their food needs are related to the salinity of practically stagnant water. This is also true to a certain extent of avocets. In the Coto Doñana, at a somewhat higher level than Las Marismas, there are several lagoons, lakes, and watercourses with fresh water, but these are generally quite close to the sea.

A delta is always dramatic in its dynamics, but the water conditions and seasonal changes in the landscape of the Coto Doñana and Las Marismas are probably without parallel in Europe.

THE COMING OF SPRING

By summer Las Marismas has been largely transformed into dry land. How different it then is from the watery region of autumn, winter, and spring. For four months or more, Las Marismas is first a flowering and then a green heath.

Sun, wind, and water have, for thousands of years, fostered the natural life of the Coto Doñana and Las Marismas, while man's role has proved insignificant, restricted almost entirely to the minor effect of his cattle. These black, sharp-horned beasts—perhaps direct descendants of the prehistoric aurochs—are not very numerous and graze as individuals or in small widely-scattered herds, so there is no question of their trampling down vegetation or destroying the soil.

In some parts of Andalusia the luxuriant vegetation reminds one that Africa is not far away. Neither the Coto Doñana nor Las Marismas can claim such rich vegetation; nevertheless, the flora is surprisingly abundant and varied. It would not be difficult to make an inventory of the flora, for the plant communities are rather distinct, and the species easily identifiable. The several British expeditions that have worked in this corner of Spain have reported that about eighty per cent of the plants of the Coto Doñana and Las Marismas are also widely distributed in Europe and Africa.

It is a fascinating experience to meet spring in the south-western part of Andalusia, for it is then that the exotic nature of the region is most manifest, forming a tapestry of colors and a symphony of sounds unparalleled elsewhere in Europe. Between two entirely different aquatic worlds, the Atlantic to the west and Las Marismas to the east, is the Coto Doñana, the home of many species of animals and plants. In spring, when the area is invaded by thousands of birds on their way northward from Africa, there is at times an indescribably rich bird life in shrubs and trees, on beaches and meadows.

A walk from the Atlantic coast to the marshes takes one over enormous sand dunes, through coniferous woods, deciduous woods and shrubs to Las Marismas, which in itself, as we have seen, changes from marshes into a dry plain. It is this infinitely differentiated landscape that, in spite of its flatness, gives the region its diversity of animal and plant life. Generally, the Coto Doñana, consists of sandy soils. The topsoil of Las Marismas is a clayey earth deposited when the Guadalquivir overflows its banks.

The whole stretch of coast from Huelva down to the wide estuary of the Guadalquivir at Sanlucar de Barrameda is virgin land, where the only signs of man's influence are stone watchtowers built in the Middle Ages for defense. It is unfortunate that a projected highway along the coast now threatens to disturb this series of natural environments.

DESERTED BEACHES AND MOVING DUNES

Where the Coto Doñana and the sea meet, the waves of the Atlantic roll over Playa Castilla, an almost perfectly straight, smooth beach about thirty-eight miles long. Only a few plants grow, precariously, above the high-water level. The simple elements of sand and water create a true grandeur. Looking out to sea or along the pale sandy beach into the misty distance, the interior hidden by the ridge of dunes to the east and northeast, one feels just as dwarfed as in the shadow of high mountains.

Now and then birds enliven the generally deserted beach. Migrating waders—gray plovers (*Charadrius squatarola*), sanderlings (*Crocethia alba*) and oystercatchers (*Haematopus ostralegus*)—linger in November. The Kentish plover (*Charadrius alexandrinus*) breeds on the sandy beach. Caspian terns (*Hydroprogne tschegrava*) appear. A pair of peregrines (*Falco peregrinus* occupy one of the medieval watchtowers, which have never before housed such keen-eyed watchmen. The hunting territory of the peregrines is inland, over dunes, woods and marshes. Other occupants of the watchtowers include kestrels, barn owls (*Tyto alba*), little owls (*Athene noctua*) and jackdaws (*Corvus monedula*).

When one leaves Playa Castilla to climb up the first dunes, one comes upon an expanse of sand that stretches as far as the eye can see. The dunes close to the sea are covered with marram grass (*Ammophila arenaria*), faithful colonizer of sandy beaches, but inland the tufts of plants become less dense and then disappear completely. The dunes are the highest points in the region, rising to more than three hundred feet, but ranging topographically from high ridges to deep hollows. The vegetation varies with height, sand-drift, exposure to wind, and moisture. A walk over the dunes is indeed a journey of discovery. Sand is everywhere, but the scene is far from monotonous.

Some areas are completely barren; on these mobile dunes one could imagine oneself suddenly in the Sahara. The dunes are constantly on the move, smothering fertile land, whether

Pines and junipers climb the cliffs of the Costa Brava at Golfo de Rosas on the Spanish Mediterranean coast. The famous blue water of the Mediterranean is the result of its high salinity. (Erich Andres)

Besides this griffon vulture, two other species of vultures, the bearded and the Egyptian, live in the Pyrenees—a high concentration for Europe. (Michel Terrasse)

natural vegetation around small ponds left from the annual floods, or planted pine woods. In one area the dunes extend all the way from the sea to Las Marismas. This is Europe's desert, a true desert, including oases here and there.

Elsewhere in the Coto Doñana colonization by plants and trees has partly or wholly stabilized the dunes. Static and moving dunes form a mosaic pattern rather than two distinct regions. In such marginal areas the desert has some unusual inhabitants. It is traversed not only by snakes and lizards, but also by hares *(Lepus capensis)* which cross the bare sand between green patches. It may be that some reptiles live more or less permanently in the sand dunes, hunting insects or each other at the edge of the areas of vegetation. There are several species in North Africa that make this kind of adjustment.

Pioneer among the plants that have succeeded wholly or partly in binding the moving sand is a kind of heather-like shrub, *Corema album*. As the sand becomes stabilized, this shrub is followed by *Halimium halimifolium*, a rather low plant which transforms the bare sand into a kind of sand heath. Elsewhere in the Coto Doñana it reaches a height of three feet. The animal life of the corema community is poor but becomes richer farther from the sea, where halimium dominates. Thekla larks hunt insects, and red-legged partridges *(Alectoris rufa)* fly up in fright now and again, but are much more frequent where the vegetation is denser. Stone curlews *(Burhinus oedicnemus)*, which favor dry heaths, stand with their necks stretched up, staring at the intruder before they finally take to flight, revealing the characteristic white stripes on their wings. As is indicated by their remarkably large eyes, these waders are chiefly nocturnal. Both thekla larks and stone curlews are also found among the thinly-covered corema dunes toward the Atlantic, and even visit the almost naked dunes near the sea, where only sporadic tufts of marram grow.

In spring and summer birds and insects avoid the hot air immediately above the dunes and hide in whatever shade the scanty vegetation provides. Higher up in the blue sky soar two species of birds of prey—the short-toed eagle and the imperial eagle—their presence indicating that these dunes are not wholly devoid of life, since the former lives on reptiles and the latter on small mammals.

AN ABUNDANCE OF REPTILES

As often in deserts and extremely dry zones in subtropical areas, reptiles are remarkably abundant. Indeed, there are more species of reptiles than of birds on the corema and halimium dunes. Two lizards, two snakes and a tortoise are found there regularly. One of these lizards, the spiny-toed lizard *(Acanthodactylus erythrurus)*, is a typical desert species in Africa and Asia. This creature, about six-and-a-half inches long, is adapted to life in soft sand. Its toes, as its name implies, are equipped with a fringe of spiny scales which, like snowshoes, enlarge the bearing surface and facilitate movement over and digging into sand. American desert lizards of the genus *Uma* show a parallel development. The other lizard in the Coto Doñana is the Algerian sand-lizard *(Psammodromus algirus)*. This species, which also occurs in northwestern Africa, where it is a characteristic inhabitant of dry heaths and bushland, has keels and nodules under its toes—another form of adaptation to sandy habitats. The male is a glossy brown, which in some individuals is tinged with red or bronze-green, while the forepart of the body is speckled with blue spots surrounded by white rings. This lizard's body is somewhat less than four inches long, but its tail is about twice that length and adds to the animal's grace. Another member of the dune fauna is a tortoise *(Testudo graeca)* that is mainly vegetarian. A species typical of semideserts and steppes, its presence in the Coto Doñana implies that it has adapted itself to such plants as corema and halimium. Most likely it also feeds on insects on the dunes.

The Montpellier snake *(Malpolon monspessulanus)*, widely distributed in southern Spain, abounds in the Coto Doñana and Las Marismas. It has colonized the dune region, where it lives on lizards and snakes and perhaps on young thekla larks. It is one of the three venomous European species that has its poison fangs in the rear of its mouth. It must therefore draw the prey into its mouth before it can inject venom into its victim. Death occurs within three or four minutes—which is very fast for a cold-blooded reptile. Although the Montpellier snake is surely very venomous, its bite is not likely to prove dangerous to a human being because its poison fangs could not come into play. This snake may attain a length of six feet and it snaps wildly when attempts are made to capture it. Even as late as November, when the temperature generally has a calming effect on reptiles, a violent struggle resulted when six of us tried to capture one.

Another most interesting reptile of the sand dunes is Lataste's viper *(Vipera latasti)*, found only in the Iberian peninsula and northwestern Africa. Its tracks suggest that it moves in the same way as the sidewinder of American deserts and some African vipers that live in a sandy environment. Although its sidewise glide looks strange, it is a very effective means of locomotion in soft sands. The development of such an unusual method of locomotion on different continents and in various species is further evidence of parallel evolution.

UMBRELLA PINE FORESTS

On the land side of the dunes, umbrella pines *(Pinus pinea)* form a belt of varying width. Lone groves of pines also form oases in the desert landscape. These dwarfed trees are found in the hollows, yet most of them will nevertheless probably be killed off by the sand. There is some doubt whether these pine woods are native or not. The planting of such forests is said to have taken place in the eighteenth and nineteenth centuries. But the pine is indigenous to this part of Spain, and is found north of Las Marismas, so its presence on the dunes in this environment cannot be considered unnatural.

Animal life in the pine oases is rich, contrasting with that of the surrounding dunes. At migration seasons the woods are filled with birds that rest there for a day or so before continuing on their way. The air is then full of the songs of small warblers, flycatchers, and shrikes—a desert chorus. Carrion crows *(Corvus corone)*, rare in this corner of Europe, have, curiously, chosen among the many environments of the Coto Doñana these poor pine woods as their principal habitat. The reason for this may be that it is easy to catch prey on the ground there. If so, these crows, like the short-toed eagles breeding here, probably feed mainly on reptiles. That these birds live here is evidence in itself of the wealth of reptile fauna in this seemingly poor environment. The number and species of birds increase dramatically where the pine belt is continuous, and continues to increase the farther inland one gets until, in Las Marismas, the crescendo of birds' songs and clashing wings is almost deafening.

The struggle of the pines for survival in the unfertile soil is desperate, and although the trees bolster the fertility of the soil, man does nothing to help. Instead, he hampers their growth by cutting off branches and collecting twigs for making charcoal, thus depriving the soil of needed waste material.

Only in the southeastern part of the Coto Doñana do the pine woods extend as far as the marshes of Las Marismas. In the northeastern section the stands of pine are gradually replaced by heaths colonized by halimium. Here and there the pine woods border on freshwater lagoons, thus contributing to the pleasing variety of Las Marismas.

How much life this poor pine wood on the edge of the dune desert contains! In spring it is alive with birds, including species to delight the most discriminating ornithologist. First there is that master singer, the orphean warbler *(Sylvia hortensis)*, which nests in bushes and on the lower branches of trees. The Sardinian warbler, its near relative, which we saw in winter, sings diligently, and, while singing, sometimes makes a flight above the scrub. The melodious warbler *(Hippolais polyglotta)* is impressive for its varied song and its mimicry. Over the pine wood the wood lark *(Lullula arborea)*, found in other environments in most parts of Europe, utters its lovely song. Other small birds one can descry or hear in the bushes include the Dartford warbler and the nightingale. The trill of the serin *(Serinus serinus)* is heard occasionally, but this bird prefers cultivated country and seems not too common

in this wild region. Goldfinches visit the pine woods but prefer the vicinity of settlements. The raven *(Corvus corax)* breeds here, and the azure-winged magpie not only breeds here but is common among the pines; its pale brownish-gray body and light-blue wings and tail contrast with its blue-black cap, forming a glorious sight against dark-green pines and sunlit sand. This magpie seems able to compete successfully with the common magpie *(Pica pica)*, which has been forced to the outer fringes of the pine woods. The great gray shrike and the blackbird *(Turdus merula)* are among the other passerines often seen here.

The woodchat shrike *(Lanius senator)*, with red, black, and white plumage, sits in the shade of the umbrella pines, where its contrasting colors give it excellent camouflage. Hobbies *(Falco subbuteo)*, black kites, and at least two pairs of imperial eagles, a normal number in territories of this size, also live here, not to mention such other birds of prey as buzzards *(Buteo buteo)*, booted eagles, kestrels, and kites. In fact, no fewer than one-third of the birds breeding in the pine woods

Cattle egrets nesting on a platform of reeds. In Europe this small heron occurs only in the southwestern Iberian peninsula, its main distribution being in Africa and Asia. (G. K. Yeates)

of the Coto Doñana—a remarkably high percentage—are birds of prey.

The ring dove *(Columba palumbus)* is common here, but prefers to nest in such shrubs as *Rubus* and *Pistacea lentiscus* rather than in the pines. One of the Coto Doñana's rarest birds, the red-necked nightjar *(Caprimulgus ruficollis),* appears in these woods. Remarkably enough, the green woodpecker *(Picus viridis),* which prefers deciduous woods, lives in holes in the pines. A bird mainly found in Africa, the great spotted cuckoo *(Clamator glandarius),* is also found here. Like the European cuckoo *(Cuculus canorus),* it is parasitic, usually laying its eggs in the nests of magpies and crows.

At times the pine woods are alive with lizards and snakes, but the number of species is no greater than on the scrub covered dunes. The same species appear in both habitats, but evidently the pine wood is their favorite environment. From here the reptiles colonize the pine oases, and from the oases they make dangerous excursions over the open sand. Probably the reptiles leaving the pine wood are surplus members of the population. This illustrates a fundamental principle of the animal world: namely that mainly excess individuals leave the optimum environment owing to lack of space and competition for food. Spreading over less favorable areas, these are subjected to greater persecution by predators than in their original habitats. And so in summer birds of prey constantly patrol the semidesert dunes.

Besides the hare already mentioned, several mammals inhabit the pine woods. Before the lethal virus, myxomatosis, killed them off, wild rabbits *(Oryctolagus cuniculus)* abounded, and were a staple food of various birds and beasts of prey. The mongoose *(Herpestes ichneumon),* an African animal and a relative of the Asian mungo made famous by Kipling, lived largely on these rabbits. In the damp hollows of the pine belt, where the brush vegetation is dense, there are deer and wild boar, both also found in the interior of the Coto Doñana. And the black rat *(Rattus rattus)* lives among the pines, apparently having learned to feed on pine cones and to get along without human beings. This is also true to a certain extent of the dormouse, which in this area belongs to the species *Eliomys lusitanicus.*

THE HALIMIUM HEATH

The greater part of the woods of the Coto Doñana open onto a heath colonized mainly by *Halimium* thickets, the dominant vegetational environment, or biotope, of the Coto Doñana. This pale green heath is most beautiful when covered with flowers, especially the yellow *H. halimifolium,* but also various kinds of broom *(Genista)* and gorse *(Ulex).*

The shrubs on the halimium heath grow in thickets three to five feet high and are so dense in places that they form a low, closed canopy. The only way to study wildlife here is by creeping and wriggling, but one soon stops trying, for the thickets are truly impenetrable. Perhaps for that very reason they contain a rich animal life, made up not only of insects and other invertebrates, but also of birds (particularly warblers of the genus *Sylvia),* lizards, and some batrachians.

Among the latter I found, to my surprise, considering the environment, the natterjack *(Bufo calamita).* The thickets are also a favorite haunt of the pardel lynx.

Thekla larks, red-legged partridges, and stone curlews are found on the fringes of the heath, but they do not penetrate far into the halimium thickets, probably because there the thickets are much more dense than on the dunes. The Dartford warbler is the typical bird of these thickets. Its characteristic profile, dark-red breast, and cheerfully wagging tail may often be seen as it alights for a moment on top of a bush.

In the halimium thickets the number of mammals, in species and in individuals, is higher than in habitats already described. Here there is clearly more suitable food and shelter for such animals than in the sparse ground vegetation of the pine woods. Of the smaller carnivores found here, the pardel lynx and the wildcat *(Felis sylvestris)* are the most remarkable. The fact that the shrubs of the Coto Doñana harbor two species of Europe's wild cats indicates how remote and isolated the region remains.

The Coto Doñana is one of the last secure retreats of the pardel lynx. It has been estimated that there are still about 150 of them there—a goodly number, considering that the whole region encompasses only about sixty-two square miles. Dr. Valverde has calculated that each individual possesses a territory with a diameter of two-and-a-half to six miles, but that the animals sometimes travel twelve to eighteen miles.

The pardel lynx is another animal that fed on wild rabbits until myxomatosis greatly reduced the number of rabbits. This was an unfortunate development, for Spain is the only place in Europe to which the wild rabbit is indigenous. But the number of pardel lynxes has not been affected by the sudden decimation of wild rabbits, since hares, red-legged partridges, and other small animals have filled the gap. Neither do the lynxes appear to be greatly affected by predation. The dense populations of red deer, fallow deer, several species of small game, and the large number of cattle, that coexist with a relatively large population of pardel lynx show that it is in general not necessary for man to persecute predators. Other carnivores here include the weasel *(Mustela nivalis)* and the polecat *(M. putorius),* both rare, and the genet *(Genetta genetta)*—a lithe creature of African origin—and its relative, the mongoose. The fox *(Vulpes vulpes)* has also found its way here to hunt small rodents. The hedgehog *(Erinaceus europaeus)* hides under the dense vegetation. Red deer visit the area all the year round.

There are also more reptiles, or at least a greater number of species, on the halimium heath. But in the dense thickets they cannot be observed as often as in the open pine woods. The reptiles have a thousand hiding places and are quick to take cover when a vibration of the ground warns them of another creature's approach. In addition to the reptiles already mentioned, two species of snakes and three of lizards exist on the heath. Among the latter is the strikingly beautiful pearl lizard *(Lacerta lepida).* It sports a mosaic pattern in emerald green, yellow, and black, a series of blue dots along the sides of its body, and a rose-colored gape. It is a giant for Europe and for its family *Lacertidae,* sometimes attaining a length of thirty inches. A formidable predator, it eats insects, reptiles, and small rodents.

Here and there the flora of the heath alters to a macchia type of vegetation. Bramble *(Rubus)* and tree heather, reaching up to ten feet in height, mix with, or replace, the halimium. There the stonechat abounds, and the curious "knocking" call of the red-necked nightjar sounds on spring nights.

Granite rocks sculptured by sand bear witness to the tremendous effect of wind erosion during millions of years. (Erich Andres)

THE CORK OAK SAVANNA

One of the most interesting parts of the Coto Doñana is the savanna-like country beginning where the great treeless halimium plain ends. The halimium dominates the savanna, too, but the presence of many cork oaks gives the area its characteristic savanna features: tree heather, blackberry bushes and a few olive trees also grow there. In this parklike area the wide crowns of the cork oaks soar to heights of from thirty to fifty feet. Many of the trees are hollow. In one such hollow tree, near the ground where the great trunk encloses a cavern-like niche, a pardel lynx had reared its young. The cork oaks are sometimes resting places for the largest of the Coto Doñana carnivores, which are then close to their favorite territory, the dense macchia.

The interior of the old cork oaks provides a good nesting place for many birds: jackdaws, great tits *(Parus major),* green woodpeckers, little owls, and barn owls, as well as bats, breed there. In the branches of the oaks or in the shrubs in their shade, large and small birds build their nests or take over those built by others. These include ringdoves, imperial eagles, booted eagles, buzzards, kites, black kites, kestrels, golden orioles *(Oriolus oriolus),* great gray shrikes, and wood-chat shrikes. Here, too, the great spotted cuckoo lays her eggs in magpies' nests.

Many other birds fly through or over the cork oak savannas on their way from their breeding grounds to feeding places in Las Marismas. Among them are several species of herons, which are seen continually over the savannas at breeding time. Their nests are concentrated in a part of the savannas containing small pools of water protected by a fringe of tree heather and bramble bushes, together with an occasional cork oak. The latter contain many nests, but most marsh birds build in the tree heather and bramble thickets. At breeding time the pools of water seethe with life, their muddy shores ploughed up by rooting boars and the hooves of red deer. White storks *(Ciconia ciconia),* night herons *(Nycticorax nycticorax),* cattle egrets *(Ardeola ibis),* and squacco herons *(A. ralloides)* also live here. The storks and herons build their nests in large cork oaks, while the night herons and little egrets use both trees and shrubs. Cattle egrets build nests mainly in thickets, but only exceptionally in trees, whereas squacco herons build nests only in shrubs.

Many insectivorous birds, such as warblers and flycatchers, leave the shrubs near the cork oak savannas to hunt for food in the rich insect fauna of the old oaks. This wealth of insects attracts a lizard, *Lacerta hispanica,* which may be seen climbing about the trunks and branches. This species, found only in the Iberian peninsula and northwestern Africa, is represented in the Coto Doñana by a race distributed only in

43

A male black-eared wheatear, common on the arid, stony plains of the Spanish sierra, brings food to the nest. (G. K. Yeates)

southernmost Spain and the most northwesterly parts of Africa. There are indications that this lizard has colonized Africa from Europe.

Sometimes a chameleon, *Chamaeleo chamaeleon*, appears in the Coto Doñana, introduced from the woods of Puerto de Santa Maria, but it does not survive. This species is also found in North Africa and western Asia, but southern Spain is the only part of Europe where it occurs.

FRESHWATER LAGOONS

About a mile from the Atlantic there is a freshwater lagoon, the first in a series of seven small lakes running from west to east through various environments almost as far as Las Marismas. These lakes contribute much to the variety of Coto Doñana's scenery. They form a boundary between the halimium heath and the pine belt, the lagoons being thus surrounded by two different types of natural setting. The series probably represents the remains of a natural channel that carried some of the water from the Guadalquivir through the delta to the sea before sand dunes closed the outlet.

The lagoons are immediately surrounded mostly by meadows of rough grass, which provide good hunting grounds for the yellow wagtail *(Motacilla flava)*. The meadows are fringed at the water's edge by bullrushes *(Scirpus lacustris)*, now standing on land, now in water, depending on the water level. In dry years, by August and September some of the lagoons are almost empty of water. Reed-mace *(Typha)* and water reed *(Phragmites communis)* grow in most of them. Many species of birds breed there, while others winter there. The moor hen *(Gallinula chloropus)*, the coot *(Fulica atra)*, and the rare crested coot *(F. cristata)*, which breed only in southern Spain, are among the water hens of the lagoons. Purple herons *(Ardea purpurea)* breed in the rushes of the Laguna de Santa Olalla, the largest of these freshwater lakes. The silhouettes of the little grebe *(Podiceps ruficollis)* and the great crested grebe *(P. cristatus)* can be seen on the open water, and the black-necked grebe *(P. nigricollis)* also turns up there. The waters prove naturally suitable for ducks, some of which are very rare in Europe. The white-headed duck *(Oxyura leucocephala)* breeds there, and so probably do the red-crested pochard *(Netta rufina)*, the white-eyed pochard *(Aythya nyroca)*, and the marbled duck *(Anas angustirostris)*.

During the spring and autumn migrations, many waders, terns and insect-eating pratincoles *(Glareola pratincola)* are seen here, but the number of birds can never mount as high as in the vast Marismas, where really extensive sheets of water and meadows attract passing aquatic birds. Along with an abundance of water insects and other small forms of animal life, there are of course other vertebrates in and around the freshwater lagoons. Large lake frogs *(Rana ridibunda)* sit in rows along the beaches when the sun is not too strong, natterjacks hop over the sand and meadows, and tree frogs *(Hyla arborea)* croak in spring and summer nights. A water lizard, the pleurodele newt *(Pleurodeles waltli)*, which is very large for Europe, attaining a length of a foot or so, lives in the lagoons of the Coto Doñana and on the periphery of the region, near Las Marismas. Two species of tortoises, the European pond tortoise *(Emys orbicularis)* and the Spanish terrapin *(Clemmys caspica)*, make an appearance on the lagoons. The water snake *(Natrix maura)* is common, and among the fish are eels *(Anguilla anguilla)* and the crucian carp *(Carassius carassius)*.

BETWEEN DRY LAND AND MARSH

The dry land of the Coto Doñana meets the marshes of Las Marismas along an expanse of about nineteen miles. In the southeastern part of this border area the pine wood reaches almost to the marshes, whereas to the northeast the halimium heath borders on Las Marismas. At Lucio del Membrillo, in the southern Coto Doñana, woodland and marshland meet, and still elsewhere the bare sand reaches to the water's edge. The juncture of varied habitats means that such birds as azure-winged magpies and flamingos, orphean warblers and marbled ducks can all be seen at one time.

Meadow, with tussocks of rush *(Juncus)*, forms the greater part of the transitional zone between pine woods and marsh. But the halimium heath, the cork oak savanna, and the macchia country border directly on Las Marismas.

Animals abound along almost the entire boundary zone between the Coto Doñana and Las Marismas. In the first place, the zone is traversed by inhabitants of two entirely different worlds. Animals living in the Coto Doñana often seek food in Las Marismas, and those of Las Marismas often hunt in the Coto Doñana. The boundary zone, furthermore, is very productive and this has encouraged an increase in the number of species there.

Rodents of different kinds are very common, as are those frogs that breed in water but otherwise live on land. One example is the southern mud frog *(Pelobates cultripes)*, which spawns in great numbers in the marsh, and whose eggs later hatch into thousands of larvae. The young frogs leave the water and spread out over the shore meadows, where they find an abundance of food. During a resting period they hide in fissures in the dried clay. In this zone, the frogs are the staple food of the water snake, the black rat, the black kite, the barn owl, several species of herons, and many other small animals, and these are in turn the quarry of still other predators. Many reptiles besides the water snake prefer to live near water; it is thus no surprise that many birds of prey are concentrated here. Buzzards, imperial eagles, kites, and booted eagles all breed here in great numbers, and black kites in even greater numbers.

Rabbits were formerly very common in the Coto Doñana near Las Marismas. There they always found fresh grass. Other rodents living in the border area that are largely responsible for the wealth of birds of prey include the Mediterranean pine vole *(Pitymys duodecimcostatus)*, the water vole *(Arvicola terrestris)*, long-tailed field mouse *(Apodemus sylvaticus)*, and dormouse. Wild boar and fallow deer come regularly at night to root and browse, sometimes accompanied by red deer. And foxes make regular trips to hunt for food. Several times I detected the footprints of the pardel lynx—even in the bare sand dunes.

Lapwings *(Vanellus vanellus)* breed on the meadows, where short-toed larks *(Calandrella cinerea)* trip about or rise singing a staccato song. This area is also a favorite haunt of yellow wagtails, which keep company with the half-wild cattle grazing there. These birds undoubtedly lived in association with the aurochs long ago, just as they now live alongside buffaloes, antelopes, rhinoceroses, and elephants in their African winter quarters. Small quails *(Coturnix coturnix)*, the smallest of gallinaceous birds, also frequent the meadows.

From the tussocks of rush at the shore of the marshland sounds the Savi's warbler *(Locustella luscinioides)*. And there the fan-tailed warbler *(Cisticola juncidis)* alights between its "flights of song."

SPRING IN LAS MARISMAS

Although the Coto Doñana, despite its flatness and its desert-like dunes, teems with life, it must perhaps take second place in this respect to its neighbor Las Marismas. As a unit, Las Marismas and the Coto Doñana are a wonderful and unique combination of dry land and marshes—a sort of European Eden, where the greatest number of vertebrate species abide.

Even though these vast marshlands turn into an almost continuous sheet of water in autumn and winter, and become a parched heath in summer, and despite seasonal contrasts that could hardly be greater, there is life there all the year round.

Two main zones characterized by their vegetation can be distinguished in Las Marismas. One is covered with fresh water practically all the year round and is marked by bullrush *(Scirpus)* and sedge *(Carex)*; the other consists of land that is dry most of the year, is overgrown by glasswort *(Salicornia fruticosa* and *Arthrocnemum marcrostachyum)*, and covers the greater part of Las Marismas. During November and December, and in some years even longer, the salicornia heath

The coloration of a bee-eater seems particularly exotic as it stands on material it has dug from its nest hole. (Walter E. Higham)

is wholly under water. Some parts of Las Marismas do lie so high that they are only rarely flooded. Such islands, called *vetas,* have been colonized by sea blite *(Suaeda maritima),* grass, and thistles, and are inhabited by numerous birds, primarily waders, pratincoles, ducks, and terns.

The vegetation of Las Marismas, logically enough, consists largely of salt-loving species of plants. But great volumes of fresh water flow out over the marshes when the Guadalquivir overflows its banks. This fresh water (La Madre de las Marismas) reaches the delta through a natural channel running parallel to the "coast" of the Coto Doñana at a distance of between five hundred and one thousand yards from the dry land. When Las Marismas is flooded, this stream of fresh water can be distinguished only by the denser vegetation of water reed and reed-mace growing along its channel.

Las Marismas in spring can compete with the lakes of tropical Africa and the marshes and lakes of Florida in respect to number of birds and bird species. It is such a favored region because periodically flooded land is nearly always rich in organic life, providing an abundance of food for birds adapted to take advantage of aquatic storehouses. It is also full of shallows and places where birds of different kinds can build their nests and rear their young.

Hence, most species of the marsh birds of Europe are to be found in and around Las Marismas. In the flocks of breeding birds are migratory species from North Europe and Asia. And here birds from the temperate and arctic zones meet.

In this vast marsh expanses of water and salicornia heaths alternate as far as the eye can see, and marsh and sky merge in the distance. On the west side of the Guadalquivir, Las Marismas is 25 miles wide (from El Rocio) and more than 43 miles long. Its total area is about 525 square miles.

The blue sky is flecked with birds, mostly drakes that have flocked together while the females sit on their eggs. (And the ducks in spring are only a fraction of the multitude present in autumn and winter.) On the grassland of shores and islets, yellow wagtails hunt flies among flocks of Kentish plover, lapwings, stone curlews, and pratincoles. Nervous redshanks fly up, yelping their note of alarm as soon as an intruder gets within thirty yards of them, disturbing avocets and black-winged stilts. On some islets little terns (Sterna albifrons) and gull-billed terns (Gelochelidon nilotica) breed.

The most common waders in Las Marismas are probably black-winged stilts; it is certainly the species one notices most among the waders. These stilts breed not only on islets, but also among the salicornia tussocks on dry land near the water. Pintails, mallard, teal, marbled ducks, gadwalls, and garganeys graze in the shallow water around the low islands. The graceful silhouettes of bee-eaters (Merops apiaster) can be observed on vetas and meadows, where they build their nests in tunnels in the ground. Sometimes they have pin-tailed sand grouse as neighbors. On the shore, black kites feed on carrion while other kites swoop down to join the feast.

From the groves round La Madre de las Marismas sounds the rather harsh song of the great reed warbler (Acrocephalus arundinaceus), and in the reeds one can see the exotic colors of the purple gallinule (Porphyrio porphyrio)—blue plumage and bright red bill and frontal shield. Spoonbills, night herons, and purple herons also dwell there.

Farther out in the marsh, where the breeze sways rush and sedge in time to the rippling water, birds appear that prefer to breed in this sparse vegetation than in the denser belts of reeds. Marsh harriers nest here, but fly far afield along the shores of Las Marismas. The bittern, surprisingly enough, builds its platforms in small tussocks, and, close by, the nests of great crested grebes rise and fall gently with the water. Several species of ducks are found here, and still other species of crakes—moor hens, coots, crested coots, and the little Baillon's crake (Porzana pusilla). Nearby are whiskered terns (Chlidonias hybrida) and black terns (C. niger)—small, dark birds that fly around hunting insects on and above the water.

Many species of birds breed on the salicornia heaths. These heaths are dry in summer, but because of the rich animal life roundabout, this salt environment is densely inhabited. The larks have adapted themselves to the dryness and no fewer than three species breed here, namely the calandra, the short-toed, and the lesser short-toed. Another heath-dweller is the yellow wagtail, which nests like an aquatic bird in glasswort tussocks surrounded by water. The Montagu's harrier (Circus pygargus) also lives in this heathlike region. Pin-tailed sand grouse, stone curlews, pratincoles, bee-eaters, and the Kentish plover, whose young may be seen on the cracked clay in May, complete the breeding bird fauna.

Various species of herons appear everywhere in Las Marismas, fishing, hunting, or flying to and from their nesting places in the Coto Doñana. Traffic is especially heavy during the breeding season when the young must be fed. The heron colony then numbers about thirty thousand birds. Although this impressive community of five species of herons is spread over a rather wide area, it must still be reckoned a major and remarkable concentration, particularly since the main body nests in the rather restricted area of the Coto Doñana.

Among all these herons, including purple herons and bitterns breeding in other parts of Las Marismas and in the lagoons, there is no competition for food. Some herons even fly as far as the Guadalquivir to fish; the proof of this is that they feed river fish to their young in Coto Doñana nests.

The pochard (Aythya ferina) occurs in Las Marismas and is most common in Las Nuevas, the central part of the marsh where the water is deeper. Las Nuevas has colonies of purple herons and what is probably Europe's largest population of marbled ducks, black-necked grebes, and whiskered terns. Many little crakes nest among the colonies of whiskered terns. Flamingos have been numerous in Las Nuevas in recent years, and have attempted to breed there. Here too appear the greatest numbers of wintering ducks and graylag geese; in spring and autumn waders are numerous.

There are of course many animals that cannot be assigned to one habitat in particular. Among these are the vultures that sail over the whole region, appearing wherever there happens to be food. There are also the multitude of waders resting in Las Marismas in spring: in April and early May one meets these birds everywhere. Flocks arrive, feed, sleep, and move on, to be succeeded the next night by newcomers. The waders include black-tailed godwits, curlews, whimbrels, greenshanks, common sandpipers, wood sandpipers, green sandpipers (Tringa ochropus), little ringed plovers, ringed plovers, black-bellied plovers, ruffs (Philomachus pugnax), curlew sandpipers (Calidris ferruginea), dunlins (C. alpina), and turnstones. They return in autumn, when I have also heard spotted redshanks (Tringa erythropus) among them. Sometimes at the end of summer an impressive concentration of bank swallows (Riparia riparia), estimated in hundreds of thousands, has been seen.

Many of the waders are at home on the tundra and mountains as far away as the coast of the Arctic Ocean. Las Marismas to them is just a resting place on their long flights between the equator and a point far beyond the Arctic Circle. The Coto Doñana is also a busy place during the migration season. But there it is mostly passerines that fill shrubs and trees with the flutter of wings, and the air with music.

THE VALLEYS OF ANDALUSIA

In terms of landscape, the magnificent marshes of Las Marismas form a climax region, that is, a stable and self-perpetuating natural community. Around the marshes lie the fertile valleys of Andalusia, which contrast brilliantly with the devastated wastes in Spain's interior. It is highly probable that the abundance of the valleys and the impoverishment of the highlands are related. For centuries the wind has transported soil from the eroded mountains and deposited it in the valleys, leaving one to die while giving life to the other.

Below the Sierra Morena, the whole wide basin of the Guadalquivir is a green oasis without equal in Spain. Ap-

The Pyrenees between Spain and France are still a wilderness area, with few roads and with long distances between villages. (Michel Terrasse)

In a stone pine in the Coto Doñana, a short-toed eagle feeds a water snake to its young; this species preys exclusively on reptiles. (Eric Hosking)

proaching Andalusia by air from Africa or northern Europe, the land below appears to be entirely sterile and desert-like until, as if by magic, the green land of Andalusia appears. But once on the ground, one can see that the entire landscape of Andalusia is the result of man's cultivation. What looked like forest land from above proves really to be orange groves and olive plantations, covering great areas with delightful park landscapes. Andalusia is a kind of cultivated savanna, where groves of trees alternate with fields of cotton, wheat, corn, and tobacco.

Vine stocks and tomatoes grow everywhere, sugar cane rises up where least expected, orange trees richly offer shade, and, above, the great leaves of the date palms rustle in the breeze. At night the song of the nightingale floats from small gardens. The territories of these birds are close together, so the singing of a dozen males may be heard at once. Even in the valleys higher up the mountains, the sound of the nightingale reigns. On quiet spring nights their singing in Granada can be heard on the heights of the ancient Alhambra. Their voices seem to permeate all of space and blend with those of Alhambra's own innumerable nightingales.

LAND OF TWO SPRINGS

Andalusia has two springs—one in the early months of the year and one in autumn. This latter season is also one of awakening. After the burning sun and the drought of summer, autumn rain transforms the parched landscape into a green paradise in October and November. The golden hues of autumn tinge some trees, the ground is carpeted with bright green grass, in the fields the pale green winter wheat appears, and many trees are clothed in silver-gray foliage, just as in the earlier spring. The groves abound with birds, many of them on their way to Africa, singing as though it were true spring.

This autumn-green Andalusia makes a deep impression on any visitor accustomed to the annual rhythm of northern landscapes. Winter in Andalusia—the season of oranges—is wonderful, too. As the fruit changes from green to orange, the whole area is filled with a most exquisite perfume, so penetrating as sometimes to be detected far up the slopes of the surrounding mountains.

Olive trees, found in most parts of the valley of the Guadalquivir, are probably the commonest trees in Andalusia. They are sometimes planted in orderly rows but sometimes less uniformly, as in former times. Seen from a height, the undulating valley country clothed in silver-gray olive trees looks like a grayish-green sea. Olives are one of the most important products of Spain and they comprise nearly half of the total world production. There are about 32,000,000 olive trees in the region round Jaén and Martos, east of Cordoba.

A landscape fusing the cultivated and the natural is found in other parts of Andalusia, too, but on a smaller scale. There are many similar valleys in Granada, where a network of rivers runs down from the mountains. These have also collected and stored washed-out soil; the result is often vegetation of almost tropical richness, but influenced everywhere by cultivation. In such valleys appear lush landscapes unique in Europe, while only a few hundred yards higher up, the mountain slopes are naked and almost empty of life.

Although the old bed of the Guadalquivir, built up by the soil washed down into it, produces excellent farmland, there is still marshland present among the groves and fields. Between Cordoba and Seville in particular, the river sporadically swells out to form such marshes, thereby attracting a variety of birds, including many species of herons—little egrets, cattle egrets, night herons, herons, purple herons, and marsh harriers. The cattle egrets flock round grazing cattle, profiting from the fact that the animals attract insects. It is beautiful to see jet-black, massive bulls surrounded by graceful white herons in a fusion of natural and cultivated landscape. Small Montagu's harriers hunting larks complete such a picture.

Nature has not been completely expelled from the thousand-year-old cities here. Both Cordoba and Seville have famous cathedrals, wonderful structures that tourists come great distances to see. On these cathedrals appears a living thing that is almost as interesting to a lover of nature as the architecture—*cernicalos,* a small falcon, or more exactly, a colony of lesser kestrels *(Falco naumanni).* The bird breeds on the cathedrals of both Cordoba and Seville. On the latter we found the lesser kestrels still present in November, when most of their kind had already reached winter quarters in tropical Africa.

The lesser kestrels on the Seville Cathedral are diurnal birds, but because the cathedral is floodlit at night, which attracts many insects, a score or more of the kestrels were energetically hunting flying insects above the towers.

Brightly illuminated by the floodlight, which made their pale underparts appear almost white against the dark November sky, they made a rare after-dark spectacle.

THE MONKEYS OF GIBRALTAR

Spain is a country of contrasts—Atlantic and Mediterranean coasts, subtropical marshes, fertile valleys, dry plateaus, stark mountains, and snow-covered peaks. Its wide topographical range corresponds to the range in climate.

But mountains and plateaus occupy much of the Iberian peninsula. These highlands are, with few exceptions, nothing but denuded, sterile land. Woods and other vegetation were long ago destroyed, leaving a large part of Spain desert or at best semidesert.

The mean height of Spain is about 1900 feet above sea level. This is the second highest in Europe, exceeded only by Switzerland and several tiny mountain states. But the most famous cliff in the area is not in Spain's highlands, nor even on the Spanish mainland. The limestone rock of Gibraltar rises 1380 feet above the Mediterranean, where Great Britain commands the passage between the Mediterranean and the Atlantic.

It is only nine miles between Europe and Africa across the Straits of Gibraltar, but more important is the fact that the water is only 1050 feet deep. This is very little when one considers that the Mediterranean is generally about 6500 feet deep close to the shore and about 9800 feet or more farther out. The comparative shallowness off Gibraltar provides a threshold in the Strait that prevents the tides of the Atlantic from affecting ebb and flow in the Mediterranean.

The east face of the rock of Gibraltar is precipitous, but the west side slopes down in a series of terraces toward the Bay of Algeciras and the town of Gibraltar. The rock is not the most southerly point of Europe; that it is Punta Marroqui, which extends south almost to latitude 36°.

In natural history terms, Gibraltar is most famous for its monkeys. It is the only place in Europe where such animals are found wild. They live mostly on the gentle slopes of the west face of the rock. The Gibraltar ape is a magot or Barbary ape *(Macaca sylvana),* a species which is also found in northwestern Africa, but nowhere else. The Barbary ape is remarkable because it alone among the apes in Africa lives north of the Sahara. Most likely the magot once had a wider distribution but has become isolated in northwestern Africa by the spreading of the desert. Once, the magot was probably more widely distributed in Europe, too. Indeed fossilized remains of macaques, a species closely related to the Barbary ape, have been found in Europe as far north as England.

Apart from being—along with the anthropoid apes and gibbons—the only tailless monkey, the magot is the only macaque in Africa. Not until we reach Pakistan do we find related species—and they have tails. The isolated distribution of the magot has led to speculation that it was brought to northwestern Africa and Spain by Arabs. This is unlikely, since magot-like macaques existed in former times in many parts of Europe.

During World War II there was some danger that the Barbary ape would disappear completely from Gibraltar. When Winston Churchill learned of this while on a visit to the rock during one of the most critical phases of the war, he ordered the magot population augmented immediately to ensure the future of the ape on Gibraltar. Specimens were then imported from Morocco. It is said that the older magot population persists in a small area on Gibraltar, has become quite wild, and does not associate with the newcomers, which have become acclimatized and half-tame.

The finest natural feature of the Gibraltar area is not the rock with its apes, but the dense, magnificent woods at Almoraima. There Europe truly meets Africa, in an encounter celebrated by the songs of the many birds in the woods. The long-tailed tit *(Aegithalos caudatus),* the firecrest *(Regulus ignicapillus),* the chiffchaff *(Phylloscopus collybita),* and the Bonelli's warbler *(P. bonelli)* are European birds that here associate with such African species as the rufous warbler *(Agrobates galactotes),* the olivaceous warbler *(Hippolais pallida),* the Sardinian warbler, and the Spanish sparrow *(Passer hispaniolensis).* Despite its name, the Spanish sparrow is mainly an African species.

THE SPANISH SIERRAS

The valley of the Guadalquivir is surrounded by the highlands of Granada to the south and the Sierra Morena in the north. From the valley bottom, through the openings of tributary valleys, the contours and icy caps of these sierras can now and then be seen. Like all high land in the Iberian peninsula, the Sierra Morena has been impoverished. It does not however reveal the same degree of erosion as other Spanish mountains. This is also partly true of the Sierra Nevada, as far as could be judged from an airplane. One cannot help wondering why these two southern sierras have escaped as much as they have. Among the desert-like plateaus of the Sierra Morena and on the greatly eroded slopes, green patches can be seen, where sparse vegetation has draped the naked rock. One's first thought is that these green oases are places not yet destroyed by grazing goats, until, in another part of the mountains, one comes upon more or less open macchia vegetation on similar sites. Sometimes the shrubs are dense enough to warrant the name of thickets. Evidently such oases are not the remains of former vegetation, but recolonization of previously naked ground which, owing to topographical features, has been able to catch and accumulate fugitive soil. It is such evidence that allows us still to hope that this land may recuperate if it is allowed to develop without harmful interference from man and his goats. With the right treatment, convalescence could perhaps even be accelerated.

Up in the sierra the principle of the gradual recovery of vegetation can be studied. Here various topographical features begin to trap the particles of soil and make vegetation possible again. Such a recovery will take centuries—perhaps thousands of years—in the Sierra Morena. The few green patches in these sierras have probably survived because they are so far from the villages in the valleys, and so isolated by the mountain deserts that goatherds no longer go to them with their animals.

Gradual recovery of vegetation is likewise taking place in the lower parts of the Sierra Morena, where the earth is cultivated and is being constantly renewed by airborne particles of soil, but here crop rotation by man allows fallow periods that are long enough for arable land to revert to bush and forest.

The high plateaus of Spain are geologically older than most of the Mediterranean lands, although they were lifted to their present altitude during the Tertiary period. A folded part of the Sierra Nevada range shows fearful erosion. (Gerhard Klammet)

Almost everywhere in Spain, one or another dazzlingly snow-covered mountain range looms near at hand or in the distance. Close up to such ranges in central Spain as the Sierra de Gredos or Sierra de Guadarrama, the vista almost everywhere is dismal: exhausted land, and without the green spots that in the Sierra Morena and the Sierra Nevada provide some slight hope for the future. Conditions are not much better on the plateau around Madrid, almost the center of the arid country. The land here, once cultivated, was deserted after it had been exhausted. Now vegetation is attempting to take possession again, but it is, alas, fighting a losing battle against grazing and trampling by livestock.

The vertical distribution of vegetation and animals on a mountainside, is always interesting. Judging from visits to a couple of mountains, it is surprising, considering the poor environment, how many species of birds are found there. The number increases astonishingly wherever patches of deciduous or coniferous forest still remain, indicating how rich the bird life must have been when trees covered the mountains. We are indebted to the Spanish ornithologist Professor Francisco Bernis for much of our knowledge of the vertical distribution of birds in these mountains. According to him, twenty-one species were found in the deciduous forest belt of the Sierra de Gredos, the most common being the great tit, the blue tit *(Parus caeruleus)*, and the chaffinch *(Fringilla coelebs)*. Nineteen species live on the Sierra de Guadarrama, with the chaffinch the most common bird. In the subalpine

coniferous forest zone the figures were twenty-two and thirty-two species respectively, with the coal tit and the chaffinch as the most usual birds. On the alpine heath above the tree line, there were eight species on the Sierra de Gredos and nine on the Sierra de Guadarrama; in both places the hedge sparrow *(Prunella modularis)*, the bluethroat *(Luscinia svecica)*, and the ortolan bunting *(Emberiza hortulana)* were commonest. There were thirteen species in the highest belt of the Sierra de Gredos and twelve in the Sierra de Guadarrama. Of these species the following also bred in these mountains: the griffon vulture, the Egyptian vulture, the golden eagle *(Aquila chrysaëtos)*, the kestrel, the lesser kestrel, the crag martin *(Ptyonoprogne rupestris)*, the raven, the chough *(Pyrrhocorax pyrrhocorax)*, the rock thrush *(Monticola saxatilis)*, the black redstart *(Phoenicurus ochruros)*, the alpine accentor *(Prunella collaris)*, the rock pipit *(Anthus spinoletta)*, and the rock bunting *(Emberiza cia)*.

The above distribution is probably representative of the sierras of the Iberian peninsula. But it must of course be corrected for mountain ranges that have been deprived wholly or partly of their forests, as for example the Sierra Nevada and the Sierra Morena.

Crag martins may often be seen hunting over ravines and at the bottom of precipices in southern European mountain regions, sometimes together with the Alpine swift *(Apus melba)*. The pallid swift *(A. pallida)* occurs in the Sierra Morena and the Sierra Nevada, but is almost impossible to distinguish in flight from the swift, which occurs almost everywhere in Europe.

The easiest birds to detect as they sail over the open stony plains of the sierras, or perch on granite rocks worn smooth by wind-blown dust, are the large birds of prey. Several of these have been mentioned; of the others, the buzzard is most common. Also present are kites, black kites, short-toed eagles, booted eagles, Bonelli's eagles *(Hieraëtus fasciatus)* and, where groves of conifers have been allowed to remain, an occasional sparrow hawk *(Accipiter nisus).*

Wheatears of various kinds thrive in the endless stony wastes, among them are the so-called wheatear, *Oenanthe oenanthe,* and at times also the black-eared wheatear *(O. hispanica)* and the black wheatear *(O. leucura);* the latter, with its dark plumage and white rump, can be seen at great distances against the pale ground.

The wolf *(Canis lupus)* occurs here, as in several other mountain regions, but is very rare everywhere. Trout *(Salmo trutta)* live in many of the rivers of the Sierra de Gredos. There are also isolated populations of the ibex *(Capra pyrenaica)* among these bare mountains, some of them at rather low altitudes. Formerly the species was probably not the alpine animal it seems to be nowadays. Most likely it was driven up into the highest mountains by man. In other words, the ibex could have a much wider distribution and might even be made useful as a game animal to man. It is much more worthy of encouragement than the tame goat, for it does not destroy its environment and its population can be kept within desired limits.

The ibex is now found in Spain in eight main regions, among them the Sierra Morena and the Sierra Nevada. The total population is probably about 2500 animals.

CATALONIA AND THE PYRENEES

The two great green areas of Spain are at opposite corners of the country: Andalusia in the southwest and Catalonia in the northeast. After a sojourn in the semideserts of Castille, the fresh, living landscape of Catalonia is truly a relief. Large-scale reforestation has succeeded here. Cork oaks, evergreen oaks *(Quercus ilex),* and olive trees spread over the undulating country between the Mediterranean coast and the mountain ranges. The coastal plain teems with life. Gardens and rich arable land abound. Choirs of birds seem to sing songs of praise. Again, this is a cultivated landscape.

The Pyrenees rise like a mighty barricade, more than 10,000 feet high, between France and Spain. Like the Alps,

they form a climatic boundary: south of the range it is often sunny and hot, while to the north it is rainy and cold.

Of all the mountains in Europe, outside of the Caucasus, the Pyrenees give the greatest impression of wildness, not only because of their height and majesty, their peaks piercing the clouds, but even more perhaps because they are so fresh—almost virgin country. Few roads wind through the mountains; rivers and lakes, valleys and heaths, dot the wilderness—the whole framed by alpine walls. The Pyrenees fall steeply toward Spain; on the French side the slope is gentler. Consequently the south side has the fewest roads and the most interesting natural features. Different in many ways from the sierras farther south, the Pyrenees are wilder and less eroded, their slopes being covered with vegetation. They also have a partly distinct fauna. The chamois *(Rupicapra rupicapra)* lives here as well as in the Alps. Both species also occur in the Cantabrian Mountains, west of the Pyrenees, but not elsewhere in Spain. The bear *(Ursus arctos)* is to be found in these habitats too.

The vegetation of the Pyrenees has not been destroyed to the same extent as in the southern mountain ranges. Vegetation belts can be clearly distinguished, with conifers, as usual, growing farthest up the mountains. Many species of birds found here do not occur in the sierras, or south of the Pyrenees for that matter: e.g., (in the order they are met with from the lower slopes up to the peaks), the willow warbler *(Phylloscopus trochilus),* the bullfinch *(Pyrrhula pyrrhula),* the tree creeper *(Certhia familiaris),* the whinchat *(Saxicola rubetra),* the song thrush *(Turdus philomelos),* the capercaillie *(Tetrao urogallus),* the wood warbler *(Phylloscopus sibilatrix),* the woodcock *(Scolopax rusticola),* the wall creeper *(Tichodroma muraria),* the ring ouzel *(Turdus torquatus),* the alpine chough *(Pyrrhocorax graculus),* the partridge *(Perdix perdix),* the rock ptarmigan *(Lagopus mutus),* and the snow finch *(Montifringilla nivalis).*

The bearded vulture *(Gypaëtus barbatus)* is another of the birds of the Pyrenees. It inhabits other remote mountain ranges in Spain, but there are said to be only about twenty-five pairs in the whole country. A magnificent bird, it soars high up in the air on long and—for such a large bird—narrow wings. Its eating habits are strange indeed, for it has learned to live on bones, and begins feeding on carrion only after other vultures have eaten their fill. It swallows small bones at once, but must break up the bigger ones, carrying them high in the air and dropping them on rocks below. It digests its remarkable diet completely, disgorging only remains of horn and hair. Among other vultures in the Pyrenees, the griffon and the Egyptian are most numerous.

Subtropical Lagoons

The Camargue in the Rhone Delta

4 The Rhone rises in the Swiss Alps and reaches the Mediterranean west of Marseilles. Its source is in glaciers in a Central European but nonetheless arctic region, and its course ends in two arms embracing a subtropical area, La Camargue. The latter is delta land built up of mud brought down by the river from the highest mountains. The Camargue is the result of centuries during which mountains were slowly being worn down while land at the edge of the sea was being built up. The Camargue is land still in the process of creation, changing in appearance almost from month to month.

During recent decades, when interest in nature and recognition of its value have increased everywhere, the Camargue has become famous far beyond the boundaries of France for its remarkable natural features, its unique flora, and its rich fauna, particularly birds. It is difficult to imagine a more exciting environment for the study of natural history than this complex combination of water and land. Man's interference in the natural processes of the area since Roman times has had a great effect on the development of the delta, but on the whole it has followed its own tendencies.

Although the Camargue is most appealing in spring and early summer, with its colorful pageant of flowers and birds, the scents in the mild nights, and the morning chorus of birds in reeds and groves, it is November, the rainiest month of the year, that reveals far more clearly the significance of marshy land for resting and wintering birds.

During the autumn, an immense number of ducks congregate in the lagoons of the Camargue. The most common are teal, mallard, widgeon, gadwalls, shovelers, pochards and red-crested pochards, and tufted ducks. Among the waders, redshanks are common. Flamingos, one of the most spectacular attractions of the Camargue, remain there despite the cold rainy weather. Marsh harriers and buzzards are visible every-

The greater flamingo, prize bird of the Camargue, is here seen in the Petite Camargue. The species has only a few more or less permanent breeding places on the five continents. The Camargue is the only one in Europe. (Charles Vaucher)

Left: The Camargue in southern France, a land of shallow lagoons, half-flooded meadows and rice fields, extensive salines and plains, is a paradise for birds. (Weber and Hafner)

Left below: Black-headed gulls are found all over the Camargue. (Weber and Hafner)

Below: A pratincole incubates its eggs on a simple nest among salicornia and arthrocnemum plants on hard, sun-cracked mud. One of the best known birds of the Camargue, it is found only here in France. (G. K. Yeates)

Above: Although the dry and stony plain of La Crau contrasts sharply with the adjoining wetlands of the Camargue, it is also inhabited by many species of birds. (Weber and Hafner)

Left: Wild boar are quite common in the Camargue, where they dwell in wooded areas as well as on the plains. (Weber and Hafner)

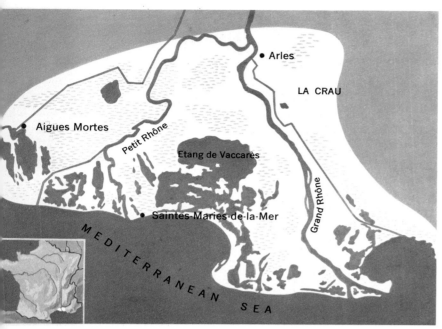

Strictly, the Camargue is only an island in the delta between the Petit Rhone and Grand Rhone, but among naturalists it includes the whole region from Aigues Mortes in the west to La Crau in the east.

where high above reeds and meadows. We even saw a spotted eagle *(Aquila clanga),* a very unusual visitor at this time of the year. It remained for several days, sometimes resting on a grassy hillock in the water, with teal swimming peacefully all around it and various kinds of ducks flying over it all the time. Even though it was late autumn, Cetti's warblers, fantailed warblers and wrens voiced their clear songs from reeds and tamarisk bushes.

The Camargue has fascinations all the year round. The beautiful autumn days with myriads of ducks quacking, chattering, and whistling in chorus, the cries of the waders, and the flight of predators over golden-brown heaths and glistening water in the rays of the low sun provide an outdoor spectacle second to none in Europe. But it is nevertheless surpassed in the spring.

Between the two arms of the Rhone the Camargue covers an area of 138,000 acres, of which 35,000 acres is cultivated land. Shallow lagoons cover about 25,000 acres. One finds a rapid succession of arable land and pastures, steppe-like heaths, plains with macchia vegetation (sometimes astonishingly like the African bush savanna), extensive salines, channels, half-flooded meadows and fields of rice, sand dunes, pine groves, gallery woods and screens of shrubs around the arms of the river, lush groves, and deciduous woods.

Practically all nature in this region has been affected directly or indirectly by cultivation, yet the area still strikes the visitor as wild. In any case, few wild areas in Europe can boast such a wealth of birds. Except for large sections that have been made into nature reserves, almost every yard of the region is traversed by hunters. In the fall, the sound of shooting is heard day and night. Apart from the fact that shooting at night is illegal, one wonders how it is possible to shoot at such a time without leaving many injured birds behind, and how dead birds can be recovered after dark in these watery wastes.

Geographically, the Camargue is an island separated from the mainland by two arms of the Rhone and is bounded to the south by the Mediterranean Sea. Biologically, the Camargue also includes the marshy land stretching east and west of the arms of the Rhone.

One is tempted to compare the Camargue with Las Marismas and the Coto Doñana of Spain. The flora and fauna are similar in many ways; but there are major differences. The climate—and even more, the hydrography—of the regions differ. Furthermore, the Coto Doñana and Las Marismas, near the Atlantic, are more African in character than the Camargue, which is typically Mediterranean. The Camargue has been more affected by cultivation and by human influence in general. The many highways and human habitations in the Camargue contrast with the trackless, almost uninhabited marshes of southwestern Spain.

Even though from a naturalist's point of view there are too many roads in the Camargue, one must admit that they have not destroyed the land and water of the region. And the roads make nature's beauties more accessible—almost every species of bird can be seen from the roads; there is no need for expeditions or for permission to visit the reservations. The nature reserves in the Camargue are intended not only to protect the flora and fauna, but to make them available for scientific research; only those carrying on approved research are allowed in some parts of the reservations.

A land wind, the famous mistral, often blows over the Camargue for long periods during the year. Beginning in the Massif Central, a mountain range more northward in France, it storms unimpeded over the plains and marshes of the Camargue. Waves run high in the lagoons, and birds take shelter. Sometimes the storm is so violent that it is almost impossible for anyone caught in it to stand upright. When it blows continuously for a week or so, it is certainly a strain on one's temper—particularly if one has come for a few days to study the birds.

The rice fields of the Camargue are flooded throughout the growing period of the rice, i. e. from April to September, by water pumped from the Rhone; this periodically increases its attraction for aquatic birds. The lagoons in turn receive the run-off from the rice fields, which increases their size while reducing their salinity. What effect these changes will eventually have is uncertain.

The first thing one sees in driving down to the Camargue on a spring day is whiskered terns hunting over the shallow water; it does not seem to matter whether the water covers young rice or soft mud, whether it is fresh or brackish. Migrating greenshanks and wood sandpipers also hunt for food here, searching just as energetically in artificial as in natural water meadows. Along with the cows grazing on the moist bright-green meadows, yellow wagtails trip, and above them lapwings, calling plaintively, engage erratically in acrobatic mating flights. Kentish plovers are found near small pools of water and salines, and along the beaches of Etang de Vaccarès.

The Camargue is the only place in Europe where flamingos nest almost every year, up to 25,000 congregating there in the spring. Characteristically, they do not have regular breeding habits. A unique attraction, these are the birds that almost all visitors ask about first.

There are many pieces in this jigsaw-puzzle of land and water, but eventually a certain natural, historical zonation

The black cattle of the Camargue live in a half-wild state, grazing especially on the glasswort that covers large parts of the Camargue. (Serge Holtz: IKO)

can be discerned, and one begins to understand how this extraordinary lowland functions ecologically.

The sea and beaches form a distinct zone, behind which are low-lying saline areas with shallow salt lagoons surrounded by temporarily flooded lands. The next zone consists of freshwater lakes and ponds and ground that is only rarely flooded. Beginning with the inland or northernmost zone, we find that this part merges almost imperceptibly into farmland, but is soon succeeded to the south by damp meadows and fields of rice alternating with vineyards. In autumn and winter the vines are kept partly under water in order to kill insect parasites *(Phylloxera)*, which live in the roots. In this northern part, the flat country is often broken by groves of trees on the farms, cypresses and poplars being planted to give protection from the mistral. Such trees form sanctuaries for birds of a kind not common in the wetter parts of the Camargue. Crested larks trip around, corn buntings *(Emberiza calandra)* hop about in the fields of grain, wood larks in spring migration sing above the trees, and orphean warblers call from the tangled hedges. Along the roads lesser gray shrikes *(Lanius minor)* sit on the lookout and serins fly singing from grove to grove. From the crowns of trees golden orioles call.

A farmer with whom I spoke was understandably astonished to learn that people crossed all of Europe just to look at the birds round his house. He admitted that he did not take much interest in the birds, except in the shooting season, when he helps himself to a few of the many ducks. Suddenly a flock of lovely rosy-white flamingos came flying over the farm. Immediately the farmer began talking about these birds. He knew a great deal about them and was very proud that they lived in his neighborhood.

Moving on, one comes to the Grand Rhone, which, like the Petit Rhone, is bordered here and there by a narrow belt of gallery woods and bushes, the lower parts of which often stand in the water. Huge poplars *(Populus alba)* covered with ivy *(Hedera helix)*, white willows *(Salix alba)*, alders *(Alnus glutinosa)*, and weeping willows edge the banks of the river, while higher up, where the flood seldom reaches, is a rich wood of oaks *(Quercus pubescens)*, elms *(Ulmus campestris)*, and ash *(Fraxinus oxyphylla)*. Under the canopy of trees is a dense thicket of shrubs divided by paths like narrow corridors. It is fascinating country, almost tropical in character, and of course full of birds. Only occasionally do the sun's rays penetrate the dense shrubs, the branches and twigs of which make a fine pattern of shadows on the pale clay soil. The privet *(Ligustrum vulgare)*, the hawthorn *(Crataegus oxyacantha)*, the dogwood *(Cornus sanguinea)*, and brambles are the principal elements in the thickets along the banks.

57

The night heron usually nests in trees in the Camargue. It spends the day in trees or thickets and then sets out at dusk or in darkness to feed in shallow water. (G. K. Yeates)

On the river side, the shrubs and trees are like a green wall, embellished here and there with beige-white squacco herons, black-white-blue night herons, and pure white little egrets. All three species breed in the woods along the Rhone, but their main habitat is elsewhere in the Camargue. We came upon their nests of twigs in colonies in the shrubs.

This jungle of shrubs is the principal haunt of small birds. Male golden orioles flash in the gloom beneath the canopy of trees when a ray of sun strikes their golden feathers. Among the multitude of songs rising from the foliage, one is tantalized by the chattering and musical tones of the melodious warbler. Hobbies *(Falco subbuteo)* live in the woods but hunt over open ground. Turtledoves *(Streptopelia turtur)* call and woodpeckers hammer under the canopy of deciduous trees. There are at least three species of the latter group: the lesser spotted woodpecker, the great woodpecker, and the green woodpecker. The presence of the beaver *(Castor fiber)*, the most remarkable animal in the narrow belt of woodland round the Rhone, is betrayed by its characteristic spoor. Along the wooded banks of the two branches of the Rhone the beaver is quite common; this area is one of its few remaining haunts in western Europe.

Leaving the fragrant semidarkness of the cool enchanting gallery woods, with its multitudes of singing birds, for the open plain and the expanses of sparkling water—the air above vibrating in the heat of the sun—is like entering another world.

HEATHS AND WOODS

East of the Grand Rhone is the broad plain of La Crau—dry and stony, almost the opposite of the Camargue. A semidesert, the ground in spring is covered with dwarf plants and a species of grass, *Stipa capillata.* Here sheep graze. Around these are many birds of species peculiar to dry heaths. There are numerous larks—short-toed larks, skylarks, crested larks, and calandra larks. The black-eared wheatear seems to have found an ideal habitat here, as has the tawny pipit *(Anthus campestris).* Hoopoes *(Upupa epops),* common in many places in the Camargue, particularly where old oaks provide nesting places, have settled here to haunt the sheepfolds, and hunt insects and lizards on the heath. The lesser kestrel (in 1956 this bird was observed breeding here for the first time) and the kestrel have much the same habits. These three birds —the hoopoe in reddish-brown, black, and white; the two kestrels in red, brown, and blue—make charming splashes of color in the open country landscape. Other denizens of the stony plateau of La Crau are pin-tailed sand grouse, little bustards *(Otis tetrax),* pratincoles, stone curlews, and red-legged partridge.

From La Crau the ground slopes down toward the marshes of the Camargue. On this slope, especially on the southern parts, are rather large woods of evergreen oaks *(Quercus ilex),* interspersed with a variety of shrubs. The woods are full of birds, especially nightingales and subalpine warblers *(Sylvia cantillans).* Brown hares frisk about in the glades, where they find plenty of food. Many holes in the ground bear witness to the former abundance of rabbits. Now they have disappeared, as they have practically everywhere on the Continent, as a result of myxomatosis. As we moved through the area, a hedgehog hurried by, snuffling as it moved, examining hollows under the roots of the oaks. We hastened to get a better view of the animal, for in this part of Europe it was possible that it would be the Algerian hedgehog *(Aethechinus algirus),* which has spread from Africa and Spain as far as east of the Rhone; but it turned out to be the common hedgehog *(Erinaceus europaeus).* It was so absorbed in its business that when we bent over it, it did not curl up, as hedgehogs usually do when frightened, but looked up for a moment with its little bright eyes, and then went on its way.

DELTA COUNTRY

So far we have described only the periphery of the Camargue. The Camargue proper begins on the lowland plain, where land and water embrace with innumerable intertwining arms. But even such country has areas that can be called dry land, in that they are never flooded though they are at times surrounded by water.

It is astonishing that such a flat region, almost at sea level, can vary so much. The reason for this is variations in elevation, even though the difference between the highest and lowest points is only about twenty inches. What makes a difference of a few inches so significant is the salty subsoil water. The distance between the subsoil water level and the surface of the land is decisive for the forms of vegetation here. Further, on land that is never flooded, that is above the high-water level, even though only slightly above, it is possible for several species of plants to survive. In some places such patches of soil may not be larger than a square yard or so, but elsewhere they may form widespread heaths.

Ground that is flooded periodically may be a vast swamp in spring and autumn and a region of sterile dry clay during summer droughts. Other stretches of water are permanent, but may be fresh, brackish, or salt. Both cattle and horses, which lead a more or less wild life in the Camargue, show almost aquatic habits. These animals are often seen wading through the marshes, the horses grazing on subaquatic plants, sometimes, like moose, with their heads almost submerged.

Many of the freshwater marshes are overgrown with rushes, reed-mace, and reeds, and surrounded by tamarisk bushes. In this sighing, rustling world there are not only innumerable small warblers, but also bearded tits *(Panurus biarmicus)*, charming in their brown, beige, yellow and black plumage. This tit haunts the outer edges of the reeds together with the reed bunting *(Emberiza schoeniclus)* and the sedge warbler. From the almost inaccessible reeds sound the songs of the reed warbler and the great reed warbler, whereas the mustached warbler *(Lusciniola melanopogon)* seems to prefer to nest in reed-mace.

Rich both in vegetable and animal organisms, the freshwater marshes of the Camargue are home to many aquatic and marsh birds. The marsh harrier appears almost constantly above the reeds where such birds as the little bittern, the water rail, and several species of small crakes *(Porzana)* hide. Moor hens also abound, and the trombone-like hoot of the bittern is a frequent note in the music of the marshes. The most common birds in and around the marshes, which are made up predominantly of fennel-leaved pondweed *(Potamogeton pectinatus)*, spiked water-milfoil *(Myriophyllum spicatum)* and rushes, are whiskered terns and black-winged stilts. Coots, little grebes, great crested grebes, and red-crested pochards can be observed on the open water, while garganeys, gadwalls, and mallards search for food in the aquatic vegetation.

The water level in most of the Camargue's freshwater marshes fluctuates considerably. Many marshes dry up in early autumn, or are transformed into great mudflats where migrating waders hunt for food. The pond tortoise, which may be seen sunning itself on a tussock surrounded by water, is an inhabitant of some of the marshes. Among batrachians is a palmate newt *(Triturus helveticus)*, and, on spring nights, tree frogs *(Hyla arborea)* sing in chorus from trees, bushes, and water. But the marsh frog is the amphibian seen most often in the many watery parts of the Camargue.

The uncultivated parts of the upper Camargue consist largely of meadows, the higher parts of which become bushy heaths. Groves of trees and tamarisk bushes grow here and there. The predominance of maritime plants, even in the interior, indicates how near the sea is. Two of the principal plants are the sea lavender *(Limonium vulgare)* and its relative *L. virgatum,* which cover large areas. Yellow dandelions are visible from great distances in spring, whereas the field forget-me-not *(Myosotis arvensis)* and the daisy *(Bellis)* are seen only when one is close upon them.

A walk over these meadows provides a rich variety of natural entertainments. Flocks of bee-eaters *(Merops apiaster)* hunt insects in the air, darting as gracefully as swallows, or gliding on still wings as if independent of gravity. They display a kaleidoscope of color—shades of green, golden yellow, and reddish-brown—and, depending on the angle of the sun, their undersides change from emerald green to Vienna blue

Little egrets balancing in the top of a stone pine. These herons feed in water, catching small fishes, crustaceans and insects along the shores. (Charles Vaucher)

and ultramarine. The bee-eaters congregate at breeding time and build their nests in tunnels in the ground or in the banks of canals. There are many such colonies in the Camargue, but the bee-eaters seem to prefer the open fields around Etang de Vaccarès, where one may see a score of them sitting on telegraph wires or perched decoratively in tamarisk bushes, resting from work on their nests.

Twittering linnets *(Carduelis cannabina)* move in small flocks over the bushes, and whitethroats *(Sylvia communis)* fly up from them singing now and again. A great gray shrike may be seen on the lookout on a shrub. The only waders that nest on the dry meadows and heaths are stone curlews and lapwings. Vultures, looking for carrion, glide overhead constantly. The most common species here is the small Egyptian vulture. The bird of prey seen most frequently on patrol is the black kite, occasionally in company with the Bonelli's eagle *(Hieraëtus fasciatus)*.

But the cluster of trees and shrubs in the lavender meadows attracts the birds most. This is especially true of the groves of tamarisks *(Tamarix gallica)* around the innumerable pools of fresh water. These pools seem to have resulted from former branches of the Rhone River and from artificial drainage ditches that have been allowed to run off at will. Around the pools or canals colonized by tamarisk bushes, brambles, elms, and poplars soon appear, and in places they form woods.

The penduline tit *(Remiz pendulinus)* hangs its skillfully

Above: In the Camargue, half-wild horses (shown here at Etang de Vaccarès) graze freely not only on grasslands but also in flooded areas, where, like amphibious mammals, they feed on aquatic plants. (Othmar Stemmler)

Right: A male edible frog, whose croaking can be heard from early spring to late summer in the Camargue, inflates air sacs as large as hazel nuts. (Julius Behnke)

Right above: Black-winged stilt on its nest. True marsh birds, these long-legged waders prefer to breed on tussocks surrounded by water. (Walter E. Higham)

Right: Like jewels in a crown, five bee-eaters, European representatives of a group of tropical birds, perch on a shrub. (Ingmar Holmåsen)

constructed nest like a great pear on the delicate branches of a tamarisk bush. Fan-tailed warblers and Cetti's warblers are attracted to such habitats, but they also haunt the reeds in the ditches, from where their melodies are heard in autumn as well as in spring and summer. At night the pleasant hooting of owls bespeaks the presence of little owls and scops owls *(Otus scops)*. The latter call incessantly and rhythmically "choo-choo-chooi-choo-choo." If there is a farm in the neighborhood, the nocturnal choir is sure to be augmented by two more owl songs: those of the barn owl and the tawny owl. Turtledoves live in the groves, too, apparently preferring brambles as nesting sites. The cuckoo *(Cuculus canorus)* is common here, where it may be parasitic on a great many bird species. Since the hoopoe and its companions, the roller *(Coracias garrulus)* and the green woodpecker, all nest in holes, it is not difficult for them to find suitable dwelling places in these deciduous woods. When there are young in the nests, the three species of birds flying to and fro in search of food provide a rare spectacle in color, especially if the sun is shining over the glade.

THE SMALLEST MAMMAL IN EUROPE

The broken terrain in the Camargue forms an excellent habitat for many mammals. The woods afford shelter, nesting places, and food, and during certain seasons the plains provide a complement to their diet. One species, the fox, even takes advantages of waste from the farms. Both the fox and badger are common in the Camargue, digging their dens in the groves.

Among the smaller mammals is one fascinating Lilliputian creature, the Etruscan shrew *(Suncus etruscus)*. The smallest mammal in Europe, one-and-a-half to two inches long, it competes with a species of bat for the title of the smallest mammal in the world. The Etruscan shrew occurs in many environments in the woods and open fields of the Camargue. Its habits are almost unknown. Its nest containing young has been found in earthholes and between the roots of trees. The known life expectancy of most shrews is very short—only up to one-and-a-half years—and this is probably also the case with the Etruscan shrew.

Among other shrews in the Camargue are the lesser white-toothed shrew *(Crocidura suaveolens)*, the common European white-toothed shrew *(C. russula)*, the common shrew *(Sorex araneus)*, and the pigmy shrew *(S. minutus)*. There are, of course, many small rodents in the woods. These in turn help account for the number of owls, foxes, and—especially—weasels.

HALF-WILD HORSES AND BULLS

The most famous mammals of the Camargue are the half-wild horses and bulls that roam freely all the year round. The horses gallop about in great herds, a reminder of the time when wild horses inhabited the plains of Europe. The black bulls are very imposing; we gave them a wide berth. It is mainly during breeding time in July and August that the bulls and cows form large herds in which a strict social order is recognized. The animals show a marked tendency to defend certain vital territories, e.g., pastureland and the places where

they drink, rest, or go through performances related to maintaining the order of precedence. They thus possess a kind of territorial system, guarding their territories from trespassers of their own kind. This illustrates how wild these bulls and cows have become, and gives us some idea of the habits of the now-extinct aurochs. The semiwild bulls of the Camargue are caught and used at bullfights in Arles.

The Camargue is also rich in reptiles, which find very suitable habitats in the combination of groves and water. Lizards dart about in the grass or on the trunks of trees. Several of them are of the same species as those mentioned in our account of southwestern Spain. The green lizard *(Lacerta viridis)* is common. At mating time the males, which are then bright green or greenish-blue, fight viciously with each other, during which struggles their colors become even brighter. Among the more common snakes are the Montpellier snake, the grass snake *(Natrix natrix)*, and that skillful climber, the ladder snake *(Elaphe scalaris)*.

On low-lying land, the limonium vegetation gives way to such salt-loving plants as *Salicornia fruticosa*. Parts of these meadows are flooded during winter. Here, too, are numerous pools, some of them brackish, others more saline. In time of drought such places are left dry with only the crust of salt deposited as the water evaporates. The plants on the meadows are dwarfs compared to those on higher land, and birds that spend much time on the ground are therefore more common here. Skylarks, short-toed larks, and crested larks are numerous. Occasionally a tawny pipit may be seen among them. The spectacled warbler breeds in the low salicornia thickets, whence sounds its simple song, reminiscent of the whitethroat's. Pratincoles, for which this is a favorite haunt, breed in spring among the tufts of grass on the rapidly drying ground.

Of all the birds in this open country, the skylarks are most numerous and sing their sweet songs everywhere. Also very common and perhaps the most attractive are the yellow wagtails. One can spot them easily from a distance, their bright yellow breasts standing out like flames against the green saltwort tussocks and the dry naked ground.

THE MIRACLE OF BIRD MIGRATION

When the yellow wagtails come flying from tropical Africa in spring, they rest in the fields of the Camargue. Many of them stay there to breed; others continue northward. Thus, for these birds the area is either goal or resting place. For the yellow wagtails that breed north of the Arctic Circle, the Camargue represents the halfway mark on their long journey from the equator. Several races come together here during migration, including *Motacilla flava iberiae* and *M. f. cinereocapilla*, breeding on the Iberian and Apennine peninsulas respectively, and *M. f. flava*, breeding in other parts of France and elsewhere in Europe. A northern race, *M. f. thunbergi*, and possibly also other subspecies, stop off at the Camargue during their migration.

For many years, I numbered the yellow wagtail among my

Flamboyant flamingos, shown in Etang de Vaccarès, are the most numerous of the birds breeding in colonies in the Camargue. (Ray Delvert)

close acquaintances. Almost daily for four winters we shared the pleasures of the marshy meadows and savannas of tropical Africa. I have also watched these birds hurrying, with only brief pauses, over North Africa, in the Camargue, on the spring-wet meadows of Flanders, on the seaside pastures of southern Sweden, and in arctic Alaska. During many summers we have been neighbors in the mountains of Swedish Lapland. Although I am quite well acquainted with the habits of the yellow wagtail, I have yet to learn many of its secrets. I have cultivated its acquaintance because alone of all the European and Asiatic birds that winter in the tropics it can contribute to the solution of various special problems of bird migration.

Migration takes place periodically with incredible precision. The departure from the tropics is coordinated with the length of time it takes for the birds to fly to their breeding grounds in northern Europe, and with the number of days that spring has progressed in the latitudes where the birds live. Their orientation across half the globe is nearly always perfect, whether they fly by day or by night. The timing mechanism within the bird, regulated by inner or physiological—and outer, or ecological—factors, sets off the migration, steers the bird over seas and continents, and makes it stop at the right moment in the right place. Later it returns to its winter quarters of the year before. How has this remarkable performance developed? Adaptation by selection is probably the answer; Operating over a long period of time this has probably made it possible for certain species of birds to utilize the different environments most favorable to them during the various seasons.

It would appear that the physiological machinery of a bird is "wound up" once a year or "set" at birth, after which it works faultlessly, adapting to the changing seasons throughout the bird's whole life. But the cycle varies considerably, even within a species. The yellow wagtails wintering in the Congo are a good example of this. Several races of the species, representing different Eurasian ranges, winter there. The birds appear in flocks composed of several subspecies. Although all these birds are subject to exactly the same external influences for several months, both molting and migration differ in each race. When molting is almost completed, race characteristics have begun to appear, and when the gonads begin to swell, it usually means that the time for migration is near. Yet while all this is happening with some yellow wagtails, others have not begun to molt, have quiescent gonads, and will not be ready to migrate northward for another month or two.

The extraordinary feature of the secretory rhythm of these birds is their ability to synchronize their arrival at their breeding grounds—for some races more than 5,000 miles distant—at the ideal season. If in good health, the birds usually reach their goal just on time. It may seem paradoxical that birds with a long way to fly start later than those that migrate only a relatively short distance, but this is because the farther north their breeding ground lies, the later spring will arrive there. Thus some yellow wagtails linger in the Congo as late as the beginning of May; these belong to the race *thunbergi,* which breeds in northernmost Europe, where snow still covers the ground. By that time the Central European yellow wagtails have been at their breeding places for a few weeks, and others have already arrived in southern and central Scandinavia.

SALT STEPPES, LAGOONS AND SALINES

Natural sand dunes separate the lowest land in the Camargue from the sea. Much of this region consists of large and small lagoons, some of them as large as lakes, others mere pools. Many of them are connected by meandering channels, in a maze of land and water that is not easy to traverse. This lowland is the genuine Camargue, a synthesis of marshes and savannas, saline areas and semideserts, where one can take in a multitude of birds at a glance, since there is hardly anything to hide them.

Around the lagoons the ground has such a high salt content, due partly to the salinity of the subsoil water and partly to annual floods, that only the highest parts—those a few inches to a foot or so above water—have been colonized by plants, and then only by *Arthrocnemum glaucum,* a near relative of saltwort. Between the tussocks of this plant the ground lies naked, and in June is baked to a hard crust that may crack and form large cakes. The blazing sun shines down pitilessly day after day. Animal life consequently is very poor. But the Kentish plover breeds here, seeming to thrive on the sun-baked earth. The skylark sings exultantly overhead, while short-toed larks and yellow wagtails trip over the dry ground. But even the pratincole, which seems not to mind a hot sun, does not willingly frequent such parched, salty ground.

Though the dry land of the Camargue cannot support much animal life in summer, multitudes of birds congregate throughout the year on and around the innumerable lagoons. In winter huge flocks of ducks rest there, and the cormorant *(Phalacrocorax carbo)* remains from autumn till the following spring. During spring and autumn migrations, waders rest there for a time to feed on the wealth of small animals. Dunlins, little stints, ringed plovers, gray plovers and ruffs are the most common members of this lively congregation, which also contains redshanks, wood sandpipers, greenshanks, and an occasional spotted redshank.

Now and again in spring, great numbers of black terns *(Chlidonias niger)* arrive in the Camargue. They dance gracefully with their reflections, catching insects on or close to the surface of the water. A few days later they disappear, but a near relative, the paler whiskered tern, remains, hunting insects in the same elegant manner. All day long the dark-gray and white whiskered terns fly backward and forward over the lagoons. Thus there is a constant swarm of white wings over the salines of the Camargue in summer. Gull-billed terns, Sandwich terns *(Sterna sandvicensis),* common terns *(S. hirundo)* and little terns breed in large or small colonies, often together with black-headed gulls *(Larus ridibundus),* avocets, and occasional redshanks. Now and again black-winged stilts lay their eggs by the lagoons, as do the Kentish plover and an occasional oystercatcher. Black-winged stilts prefer flooded ground, building their nests in salicornia tussocks surrounded by water, where their long legs prove useful indeed. The herring gull *(Larus argentatus)* has increased its numbers during recent years, both in the Camargue and elsewhere.

All these gulls and waders usually occupy the periphery of the lagoons, while ducks haunt the higher regions in the center of the islets, with their richer vegetation. Almost without exception the ducks' nests are found on these flat islands, where birds can usually live in peace, although a fox or other animal, or even a human being, may occasionally find their way through the mud to raid their homes. Red-crested

The Camargue is a lowland plain and a delta where land and water embrace between the Mediterranean Sea and the dwindling branches of the Petit and the Grand Rhone. (Ray Delvert)

pochards, mallards, and gadwalls are among the most common ducks breeding in the Camargue, but shelducks *(Tadorna tadorna),* shovelers, and pintails also occur there. And sometimes such rare birds as the roseate tern *(Sterna dougallii)* and the slender-billed gull *(Larus genei)* join the colonies of gulls and breed in the Camargue.

Out on the lagoons are small birds not met on the dry mainland—skylarks, yellow wagtails, and spectacled warblers.

The most striking birds found in and around the lagoons are flamingos and herons, the former all the year round, though less often during the winter months. Herons are summer visitors, except for the gray heron, which stays in the Camargue from late summer until spring.

Many of the lagoons are exploited for the production of salt. Sea water is conducted into the lagoons, where it spreads over large areas and is allowed to evaporate, leaving a residue of salt. Some of the salines have the same salt content as the Mediterranean; others have an even higher salinity.

There are low islands in the salines, too, where nests, sometimes in the thousands, lie even closer together than in the lagoons. The species present are largely the same as those in the lagoons, but two species, the flamingo and the avocet, show a predilection for these areas. Several of the islands are inaccessible to such animals as the fox, one of the largest predators in the Camargue, which cannot swim or wade through the shallow water. Only waders' feet are adapted to the soft mud bottoms.

The location of the breeding sites chosen by the marsh birds is influenced by the effect of the mistral. The nests must be out of reach of the high waves generated by the big wind in lagoons and salines. Low islands, over which waves wash, are unsatisfactory. The birds choose not only islands that are a foot or so above the level of the water but quite often build in the middle of an island, or on the southwestern side, protected from the waves.

The flamingos of the Camargue usually nest in one huge colony, selecting an island in the salines where no other birds, except the herring gull, breed. By April each pair of flamingos has usually produced its one egg, which hatches after about a month. The flamingo colony consists of about four thousand pairs, the average during the years from 1955 to 1957. The number may, however, vary greatly from year to year.

Even a single flamingo is an impressive sight, with its grotesquely curved beak, its long, snakelike neck, its horizontally held body, and its long legs. But flamingos almost always gather in huge communities if the environment is a suitable one. The mass effect of a flock of a thousand flamingos, all moving slowly in the same direction through the water, is stunning. When the flock takes wing, it is a magnificent sight —a vision in white, rose and black, against the clear blue sky. Only in flight is the full glory of the flamingo's lovely wing colors revealed.

As one approaches a flock of flamingos, they retreat from the shore and are careful to keep at a safe distance. Not until one succeeds in getting quite close to them is it possible to see that the forest of red legs conceals grayish-brown young birds that seem ridiculously small in comparison with their long-legged parents. The older birds move slowly and

The hoopoe, a common bird in the Camargue, often nests in holes in trees, especially in oaks, as shown here. (Eric Hosking)

mainly the abundance of animal organisms in brackish water, such as amphipods *(Gammarus locusta)* and isopods *(Sphaeroma hookeri)*, that provides the basis of the rich bird life of the Camargue. Where the salt content mounts, the number of marine organisms rises. A bristle-worm, *(Nereis diversicolor)*, a beautiful creature whose red blood vessels are visible through the thin skin of its back, is very common in muddy bottoms. Several mollusks (e.g., *Cardium*) dwell there, too. Some shores are covered with a carpet of shells. Microscopic planktonic forms are important as food for large and small animals living in these shallow brackish waters. Other marine forms occur in the salines, among them a phyllopod *(Artemia salina)*, which is found periodically in very great numbers. It usually multiplies parthenogenetically.

Periodicity characterizes the occurrence of invertebrates in the brackish waters of the Camargue. The lagoons, above all in late spring and early summer, are replete with small animals very important for breeding birds. It is the same in the salines, but there the abundance of invertebrates in spring and summer is followed by an almost complete absence of them in autumn and winter. But the lagoons still contain many active lower forms of life.

The lagoons of the Camargue teem with fish. The brackish water contains no fewer than twenty-two species, a delight for the fish-eating birds. The fish fauna of the lagoons is so remarkable that a provisional list of species is given here. It reveals that the brackish waters contain surprisingly many Mediterranean species. Most of the fish living in the brackish lagoons are of marine origin. As far as is known, only sea fish live in the salines.

Fish in the Brackish Waters of the Camargue

Pilchard *(Clupea pilchardus)*	Marine
Carp *(Cyprinus carpio)*	Fresh water
Gambusia *(Gambusia affinis)*	Fresh water (introduced)
Pike *(Esox lucius)*	Fresh water
Catfish *(Ameiurus nebulosus)*	Fresh water (introduced)
Eel *(Anguilla anguilla)*	Fresh and marine water
Garfish *(Belone acus)*	Marine
Pipefish *(Sygnathus abaster)*	Marine
Sea perch *(Morone labrax)*	Marine
Pike perch *(Lucioperca sandra)*	Fresh water
Perch *(Perca fluviatilis)*	Fresh water
Dorado *(Sparus auratus)*	Marine
Golden gray mullet *(Mugil auratus)*	Marine
Gray mullet *(M. cephalus)*	Marine
Thin-lipped gray mullet *(M. capito)*	Marine
Goby *(Gobius* sp., probably *G. minutus)*	Marine
Stickleback *(Gasterosteus aculeatus)*	Marine and fresh water
Smelt *(Atherina mochon)*	Marine
Brill *(Scopthalmus rhombus)*	Marine
Turbot *(S. maximus)*	Marine
Plaice *(Pleuronectes platessa)*	Marine
Sole *(Solea* sp., probably *S. solea)*	Marine

cautiously, step by step, while the young flow along like a floating carpet under them, doing their best to keep up with the older birds.

The flamingo is the most numerous of colony breeding birds in the Camargue. During the years from 1955 to 1957 the number of black-headed gulls was calculated at about three thousand pairs, the common terns at two to three thousand pairs, the avocets at six to eight hundred pairs, and the little terns at three to four hundred pairs. Ducks number in hundreds of pairs, but this total swells enormously in winter, the most numerous being widgeon, teal, and mallard, which stay in the Camargue from October until spring. Remarkably enough, the teal, which breeds next to water, leaves the Camargue during the summer.

It is easy to understand that the flooded land suits ducks, accounting for much of the astonishing bird life of the Camargue in winter as well as the meeting of waders there in autumn and spring. But may the flooded land also account for the great congregation of breeding birds in lagoons and salines? The answer is both yes and no. A great many of the birds living in the marshes of the Camargue base their way of life on the food they find there, but others, which breed on islands in lagoons and salines, live on food they must seek elsewhere.

The most common plant in the lagoons and salines is the rassel pond weed *(Ruppia maritima)*. In less saline water, other species of pond weeds *(Potamogeton)* are found. It is

Some of the many herons as well as cormorants and herring gulls of the Camargue fish in the lagoons, while others seem to prefer the salines. Their prey consists chiefly of flatfish, eels, and mullets. The little egret is seen about as often in salines as in lagoons. Its diet consists mainly of small fish, crustaceans, and insect larvae.

Since the dense colonies of birds breeding on islands in lagoons and salines search for food all over the Camargue, even in the sea, competition between the species is not keen, even though colonies may crowd together when breeding. As a rule during breeding only redshanks, avocets, shelducks and flamingos take all the food they need from the brackish lagoons. The Kentish plover and the oystercatcher feed in lagoons and salines and on the seashore. Gull-billed terns, black-headed gulls and ducks seek their food in fresh water and on inland meadows. Little terns fish along the seashore, in lagoons and salines. Sandwich terns and common terns also fish there although they often go quite far out to sea.

THE VIRGIN CAMARGUE

Even though much of Camargue is greatly influenced by human activities, some fragments of landscape that may be called virgin persist in the heart of this area. From Salin de Badon westward to Bois des Rièges, and southwestward to Pointe de Beauduc, one may travel for hours through genuine marshland, heaths, scrubland, woods, and old stabilized dunes that have a typical Mediterranean vegetation of junipers *(Juniperus phoenicea)* up to twenty feet high. The latter are often covered with lichens, and these, together with pistachio *(Pistacia lentiscus), Rhamnus alaternus,* and *Phillyrea angustifolia,* form a patchwork quilt of shrubs in which grasses grow high and many flowers, such as the asphodel *(Asphodelus cerasifer)* and the narcissus *(Narcissus tazetta),* hide. At some points a pine wood *(Pinus pinea)* rises above the shrubs, and there the flowers are even more abundant.

Of singing birds, the Sardinian warbler is the one heard most often in the daytime in the treeless macchia terrain, and the nightingale at night, but the small bird seen most frequently is the goldfinch. Other common birds in the dense shrubbery are red-legged partridges, magpies, and kestrels. Another species of the pine wood is the hobby. Colonies of herons attract one's attention, and a few squacco herons and many little egrets and night herons nest here.

There is a sizeable population of wild boars in the regions all around Etang de Vaccarès, where they may sometimes be seen in the open country between lake and dunes. Here the wild boar is mostly a creature of the plains. The little Etruscan shrew is found here, too. Thus the largest and smallest completely wild animals of the Camargue are neighbors.

The sand dunes of the Camargue vary in width from one or two hundred yards to a few miles. The highest of these, which is also the highest point in the Camargue, is almost thirty feet above sea level. Outside the shrub layer the sand has been colonized by plants which, when they flower in May and June, give color to the dunes. Short-toed larks and tawny pipits breed there, and in summer many other species of birds go there to hunt insects, especially grasshoppers.

Beyond the dunes one comes at last to the Mediterranean. Almost the whole of the sandy beach here is free from buildings, except in Saintes-Maries-de-la-Mer, the "capital" of the Camargue. Nothing on the beach reveals to the visitor that immediately beyond the first rows of dunes lies one of the most remarkable natural regions of Europe. There are never many birds on the beaches of the Mediterranean; only a few gulls and terns fly along the shore and out to sea. Only two birds breed on the beach, the Kentish plover and the oystercatcher, and both species seem to be more common in the interior of the Camargue than along the seashore.

The most valuable parts of the Camargue now are protected by the Société Nationale de Protection de la Nature et d'Acclimatation de France, an organization that has done much to increase our knowledge of the area. During the past decade, the Station Biologique de la Tour du Valat, with its enthusiastic team of workers directed by Dr. Luc Hoffmann, has been conducting valuable research work, and in 1962 it became the headquarters of the International Wildfowl Research Bureau. A more strategic position for such a research station could hardly be found.

Ancient Woods and Great Volcanoes

The Italian Peninsula

5 Geographically, Italy is the most Mediterranean of all European countries. Bordered on all sides but the north by the Mediterranean, it has a longer shoreline than any other European country; everywhere there are sandy or pebbly beaches and rocky coasts.

From the south coast of Sicily to the most northerly point in the Italian Alps, it extends about 750 miles, comprising many different types of terrain. No other place on earth has been so fully covered in records over a period of two thousand years. Thus we know much about the natural features of the Apennine peninsula, century by century, from Roman times. An oft-repeated theme in these records is the devastation of nature through the cutting down of forests and overgrazing by livestock. Nevertheless, even as late as the Renaissance, Italy was rich in wildlife. The many accounts of the hunts organized by noble families bear witness to this. From Piedmont, Lombardy and the Three Venetias in the north to Calabria and Sicily in the south, deer and other animals were hunted. Such a wealth of wildlife cannot exist without extensive forests, and we know with certainty that there were many woods in the various provinces; but few of these remain. Fragments of lush deciduous forests, which in variety of species and in luxuriance give us some idea of the primeval forests of Italy, may still be found here and there, including such regions as Latium, Rome's province, which, along with Campania, has undoubtedly been most affected by man.

It is remarkable that in Italy, with its rich history, so many natural regions should still remain. Often, while visiting Latium, Umbria, or Tuscany, I was able to imagine myself in virgin country. But no matter how luxuriant the wood, how wild the ravine, or how extensive the marsh, sooner or later I found traces of human culture. It was the same throughout Italy. South of the high mountains, the Apennines and the Alps, the land is one immense memorial to ancient and medieval times, a synthesis of nature and civilization. It is indescribably fascinating to wander about the Roman countryside, on the Roman Campagna, and everywhere to find traces of the ancient imperium or of the Renaissance. Architectural remains date the sites and help us to understand the history of the present woods, the denuded earth, and the gentle slopes.

Much of the cultivated landscape of ancient Tuscany would be beyond our understanding if the writings of the Renaissance masters did not contain so many descriptions of scenery. The joy of life, which is such a conspicuous feature of life in Italy, and which appears so richly in the Golden Age of Florence under the Medicis, owed much to the natural surroundings. Although humanistic interests dominated the Renaissance, the natural environment always formed the background to brilliant spectacles and dramatic events. The forests were still so large and dense in fifteenth-century Italy that they could conceal whole armies.

A feeling for and interest in natural history can be discerned throughout the centuries and was at a peak in ancient Greece and Rome, memorably so in Aristotle and Pliny. In the Renaissance there was a rebirth of curiosity about nature.

This new philosophy is nowhere so marked in Renaissance Italy as in the circle around Lorenzo de Medici. In his poem "Falconry," Lorenzo describes an early morning hunt and gives us a vivid picture of the landscape—the rosy first light, the gentle breeze rising slowly as night gives way to day and making the leaves tremble and the crowns of the trees sigh, the awakening of the animals and so forth. All this is described with a sensitivity that stamps the author as a learned and trained observer.

Interest in natural history spread from Tuscany to other cultural centers of Italy, so that the Renaissance in general reflects constant contact with nature. That is why Italy has become so important in helping us to understand the natural history of the whole Mediterranean landscape of the past.

The writer was fortunate enough to have lived in Rome and to have attended school there. Although it was difficult to get away from the urban environment of the city with its memorials of thousands of years of history, the environs of the city were fascinating. That was in the 1930's, before Rome had begun to develop so explosively in all directions. At that time beaches, lakes, marshes, plains, woods, and mountains, with scenery that was in some places surprisingly wild, were within reach of the people of Rome, even if only a few took advantage of them. One could, after a few hours' journey out of the city, wander all day long without meeting anyone but a shepherd, a farmer or, on a Sunday, a hunter. There was the great expanse of the Pontine Marshes, with, at times, a rich bird life; there were deciduous woods on Monte Circeo, full of four-footed creatures and birds; there were mountain woods climbing to an altitude of more than six thousand feet.

Much of this is changed now. The Pontine Marshes, a source of malaria, have been transformed into a flourishing agricultural region with forty thousand inhabitants and five towns. The woods have shrunk or disappeared.

Leaving Rome and driving westward one moves along the highway to the sea. The road runs parallel to the Tiber and the old Roman military road that led to Ostia Antica. Two thousand years ago this city was on the coast at the mouth of the Tiber, and it was the most important harbor in the Roman Empire; today it is about three miles inland. The explanation for this is that the river, with the four to five million cubic yards of mud that it carries down every year, has been build-

The vivid blue of Lake Carezza in the Dolomites is framed by conifer forests with the rugged Latemar Pinnacles towering above it. (Josef Muench)

Italy is a mountainous country, with the Alps in the north and the Apennines running down the entire peninsula. Lowlands extend through the valley of the Po, along the coasts, and in Italy's southeasternmost province, Puglia. Corsica, Sardinia and Sicily are also mountainous.

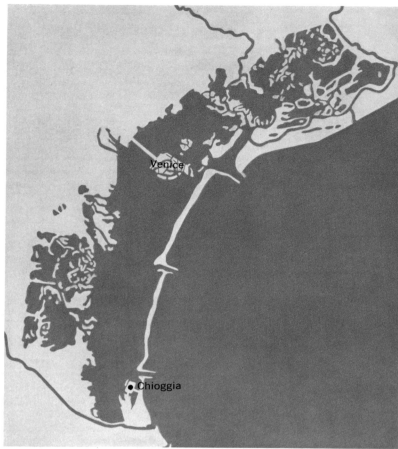

The Adriatic coast of Italy from the River Isonzo west and south demonstrates delta growth. The Venetian lagoon and the surrounding lands, shown on the map, did not exist at the time of the Roman empire, because the coast was then about eight miles west of the present western shore of the lagoon.

ing up a delta, creating new land, in effect thus pushing the coast westward at the rate of three yards a year. This was going on during Roman times, and the Romans several times were compelled to relocate harbors cut off from the sea.

Deltas nearly always provide suitable habitats for birds, so I often made trips to the delta meadows farther inland from the present Ostia and Fiumicino. During migration periods some waders and a very few ducks appeared there, but otherwise there was no animal life at all. What were formerly vast stretches of marshland and bogs, the once famous *maremme,* are now flat pastures and arable land. Here and there are groves of trees, like oases on the delta plain.

I also visited the area south of the Tiber and Rome. According to maps drawn in the 1930's, almost no roads cut through this region. There were few villages between Lido di Roma (modern Ostia) and Anzio, another ancient Roman harbor, made famous in World War II, a distance of twenty-five miles. I went there, found an undulating pastureland, typical of the Roman Campagna, and spent wonderful winter days among singing skylarks, whirring quails, and kestrels. I came upon the half-overgrown Via Severia, the old Roman road running from Ostia along the coast of the Mediterranean. There were no marshes, but charming groves and small woods, stretching like a border along the coast, a type of landscape found in many places north of Ostia.

THE PONTINE MARSHES

I had often heard about the great marshes south of the Tiber, but I had been told not to venture into them lest I drown in the swamps or come back with malaria. As a matter of fact, these marshes were much farther south than the Tiber basin and had no connection with the river. My stay in Rome coincided with the draining of the Pontine Marshes, a gigantic project, and large areas of the vast swamps were made accessible by car or bicycle. In the early 1930's, much of the region was still wild, with plains, bushy heaths and woods inundated for long periods every year; the marshes and lakes did not dry up completely even in summer, though they were sometimes transformed into wastes of mud.

The Pontine Marshes were regarded with loathing for centuries, but they represented a fascinating aspect of nature, completely different from anything I had seen elsewhere in Europe. It seemed incredible that such a wilderness, so like the swamps at the dawn of the world, could be found only sixty miles from Rome. The few inhabitants of the area only underlined the unreality of the region. They lived on the highest hills in very primitive huts made of reeds and earth reinforced by boards and branches. The total population of the marshes was about a hundred persons, spread over some fifty thousand acres. Their livestock consisted of pigs, which often showed signs of having interbred with wild boar, and Indian water buffaloes, the only domestic animals that could move about in the quagmire. The buffaloes were also used for draft. It is not known when these cattle were introduced into Italy, but it was probably very long ago. The same domestic animals are also found today on the Balkan peninsula.

The water buffaloes were the largest mammals in the marshes, strengthening the visitor's feeling that he was in an alien world. In the middle of the water-logged land lay islands overgrown with jungle-like brush, surrounding luxuriant virgin deciduous forests in which a few giant trees rose high above an almost unbroken canopy of leafy crowns. It was a paradise for wild boars and for multitudes of birds. Although wolves had been reported in this forest, there was no convincing evidence of their presence. Foxes, brown hares, small rodents, snakes and frogs were everywhere.

The history of the marshes in pre-Roman times is lost in the mists of the past, which is not surprising, for the whole region was probably shunned as much in that day as in the next two thousand years. We do not know whether the marshes were once part of the sea or were the remains of a prehistoric lake filled, with infinite slowness, by sediment brought down from the hills or formed by the sinking of the land. When the Via Appia was begun in 312 B.C. it was built straight through the marshes. As the busiest road in the Roman Empire, it brought the region into history, but the marshes remained intact in spite of all attempts to drain them. The Via Appia lost its usefulness with the fall of the Roman Empire, and the marshes were again totally isolated. The region was later annexed by the papacy, and for twelve centuries various popes tried in vain to conquer the marshes.

At the end of the 1920's it was Mussolini's turn to attempt to drain the swampland. It took less than ten years. For those who saw the trackless marshes at the beginning of the 1930's, the transformation to rich arable land with four thousand farms and five towns, is extraordinary. Although one rejoices with those who have thus been able to gain a livelihood, it is difficult for a naturalist to suppress a feeling of regret that this last fragment of primeval country is lost forever.

When I first went into the Pontine Marshes, one misty winter's day, walking along a narrow, muddy path just above the level of the water, it was a drowned country—leafless trees and bushes stood in water, as far as the eye could see. But when I returned in early summer, the quagmire had come to life. Every patch of high ground was covered with luxurious meadows; on the higher heaths the macchia vegetation had been transformed into a pageant of color, and the fringes of the woods formed an almost impenetrable green wall. Many of the permanent lakes were fringed with reeds, and behind this border of vegetation a belt of date palms *(Phoenix dactylifera)* made the region seem tropical. How did the palms get there? Were they descended from trees planted around the villa of some noble Roman two thousand years ago?

Some of the marshes were completely overgrown with reeds, extending like a billowy green sea to the horizon. I could tell from the behavior of the birds I could see and from the distant piping of coots that somewhere nearby was a sheet of open water. Wherever we went in the reeds the cackling

of moor hens and the grunting of water rails followed us. The booming of the bittern was often heard here and the marsh harriers had excellent hunting grounds. Everywhere were narrow paths made by wild boars; out on the sea of reeds these creatures became veritable marsh animals. On all sides were islands of every kind, with tussocks of juncus forming the core of all of them. Immense swampy areas alternated with lagoons and with small freshwater lakes.

The topography of the outer parts of the marshes was similar in many ways to that of the delta of the Guadalquivir, except that the Pontine area had many groves of deciduous trees as well as such majestic woods as I have not seen anywhere else in Europe. The mighty canopy included evergreen oaks, holly oaks, Turkey oaks *(Quercus cerris),* which grow about one hundred feet high, hornbeams, sycamores, limes, ash and elms. The damp ground under these trees was covered with tall ferns, with the royal fern *(Osmunda regalis)* so dense that it formed a green world of its own, smelling of decomposing vegetation and spongy soil.

Many bee-eaters flew in the glades and above the trees. Golden orioles could be seen everywhere, and hosts of small birds sang throughout the spring and summer. In some places the wood was almost like tropical rain forest. Ivy completely enveloped the trunks and branches of trees. Ci-

Chestnut woods, some quite old, occur in various parts of Italy. (Benedikt Rast: Bavaria Verlag)

cadas chirped, bees buzzed, and clouds of horseflies congregated in the glades, while in the shade of the ferns mosquitoes went to the attack. Gigantic trees had fallen under the weight of years, had been struck by lightning, or toppled by spring and autumn storms, leaving monumental, naked trunks. Owls, woodpeckers and other birds had built their nests in the hollow dead trees. In the sunlit glade left by fallen giants, young trees began growing at once. As I forced my way through the woods, I sometimes found my path barred by a massive, moss-covered wall of soil—generally the unearthed roots of huge fallen oaks; they were nearly always inhabited by wrens.

This region, an example of climax vegetation unique in Europe, gave me a glimpse of what the countries around the Mediterranean were once like. With the draining of the marshes, wood after wood was cut down, the trees being used mainly for railway ties. Nothing now remains of the majesty of Agro Pontino.

The remarkable thing about these deciduous woods was that they could stand in water for several winter months each year and still survive. What happened to all the ground animals then? Perhaps the reptiles took refuge in hollow trees or migrated, like the small rodents, to dry ground.

Reptiles were very common in the moist woods, and hunted both in water and on land, and sometimes in the trees. The water-loving grass snake, often beautifully patterned, with rows of dark spots on its pale sides, was found almost everywhere. The Aesculapian snake *(Elaphe longissima)* could often be seen gliding quickly into the dense vegetation, or climbing up a tree when its siesta was disturbed. The only venomous snake I saw was the asp *(Vipera aspis),* and I remember that it seemed to have a preference for the many places where wild strawberries *(Fragaria vesca)* could be found.

Now and again I came across straying water buffaloes. Generally they stood or lay in small pools in the woods, with only their heads above water.

Right: A luxuriant canopy of leaves in Italy south of la Spezia indicates what the country looked like in the far past. (Stefano Robino) Below: Many species of snakes, such as this water-loving grass snake, occur in Italy; only a few of them are venomous. (R. P. Bille)

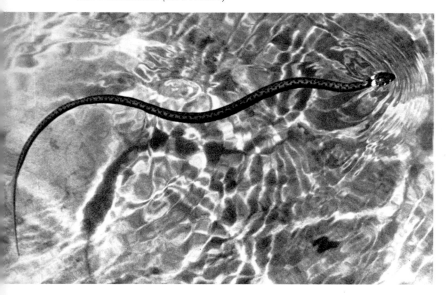

The most interesting birds I observed were four marbled ducks, a species seldom seen in Italy. They were in a swamp together with mallards and shovelers. Besides mallards, the most common ducks in the marshes were teal and garganeys, the former occurring in flocks of a thousand or more. Pochards visited lakes deep enough to allow them to dive for food without being hampered by vegetation. The snipe was the wader most suited to the flooded land in winter, and in spring many great snipe (Gallinago media) rested there. Woodcocks (Scolopax rusticola) inhabited all the groves and woods; there, all winter, they could drive their long, sensitive beaks into the soft ground in search of worms. One winter I counted six avocets—which do not breed in Italy—in the marshes. Geese appeared regularly every winter, but were extremely timid and grazed or rested too far away in fields or on water to be identified.

Of course, there were many herons in winter. They spent most of their time in the lakes and juncus marshes beyond the dunes, together with cormorants, which divided their time between the sea and fresh water. In spring, night herons could be observed here and there on wooded islands, where they probably bred.

The lakes near the dunes are now the only expanses of wetland left of the Pontine Marshes. Next to one of the largest lagoons, which was still a deserted area in the early 1930's, is the town of Sabaudia, not far from Circeo, one of the most beautiful woodland regions near Rome. The remaining lagoons extend continuously for miles along the coast.

The greater part of Agro Pontino consisted of marshes with stagnant water. Even where the water was several feet deep it was completely covered with a rich vegetation of Ranunculus, pondweed and other aquatic plants. A great many fish inhabited the marshes, but as far as I know they were all of one species, Gambusia affinis, 24 specimens of which had once been introduced to control mosquito larvae. These twenty-four fish had become millions and spread all through the marshes, a staggering illustration of how an ecological vacuum can be filled. Favored by climate, an unlimited supply of food, plenty of space, few enemies and no competition from other species of fish, the Gambusia soon became the most common vertebrate in the Pontine Marshes.

As far as I know, no comprehensive study was ever made of the flora and fauna of Agro Pontino before it was drained and transformed into agricultural land. It is therefore probable that the legends about the marshes will live on, but I doubt whether they can surpass the reality.

THE WOODS AROUND ROME

Under the wide semicircle of mountains around Rome is an undulating plain, the Campagna di Roma. It is ancient pastoral land. Once, perhaps after the woods had been cut down, it was farmed and gave rich harvests of grain. It then became pastureland again; but it is now so impoverished that in many places only sheep and goats can get any nourishment from the ground. The pastureland has crept up and transformed the mountainsides, too. The consequences there are even more disastrous; the destruction of the woods, the grazing, and the trampling down of vegetation open the way for erosion and the conversion of fertile country into barren land.

The Campagna extends for miles around Rome, an immense heath with great flocks of sheep in winter, but almost without life in summer. There are a number of groves here, but mainly along the deep river beds. Their luxurious growth is a reminder of the gallery woods of the Campagna of the past and the woods that can still be found in the mountains. The thickets are full of singing birds, snakes sunning themselves, and choirs of frogs at night; in June they begin to dry out, silence falls over the shrubbery, and insects are almost the only living creatures left.

There are still a few wooded dales in the mountains around Rome where one can wander under a leafy canopy. The sun pours down on the trees and the warm brown earth underfoot is delicately patterned with sunshine and shadow and smells of damp humus. Few or none of these groves are primeval forest, but they give some idea of what such forests looked like. Many of them must be several hundred years old. Venerable, gnarled olive trees (Olea europaea) grow at random on some slopes, and one wonders whether they were planted or came up of themselves. In other places there are even denser groves of mighty chestnut trees (Castanea sativa) that must be five or six hundred years old. They form relatively open woods, and although their crowns meet, the sun can shine through. Animals have usually grazed the ground underneath, so vegetation is kept down and the chestnut trees have no chance of renewing themselves; nevertheless, the yield of these groves is often so great that the ground is quite covered with shiny brown nuts. In October, when the shells split with a crack, and the yellow, bristly cups open, the woods are filled with the sound of falling nuts.

One day, in the ancient Alban Hills, I followed a path that gradually lost itself in a tangle of ferns, tall grass, and herbs. The hesitant notes of the subalpine warbler (Sylvia cantillans) could be heard from the dense thicket, and from the crowns of the trees the Bonelli's warbler (Phylloscopus bonelli) sang, its notes blending with the sweet utterance of orphean warblers, blackcaps, melodious warblers, nightingales, wrens. It is a remarkable experience to walk through woods and listen to birds that once charmed Virgil.

FAMOUS COASTS
AND SPECTACULAR ISLANDS

The coast south of Rome, from Lido di Roma and Lido di Lavinio—where, according to legend, Aeneas stepped ashore—southward past the former Pontine Marshes to Cape Circeo, is mainly a meeting place of dunes and sea. Along great stretches runs a windcut border of bushes and pine woods with cork oaks and in some places fine deciduous woods. One of the latter, Circeo, with an area of about 13,000 acres, was one of Italy's best forest reserves. The greater part of it is woodland, the old selva di Terracina, and one part was originally like the swampy woods of the Pontine Marshes. Ever since the draining of the Pontine Marshes, the Parco

The entire island of Capri is a limestone cliff rising straight out of the azure Mediterranean between the gulfs of Naples and Salerno. (Bruno Stefani)

Nazionale del Circeo has gradually changed from a swamp wood, the most interesting part of the park, to something more conventional. But it still has such unique features as a variety of oaks that spread their wide crowns over a ground layer of tree heather, broom, and many other plants.

The many wild boar that lived in the marshy woods were crowded into Circeo when farmers began to cultivate their former haunts. Now the park accommodates many of these animals. During the 1930's some mouflons (Ovis musimon) from Sardinia were introduced in order to provide the park with large mammals.

Circeo is one of the best places in the province of Latium to see birds of passage. This may be due to the fact that Monte Circeo, once an island, rises quite steeply at the tip of a peninsula and is thus a landmark for migrating birds, as it was long ago for Odysseus. There the birds find shelter and food before the next stage of their long journey.

The park regulations are, unfortunately, neither comprehensive nor strictly enforced. Hunting licenses have been granted quite generously for years, and hunters have been permitted to shoot quail and turtledoves, for example, in the spring. And now buildings are invading Circeo on all sides, and it is rapidly losing its character as a national park. Instead of a tightening of control, there is talk of abolishing the national park restrictions completely.

The beach along a great part of the coast of Latium is edged with woods quite different from Circeo's light *selva*. Here, as on most of the west coast of Italy, the woods beyond the fringe of shrubs and cork oaks consist mainly of umbrella pines, with a few stands of deciduous trees,

Left: Today in many parts of Italy a tragic deforestation ruins slopes and greatly diminishes the fertility of valleys and plains, as in Lucania in southern Italy. (Gianni Berengo-Gardin). Below: In southern Italy, old olive trees, generally cultivated, form open woods, where light penetrates the canopy and reaches the ground; but the vegetation remains poor because it is grazed. (A. Renger-Patzsch)

Corsica and Sardinia are the only areas in the world where mouflons, Europe's only wild sheep occur naturally. Shown here in Corsica is a three-year-old ram in mixed pine and macchia vegetation at an altitude of about 3000 feet. (Pierre Pfeffer)

mostly oaks. The short-toed eagle and hobby live in the pine woods—the former feeding on reptiles, the latter on insects.

The coastal areas are probably the best known and certainly the most photographed scenery in Italy. There are few people who would not recognize the spectacular view of the Bay of Naples—the cone of Vesuvius in the background, sometimes with wreaths of smoke rising from the crater, and the steep cliffs of Ischia and Capri thrusting up out of the blue sea. Undeniably the sweep of the bay, the terraced slopes, the majestic contours of the volcano, the play of light on blue waters and green hills combine to make one of the most beautiful scenes in the world.

THE VIOLENT HISTORY OF VESUVIUS

From the viewpoint of natural history, Vesuvius is perhaps the most interesting phenomenon near Naples. Although the volcano has frequently caused major catastrophes and buried whole towns under lava and ashes, its slopes have always been cultivated anew, and houses and villages built around it. The ash-covered sides of the volcano have been colonized by wild plants, and vineyards have been planted

there. Probably airborne particles of soil from the mountains of Campania and the Apennine range accumulate on the lava slopes of Vesuvius and help to make them so fertile. At times the woods have advanced high up the slopes of the volcano, but they have been repeatedly destroyed by molten lava. The uppermost parts are barren and dark, few or no plants having gained a foothold there.

Seething movement and naked death represented by black streams of lava, often in bizarre formations, are the extreme features of active volcanoes. Growth and desolation may often be found side by side. Wild vegetation and vineyards cover old fields of lava with a green mantle; nearby a new field of lava does not have even a single plant on it.

High up on Vesuvius, far above the cultivated land, one finds wide streams of lava that have hardened in their course and created monuments to a dramatic moment in the volcano's past. Here and there, vegetation has begun recolonizing the fields of lava. Algae, lichens and mosses have spread cautiously over lava rocks. In other places the flora is further advanced. These variations in colonization are chiefly the work of the wind. Although the lava underneath may be the same, it is the wind that wafts fertile volcanic ash and seeds into fissures and niches in the lava. The ash absorbs moisture from the air, and the seeds begin to grow.

In the 1930's, when I first climbed Vesuvius, the volcano was in a period of quiescence. Every three minutes or so there was a rumbling and a hissing explosion in the crater; greenish sulphurous smoke and grayish-white steam shot up from the bowels of the earth; and stones and particles of lava were thrown up and fell with a patter around the crater. At times the pillar of smoke seemed to be on fire; this was usually due to a reflection of the molten lava in the crater, but sometimes combustible gases caused genuine flames. Now and again molten lava from the crater or from a breach in the side of the cone ran down the slope in a narrowing stream until it stopped and began to cool off; eventually it became hard.

These eruptions did not prevent spectators from viewing the spectacle from a distance of only fifty yards or so, just beyond the range of the falling stones. Even at that distance from the crater the ground was so hot that the heat could be felt through the soles of one's shoes. Sulphurous smoke and gas escaped through small fissures in the slope below the crater.

Vesuvius the only active volcano on the mainland of Europe, is the most famous volcano in the world partly because it has erupted at least seventy times since the beginning of history, and sometimes with catastrophic results. The most famous of these eruptions is of course the one that destroyed Pompeii in A.D. 79. The volcano had been inactive for a long time and was regarded as extinct. Its slopes were cultivated and wooded to the very top, and towns and villages lay at its foot. Without warning an eruption and an earthquake occurred simultaneously. The top of the volcano blew up, and a cloud of steam and ash poured from a breach in the crater, blacking out the whole area. Explosion after explosion threw great stones into the air, and small pea-size stones *(lapilli)* fell like rain. Ash, like a snowstorm, buried houses and roads. The eruption lasted three days and nights, and when the sky cleared, Pompeii and sixteen thousand of its people lay buried under volcanic ash nearly twenty feet thick. The neighboring town of Herculaneum was destroyed in the same way. There rain and steam turned the ash into a semiliquid mass that penetrated into all the houses and finally enveloped the whole town. The mud, hardened to rock, has made the excavation of Herculaneum much more difficult than that of Pompeii.

The outburst in 79 was the beginning of a period of activity lasting until the twelfth century, but no later eruption exceeded the one that destroyed—or, for the archaeologists, preserved—Pompeii. For a few centuries the volcano slumbered; the plants again climbed to the top of the cone, the slopes were cultivated, and flourishing towns grew up at the foot of the mountain. Then, on December 15, 1631, an earthquake began and was followed during the next few days by a violent eruption. Again the surrounding land was covered with ash, and a stream of lava flowed quickly down the slope of the volcano, reaching the sea in less than an hour. Several towns were destroyed and eight thousand people perished.

Vesuvius has remained active until recent years. At the moment it is passive but it probably still has surprises in store. Together with Etna on Sicily and Stromboli in the Lipari Islands, Vesuvius indicates that the crust of the earth in this part of Europe is not yet stable.

BIRDS OF CAPRI AND LIZARDS OF PAESTUM

Capri, the most famous island in the Bay of Naples and one of the most popular tourist resorts in the world, is a limestone cliff rising straight out of the sea. Monte Solaro, 1932 feet high, is the highest point on the island. The lower slopes are terraced and planted with vineyards and olive groves. Higher up is scrub, and evergreen oaks grow in some of the ravines. The shelves and ledges of the precipitous and in many places inaccessible cliffs are clothed in plants and shrubs, especially dark-green myrtle, yellow broom and blue campanula. Ivy and honeysuckle *(Lonicera)* make green patterns on the white limestone. Brightly colored, graceful lizards dart about among the plants or on the white rocks. On open, uncultivated ground numerous agaves grow, while rockroses *(Helianthemum)* adorn the highest plateaus.

Capri is an island of migratory birds. It has long been famous for the myriads of small birds that rest among its shrubs. Unfortunately, they have been pitilessly persecuted, snared or shot for centuries. Tremendous numbers of small birds on their way to breeding grounds in northern Europe have ended their careers in the cooking vessels of Italy. Bird hunting on Capri has long been a thorn in the flesh of Italian naturalists, for migratory birds are an international concern. During the 1930's, hunting birds on Capri was forbidden. Then came World War II, and the law making Capri a bird sanctuary was repealed. Now interested people are striving to protect the birds of Capri, and their work is meeting with some measure of success.

Since migratory birds form an important study for ornithologists, the Swedish Ornithological Society has a research station on Capri. It concentrates mainly on the night-flying passerines that make the island a resting and feeding stage.

From Capri one can see the Gulf of Salerno, bounded by the Sorrento peninsula and the plains around Paestum and Agropoli, behind which rise the mountains of Lucania. This area was an agrarian province colonized by the Greeks before Rome conquered the world. The magnificent remains of a Grecian temple at Paestum is a memento of this colony, and the land is still cultivated. On la campagna felice farming is more intensive than anywhere else in Europe, with four or five crops being raised annually on the incomparable soil. Although the part of Campania between Salerno and Paestum is the most densely populated agricultural area in Europe, the soil seems to retain its fertility century after century. Can this be due to the nearness of Vesuvius? Soil of volcanic tuff, fertilized by ash and wind-borne humus is known to have great fertility. In this respect volcanoes compensate many times over for the economic loss they cause.

As always in the ruins of ancient Italian towns, great numbers of lizards bask on blocks of limestone in the sun at Paestum. On its tiny legs the snake lizard *(Chalcides chalcides)* glides over the floor of the temple like a snake; wall lizards sit on carvings on the columns; and bright green lizards stand out against the white limestone. Wall lizards, now the permanent resident of all ancient ruins are particularly numerous. In the houses and streets of Paestum, Herculaneum and Pompeii, these lizards have taken the place of people. At Paestum, a beautiful snake, *Coluber viridiflavus carbonarius,* which shines like black lacquer against the white stone, occasionally catches the eye. Ancient ruins have much of interest for the naturalist.

ADRIATIC SHORES AND THE LAGOON OF VENICE

The east, or Adriatic, shore of Italy has several regions of great biological interest. Owing to the action of winds and of marine currents, some of them have become marshes—even better habitats for birds than many parts of the west coast. As on coasts everywhere, the currents along the west coast of Italy, that is in the Tyrrhenian Sea, move northward, while those on the east coast flow southward. This causes sediment transported by rivers to be deposited north of the river mouths on the west coast, but south of those on the east coast.

Apulia, the most southeastern province of Italy, is the largest plain in Italy with the exception of that around the river Po. Nevertheless, as in all the mountainous areas of Italy, hills can usually be seen in the distance. Through the plain of Apulia, south of Monte Gargano between the Gulf of Manfredonia and the Apennines, flow the rivers Candelaro, Cervaro, Carapelle, and Olfanto; these have formed widespread delta lands, with many lagoons and salines, but with only one outlet to the sea, by way of the Olfanto. This lowland country is flooded regularly, particularly around the Candelaro River. Not far away is Cannae, where Hannibal wiped out a great Roman army in 216 B.C. The marshes of Manfredonia are notable for their rich bird life. Many ducks and white-fronted as well as bean geese winter there.

Farther north along the coast of the Adriatic, in Emilia, a large lagoon more than six miles wide is surrounded by many small satellite marshes and large areas of water-logged ground, called the Valle di Comacchio. This region has been created by enormous amounts of sediment brought down by the Po River over tens of thousands of years from glaciers in the Alps. The river and marine currents have cooperated to build out the coast south of the mouth of the Po. The greater part of the delta, with its lagoons, is now well inside the shore.

The swamps and lagoons of Comacchio contain fresh, brackish, and salt water. The variety of birds nesting there is not perhaps so great as in the Camargue in France; but the number of birds that breed in these swamps—duck, waders, gulls and terns among many others—is enormous. Avocets, black-winged stilts and pratincoles also breed here.

Still farther north is another, larger lagoon, the Laguna di Venezia, about thirty miles long and six to ten miles wide; it was once separated from the sea by a narrow sand-bar, which is still being enlarged by sediment from the Piave River, and now communicates with the Adriatic by way of several openings and canals. In this lagoon is the large group of islands which form the city of Venice.

Medieval fleets sailed the waters of the Laguna di Venezia, and today ocean liners ply there. Probably a body of fresh water originally, it is now almost a part of the sea itself. Very little fresh water enters it, since all the great rivers that once formed the delta now run directly into the Adriatic beyond the lagoon. The salinity varies up to about forty per cent in different parts of the lagoon.

Here, waders, herons, ducks and coots rest and winter. More than one hundred thousand ducks and coots have been counted year after year, of which the most common are mallard, gadwalls, widgeon, teal, garganeys, pintails, shovelers, pochard and tufted ducks.

So much has already been said in the chapters on Las Marismas and the Camargue about the marsh birds of Europe that this brief account of the interesting marshes on the east coast of Italy must suffice.

SICILY AND SARDINIA

Sicily was long the granary of the Roman Empire and, still earlier, of the Greeks; in places it is still a veritable garden, particularly near Mount Etna. But mainly it is an island of mountains where, on the north coast, the mountains often rise straight from the sea. Only in the western part is there a genuine plain.

The highest point in Sicily is the snow-capped volcano of Etna, 10,739 feet in height—higher, in fact, than the highest mountain in the Apennine range, and highest of all the volcanoes in Europe. The slopes of Etna are covered with over two hundred small craters, bearing witness to innumerable eruptions from which streams of lava have flowed down to the sea. Since the year 396 B.C. Etna has erupted more than ninety times, often with catastrophic effect; in spite of the danger, people continue to live there because its soil is so fertile. The greatest natural disasters on Sicily, however, have been caused by earthquakes; these have killed far more people than have volcanic eruptions. Subterranean volcanic activity has, of course, been the direct cause in both cases. The most disastrous earthquake occurred on December 28, 1908, when nearly the whole of Messina was demolished and 83,000 people were killed.

Although Sicily has been densely populated and intensively cultivated for thousands of years, its wild, inaccessible mountains have saved many animals from extinction. There are wolves in the mountains, wildcats in the woods; and the porcupine, which may have been introduced in ancient times, has survived. Generally speaking, Sicily has only a few of the species of mammals that are common in Italy proper; it does not have the squirrel *(Sciurus vulgaris)*, the bat *(Myotis emarginatus)*, the water shrew *(Neomys fodiens)*, the stone marten *(Martes foina)* and the badger, all of which are found across the Strait of Messina in Calabria.

The birds of Sicily have also been decimated, doubtless as a result of the intensive cultivation of the land. The few lakes and bogs on the island have been wholly or partly drained, and the trees have been cut down, to be replaced by fields of wheat and olive, orange and lemon plantations, almond trees and eucalyptus. Few birds can live in cultivated habitats such as these. At present 5.1 per cent of the land is labeled "unproductive," only 3.6 per cent is natural woods, while 20 per cent of the arable land is covered by cultivated trees. The only natural habitats left on Sicily are the expanses of macchia vegetation, but these dry, bushy areas are unsuited to many species. The most common among those that can live in the macchia are robins, woodlarks, cirl buntings *(Emberiza cirlus)*, wrens, and woodchat shrikes.

On the other hand, some species have been favored by cultivation, among them the chaffinch *(Fringilla coelebs)*, the skylark and above all the serin which is probably the most common bird on Sicily. There are also large numbers of linnets and goldfinches. Since hunting is very popular and almost

Left: In the ancient crater of Mt. Solfatara at Pozzuolo near Naples steam and smoke pour from boiling mud in underground pools. This volcano has not erupted during the historical era. (Gerhard Klammet). Right: Sicily's Mt. Etna, the largest active volcano in Europe, erupts, throwing up steam, ash, lava and small stones. (G. Tomsich)

The lava flows of Etna burn off all vegetation in their path, but where they do not reach the tops of mounds, vegetation soon starts up again. (Pal-Nils Nilsson: Tio)

everything larger than a starling is considered fair game, birds of prey are practically unknown.

The richest bird life on Sicily is found in gardens, parks, and small groves around villas, so one need not go far afield to study the birds of the island.

Among the more remarkable birds on Sicily is the spotless starling, found in agricultural districts around Trapani and Agrigento. Rock sparrows *(Petronia petronia),* rock thrushes, and blue rock thrushes *(Monticola solitarius)* are seen on some mountain slopes, but the first two are more common on the mainland. Rock doves *(Columba livia)* fly in pairs over the valleys between the mountains and the fields of grain.

Sicily's most interesting lake, Lago di Lentini, near Catania, has unfortunately been drained. There were once many aquatic and marsh birds there, including the purple gallinule, which is very rare in Europe. This species is now protected on Sicily, but this is pointless since its habitat has been destroyed.

Since the shore at Ciane and Anapo, in eastern Sicily near Syracuse, has been made a nature reserve, the animal life and vegetation are partly protected. Mixed with the rushes *(Phragmites)* in the marshes along the shore are thin, wiglike stalks of papyrus *(Cyperus papyrus);* together these giants of the marsh flora form a kind of miniature jungle in the water. Papyrus also grows at Alcantara, north of Etna, making this area, as well as Ciane, seem like bits of Africa. Among the birds that the papyrus shelters is the great reed warbler.

The migration of birds from Africa over the Mediterranean in spring does not lead to any great accumulation of birds on Sicily, perhaps because of the lack of suitable habitats. Sometimes in spring, however, an impressive number of red-footed falcons *(Falco vespertinus)* arrive in Sicily from their winter quarters in Africa. After a rest, they continue over the Continent to their eastern European or Asiatic breeding grounds. I remember a few April days at Marsala when multitudes of these birds sat on the beach or hopped and flew about in gardens and plantations and along the slopes. The largest flocks, consisting mostly of males, congregated in open terrain in the macchia country. It is probable that this invasion came from Tunisia, with Cape Bon the jumping-off point.

The great island of Sardinia is of zoogeographic interest chiefly because of its isolated situation. Certain large mammals that have disappeared from other parts of the Mediterranean region can still be found there. These include the red deer, the fallow deer and the mouflon; the last-named is in fact found in natural habitat only on Corsica and in the mountains of Gennargentu on Sardinia. The species has been introduced into such countries as Italy, France, Germany, Czechoslovakia (where there are about five thousand), Poland, Yugoslavia, and the U.S.S.R. The wildcat is also still found on Sardinia and Corsica. The Cape hare, which elsewhere in Europe is found only on the Iberian peninsula and in southwestern France, occurs in Sardinia. The brown hare lives on Corsica, whereas the lesser white-toothed shrew *(Crocidura suaveolens)* and the Daubenton's bat *(Myotis daubentoni)* are found on Sardinia but not on Corsica.

Among the more remarkable birds of Sardinia are the little bustard, the slender-billed gull, the lanner falcon *(Falco biarmicus),* the white-tailed eagle *(Haliaeetus albicilla),* the black vulture, the griffon vulture, the shelduck, the white-headed duck, the white-eyed pochard, and the Manx shearwater *(Puffinus puffinus).* All of these have a restricted distribution range in Europe or in the Mediterranean region.

FORESTS IN THE APENNINES

Most of the natural world of Italy is concentrated in the Apennines, which runs like a huge backbone almost from one end of the country to the other. The Apennines belong to the Alpine mountain range system and are geologically an offshoot of the Alps. Except, however, in the northwestern province of Liguria, the Apennines are separated from the Alps by the wide valley of the Po River. The range fills the whole of the Italian boot down to the toe in Calabria, and after a two-mile gap at the Strait of Messina, continues on into Sicily.

Sardinia and Corsica belong to another formation of very old fold and plateau mountains.

The highest point in the Apennines is Gran Sasso d'Italia, 9584 feet high, in Abruzzi in central Italy. Also in this region is the Parco Nazionale d'Abruzzo, with an area of 112 square miles, one of Italy's three large national parks. Here the principal protected animal is the brown bear *(Ursus arctos).* In 1922 there were only thirty or so of these bears; the following year the national park was established and by 1935 there were more than two hundred bears. But this estimate was probably too high for in 1964 the population was found to be only about sixty animals. Although this is a small number it is more than is found in other comparable west European areas. It is astonishing that these bears live in densely populated Italy, only ninety miles from Rome.

Vesuvius raises its lava cone high over the coastal area near Naples. Its numerous eruptions have not prevented men from cultivating its lower slopes. (Erich Fischer)

The chamois, which is not found elsewhere in the Apennines, is among the other big game in the park. The wolf is found over a very wide range in the Apennines, but the family units have mobility and do not remain in the national park. In winter they pay visits to the lowlands, but generally prefer the woods.

Apparently a newcomer in the region is the white-backed woodpecker *(Dendrocopos leucotos),* which was found breeding for the first time in Italy in 1959. It occurs in the Balkans and also in eastern Europe and Scandinavia. The chough, in elegant black, with red bill and red legs, the snow finch *(Montifringilla nivalis)* in gray, brown and white, the collared flycatcher *(Ficedula albicollis)* in black and white, and the alpine accentor *(Prunella collaris)* in gray and brown are also worthy of note. In view of the disappearance of the golden eagle in many places, it is important to note that this bird breeds in the national park.

The vegetation in the Apennines naturally varies from north to south in the long mountain range. In Parco Nazionale d'Abruzzo the mountains are covered with luxuriant beech woods that climb high up the slopes. Although the bear is an animal of deciduous forests, it here seeks its food on the alpine meadows above the woods, or in the dense vegetation and juicy plants of ravines.

Unfortunately, the magnificent beech woods have been partially cut down; they will, of course, grow again, but such cutting is hardly compatible with the basic conception of a national park.

On Mt. Terminillo in the Apennines, 7300 feet high, the vegetation between 2000 and 2600 feet consists of shrubs and trees, including various species of juniper. Alder buckthorn *(Rhamnus frangula),* hazel and pistachio grow among yellow broom, here and there giving way to ash *(Fraxinus ornus),* hornbeam, and oak *(Quercus pubescens).* Travelers' joy *(Clematis)* and honeysuckle twine around the branches of the trees. Holly *(Ilex aquifolium)* is also found occasionally.

From elevations of about 3000 to 6000 feet the beech *(Fagus silvatica)* dominates completely, with a mixture of mountain sycamore, bird cherry *(Prunus avium)* and mountain ash *(Sorbus aucuparia).* Some oaks *(Quercus cerris)* are found as far up the slopes as about 4500 feet. Among the ground vegetation in the beech woods a dwarf juniper *(Juniperus nana)* begins to dominate at about 5000 feet, and above the tree line, between 6000 and 7200 feet, it forms veritable carpets. In other places at the same altitude, the bilberry *(Vaccinium myrtillus)* covers large areas. On Mt. Terminillo the beech forms the timberline.

The golden eagle, too, breeds around Mt. Terminillo, with three pairs nesting there. Unfortunately, each year men take the young from one of the nests.

Italy has two other national parks, both located in the Alps, and consisting of mountain woods: Parco Nazionale del Gran Paradiso (243 square miles) and Parco Nazionale dello Stelvio (367 square miles). These national parks are in northernmost Italy and will be dealt with in the chapter devoted to the Alps.

Mountains and Archipelagos

The Balkan Peninsula

6

The Balkan peninsula is a land of mountains and clusters of islands, where the few plains tend only to emphasize the rocky, broken surface of the region. The Balkans are bounded on the north by the Isonzo, Sava, and Danube rivers; this region does not include Rumania which is a Balkan nation only in a geopolitical sense.

In the mountains of the Balkan peninsula, at least three geological formations can be distinguished. The largest range, which covers much of Yugoslavia, Albania and Greece, belongs to the Dinaric system, or eastern Alps, whereas the part that runs through eastern Yugoslavia, northeastern Greece and European Turkey is a remnant of ancient fold and plateau mountains. The third formation, the Alpine ranges, penetrate into the Balkan pensinsula as a mighty continuation of the Carpathians, running across Rumania (where they are called the Transylvanian Alps) and in a crescent through eastern Yugoslavia and Bulgaria to the Black Sea.

The most important archipelagos of the Mediterranean are grouped around the Balkan peninsula. One occurs as a string of long islands along the coast of Yugoslavia from Istria in the north to Dubrovnik in the south. Farther south, off the coast of Greece in the Ionian Sea, is another cluster, and to the east of Greece, north of Crete, in the Aegean Sea, is Europe's largest archipelago, the Cyclades. Northward the islands become fewer in number; but in one sense the whole of the Aegean Sea is an archipelago. To the east the Cyclades merge into the Dodecanese, which, although they are Greek, are geographically part of Asia. Thus Greece, like Turkey and the Soviet Union, is partly in Asia.

CLASSIC ISLES AND CLASSIC LAND

The Greek islands are scattered like gems across the sparkling blue Aegean—the archipelagos that give this corner of Europe its unique character. The Cyclades are a multitude of large and small islands that lie between the latitudes 38 and 36 degrees north, the most southerly latitudes of Europe. Climatically they are subtropical, with very mild winters and hot summers.

The Cyclades are unique in Europe. There are archipelagos in the northern parts of the continent, too, but they are usually young areas, only recently liberated from ice and colonized by plants and animals, and their severe climate has discouraged exploitation by man. By contrast, the mild climate of the Greek archipelagos has for centuries favored man, so that he has left little room for other creatures. This retreat of flora and fauna will eventually handicap human activities rather than help them.

As a refuge for plants and animal life, the Greek archipelagos have been of great importance. Northern species found a haven there during the Ice Age, and in warmer epochs there was some expansion southward. Several northern and southern species became isolated, and remained there longer than anywhere else. Besides this, the Mediterranean flora and fauna have themselves been rich in species, and remnants of the original plant and animal world still remain on some islands. Isolated islands are often extremely interesting from the aspect of evolution; for example, a great number of lizard forms have developed on some of them. All this life, however, is doomed to disappear with the continuing impoverishment of the environment.

The beauty of the archipelagos is justly famous and irresistible. There are not so many islets as, for instance, in the Scandinavian skerries, but by the same token each island is more isolated than in northern archipelagos. Where in the northern archipelagos the islands dominate, around Greece the sea dominates. The islands themselves are usually mountains rising from the blue water, with inlets sometimes penetrating the land almost like fjords. In some places the slopes are bare; in others they are covered with olive trees and cypresses, or with macchia vegetation.

It is astonishing that such devastated, rocky islands can be so beautiful. Light and color play softly over them, the blue of the sky and sea forms a dazzling frame for the yellowish green and terra-cotta red of the land. An island such as Paros, whose marble has made it famous, seems at times to be a gleaming white. Another, Thera, one of the southernmost of the Cyclades, is volcanic in origin, and its red earth and black tuff, and the white dune at the crown make a striking color combination. It is about 900 feet at its highest point and one cliff, which is really the wall of a crater, rises 600 feet vertically from the sea. This precipice is made up of pale pumice stone embedded like arabesques in the brown cliffs. Thera is still active below sea level, and its submarine crater from time to time creates or transforms small islands, or even swallows them altogether. Not infrequently one sees mighty banks of snow-white cumulus clouds above the island, like a natural continuation of the mountain tops.

After a visit to the Cyclades, one realizes that these islands are much richer in the remains of ancient buildings than in wildlife. Scarcely any mammals live on the barren slopes and plateaus, and birds, too, are rare. Among the few interesting species here is the Eleonora's falcon *(Falco eleonorae)*, which is most at home in these archipelagos, although it is found also on Sardinia and in the Balearic Islands in the western Mediterranean. This falcon prefers mountainous islands, where it feeds on insects and small birds. Since it does not depend

Macchia scrub with yellow gorse (Ulex), white shadbush and stone oaks on Mt. Parnassus. (Gerhard Klammet)

The Balkans, bounded to the north by the Isonzo, Sava and Danube rivers, are characterized by mountains, river valleys and archipelagos. Rumania is a political but not a geographical part of the region. The island of Crete is the southernmost part of Europe.

rounding Cyclades and the Balkan peninsula are inhabited by another race. Still a third species, *L. erhardii*, including many subspecies, is found on the Cyclades.

What does this rich differentiation of races of lizards tell us? Many lizards may have reached the islands with the help of man; but it is also quite possible that many colonized the archipelago by swimming from one island to another or floating on branches, roots and the like. It should, however, be noted that no such transportation has been reported from any part of the world, despite the fact that lizards have shown a unique ability to colonize islands. It should also be remembered that many of the islands were undoubtedly cut off from the mainland in comparatively recent geological periods, so that the isolation and differentiation of the lizards could have taken place at this latter time.

Other factors besides purely geographical ones have contributed to this development. Recessive hereditary factors make themselves felt and become permanent more easily in a small population than in a large one. For this reason, the islands probably favor the occurrence of mutations among lizards; their distribution has probably taken place slowly and, in fact, the colonization of many islands has doubtless been based on only a few specimens.

The remarkable evolution of the many lizards of the Cyclades has a parallel in the plant life; no fewer than thirty-three endemic or local plants are found here.

One also sees many marine animals among the islands, conspicuous among them the dolphins *(Delphinus delphis)*. Inhabitants of warm seas, they may grow to a length of ten feet; their principal food is fish and octopuses. Frequently the dolphins will approach a boat and with indescribable grace and speed play around the bow, weaving in and out as in a ballet, leaping high in the air and plunging back into the water. It is easy to understand why dolphins caught the imagination of ancient mariners and generated many legends, why they occur so often in Greek mythology as a symbol of the sea, and why Poseidon and other gods were shown riding them over their marine domains.

As we have already noted, the Cyclades are the favorite European haunt of the monk seal; it can even go ashore on some of the more remote islands.

A bird often seen following in the wake of boats in the Mediterranean is the herring gull. But perhaps the most beautiful sea bird in the Cyclades is the shag *(Phalacrocorax aristotelis)*, which nests on the cliffs of some of the islands. If one is lucky, one may also catch a glimpse of a pair of Audouin's gulls *(Larus audouini)*.

GRECIAN MAINLAND

We have seen how the Mediterranean landscape of Italy and Spain has been destroyed. Greece has not been exempt: it has suffered even more than Italy from the destruction of forests with consequent erosion.

The records testify amply to the richness of nature in ancient Greece. When Greek civilization was at its height, about sixty per cent of the country was covered with forests. Now only about five per cent is wooded and only a small percentage of the fertile land is intact, due to erosion following the destruction of trees and ground vegetation. The country around Athens today resembles a mountain desert.

on food from the sea, its predilection for islands must be due to other factors. Almost wholly black, it is an arresting sight against the pale cliffs where it loves to nest, and where, on some islands, it breeds in small colonies. Less common is the peregrine.

Black-eared wheatears find favorable conditions on these treeless islands, frequenting slopes and plateaus wherever thin grass or shrubs grow. The population of swifts in the Cyclades must also be huge for they are always to be seen hunting insects over islands and sea. Ravens, kestrels and house martins breed on precipices facing the sea, and crested larks appear on grassy slopes around the villages. White wagtails *(Motacilla alba)* are found in all harbors and along natural beaches.

As we pointed out in Chapter 2, Andimilos is the only island in the Mediterranean on which the wild ibexes have not interbred with domestic goats. Many lizards have, through isolation, evolved a large number of local subspecies. Since this evolutionary process is still going on, many islands may contain surprises, for they have not all been studied herpetologically. For instance, a subspecies of the green lizard *(Lacerta viridis citrovittata)* is found only on the large island of Tiros. Three adjacent islands, Milos, Kimolos, and Siphnos, are the habitat of the giant green lizard *(L. trilineata)*, which may attain a length of twenty inches, whereas the sur-

Shallow lakes on the plains of Greece dry up completely during some summers, but in autumn they fill up again with rain water from neighboring mountains. (Werner Bischoff: Magnum Photos, Zurich)

It has been claimed that climatic changes have been the principal cause of the transformation from fertile to barren land, and one of the causes of the decline of Greek civilization. But if developments during the past few thousand years from Iran to Greece are analyzed, we find a number of reasons to believe that man rather than climate is the main cause of the ruin of the Mediterranean countryside. First the woods were cut down; then generations of sheep and goats grazed and trampled the vegetation, leaving the ground unprotected and allowing water and wind to erode the soil. With fertile topsoil gone, the landscape, and therefore man, became impoverished. (Goats graze by tearing up young plants by the roots, thus preventing the vegetation from recovering. They also climb low trees and shrubs and eat all the leaves. The quaint little goat of schoolbooks is, in fact—and especially in Mediterranean countries—man's greatest enemy.)

In 1958, at a meeting of the International Union for Conservation of Nature and Natural Resources in Athens, a discussion was held on the effect of erosion on the decline of ancient civilizations. A biologist, Professor Théodore Monod, analyzing the transformation of Greece from a flourishing country to the present impoverished land, concluded that climate had not been responsible for the change. On the same occasion, two historians, Professor E. Janssen and Professor Gaspard G. Mistardis, reached much the same conclusion in a discussion of Argolis, the northeastern part of the Peloponnesus and one of the oldest regions of ancient Hellas. However,

Janssen believed that cutting down forests and excessive grazing could not alone have caused the destruction of the landscape and the fall of Greek civilization; he considered man and his domestic animals contributory but not decisive factors in this decline. Janssen called attention to such other factors as invasions, political and social struggles, and irresponsible administrations. Professor Mistardis too, rejected the theory that purely climatic factors were responsible. He held the view that man started, continued, and aggravated a process that, once begun, could lead only to reduced fertility of the soil and eventually economic and social ruin.

As far back as 2500 years ago Plato (in a passage quoted by the Swedish scientist Carl Fries) described the erosion taking place even then: "Compared with what it was formerly, there now remains only, so to say, the bones of a body emaciated by illness: the soft, rich soil has been washed away and only the skeleton of the land remains." It is evident that even at the height of Hellenic civilization Greece was becoming a worn-out land and that Greek civilization was largely dependent on other countries for its material well-being.

The Greek countryside of today may be roughly divided into three levels: first, the cultivated valleys with olive groves and other plantations; then the plains on which sheep graze; and above these, the naked mountain slopes. That is the situation in spring, when vegetation is most lush. In summer and early autumn, the plains in many places are scorched and dry, the grass is worn down and the soil has blown away.

Not much is left of Greece's original flora and fauna; a few pine woods in Pindus and other mountain regions are exceptional. In spite of this, the country is still rich in both plants and animals, with a flora of 4100 species in about 6000 forms—far more than that of Switzerland, France and Belgium combined. Of this great number of plants, shrubs and trees, as many as 676 species are found nowhere else in Europe. Although many rare species occur on the mainland, the archipelagos and isolated islands have added to the great number of endemic plants. There are 213 such plants on Crete alone.

Many of these rare plants are now threatened with extinction by goats, whose pastures extend to remote ravines and the ledges of cliffs. The effect of the grazing of goats is catastrophic not only from the economic but also from the scientific viewpoint. Entire areas are being turned into deserts, with goats dévouring the last specimens of plants found nowhere else. Just prior to World War II, the Greek Government endeavored to do away with goat breeding completely, but the war interrupted this plan, and later governments seem to have had neither the courage nor the desire to revive it. The advantages of banishing goats may be seen in Mount Athos, a monastic community located on a promontory jutting into the Aegean Sea. According to an old monastery rule, no female of any kind, including goats, sheep and cattle, is permitted there. The result is an environment in equilibrium, with a richer wild vegetation than anywhere else in Greece.

There are also many endemic, or local, mammals in Greece. Most of these are small rodents, such as the greater mole rat *(Spalax microphthalmus graecus)*, which is here isolated from the rest of its distribution range; the spiny mouse *(Acomys cahirinus minous),* found only on Crete; and the gray hamster

Left: On the steep cliffs of Corfu in the Ionian Sea the vegetation is undisturbed; the result is a thick cover of junipers, broom and other shrubs. (Gerhard Klammet). Below: European pond tortoises in a lake on the Aegean island of Euboea. A sun-loving species, they often expose themselves on stones or on the shore. (Walter Fendrich)

Characteristic scene on the island of Crete: near Khania a high plateau covered by macchia vegetation, a cultivated valley and an 8661-foot peak, Levka Ori. (Toni Schneiders: Coleman and Hayward)

(Cricetulus migratorius atticus), a European representative of a species found mainly in Asia.

Apart from these unique endemic races, there are several mammals in Greece that have a restricted distribution in Europe. Among these are the European free-tailed bat *(Tadarida teniotis),* the only member of this genus in Europe; the Mediterranean pine vole *(Pitymys duodecimcostatus),* found chiefly in Spain; the snow vole *(Microtus nivalis),* which occurs in isolated groups in the mountains of southern and Central Europe; and the broad-toothed field mouse *(Apodemus mystacinus),* found chiefly in Asia.

The chamois occurs in some mountain ranges. Roe deer *(Capreolus capreolus)* are found locally but only in small numbers. Bears and wolves occur from time to time in the woods in the northern mountains, whereas the jackal *(Canis*

aureus) has a somewhat wider distribution. The fallow deer and the red deer have been exterminated on the mainland of Greece, but still persist on Rhodes. It is thus evident that although few large mammals have survived, numerous small ones remain. The relatively great number of species is due to the proximity of Africa and Asia, from which many have migrated.

The bird life of Greece is concentrated mainly in cultivated regions, where gardens and groves of trees around villages and farms are often the only green patches in an otherwise stony and, in summer, parched landscape. Hardly a village is without at least one plane tree *(Platanus orientalis),* and birds are always found in them. Naturally, most birds also haunt the olive woods and the groves or thickets of citrus and walnut trees; among them are such species as the black-eared wheatear *(Oenanthe hispanica),* the goldfinch, the greenfinch *(Chloris chloris),* the cirl bunting *(Emberiza cirlus),* the blackbird *(Turdus merula),* the spotted flycatcher *(Muscicapa striata),* the woodchat shrike *(Lanius senator),* the cuckoo, and the turtledove *(Streptopelia turtur).*

DELPHI AND PARNASSUS

When one looks out from the slopes of Parnassus (whose highest summit is 8068 feet) over the country around Delphi and Amphissa, the valley between the two places looks like a broad green brushstroke across a yellowish-brown background, framed by the azure inlets of the Mediterranean and the snow-capped mountains in the distance. This green belt in the valley is the largest olive forest in Greece. A few half-wild olive trees have ascended the mountain slopes and grow at random near Delphi's famous amphitheater.

Seldom can one find a place in Europe where civilization and nature have combined so harmoniously as at Delphi. Close by the ruins of ancient temples, now invaded by weeds, grasses and shrubs, to form a mosaic of gray stone and green vegetation, the wild cliffs of Parnassus rise steeply toward the sky, and vultures on broad wings soar over the mountain.

The birds found even in the truly wild country of Greece, such as the mountains of Macedonia near the Albanian border, cannot compare with those of Delphi, the lower parts of Parnassus or the olive groves of Amphissa. Of the species that can be heard in the shrubs, trees and ruins of Delphi in the spring, the most common is the whitethroat *(Sylvia communis).* The finest singer, a competitor of the nightingale, is the blackcap, whose silvery soprano blends with the songs of other birds. Other singing birds are the Sardinian warbler, the lesser whitethroat, Rüppell's warbler *(S. rüppelli),* the subalpine warbler and the orphean warbler, all belonging to the *Sylvia* species, as well as various finches, the black redstart and the rock sparrow.

Commonly seen in the area is the rock nuthatch *(Sitta neumayer),* which runs about on cliffs and among the ruins. The stone nuthatch, unlike the common nuthatch *(S. europaea),* seldom visits the nearby olive trees, but nests in holes in cliffs; here it reduces the size of the entrance with mortar made of mud, much as the common nuthatch does with holes in trees. Like water gurgling from Kastalia's ancient spring, the nuthatch fills the air with music. Another striking bird is the beautiful rock thrush *(Monticola solitarius),* which visits the loftier ruins as well as the precipices of Parnassus.

For millions of years the fabled mountains at Meteora in Thessaly have been sculptured into gigantic towers. (Gerhard Klammet)

At Delphi one may become acquainted also with the somber tit *(Parus lugubris),* which resembles the Siberian tit *(P. cinctus)* more than it does its nearer European relatives. In the ruins high up in the hills, just below the steep cliffs, where trees and shrubs are sparse, one finds the ortolan bunting, the Cretzschmar's bunting *(Emberiza caesia),* a Balkan bird that differs from the ortolan only by a few shades of color, several rock buntings *(E. cia),* and an occasional cirl bunting *(E. cirlus).*

Swallows are numerous at Delphi. This group has not been discouraged by the destruction of the landscape, since it nests on buildings or cliffs and takes food while airborne. House martins *(Delichon urbica)* attach their mud nests to cliffs and buildings, while the swallow *(Hirundo rustica)* haunts buildings everywhere. Its relative, the red-rumped swallow *(H. daurica),* nests in tunnels, in caves, and under bridges. The most common martin at Delphi, however, is the crag martin *(Ptyonoprogne rupestris),* which in summer flies above the ruins, its tracks sometimes crossed by darting alpine swifts *(Apus melba).*

Many birds breed among the crags of Parnassus, and it is pleasant to lie on a stone bench in the ancient amphitheater admiring an avian spectacle the Greeks might have watched three thousand years ago. Rock doves, kestrels, peregrines and buzzards fly to and fro while, high above, griffon vultures glide in wide circles, lifted by currents of warm air from the mountain slope. The air currents begin to rise early in the morning, whereupon a wonderful exhibition begins. The vultures, which spend the night in rocky crevices, dive out one at a time until there is a considerable flock circling in the air. Although an occasional golden eagle *(Aquila chrysaëtos)* passes over Parnassus, the faithful sentinels here are the vultures. The griffon vulture is the most common; small Egyptian vultures and large black vultures sometimes accompany them. Occasionally the bearded vulture, most elegant of the genus, may be seen.

Parnassus has several levels of vegetation. On the lower slopes above the village of Arakhova, where an ancient pathway ascends the legendary mountain, the visitor is surrounded by occasional deciduous trees and shrubs, but they soon give way to almost bare earth. Farther up, on a wide, sheep-grazed plateau about three thousand feet above sea level, the raven's harsh cry emphasizes the wild character of the stony desert. Still higher is a wood of conifers *(Abies cephalonica)* where the meager vegetation has been almost entirely eaten by goats. The nuthatch is common in this wood, which also shelters the firecrest *(Regulus ignicapillus)*, coal tit *(Parus ater)* and two species of tree creepers *(Certhia familiaris* and *C. brachydactyla)*. Larger birds found here are the black woodpecker *(Dryocopus martius)*, the alpine chough *(Pyrrhocorax graculus)*, and an occasional bird of prey.

The little fire-bellied toad *(Bombina variegata)* and the Greek frog *(Rana graeca),* which are both common throughout Greece, are found high on Parnassus. The tortoise *(Testudo marginata)* which lives only in southern Greece, prefers a mountain habitat, living on Parnis and Olympus as well as Parnassus.

The country below Delphi is richer in natural vegetation, although it too shows the effect of cultivation. In the valley, widening rapidly to a plain around the small Pleistos River, the branches of huge, ancient olive trees intermingle so that they form a thick green canopy. The local people claim that these trees are thousands of years old, and—whether this is an exaggeration or not—the wood is mentioned in writings of the seventh century B.C. While wandering in the shade of these mighty trees, listening to the songs of birds, and surrounded by the heights of Delphi, one gets an idea of the former grandeur of this ancient place and the once virginal and generous Mediterranean landscape that inspired the classical poets. This olive wood at Amphissa is full of birds. The olivaceous warbler, found only in this southeastern corner of Europe, lives alongside the red warbler, and the cooing of turtledoves is heard incessantly.

THE PLAIN OF THESSALY

The cultivated plain of Thessaly is the largest of its kind in Greece. In ancient times, after the topsoil of the uplands eroded, it supplied most of the agricultural produce in the Greek kingdoms. The woods of Attica—that is, around Athens —had been cut down in prehistoric times, and we know that

Facing: Karst landscape on the Adriatic coast near Jablanac in Yugoslavia. The karst, a limestone, covers a large plateau in the northwestern Balkan peninsula. (Gerhard Klammet)

Above: The Montpellier snake (Malpolon monspessulanus), *one of Europe's largest venomous snakes, is back-fanged, so its bite is not usually harmful to man. Center: The leopard snake* (Elaphe situla), *one of the most beautiful reptiles of Europe, occurs in southern Italy, the southern Balkan peninsula, the Greek archipelagos, the Crimea and the Caucasus. Below: Four of the five European species of the snake genus* Coluber *are found in the Balkans. Of these the arrow snake* (C. jugularis), *shown here, is distributed in mountains, steppes and archipelagos. (All by Erich Sochurek)*

Drought is normal in Greece in summer. Even in April this river near Asprovalta in northern Greece is nearly dry. (Ingmar Holmåsen)

even before Pericles (490—429 B.C.) few trees remained in this region.

The Thessalian plain was therefore of great importance as the granary of Hellas; however, even by the fifth century B.C. its fertility could be maintained only artificially. Soil brought down by wind and water from surrounding mountains contributed unexpectedly to this fertility. This phenomenon, called *terra volante* or "flying earth" by the Italians, has played a vital role in maintaining the fertility of the plain for at least two thousand years.

Today, cotton, potatoes, tobacco, and grain are grown in Thessaly, but most of the plain is unsuitable for agriculture and has been converted to grazing land for sheep and goats—the same negative development we noted in Castille in Spain and in the Roman Campagna in Italy. When I visited the Thessalian plain one September, practically the only signs of life were flocks of sheep and their shepherds. In spite of the heat, the latter were wrapped in huge black furs—probably very welcome during the chilly nights.

In traveling over the plain, one is astonished at the dearth of dwellings or farms. One wonders where the homes are of the farmers who must attend to their fields at least a few times a year; it turns out that they prefer to live in neighboring villages, even though several miles from the fields.

It is interesting to note that when the armies of Caesar and Pompey fought one of the most decisive battles in Roman history (in 48 B.C.) on this plain it was probably a fertile, flowering region.

Birds are few and easily detected here. On the plain proper we noted only the crow, corn bunting *(Emberiza calandra)*, calandra lark, kestrel and lesser kestrel. But around Larissa, the capital of Thessaly, the bird life is richer because the trees and shrubs provide greater variety in food and shelter. The green valley of the River Pinios, west and north of Larissa, attracts the colorful hoopoes, rollers and bee-eaters, as well as the cuckoo, quail, woodchat shrike, black-headed bunting *(Emberiza melanocephala)* and white stork.

The white stork is common along the river valleys on the plains. It nests in dense colonies, both in trees and on roofs of village houses. We counted thirty-three nests in the churchyard of Stephanobiki, fourteen of which were in one tree. Among other birds in the area were the sparrow hawk *(Accipiter nisus)*, which preys on nightingales, great tits or house sparrows; the dipper *(Cinclus cinclus)* over the river; and the yellowish gray wagtail *(Motacilla cinerea)* which hunts insects at the edge of the water. Little owls *(Athene noctua)* and scops owls *(Otus scops)* were observed in the valley.

Although the rivers in many of the plains of Greece dry

up in summer, their valleys sometimes form oases rich in vegetation. Among the trees, species of *Populus* dominate, though one also finds cypresses *(Cupressus sempervirens)* and platans. On the river banks grow willows and other species of *Salix,* as well as tamarisks and the pink-flowering *Nerium oleander.* Nearby, terrapins *(Clemmys caspica)* sun themselves on stones, while the glass snake *(Ophisaurus apodus),* a powerful, legless lizard, often more than a yard long, hunts snails and insects.

Because of its bird life, Lake Karla, in the eastern part of the plain of Thessaly, is one of the more interesting lakes in this area. A shallow body of water, only about twelve miles long and three to four miles wide, and sometimes likely to dry up completely, it is supplied by streams from Mt. Osa (6500 feet) and Mt. Pelion (5300 feet). In spite of its inconstant water level, the lake is excellent for wintering ducks and waders. While visiting in March we observed many surface-feeding ducks, mainly teal. In February 1964 more than 400,000 ducks were counted in Lake Karla.

MT. OLYMPUS AND THE PINDUS RANGE

Olympus, the highest mountain in Greece (9753 feet), raises its snow-clad summit north of Lake Karla and the Thessalian plain. The natural zonation on the mountains of Greece are difficult to interpret, since the woods have been either partially or completely destroyed. However, on some mountains, two or three principal types of vegetation can be distinguished; for example, such southern mountains as Parnis in Attica, Parnassus, Pelion, Olympus, the mountains of western Macedonia, and Epirus in the Pindus range. The southern mountains are Mediterranean in character, while the northern ones (with the exception of the wooded slopes of the Pindus range, which have a character of their own) are often mantled in Central European types of forest.

The mountains of the Mediterranean type usually show the following zones: At lower levels there seems to be no natural vegetation anywhere. Where the slopes are not altogether bare, there is evergreen macchia vegetation up to altitudes of 2500 to 3000 feet. Pines grow sparsely up to about 650 feet, and a related species *Pinus halepensis* up to 1000 feet; at that height it is joined or replaced by oaks *(Quercus aegilops, Q. coccifera* and *Q. ilex).* Somewhat higher are pure deciduous woods, with four other species of oaks *(Q. petraea, Q. pubescens, Q. robur* and *Q. lanuginosa),* beeches, chestnut *(Castanea sativa),* and ash trees, which ascend to an altitude of from 2600 to 3250 feet above sea level; after this, a species of fir *(Abies cephalonica)* forms the highest vegetation zone. Occasionally, pines *(Pinus nigra)* grow in the highest zone on some mountains.

The mountains of northern Greece usually lack the macchia vegetation, which is basically Mediterranean, but are covered with oaks of the species mentioned above, and with *Quercus cerris.* The ash, maple and elm appear between 2500 and 3250 feet, but are supplanted above this altitude by pure beech woods, which appear up to an altitude of 6000 to 6500 feet. Above that, conifers, the silver fir *(Abies alba), Pinus nigra,* and the spruce *(Picea abies),* take over. Coniferous woods, unlike northern forests, occupy a relatively large area of the Pindus range, including *Pinus nigra,* which attains a height of about 120 feet, and *P. leucodermis.* In parts of the

The species Ramondia nathaliae, *found in Greece and Yugoslavia, is one of many plants found only in the Balkan mountains. (Wilhelm Schacht)*

Pindus the deciduous woods even on the lower slopes are, for southern Europe, rather well preserved. They consist mainly of beeches, impressive horse-chestnut trees *(Aesculus hippocastanum),* walnut trees *(Juglans regia),* limes *(Tilia tomentosa),* and occasional groves of hazel *(Corylus colurna).*

Mt. Meteora lies between Trikkala and Metsovon, where the plain begins to rise into the uplands. It differs from other Greek mountains in that it is composed of conglomerate, which has been sculpted over the years into a series of fantastic pillars rising from the Pindus valley to a height of about 2500 feet. At the top, the visitor finds himself level with hovering vultures, buzzards and eagles, and far above the black and white storks. Meteora, meaning "floating in air," refers to the cloisters built in the fourteenth century, like swallows' nests, into the walls of the cliffs or on the mountain top.

It is in these mountains in the interior of Greece that one may see nesting birds of prey that are rare elsewhere in Europe. Besides the species found around Delphi and Parnassus, the short-toed eagle, booted eagle *(Hieraëtus pennatus),* Bonelli's eagle *(H. fasciatus),* and lanner falcon *(Falco biarmicus)* breed there. The long-legged buzzard *(Buteo rufinus)* also breeds in eastern Greece.

Pindus is still inhabited by some of Europe's rarest mammals, such as the wildcat and bear. The ibex allegedly lives there, and if this is true, it is the only place on the Balkan mainland where it is found.

Lake Ioannina, in the mountains of Pindus in Epirus, is a gathering point for birds of passage. When I once visited the lake at the end of September, about five hundred lesser kestrels had congregated there. In their hunt for small, winged creatures, they gave a spectacular aerial exhibition above and around the trees on the shore. At the same time, hundreds of small dark terns *(Chlidonias)* flew to and fro over the lake. Since they were all in molt, it was impossible to determine whether or not they were black, whiskered or white-winged terns, all of which breed in the Balkans. I am still wondering how these small water birds flew over the Pindus range, 6500 feet high, to Lake Ioannina.

From the herpetologist's point of view, the Balkan peninsula is a paradise, for no other place in Europe has so many species of batrachians and reptiles. Marsh frogs *(Rana ridibunda)* swim in the vegetation along the shores of the lake. Around the lake and on its islands lizards scurry about in search of insects. Among the lizards are the giant green lizard *(Lacerta trilineata),* which is one of the largest species; the wall lizard *(L. muralis);* the spectacular lizard *(Algyroides nigropunctatus);* the water snake *(Natrix natrix);* and its near relative, the diced water snake *(N. tessellata).*

In the areas of Greece already mentioned, Parnassus and Olympus are national parks, established in 1938; unfortunately, the war and its aftermath made it impossible to carry out protective regulations. Mount Parnis, too, is the center of a natural reserve of about 15,000 acres. A national park in the Pindus is projected by the Greek Government and encouraged by the Council of Europe. Finally, several small reserves have been established in the Aegean archipelagos and on Crete.

Right: A magnificent forest of beech, oak and other deciduous trees in Yugoslavia's Sava Valley. In May, the river, a tributary of the Danube, floods the forest for several weeks. (Ingmar Holmåsen). Below: Black-winged stilt nesting in Lake Karla on the plain of Thessaly. (Walter Fendrich)

White storks nesting in a lone tree in Thessaly. This bird often nests on the roofs of houses, sometimes in dense colonies. (Toni Schneiders: Coleman and Hayward)

MOUNTAINOUS REALMS: YUGOSLAVIA AND ALBANIA

The Pindus is the Greek section of the mountain range stretching across the western part of the Balkan peninsula through Yugoslavia and Albania. Yugoslavia is, in fact, mainly mountainous. However, the Central European plain spills over into northwestern Yugoslavia and wide, cultivated plains are also found in the valleys of the great rivers, particularly of the Danube, Sava, Drava, Tisa, and Morava. Despite the thickly-wooded mountains, Yugoslavia is primarily an agricultural country. The southern mountain range, having vegetation of the Central European type, occupies about half of Yugoslavia. In the northern part of the country—that is, in Slavonia, Croatia, Dalmatia and Slovenia—lie several mighty ranges; of these, Velebit Planina along the Adriatic coast is marked by Mediterranean vegetation and the Karawanks on the border of Austria resemble the Alps.

The upper Velebit range, rising high above the Adriatic in Dalmatia, is wooded; oak at the lower levels, then beech, and finally, at the heights, spruce. Large mammals found there are bears, wild boar, and roe deer. The outstanding bird is the nutcracker *(Nucifraga caryocatactes),* which ordinarily lives in the coniferous forests of Europe, but is very spottily distributed on various mountains, probably as a relict from the period when conifers were more widespread in Europe.

Wolves, bears and jackals live in the isolated mountains of both northern and southern Yugoslavia, and a few pardel lynx are still found in the range between Yugoslavia and Albania, in Macedonia and in the neighboring corner of Bulgaria. An interesting rodent, found only in Yugoslavia, is the Nehring's snow vole *(Dolomys bogdanovi),* five races occurring in as many mountain ranges. It inhabits fissures in calcareous rocks, where vegetation is rich. In color it differs from all other small European rodents, its fur being a beautiful pale gray and white.

Yugoslavia's outstanding national park, Plitvička Jezera, is in the Croatian Mountains. Its magnificent beech and spruce woods are like virgin forest, and provide a habitat for eight species of woodpeckers, several of which also breed farther north in Europe and Asia. The three-toed woodpecker *(Picoïdes tridactylus),* the black woodpecker, the gray-headed woodpecker *(Picus canus),* and the white-backed woodpecker *(Dendrocopus leucotos)* share the woods with the great spotted woodpecker *(D. major),* the lesser spotted woodpecker *(D. minor),* the middle spotted woodpecker *(D. medius)* and the wryneck *(Jynx torquilla).* Moreover the green woodpecker probably lives in these woods; if so, only the Syrian woodpecker is not found in Plitvička—but it will doubtless find its way across the Balkans and reach western Yugoslavia in the near future. Another bird with primarily northern distribution, the Ural owl *(Strix uralensis),* should be mentioned among the denizens of Plitvička. As a southern contrast to this northern bird, the sand viper *(Vipera anmodytes),* a venomous reptile, is common in Plitvička.

LAKE OHRIDA AND THE KARST CAVES

From the point of view of natural history, the most striking features of Yugoslavia's mountains are Lake Ohrida in the south—partly in Albania—and the karst caves in the north.

Lake Ohrida is remarkable among European lakes for the evolution of animal species corresponding to that of Lake Baikal in Asia and Lake Tanganyika in Africa, the deepest lakes in the world. Lake Ohrida has fewer animal species and local forms than the other lakes, and it cannot be compared with them in area (134 square miles) or depth (938 feet); but from a biological standpoint it is unique. Situated 2265 feet above sea level, it is surrounded by precipitous mountains. Cormorants fly over the surface, indicating that, despite its isolated situation, it is rich in fish. The lake contains thirteen species of the carplike cyprinids; one of which is found only there and in Lake Scutari, near the Adriatic between Yugoslavia and Albania. A species of eel, *Anguilla anguilla,* dwells in Lake Ohrida; it is unusual in that, although being born in the sea, it finds its way up the River Drin to the mountains.

Salmonids are the most remarkable fish in Lake Ohrida, presenting some interesting problems. One species, *Salmothymus ohridanus,* is found nowhere else. A species of trout, *Salmo letnica,* occurs in three, or perhaps four, distinct populations, which do not interbreed because they have different spawning periods and places. In a study made in 1960 these trout were regarded as subspecies, although they can be distinguished only by the state of their sexual organs at a certain time. The various races of *letnica* in Lake Ohrida provide an interesting parallel to another salmonid, the whitefish *(Coregonus)* of Lake Hornavan in Sweden, which is also represented by four populations that do not mingle.

Most of the animal species peculiar to Lake Ohrida are invertebrates, mainly snails *(Gastropoda)* and worms *(Oligochaeta* and *Turbellaria);* these have undoubtedly been isolated in the lake for a very long time, during which they have evolued and become specialized in different ways.

Caves are found in great number in Rumania and on the Balkan peninsula. They appear in various types of formations, most commonly in the karst formations of northwestern Yugoslavia. Some are very large, penetrating several miles into the limestone mountains. The term *karst* is derived from the name of a limestone plateau in Carso, or Kras, and Istria in western Slovenia and Croatia. The caves there were cut by water that penetrated the mountains and the dolomite, gypsum and limestone of which the rock usually consists. Long tunnels and high vaults have been formed, occasionally widening into gigantic underground chambers. They resemble such other caves, for instance, as those found in the Ardennes in Belgium and in Derbyshire and Somerset in England. A common feature of all these caves is the formation of stalactites and stalagmites by the seepage of calcareous water, the former hanging from the roof like icicles, the latter building up on the floor like fungi. Stalactites and stalagmites sometimes meet, forming columns from floor to roof, often in such numbers that the caves resemble petrified forests.

The largest of Yugoslavia's caves, and also the largest in Europe, occurs at Postojna, northeast of Trieste. There the River Pinca suddenly disappears into a hole in the limestone; close by is the mouth of the cave—the former bed of the river. The branches of the cave run about three miles underground, where the river in its former course hollowed out a number of chambers and corridors. One of the largest rooms is approximately 225 feet long, almost as wide, and 112 feet high. Occasionally one comes upon the river, racing along with a deafening roar about sixty feet below the level of the cave. It comes out into the open about three miles to the north, but soon vanishes again underground, only to reappear at Ljubljana, where it flows into the Sava, a large tributary of the Danube.

The caves of Yugoslavia, like many other caves, are inhabited by bats; but the most famous feature of the karst caves is the proteus *(Proteus anguineus).* This is a salamander that does not develop beyond the larval stage; that is, it breathes through gills and never becomes the lung-breathing animal that is the final phase in the metamorphosis of the salamander or newt. The proteus breeds in the larval stage by internal fertilization. Its gills are bright red, and its skin, though whitish, appears to have a pale red lustre due to blood vessels lying close to the surface. The skin of the proteus is not completely without pigment, and it does darken when exposed to light. Millennia of life in the eternal darkness of the caves have caused its eyes to atrophy and become covered with skin; nevertheless, as soon as a beam of light is thrown upon it, it dives to the bottom.

THE DANUBE BASIN

The Danube is second in length only to the Volga among the rivers of Europe. Its source is in the Black Forest in

The garden dormouse is widely distributed in the leafy woods of southern and Central Europe. It is nocturnal and an excellent climber. (R. P. Bille)

southwestern Germany; before the river reaches the Black Sea it flows through no fewer than seven countries and three of Europe's capitals—Vienna, Budapest and Belgrade.

Most of the plains of Yugoslavia are situated along the Danube. They are intensively cultivated and few of them can be called natural country, except fragments along the winding river and on an occasional wooded hill or mountain. A small rodent, the European suslik *(Citellus citellus),* is found on the plains around the river. It is a steppe animal, and its habitat in Yugoslavia is the most westerly outpost of its distribution range. Since the European suslik is active mainly in the daytime, its habits are easily observed. Its way of life resembles that of the marmot *(Marmota)* or the American prairie dog *(Cynomys).* Susliks live in colonies of subterranean burrows and are often seen sitting upright on their heels, looking out over the plain.

It is only natural that such an abundance of susliks and other small rodents should attract birds of prey. This is especially noticeable where the Danube meets Fruska Gora, which rises 1768 feet above the plain northwest of Belgrade. The wooded hillside provides a suitable habitat for the breeding of raptorial birds, which use rising air currents for reconnaissance flights. In this region of plains, mountains and marshlands between the Danube and the Sava, breed

several pairs of white-tailed eagles *(Haliaeetus albicilla).* In some parts of the Balkan peninsula this bird is astonishingly numerous, although it is far rarer than formerly. Other large birds indigenous to Fruska Gora are the white stork, the black stork, the imperial eagle, the saker falcon *(Falco cherrug),* and the black kite, which is common there, as everywhere else on the Balkan peninsula.

A journey down the Danube, through the surrounding marshlands of Yugoslavia and along the border between Bulgaria and Rumania to the Black Sea would be a chronicle of birds, fish, and marsh plants in the heart of a cultivated steppe. The plant and animal life observed on such a trip recurs farther down the river, in the delta, but there it is so rich and abundant that the upper river seems pale in comparison. We will deal with the mighty delta in the section on the shores of the Black Sea.

Only about three per cent of Turkey is in Europe. European Turkey is a mountainous region, bounded on the west by the Meric River of Greece, whose delta on the Aegean Sea was until recently very rich in bird life. Since the 1950's great drainage schemes have been carried out by Turkey and Greece, and the area has lost much of its ornithological interest.

Apart from this delta, it is the migration of birds over the Bosporus at the northern end and the Dardanelles at the southwestern end of the Sea of Marmara—which separates European Turkey and Asiatic Turkey—that has made European Turkey interesting to students of natural history. In September and October great numbers of birds fly over these narrow straits. The route is especially popular with large birds; as many as 4800 storks, vultures, eagles, buzzards, hawks and kites sometimes pass over in a single day. But much remains to be learned about this migration route.

Other areas of Bulgaria and Rumania will be dealt with in the chapters on the Black Sea and the Carpathians.

Lake Scutari, on the Yugoslavia-Albania border, is ringed by mighty mountains that separate it from the sea. (Michel Terrasse)

Inland Seas and Europe's Highest Range

The Black and Caspian Seas and the Caucasus Mountains

7

During one period of the Tertiary, millions of years ago, a large part of what is now southeastern Europe and south-western Asia was an inland sea or great lake. When the Caucasus range was formed, that sea was divided in two—the Caspian Sea and the Black Sea. In the Ice Age, that is, during a recent geological period, the Caspian Sea was on a higher level than the Black Sea and ran into it. Now, the surface of the Black Sea is eighty-five feet above that of the Caspian. It was during a relatively late phase of the Ice Age, perhaps even after the end of this period, that the Black Sea broke through the Bosporus and the Dardanelles into the Mediterranean, while the Caspian remained an inland sea, the largest in the world.

THE BLACK SEA: A MEDITERRANEAN SATELLITE

Geologically, the Black Sea is what is known as a graben or vast trench, its greatest depth being 6129 feet, and its area 165,000 square miles. Although it is more land-locked than the Baltic, which is of comparable dimensions, it has the characteristics of a genuine sea. The Black Sea has, none the less, preserved many of the features of a brackish water lake. Its flora and fauna are partly characterized by the freshwater epoch through which it passed, although a large number of elements have since entered it from the Mediterranean. The fact that fresh, brackish and saltwater organisms have all adapted themselves to the special conditions found here has made this area of special interest.

The salinity of the surface water of the Black Sea is approximately 1.8 per cent, but in the Sea of Azov, into which the river Don flows, it is only 0.7 to 1.1 per cent. There is very little circulation of the deeper waters in the Black Sea, and the content of hydrogen sulphide is therefore very high. In addition, the amount of oxygen decreases rapidly with the depth. This means that no organic life is found in the Black Sea below a depth of about six hundred feet. In spite of this, it is rich with fauna, but all fish and other animals,

as well as vegetable plankton, are concentrated in the surface layers of water. Thus more than ninety per cent of the water is sterile, making the high productivity of this sea all the more remarkable. The great rivers flowing into it—the Danube, Dniester, Dnieper and Don—deposit great quantities of nutritional substances there. The wealth of plankton in the Black Sea provides the nutrition essential to the survival of a profusion of fish. Calculated in pounds per square mile, this body of water produces about six times more fish than the Mediterranean, but the number of species of plants and animals is only about one-fourth of that in the Mediterranean.

GIANT STURGEON

One hundred and seventy-one species of fish are known to exist in the Black Sea, nearly all of them of marine origin; fifty-four of them are not found elsewhere. Vagrant marine mammals, the common porpoise *(Phocaena phocaena)*, and common and bottlenosed dolphins *(Delphinus delphis* and *Tursiops truncatus)*, are all found in its waters. At times, dolphins leave the Mediterranean in great shoals, chasing small fish such as anchovies *(Engraulis enchrasicolus)* and other members of the herring family. At least three species of shark swim in the Black Sea. One of them, the spiny dog-fish *(Squalus acanthias)*, a permanent inhabitant of the Black Sea, has a wide distribution range. The monk seal, occurring along the rocky Black Sea coast between Shabla and Kaliakra in Bulgaria, is considered to be a glacial relict.

The best known fish in the Black Sea are sturgeon, several species of which produce the famous Russian caviar. Many of them grow to an enormous size, the largest being the huso or great sturgeon *(Huso huso)*, a giant that reaches a length of thirty feet and a weight of up to 3300 pounds. A female of this size can provide about 220 pounds of caviar. Nowadays, however, only a few sturgeon of such a size are caught. The common sturgeon *(Acipenser sturio)* can also grow to a considerable size, about twenty feet in length and 660 to 880 pounds in weight. This species is rare in the Black Sea and does not enter its rivers. Two other species of sturgeon are found in the Black Sea and the river deltas: the pastruga sturgeon *(A. stellatus)* and the Black Sea sturgeon *(A. güldenstädti)*, while the viza *(A. nudiventris)* and the sterlet *(A. ruthenus)* live only in the Danube itself and its tributaries.

Sturgeon live on sand and clay sea beds, feeding on small animals such as worms, mussels, crustaceans, fish and vegetable matter. Like most species of the same family, they enter the deltas or wander up the rivers to spawn in spring and early summer. From April to July in the delta a female can spawn two to three million eggs, which adhere in large cakes to the clayey substratum at depths of six to thirty feet. The roe hatches after three to seven days. The small-fry are about four-tenths of an inch long and look like tadpoles. They grow rapidly to about eight inches in the autumn, when they make their way to the sea.

The Turkish and Bulgarian coasts of the Black Sea consist alternately of mountain slopes and plains, sometimes with white beaches as a transition between land and sea.

In Dobrudja, which is mainly in Rumania and forms a coastal plain between the Danube and the Black Sea, there are great agricultural regions that were genuine steppe land not long ago. The cultivation of virgin land in Bulgaria and

The shores of the Black Sea near Novorossiisk in Abkhazian below the southwestern slopes of the Caucasus. A wood of rare pines (Pinus pitiusa) *borders the beach in the foreground. (Kai Curry-Lindahl)*

Rumania is rapidly changing wild country into farmland. Here and there, groves of trees around villages or a stand of woods relieves the monotony of the flat country. One of the most interesting wooded areas of south Dobrudja, in Bulgaria, is the Baltata Forest, which separates the plain from the mountains and runs down to the shore of the Black Sea. In this deciduous forest, with its wealth of climbing and trailing plants, the European white elm *(Ulmus laevis)* is common, and among the many birds are the lesser spotted eagle *(Aquila pomarina)* and the black stork *(Ciconia nigra)*. But an even more interesting forest, a true virgin forest, lies hidden on an island in the mighty delta of the Danube.

THE DANUBE DELTA

A look at a map of Europe, and particularly at the courses of the great rivers, reveals that very large deltas have been formed in two regions: one around the mouth of the Danube, at the Black Sea, and another where the Volga enters the Caspian Sea. A map, however, can give only a faint idea of the great extent of these deltas.

Since the formation of the Danube delta during the Ice Age, the river has changed its main course several times. Thus the delta is a relatively recent formation, a result of sediment transported by the Danube on its way through Europe. This sediment is deposited at the mouth of the river and has created a number of islands totalling more than one million acres in area. During the period from 1830 to 1952, the northern part of the delta, around the arm of the Danube—called the Chilia—has been extended about ten miles into the sea, which means that in places it is increasing at the remarkably rapid rate of 410 feet a year.

The Danube divides into three main arms, the Chilia, the Sulina, and the St. Gheorghe, all flowing through the delta in divergent directions. These river arms have innumerable channels meandering in a seemingly endless labyrinth; some of them lead to lagoons, others to lakes or the sea, and still others rejoin the main river. Within this maze of river arms and channels are great expanses of reed beds and other wetlands in various stages of development. In the same way the firm land of the deltas, surrounded by water, contains many types of vegetation, from virtually naked sand to dense primeval forest. This variety is due to the very rapid sedimentation by the river and interaction with the sea. The delta is so large, and its growth so uneven, that conditions differ widely from place to place; it is thus full of surprises.

For its last three hundred miles, the Danube forms the

103

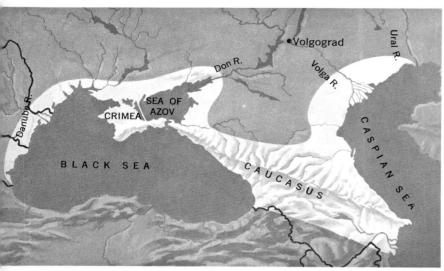

No other coastal region of Europe has such a variety of vegetation as that around the Black Sea. In Turkey there is Mediterranean macchia, in Bulgaria and Rumania deciduous woods and vast delta reed beds, in the Ukraine and the Crimea steppes and mountains, and in the Caucasus to the east, luxuriant forest groves, which to the south, in Georgia, turn subtropical.

boundary between Bulgaria and Rumania. There it swings in mighty curves in all directions, but its main course is eastward, toward the Black Sea. At Silistra, more than sixty miles from the sea, the Danube turns northeast and divides twice into two arms, one large and the other small, which completely surround the flooded areas. A little farther on these arms run due north, parallel to the Black Sea. But it was not always so: during one phase of the Ice Age the Danube flowed eastward, and its mouth was where Constanza now lies.

In many places along its winding course the river overflows its banks, forming marshes and lakes, many of which are rich in vegetation, fish, and bird life. The richest of these areas is the great marsh that surrounds the river as it flows northward through Dobrudja, from the Bulgarian boundary in the south, and to Galati in the north, a distance of almost 110 miles. This marsh, its width at various points ranging between about six to twelve miles, is flooded twice a year—in spring and autumn. Passing over the region by air, one sees a mosaic of blue and yellowish-brown water, green reeds and meadows, and brown swamps. Pelicans fly past in great flocks, sailing for hours on their broad wings, borne up by currents of warm air. At first, much of the green and brown below may be taken for land, but soon one notices the extent to which the sun is reflected by water. This gigantic marsh is only an introduction to the delta itself, which is so large that it is impossible, even from the air, to see it in its entirety. It is not easy, moreover, to travel through the delta except along the three arms of the river. Every journey into the interior, to the many islands and lagoons surrounded by aquatic vegetation a mile or more wide, must be in the nature of an expedition.

At Galati, the Danube turns sharply east and becomes the boundary to Russia. It is surrounded on both sides by large lakes and undulating country with extensive and beautiful deciduous woods, mainly of oaks *(Quercus pubescens* and *Q. robur).* The woods cover large areas and offer a contrast to

the flatness of the neighboring steppe land and marshes. The town of Tulcea marks the beginning of the Danube delta. There the river divides into its three main arms, the middle one of which, the Sulina, has been straightened out and made navigable for ocean-going vessels for about fifty miles upriver. The Chilea, about seventy miles long, and the St. Gheorghe, about seventy-five miles long, still flow in their natural courses. In a sense, the Sulina does so too, for the winding waterways surrounding the main river mark its original course.

Tulcea is about forty-five miles from the Black Sea as the crow flies. This is equivalent to the width of the delta. The delta is twice as long, extending from the Russian boundary in the north to Mamaia in the south—as great a distance as from Naples in Italy to Manfredonia on the Adriatic coast!

Immediately to the north of the Danube delta is another delta, that of the Dnieper, and several smaller rivers, all helping to change the contours of the coast.

The large motorboat placed at our disposal by the Rumanian Government during an expedition to the delta in 1963 proved to be an excellent lookout post, for its elevated deck brought us level with the tops of reed grass *(Phragmites communis)* that on the banks of the rivers and channels often attains a height of from twelve to sixteen feet. It gave us a wide, unobstructed view over the marshes.

BIRDS OF THE SALLOW WOODS

The river arms in the Danube delta are partly surrounded by narrow strips of land built up by the river; on them grows the common sallow *(Salix cinerea),* which forms a beautiful silver-gray border. In places, the land round the river widens into large islands where the sallow wood extends several miles inland. The widespread sallow woods represent a type of woodland unique in Europe, indescribably beautiful to see and delightful to wander through. Common sallow is usually found as a shrub, but here it grows into large trees that might almost be called willows. These woods have a special way of life, for they are flooded twice a year and stand in water for long periods. Farther inland, where the islands are somewhat higher, other trees begin to appear among the sallows. Alders *(Alnus glutinosa),* poplars *(Populus nigra* and *P. alba),* and white willows *(Salix alba)* give the foliage a variety of grayish-green shades.

These light and open woods, with their rich ground vegetation—on which cattle are often seen grazing—are the haunts of birds of many species. The roller is typical of these woods as of every wooded part of the delta; while hoopoes, hooded crows, starlings, cuckoos, turtledoves and stock doves are a few of the other birds most commonly seen. The black kite patrols the watercourses looking for dead or dying fish, and over the vast fields of reed grass fly marsh harriers.

If one walks through the *Salix* woods or passes them by boat, kingfishers may be seen, the grasshopper-like chirping of the river warbler *(Locustella fluviatilis)* is heard from the thickets, and, in the taller trees, sings the collared flycatcher *(Ficedula albicollis).*

But, above all, the delta of the Danube is the haunt of marsh birds: glossy ibises, herons, and, along the fringes of the salix woods, purple herons, little egrets, night herons and squacco herons. Herons are especially active toward dusk. As we moved along the channels, lagoons and lakes around

The Yaila range is the southernmost ridge of the mountains of Crimea. Its southern slopes, facing the Black Sea, are steep. (B. Gippenreiter: Institute of Geography, Moscow)

Maliuc one evening, herons rose in overwhelming numbers wherever we went. At about six in the evening, squacco herons, night herons and purple herons occupy their fishing grounds by the reed grass along the channels, about thirty feet from each other. Squacco and night herons often stand on water-lily leaves, which grow very large here and can easily bear the weight of these birds. Duck, mostly mallards, garganeys, gadwalls, and white-eyed and red-crested pochards, are common. Abundant as are the birds here, there are even more farther out in the delta, where immense colonies of them live. The entire delta is hunted over by fish-eating birds, a sure sign that the waters are well stocked with fish.

Besides the three sturgeon already mentioned, forty-four species of fish are found regularly in the delta. I list them here because they give a representative picture of the fresh-water fish of southeastern Europe: the silure *(Silurus glanis),* which may attain a length of twenty feet; perch *(Perca fluviatilis);* pike-perch *(Lucioperca sandra);* carp *(Cyprinus carpio);* crucian carp *(Carassius carassius);* tench *(Tinca tinca);* rudd *(Leuciscus erytrophthalmus);* roach *(L. rutilus);* id *(L. idus);* bream *(Abramis brama);* white bream *(A. blicca);* cosac *(A. farenus);* rapacious carp *(Aspius rapax);* bleak *(Alburnus lucidus);* plevusca *(Leucaspius delineatus);* a loach, *Misgurnus fossilis,* the spined loach *(Cobitis taenia)* and another member of the same family, *C. aurata;* pike *(Esox lucius);* ruff *(Acerina cernua)* and its relative *A. schraetser,* found only in the waters of the Danube.

The Danube is one of Europe's most polluted rivers. In its course through several countries it receives waste matter from industrial plants, sewage, and all manner of debris. But in the delta only the three main rivers are affected, and although their waters appear opaque and brown, this is due mainly to the tremendous amount of mud in them. In all the other rivers and channels the water is clean and transparent, and the bottom, with its plants and fish, is clearly visible. The water is so clear that the people living there drink it without unpleasant aftereffects. A remarkable play of color can be observed where these clear streams enter the main rivers; for a while the two currents run parallel to each other, the division of color appearing sharply defined, but gradually the brown water prevails.

Most of the fish in the delta live in the clear fresh water. The fishing villages are located on the banks of the three principal rivers, and one is struck by the precarious situation of many of the houses. When I was there in early June many of them were still surrounded by water, with the waves splashing only a yard or so from their doors, while others were flooded and had been deserted by all but white storks, which were nesting on the roofs. The stork is very common there, and nests both on houses and in trees.

The many arms of the river and channels are navigable, and it is easy to walk across the islands and banks, though the great reed beds comprising most of the delta are less accessible. But these beds can be traversed in long, narrow, flatbottomed boats, which are punted through the reeds. This is arduous work, and frequent rests are necessary, but we managed to penetrate some miles into the dense beds and thus into a strange new world. After a time, we reached a colony of squacco herons, night herons, little egrets, purple herons, glossy ibises, and pigmy cormorants *(Phalacorax pygmaeus).* Their nests are usually built in goat willow bushes *(Salix caprea),* where the various species breed in mixed colonies. The nests are very close together, not infrequently with different species at various levels in the branches. These mixed colonies of herons, glossy ibises and cormorants may contain up to ten thousand birds, representing six species, with glossy ibises in the majority. Little bitterns *(Ixobrychus minutus)* are common in the delta, where they are often seen flying over channels and lagoons, their pale coverts contrasting with their dark wings and back. Their hollow, grunting notes can be heard all day, growing in intensity as evening approaches.

In many places the arms of the river are fringed with sallows, and these may also appear in the middle of the reed grass areas. These sallows nearly always attract many herons of different species, which obviously want to build out of reach of high water. Otherwise the birds nest in the reed grass itself, even though this may be risky in the delta. The cries of two crakes, the Baillon's crake *(Porzana pusilla)* and the little crake *(P. parva),* can be heard a few yards away in the reed grass, where reed buntings *(Emberiza schoeniclus)* and Savi's warblers *(Locustella luscinioides)* are the most diligent and common singing birds. The delicate but penetrating "tsii" of the penduline tit is often heard from sallow bushes in the reed grass. The bearded tit *(Panurus biarmicus),* the tit characteristic of reed beds, is common in the Danube delta. Small black terns and whiskered terns *(Chlidonias hybrida),* hunting insects, fly side by side in graceful curves over lanes of reeds and lagoons. Elsewhere, one may see white-winged black terns and common terns. The spoonbill *(Platalea leucorodia)* breeds in the delta, but it is rare and is seldom seen. This is also true of the great white heron *(Egretta alba),* very rare in Europe, but even more rare in the delta than the spoonbill. The white-headed duck *(Oxyura leucocephala),* found in only a few places in Europe, is another of the rarities of the lagoons in the delta. The mute swan *(Cygnus olor)* breeds in the delta, but is not common; it has an isolated, very restricted breeding range in this region. The graylag is thinly distributed here and nests in reed grass and other beach vegetation.

REED GRASS AND PELICANS

The bird for which the delta of the Danube is most famous is the pelican, two species of which are found: the Dalmatian pelican *(Pelecanus crispus)* and the white pelican *(P. onocrotalus).* In Europe, the former is found only near a few lakes and marshes in the Balkans, while the only regular breeding place of the latter, outside of Russia, is in the Danube delta. The many large flocks of pelicans we saw over the Danube marshes south of Galati and Braila probably consisted of immature birds, for they do not breed there.

White pelicans are the more numerous of the two species in the Danube delta. It was estimated that about 2500 pairs bred there in 1963. Throughout the delta they are protected and at two sanctuaries even visitors are not allowed; thus the birds remain undisturbed at their nesting places. We were permitted to visit the pelican colony, and an overseer was kind enough to row and punt us along the labyrinthine channels through reed grass and over lagoons covered with water aloes *(Stratiotes aloides).* The sight we saw was magnificent—hundreds of rosy-white pelicans, as large as swans, standing out in sharp relief against a background of dense reeds. The pelicans sat or lay close together on floating tussocks of reeds which were their nests. Great armadas of them sailed around overhead on wings with a span of up to ten feet. From the colony itself could be heard their hoarse cries, resembling the grunts of the hippopotamus. Dalmatian pelicans were there, too, in single pairs on the outskirts of the colony, and had, at the beginning of June, half-grown young, while the white pelicans, which lay their eggs much later, still had eggs in their nests. In and around the colony cormorants, grebes, and ducks were breeding.

The pelicans had built their nests near a lake, which they used as a starting and landing place for flights to their fishing waters. Like swans, these great birds need much space before they can become airborne. They fish in shallow water, often swimming slowly forward abreast, driving the fish before them. Every few minutes they all dip their heads and great bills in the water simultaneously, as if on command, and swing them from side to side under the water; then they all lift their heads at the same time. All their movements are perfectly synchronized and performed in slow motion. They are seldom observed to catch fish, and although they cannot dive like the American brown pelican, they live on fish and are apparently successful in their fishing. The pelicans of the Danube delta leave their breeding ground from October through November to winter in the Nile delta. They return to the Danube in March and April.

ISLAND OF LETEA

The great reed grasses in the eastern part of the delta of the Danube enclose a number of long, narrow sandbanks that extend in various directions. They consist of old deposits that once formed the seaward limit of the delta, but have in the course of time, as the delta spread outward, become part of the marshlands. By sedimentation, some of these banks have become islands, a few of them very large ones. One of these, Letea, between the Chilea and the Sulina, is the largest island in the delta, with an area of about 518 square miles. It has one very interesting feature—a primeval deciduous forest.

We had to leave our vessel where the reed grass channel narrowed to a corridor-like passage and punt our way to Letea. I had expected that we should find some small villages on Letea, but I was astonished, when we left the reeds and entered a small lagoon, to see a village—of small and humble houses—dominated by a huge church with a high tower and a large dome. A white stork had managed to attach its great nest of twigs to the rounded roof of the dome.

To a naturalist Letea is one of the most interesting parts of the Danube delta. It has many types of environment, each representing a different phase of its growth. The shores are covered with reeds, or slope downward to open lagoons where one can hardly see the water for the water aloes and the horn nut *(Trapa natans).* In some places inlets penetrate far into the low shores. This low-lying sandy land, and the villages on it, are flooded in spring and autumn. Elsewhere is steppe,

The Danube's outlet on the Black Sea is an immense delta of reed beds, marshes, lagoons, lakes, channels and islands in all stages of plant and animal colonization. (Kai Curry-Lindahl)

where tufts of feather grass *(Stipa pennata)* sway in the breeze, and tawny pipits trip about where the grass is low. There are sand dunes on Letea, now far inland and bordering on a wood, and beach plants still grow on them. Marram grass *(Ammophila arenaria)*, sea holly *(Eryngium maritimum)*, and sea kale *(Crambe maritima)* grow there. One finds shells everywhere, a sure sign of former proximity to the sea.

The beach plants still surviving on the dunes, in spite of the nearby luxuriant deciduous woods, show clearer than words how rapid the changes are on the islands and banks in the delta. Since the virgin woods of Letea consist mostly of oaks *(Quercus pedunculata)*, they cannot be very old, probably not more than 150 years. White poplars *(Populus alba)*, whose silvery leaves are visible from a distance, and other members of the same genus *(P. nigra* and *P. tremula)* are among the many species of trees found in the oak woods. There are also magnificent ash trees *(Fraxinus bolotricha, F. holoryncha* and *F. oxycarpa)*, white willows *(Salix alba)*, maples *(Acer campestre)*, elms *(Ulmus foliacea)*, hazel, and another species of oak *(Quercus pedunculiflora)*. The ivy twining around the trunks of trees, and the lianas trailing from the branches under the green canopy of the woods, are two typical features of virgin forest in southern Europe. Space does not permit a detailed account of even a fraction of the innumerable shrubs, plants and grasses in the woods.

Farther south in the delta, between the Sulina and the St. Gheorghe, on land about as old as Letea, is another primeval forest whose development has been identical. These two young virgin forests provide unique material for study, for their ages are known and their development can be followed in detail. They show how naked sand has been colonized by various species of plants so rapidly that, within a century or so, barren land has been transformed into luxuriant woodland. But this is peculiar to this delta.

The magnificent deciduous woods in the delta shelter a rich animal life. Among the few large birds of prey, in addition to the ubiquitous black kite, are the lesser spotted eagle *(Aquila pomarina)*, the honey buzzard *(Pernis apivorus)*, and the hobby *(Falco subbuteo)*. Curiously enough, the buzzard is not found in the delta and the woods. In fact, the whole delta, like the whole of Rumania, has remarkably few birds of prey. A few white-tailed eagles live in the delta, breeding at various sites near the shore. The golden oriole inhabits the sunny woods of Letea, which are also the haunts of many small birds, including the icterine warbler *(Hippolais icterina)*, olivaceous warbler *(H. pallida)*, blackcap, and whitethroat. The thrush nightingale *(Luscinia luscinia)* is represented by the species that occurs in northern and eastern Europe. The hawfinch and red-breasted flycatcher *(Ficedula parva)* are also found on Letea.

It is remarkable that the marshlands of the delta accommodate so many species of mammals requiring different habitats. Wild boars root in the woods and make long excursions in the reed beds; brown hares are seen on the fringes of woods and in grassy meadows; and badgers are found in the woods of Letea. The otter, too, is a natural inhabitant of the delta, while foxes are sprinkled over the whole region.

There are wolves throughout the water-logged land of the delta, although their main habitat seems to be the woodlands, such as those on Letea. The wolves of the Danube delta have become so well adapted to the reeds, through which they seem to travel without difficulty, that they are called *lupi de stuf*—reed wolves—in this part of Rumania, and are regarded as a quite distinct species. They are in fact not distinct from other European wolves, but ecologically they do differ from them in their accommodation to a semi-aquatic habitat. This is evidence of the great adaptability of the wolf, even though the accommodation has taken thousands of years. The wolves of the delta have even shown that they can climb trees, an ability that is undoubtedly of great value when they are isolated by floods.

The very pale steppe polecat *(Mustela putorius eversmanni)*, whose principal range is the Russian steppe, is found here; it is an eastern European subspecies of the common polecat. Another interesting little mammal, whose principal distribution is in Asia, is the white, yellow, and brown, marbled polecat *(Vormela peregusna)*, which lives in the woods of Letea. The European mink *(Mustela lutreola)*, largely an aquatic animal which once had a wide distribution range in Europe, has survived in the delta, where it is isolated from its northern brothers. The mink *(M. vison)*, originally a North American animal, has reached the delta with the help of man, and is now more common than the European mink. The muskrat *(Ondatra zibethicus)*, another North American mammal, has now become the staple food of the mink. In the 1950's, the raccoon dog *(Nyctereutes procyonoides)* appeared in Rumania and penetrated into the Danube delta; specimens have also been observed in Poland, Finland, and Sweden. This species, which belongs to the *Canidae,* is a native of eastern Asia. It is bred in Russia for its fur, and the European specimens are probably descendants of animals that escaped from Russian farms.

The Danube delta also contains fifteen reptiles and nine amphibians. Frogs are seen everywhere in the channels and lagoons and along their banks. The frog choir at night is exceptional for Europe. Marsh frogs and edible frogs dominate with their bass voices; the fire-bellied toad *(Bombina bombina)* chimes in with its melodious "hong-hong," which in chorus sounds like church bells; the spadefoot toads *(Pelobates fuscus)* purr gently; the variegated toads *(Bufo viridis)* trill their fluty notes; and the mechanical "kreck-kreck-kreck" of the tree-frog sounds unceasingly.

The reptiles also underscore the variety of natural settings in the delta. A striking example is *Eremias arguta,* a lizard which lives on the steppes and semideserts of Russia and central Asia. The Danube delta and the Black Sea coast are its westernmost limit. Another example is the steppe viper *(Vipera ursinii),* of the flat country around the Letea woods —its most southerly habitat. This species, which thrives mainly in Asiatic regions, is also found in a few isolated areas of the Balkans, Italy and France.

FLOATING LANDSCAPES

A very special environment is that formed by great quagmires, overgrown with reeds, found here and there, but especially in the southern parts of the delta. The roots of the floating reeds bind together a mass of decaying organisms, which are rapidly colonized by the vegetation and subsequently fertilized by its debris. The narrow-leaved reed mace *(Typha angustifolia)* and a fern *(Nephrodium thelipteris)* grow on the edges of the quagmires, and here and there bay willow bushes. But reed grass, growing very tall, dominates. These quagmires are sometimes so large that they may properly be called floating landscapes. Thus, when we tried to reach the sea via the part of the delta between the main courses of the Sulina and the St. Gheorghe, we found ourselves confronted by a maze of waterways that was sometimes closed by floating islands. When our powerful motorboat forced its way through, the passage created would immediately close behind us. Steering through this mobile archipelago was very difficult. The winding streams often swung the boat completely around, making the magnificent landscape appear to revolve around us.

The marshland around this system of lakes, of which Lake Ghiolul Rosu is the largest, is extremely variegated. Vast areas of bullrushes *(Scirpus lacustris)* alternate with "floating shores," floating islands and, naturally, great beds of reed grass. These beds consist of two types of reeds, the tall *Phragmites communis* and the shorter, more graceful *P. rivularis.* They may grow side by side, with *rivularis* in the belt nearest the open water, and *communis* in another belt a few yards inside the other. The slender reed grass grows much more densely than the coarse. A third type of vegetation along the banks of the channels in this part of the delta, as seen from the water, is made up of sedge *(Carex),* rushes and reed grass.

There was nothing in the delta vegetation to suggest that we were approaching the sea, but after rounding a bend in the river, we were suddenly confronted by the wide horizon of the Black Sea, with only a sandbank between us and the sea. The sandbars have openings, the marsh and the sea communicating freely by way of thirty or so watercourses.

The southernmost part of the delta is quite different from its other areas. The largest expanse of water in the delta, Lake Razelm, twenty-five miles long and about twelve wide, is located here. To the east, the lake merges into one of the largest reed beds in the delta. To the north and west is dry land: sandy plains, grassy steppes, groves, woods and a wooded mountain, Mt. Babadag. Lake Razelm and its satellite lagoons, with their brackish water and salines, are separated from the Black Sea by a series of sandbanks.

The bird life here is quite different from that of genuine reed beds. Avocets and black-winged stilts, marsh sandpipers, Kentish plovers and oystercatchers trip around on beaches and flooded sandy land. Pratincoles nest on dry ground. In groves of trees, red-footed falcons hide. Above the heights of Babadag sail black, griffon, and Egyptian vultures. A few pairs of ruddy shelducks *(Casarca ferruginea)* breed on the island of Popim in Lake Razelm, and their relative, the shelduck *Tadorna tadorna,* is well represented. Among other birds resident here, but rare in Europe, are the Mediterranean gull *(Larus melanocephalus),* slender-billed gull *(L. genei),* gull-billed tern *(Gelochelidon nilotica),* and the Caspian tern.

In winter the delta is host to hundreds of thousands of birds of passage, geese, ducks and waders, from the northern

The torrents of the river Terek in the heart of the Caucasus photographed from an altitude of about 6500 feet. Mount Kazbeck (16,558 feet) is hidden in the clouds. (Kai Curry-Lindahl)

latitudes of Europe and Asia. For example, many of the world's red-breasted geese, which breed on the tundra of Siberia, winter in the delta.

Luckily, the Danube delta is not threatened, as are many other marshes in Europe, with destruction by draining. The Rumanian Government recognizes the usefulness of the delta and its unique nature, and strictly protects many of the most valuable parts of it. The harvesting of reeds, an important industry, is carried on at times when it will not disturb bird life. Fishing there is also of great economic importance.

THE CRIMEA'S ETERNAL SUMMER

The best known of the regions around the Black Sea is the Crimea. This peninsula is both in climate and vegetation a transitional zone between steppe and mountain. But not much is left of its pristine nature. The steppe is cultivated. and the mountains, which in many places descend directly into the sea, have been transformed into tourist centers. The climate of southern Crimea is Mediterranean, which explains its attraction as a place of recreation. On the south slope of Mt. Yaila, facing the Black Sea, the coast is always in flower, for the growing season lasts all year round. Hardly have the last autumn flowers faded before spring flowers appear. Snowdrops *(Galanthus plicatus)*. sweet violets *(Viola odorata),* crocuses *(Crocus susianus),* and spurges *(Euphorbia biglandulosa)* bloom through December and January. Thus the southern Crimea has eternal summer, its rich flowering protected from the north by Mt. Yaila, 5062 feet high.

About 1400 species of plants comprise the flora of southern Crimea—more than one-third of all those in the U.S.S.R. Only one plant, *Cerastium biebersteinii,* is unique.

The vegetation of southern Crimea is very similar to that of the European Mediterranean region, not only because of evergreen species of macchia vegetation, but also because so many exotic trees and shrubs have been introduced. Because of the latter, the Crimean riviera gives the misleading impression that it represents the original coastal vegetation of the region. Several animals are peculiar to the Crimea and do still manage to live in this partly altered habitat. Among the unique subspecies are, for example, the Crimean weasel *(Mustela nivalis nikolskii),* the jay *(Garrulus glandarius iphigenia),* and the Crimean sand gecko *(Gymnodactylus danilewskii).* Most beautiful among the reptiles is the leopard snake *(Elaphe situla),* which has a wonderful color pattern.

THE SHALLOW SEA OF AZOV

The Sea of Azov bears the same relationship to the Black Sea as the latter does to the Mediterranean, only the narrow Kerchenski Strait between the Crimea and Caucasus connecting the Black Sea and its satellite.

The Sea of Azov is remarkable in many ways. Although its greatest depth is only forty-three feet, it is fifteen thousand square miles in area. The fresh water of the Don and Kuban rivers flows into it, so that its salinity is insignificant. On the other hand, it is rich in mineral salts, which, together with other factors, have encouraged an immense production of plankton—especially mollusks. This wealth of nutriment has turned the sea into a larder, visited periodically by many of

the fish of the Black Sea. They congregate there during the summer months, so that the catches are the greatest in any European lake, the yield in some years being as great as seventy pounds per acre. This is about sixty-five per cent of all the fish caught in the Azov-Black Sea basin. The pike-perch is economically the most important fish in the region.

Unfortunately, the highly productive state of the Sea of Azov is being altered rapidly. The principal rivers flowing into it, the Don and the Kuban, are both being exploited for irrigation and the generation of electricity. Twenty-three per cent of the mean volume of water in the Don now never reaches the Sea of Azov. The dams in the rivers also stop many of the mineral salts that once enriched the sea. These salts will soon be reduced by about fifty per cent, which in turn will decrease the production of plankton by about forty per cent, while salinity will be increased to about 1.5 per cent—a higher percentage than in the Black Sea. These changes will naturally affect fish life, and the Sea of Azov will therefore lose much of its fish-producing value. This will probably have consequences for the whole of the Black Sea, since the Sea of Azov is a major source of its productivity.

The beaches round the Sea of Azov are very flat and shelved. In many places, sand reefs—one of which is about seventy-five miles long—form lagoons of a high salinity.

Both the Don and the Kuban formerly had large deltas, but the Don delta has been destroyed, while that of the Kuban has lost a part of its natural riches. The Kuban flows through a broad plain and into the Sea of Azov by way of three arms. Marsh birds still find good conditions for breeding and wintering there, and, ornithologically, the Kuban delta is undoubtedly the most interesting section of the Russian Black Sea region. The deltas of the Dnieper and the Rioni rivers are also of some importance. The latter, located between the Caucasus and Transcaucasus, consists of marshes, wetlands and large deciduous woods. Herons and ducks breed there, but the region is of little ornithological importance, even as winter quarters for birds.

SUBTROPICAL SHORES

Unlike the pale sand shores of the west coast of the Black Sea, the shores along the east coast consist of wave-polished stones, some as large as a fist, in all imaginable colors. This rich color scheme adorns the beach for miles south of the Caucasus. The stones at Batumi, near the Turkish border, are particularly beautiful.

The most striking feature of the east coast is the luxuriant vegetation from place to place on the west slope of the Caucasus from Novorossiisk southward. The vegetation becomes more and more Mediterranean in character and even richer than on the Crimean peninsula. But there, too, the number of exotic species is very great. At some points the eucalyptus tree is so dominant that one might imagine oneself in Australia.

In other places, remnants of the original forests have been preserved. One of the most remarkable reserves contains a pine, *Pinus pityusa,* which was once common along the shores of the Black Sea, growing there as long ago as the Tertiary. Bird life is, however, limited. When we were there in July, the most common species were the goldfinch, coal tit, chaffinch, and great spotted woodpecker.

Winter in the eastern Caucasus. Despite appearances, this part of the mountain range has a negligible snowfall. (B. Gippenreiter: Institute of Geography, Moscow)

Farther south the climate becomes more subtropical and this naturally affects the vegetation. Around Sukhumi, 43 degrees north, the lower slopes are covered with rich woods, but the climate is still relatively dry. Precipitation, forty-five inches a year, is, however, rather high, and hazel blooms in January. The humidity is much higher one degree farther south, which gives the woods around Batumi an even more subtropical character, far exceeding that of the northern shore of the Mediterranean. At about 330 feet above sea level, humidity is seldom below eighty per cent and precipitation is as high as ninety-seven inches.

This generous climate has made the natural woods around Batumi exceptional for Europe. There are magnificent forests full of all kinds of hardwood trees, with endemic species such as the hornbeam *(Carpinus caucasica)*, and the beech *(Fagus orientalis)*, together with oaks and chestnut. These form a canopy over a dense ground vegetation of *Rhododendron ponticum, R. caucasicum,* and at least three other species of the same genus. Yews *(Taxus baccata)* are also found there. Brooks gurgle unseen in the deep shade of royal ferns *(Osmunda regalis)* and bracken *(Matteuccia struthiopteris);* scattered here and there are the bright green blades of hartstongue *(Phyllitis scolopendrium)*, while trees are almost wholly hidden by ivy *(Hedera colchica* and *H. helix)* and lianas. In places the scenery is almost African, an impression strengthened by the red laterite soil on the lower slopes.

Blackcaps and chaffinches are characteristic birds in these subtropical forests. Thus the birdsongs heard there are like those of Europe, although the region is partly in Asia. The pheasant *(Phasianus colchicus)* is in its original home in these haunts, its Latin name having been derived from Colchis, a province of Georgia on the Black Sea. This pheasant was introduced into the Mediterranean and other parts of Europe in ancient times; it showed a remarkable ability to adapt itself to various climates and is now found in most of Europe as far north as Scandinavia.

TOWERING PEAKS OF THE CAUCASUS

Where is the boundary of Asia in southeastern Europe? The Caucasus range is usually considered part of Asia, but where on its northern slope is the European boundary? The Caucasus range is a natural boundary between the two continents, but on the other hand the whole mountain range, like the land north and south of it, is in Russia.

Hoping that I might get a conclusive answer to the question from specialists at the Institute of Geography of the Academy of Sciences of the U.S.S.R., in Moscow, I raised the question there in July 1963. The answers of the experts differed greatly. They said that a symposium on the problem had recently been held, but that no solution acceptable to everyone had been reached. They all thought that the Caucasus itself belonged to Europe. When I raised the question in Georgia, the answers again varied, a majority holding the view that Georgia was in Asia, but another group claiming that it was a part of Europe. The latter view is held by Berg in his great work on the natural history of the U.S.S.R. But children in Georgian schools learn that their republic is in Asia.

After much consideration of all opinions, I incline to the

111

view that the natural boundary between Europe and Asia is the watershed and mountains of the Caucasus range. This would put most of the highest mountains of the Caucasus in Europe as well as Asia. Since Mt. Elbrus is 14,481 feet, about 2600 feet higher than Mont Blanc, it would be the highest mountain in Europe. Many peaks of the Caucasus are, in fact, higher than any in the Alps.

Our account of the Caucasus must consider the flora and fauna of the whole range, European and Asiatic, or it will be fragmentary. The plateau around the Kura River, which rises in the Turkish mountains and flows to the Caspian Sea, is a natural continuation of the southern slopes of the Caucasus range; so we must, for completeness, trespass on Asia.

The Caucasian range is about 750 miles long and varies between 68 and 112 miles in width. Along the ridge are about 1400 glaciers, but remarkably few lakes. Many of the highest mountains in the Caucasus, such as Elbrus and Kazbeck, are extinct volcanoes, some of them active as late as the end of the Ice Age, i.e. about fifteen thousand years ago.

Although the entire range is on practically the same latitude, the climate of the mountains varies. Humidity is high in the western parts, but decreases toward the east, and this is clearly reflected in the vegetation. Since the range is also a climatic boundary between north and south, the variations in its flora and fauna are great.

The western parts of the mountains contain forests of a type not found in any other mountain range of southern Europe. An extraordinary exuberance occurs on the valley slopes down to the Bzyba River. On the lower levels, beeches, hornbeams, oaks, elms, ash, limes *(Tilia caucasica)*, chestnut and maples cluster together. At about 1650 feet the beech becomes dominant and forms continuous forests up to about 3300 feet and sometimes higher. The mixture of other deciduous trees, particularly of limes, oaks and hazel, is considerable in ravines and at the bottom of valleys. Here and there one may see mighty fir and pine trees, including the gigantic *Abies nordmannia*. Lianas, ivy and mosses cover tree-trunks. Even spruce trees *(Picea orientalis)* are clothed in ivy—something I have never seen elsewhere in Europe—and the branches have dense blankets of moss.

In places above the beech wood is a belt mainly of birch *(Betula pubescens)* and maple *(Acer trautvetteri)*, with a ground vegetation of low beeches *(Fagus orientalis)*, rhododendron, azalea, and many other shrubs. At still higher altitudes are woods of spruce and pine, with the spruce dominating, just as pines dominate in the eastern Caucasus.

It is not surprising that many animals should live in these rich woods. Chaffinches and hovering buzzards are common, but larger creatures such as roe deer, red deer, wild boars, bears, jackals, wildcats and lynx also live there. Although these animals are frequently hunted in some valleys, they have room to roam freely in forests and on slopes.

The woods in the central Caucasus are not so fully developed as those in the west, the beach is not so dominant, and spruce and pine are seen only occasionally. Two species of birch *(Betula pubescens* and *B. raddeana)*, oaks and aspens grow at the highest altitudes. Toward the east, the drier climate

A valley in Daghestan, in the eastern Caucasus, with growths of oaks, hornbeam, linden and ash. The mountain slopes in this area are entirely unforested. (Z. Z. Vinogradov)

A colony of white pelicans in the Danube delta. The birds nest close together on floating tussocks or beds of reeds. (Val Puscariu)

influences the character of the woods, and the pine woods cover large areas; but the two birches mentioned above still constitute the upper limit of trees. The southern slopes of the eastern Caucasus lack the woods, but are covered with shrubs.

As usual in Europe, man and his domestic animals have also had an influence on the extent of forest land. Immense flocks of sheep have changed the character of the central Caucasus. But the areas grazed by sheep are few in relation to the entire range, so in many places the natural vegetation grows freely, a situation unique in southern Europe. And even though the woods have disappeared from large areas, they have been replaced by beautiful green meadows, with little erosion in spite of the continual grazing and trampling to which they are subjected. The subalpine meadows above the tree limit are rich in tall herbaceous plants. Several of them grow to a height of ten feet or so, as, for instance, a monkshood *(Aconitum orientale)*. But the rhododendron is most common, so that one may speak of a rhododendron belt here.

LYNX, LEOPARD AND VOLES

The Caucasus has many interesting features as a transitional zone between Europe and Asia. Among the animals are species that are not found elsewhere in Europe and have their main distribution range in Asia. The mammals mentioned

as occurring in the dense deciduous forests of the western Caucasus are found also in the central and eastern parts of the range, although they are fewer in number.

A subspecies of the European wild bison *(Bison bonasus caucasicus)* lived in the wooded valleys of the Caucasus until about 1925, when it was exterminated. Then, in 1940, descendants of the Caucasian subspecies were sent to the Caucasus. In 1954 they were set free.

A sizable population of bear haunts the Caucasus Mountains —often in the middle of the sheep-breeding regions—apparently without coming into conflict with man. In one place shepherds pointed out a cave in a mountainside where a bear was resting; neither the sheep grazing all around nor the shepherds seemed unduly concerned.

The lynx is rather common in the Caucasus. The pardel lynx is also said to occur there, but no reliable information is available in the field or at the museum in Tiflis. Since in the Caucasus both the common lynx and the pardel lynx would be of the spotted variety, it would be difficult for the natives to distinguish between the two.

The leopard *(Panthera pardus)* belongs to the fauna of the Caucasus, but is very rare. The wildcat is more common and is found up to an altitude of about 6600 feet. The mountains also provide habitats for wolves, jackals, foxes, and badgers. Pine and stone martens are also quite common in this area. Such a rich variety of beasts of prey must have a correspondingly large number of quarry. Red deer, roe deer and wild boars are found in all the woods. Higher up the mountains are the chamois, the local Caucasian tur *(Capra caucasica)*, and the wild goat *(C. ibex)*. Perhaps there is a third species of goat, *C. cylindricornis*, in the Caucasus.

Also found here, in alpine and subalpine habitats, is a species of small mammal unique to the Caucasus—the burrowing vole *(Prometheomys schaposchnikowi)*. Other small rodents include the forest dormouse *(Dryomys nitedula)*, the snow vole *(Microtus nivalis)*, and the pygmy suslik *(Citellus pygmaeus)*, to mention a few from different families. In the southern Caucasus lives *Sciurus anomalus*, a squirrel of Asiatic origin.

High in the alpine zone, up to an altitude of about 10,000 feet, lives a large grayish bird, somewhat similar to a capercaillie. This is the snow partridge *(Tetraogallus caucasicus)*, found only in the Caucasus range. In winter it leaves its snowy kingdom among the clouds for the uppermost forests. In spite of its similarity to the capercaillie, the snow partridge belongs to the field gallinaceous birds, and is therefore more closely related to the partridge and the pheasant. The Georgian black grouse *(Lyrurus mlokosiewczi)*, found only in the Caucasus Mountains, lives in the higher spruce and birch woods and in the rhododendron belt, up to about 10,000 feet.

Some birds with an otherwise purely Asiatic distribution are found in the Caucasus and north of the watershed; they may therefore justifiably be considered European. One of these is the dwarf serin *(Serinus pusillus)*. We found this species—the male beautifully colored, with a blood-red patch on its head—at altitudes of up to about 6000 feet. Another is Güldenstädt's redstart *(Phoenicurus erythrogaster)*, which occurs on open hillsides, rocky slopes, or alpine meadows.

Other small birds commonly seen between 3000 and 6000 feet are the ring ouzel *(Turdus torquatus)*, goldfinch, coal tit, wall creeper, siskin *(Carduelus spinus)*, chaffinch, linnet, twite *(C. flavirostris)*, scarlet grosbeak *(Carpodacus erythrinus)*, rock pipit *(Anthus spinoletta)*, chough, alpine chough and, above the tree limit, the alpine accentor *(Prunella collaris)*. The snow finch *(Montifringilla nivalis)* is common above 6600 feet, where it lives in flocks. The gray wagtail *(Motacilla cinerea)* is found everywhere along the banks of rivers and brooks high up in the mountains, and so is the dipper *(Cinclus cinclus)*.

Above the mountains sail great numbers of griffon vultures. Egyptian vultures, buzzards, and kestrels ascend on rising currents of warm air, but do not usually attain the same height as the griffon vultures. Black vultures, Balkan hawks, honey buzzards, lesser spotted eagles, imperial eagles, golden eagles and bearded vultures are all native to the mountains. In winter they move down to the plateau around the Kura and are not infrequently seen flying over Tbilisi, though some of them migrate to the tropics.

Several of the batrachians in these mountains are unique to this area. Among them are the toad *(Pelodytes caucasicus)*, and the Caucasian frog *(Rana camerani)*, as well as several purely local subspecies. This is also true of reptiles. No fewer than eighteen different species of reptiles and amphibians not found in the rest of Europe, and therefore representing Asiatic elements in the fauna of the region, are found here. This large variegation is evidence that the region is a transitional zone between the two continents.

In comparison with the devastated mountains of the Medi-

Gray herons and great white herons stand in shallow water among flowering aquatic (Butomus umbellatus) *in a natural reserve in the Volga delta. (M. Redkin: Novosti Press Agency)*

terranean countries, the Caucasus range is flourishing woodland. Woods dominate this range and the Surami Mountains, which form a connecting link between the Caucasus and the highlands of southern Georgia. It is only in the mountains around Tiflis and the former capital, Mtskheta, and here and there around the broad valley of the Kura that the mountains are devoid of trees, and only in exceptional instances has erosion destroyed the topsoil. It is surprising that the ancient landscape of the Kura Valley has been able to retain its fertility despite the fact that central and eastern Georgia are much drier than the Mediterranean region and have been cultivated for thousands of years. This must be credited in part to man's care of the soil. As long ago as 1500 B.C., civilization flourished in Mtskheta, and for at least 3400 years the Kura Valley has supported an agrarian population in spite of wars and the resulting devastation. The sight of a subtropical treeless landscape in ecological equilibrium, despite man's intensive cultivation of the land for thousands of years, is truly a paradox. The explanation, I believe, is that the mountains around Tiflis and Mtskheta were covered with woods until they were cut down about a hundred years ago. A century of use has not yet exhausted the soil; also the earth's power of recovery has been maintained by the water that comes down all year round from forests on high mountains to the north and south. Great oak woods were growing in the Kura Valley as late as the 1920's; now, only remnants of these woods remain. Fortunately, reafforestation has been commenced on the mountain slopes.

The plain between the Caucasus Mountains and the Kura River is now largely a cultivated region, but it still has a rich fauna. Multitudes of partridge and quail live in the fields, pheasants and the black francolin *Francolinus francolinus)* haunt the woods, and in winter the rock partridge *(Alectoris graeca)* comes down from the mountains. Leopards are found both in highlands and lowlands, and in the latter they are neighbors of the jungle cat *(Felis chaus),* more than three feet long, which is distributed over great parts of Asia. Tigers *(Panthera tigris)* have been known to come from Iran. Thus there is a very great variety of wildlife on the south slopes of the mountains.

THE LARGEST LAKE IN THE WORLD

The Caspian Sea, largest inland body of water in the world, is about 144,300 square miles in area, 748 miles long, and 350 miles wide at its widest point. It is eighty-two feet below sea level. Since it has no outflow, its water is somewhat saline— on the average, 1.2 per cent. The greatest depth, about 3300 feet, is in the southern part. The northern part is much shallower, the average depth being only twenty feet; even far out of sight of the coast one may find depths not greater than about six feet. Evaporation is, however, considerable, amounting to a loss of about three feet per year. From 1896 to 1929 the water level decreased by about one foot six inches; while between 1929 and 1946 it was lowered more than six feet. Since 1946 the rate of decrease has been even greater. Bearing in mind the average depth in the northern parts of the sea, these changes in level are tremendous; from a biological and hydrological aspect they are catastrophic.

Several factors contribute to this, the most important being the reduced flow of water from the Volga River. As much as seventy-six per cent of the water that once flowed into the Caspian Sea came from the Volga, but now about fifty per cent of the river water never reaches the sea because it has been harnessed for generating electricity and for irrigation. Such a drastic reduction of the water supply of a lake must inevitably have far-reaching consequences. Another factor is the climate. There is much evidence that the water level has been diminishing during the whole of the Quaternary. The gently sloping shores and flat coastal regions of the north were formerly a seabed. This flat, sandy plain is constantly increasing, and of course the wetlands are drying up all the more quickly as evaporation increases. Just as the local climate is changing, so are the flora and fauna. In the long run, this development will have a great and harmful effect on the productivity of the sea and the adjacent land areas.

The Caspian Sea has many interesting biological aspects. The circulation of water makes living organisms possible in the deepest parts—unlike the Black Sea—but the amount of oxygen below 330 feet is so small that animal life is concentrated in the surface layers. The fauna, the greater part of which is of marine origin and goes back to the Tertiary period, some million years ago, is relatively poor in quality despite additions from various sources due to changes in communications with marine and freshwater regions. Of course,

animals from this long past period have in the course of evolution passed through many changes and have adapted themselves to the special conditions. This also applies to those elements of the fauna that have invaded the region from the warm Mediterranean by way of the Black Sea and from the cold Arctic Ocean during later geological epochs. The invasion from the north probably took place after the Ice Age and after the Caspian Sea had become separated from the Black Sea, which, geologically speaking, was comparatively recent. Many of these marine animals adapted themselves to the local environment when, several times in its history, the sea became almost a freshwater lake. During those periods, it was colonized by freshwater animals, which later adapted to the salinity when the region again became a salt lake.

The fauna has thus had a fourfold origin and consists of both marine and freshwater species that have lived together during long periods under continually changing conditions. Such changes, as well as a prolonged geographical isolation, favor the creation of species. Apart from parasites and birds, the Caspian contains 476 animal species which are native to the region. Of these, 222 species are found only in the Caspian Sea; to these must be added a great number of local races, which also are only to be found in this sea area. When the canal between the Don and the Volga was opened, a new migration route was created, and this has led to a great invasion of new species during the past three or four decades. Man has also introduced numerous species, so that in 1960 the total number was 557—again not counting parasites.

During recent years a large variety of fish has been introduced from the Black Sea and the Pacific Ocean and the Caspian now contains seventy-eight species; twenty-five of these are not to be found elsewhere. Some families of fish in the Caspian Sea have evolved a large number of species. This is especially true of the gudgeon *(Gobiidae),* thirty species of which are found there. Of these, fifty-three per cent are endemic forms which are unique to the Caspian. Carp *(Cyprinidae)* number fifteen species, of which nine are found only in the Caspian Sea, and, of the herrings *(Clupeidae),* fifty-five per cent are endemic. Two of these species *(Caspialosa caspia* and *C. brashnikovi)* are divided into five and seven races respectively. Salmon (the white salmon, *Stenodus leucichtys)* live in the Caspian, with near relations in the Arctic Ocean, and also one variety of trout *(Salmo trutta caspius).*

The extremely diversified origins of Caspian fauna, even before man began to interfere in its composition, gives the sea a zoogeographical transitional position so unique that many scientists consider it as a special biogeographic unit.

The Caspian has also its own species of seal, *Phoca caspica.* This seal has, it is true, been regarded as a race of the arctic ringed seal *(P. hispida),* and if it immigrated into the Caspian after the Ice Age, that view may be correct; but it is now considered a separate species. In summer these seals live in small herds in the central and southern parts of the sea. In autumn they make a mass migration to the north and congregate in great numbers on the ice, where the young are born in January. Mating time is about a month later, between the end of February and the beginning of March, after which all

Meadows and wooded slopes of the central Caucasus at the Baidary Gorge. Grazing by sheep causes the treeless patches on the ridges and plateaus. (Kai Curry-Lindahl)

116

In spring, the lower Volga River floods vast areas, including woods of black poplars. (Z. Z. Vinogradov)

the seals move southward. In 1958 it was calculated that there were about 1,500,000 seals in the Caspian Sea. During the present century about 115,000 seals have been killed annually, a total of roughly seven million.

THE VOLGA DELTA

Of the great river deltas of southern Europe the Volga in the Caspian Sea is the largest, with an area of almost 4700 square miles. It is about 110 miles wide and stretches more than eighty miles inland from the shore.

This vast delta is traversed by a large number of river arms, which branch out both at Astrakhan and upstream from it. But, as is the case with the Caspian Sea, the amount of water discharged into it by the river has declined to about half of its previous quantity. This has naturally affected the delta, which has become drier. But it is still flooded by the waters of the Volga, and sedimentation is still going on. In this respect, the delta is a living one, but large parts of its mighty marshlands are disappearing. They dry up as the level of the water sinks. Both the flora and the fauna are transformed. This development is due also to the fact that the rhythm of the river has been altered, often as a result of the regulation of the rivers for irrigation and hydroelectric power. This has upset the natural hydrography of the delta, to which animals and plants have become adapted during long periods of time.

Although the Volga delta is still fascinating, as an environment for plants and animals, it is deteriorating from year to year. Already it is a less important breeding place for birds. For example, very few ducks nest there. Nor does it play a significant role as winter quarters for migrating wildfowl, for it freezes in winter. On the other hand, it is still an important resting and feeding place during spring and autumn migrations as well as an area where many ducks molt.

Generally speaking, the Volga delta is similar to the delta of the Danube. In the interior the banks of the river are fringed with trees *(Salix alba* and others), and these, farther out, where marshland dominates, give way to vast reed beds. Between the green walls of reeds, winding channels lead to lagoons and bays. As in the Danube delta, innumerable tongues of solid land, composed of sand and clay, run in an east-west direction through the marshlands. They are usually about two hundred yards wide and from five hundred yards to twelve miles long. They may rise to a height of twenty-five feet. In some places, lakes, separated from the delta, have been formed between these banks. There are many dunes near Astrakhan. They had become stabilized, because among other things they were colonized by giant lyme grass *(Elymus giganteus),* which grows up to five feet high. This plant is popular with horses and cattle and their excessive grazing and trampling has destroyed the flora, so the sand has begun to drift again and is burying huge areas.

The delta of the Volga has a strange climate. The summers are very warm, even warmer than on the surrounding steppes. The mean temperature in July is approximately 77° F (25° C), and may rise to 104° F (40° C). The winters can be very cold, although snowfalls are usually light. The mean January tem-

perature is about 6.8° F (−14° C), which is colder than in the Gulf of Finland. Thus the Volga delta has a pronounced continental climate, influenced by the surrounding steppe and desert areas, although modified somewhat by the proximity of the Caspian Sea.

The aquatic vegetation of the delta is almost like that of the Danube delta, but its carpets of aquatic horn nuts are considerably more extensive. The Volga delta, however, is alone in having a remarkable plant, the Hindu lotus *(Nelumbo nucifera),* which grows in one lake only, where its brilliant red flowers can be seen from afar. It occurs in the Astrakhan nature reserve, where bird life is also highly developed.

White pelicans and Dalmatian pelicans, the same species as inhabit the Danube delta, breed in the Volga delta. The most common bird is the cormorant, whose largest colonies are at the tops of the white willows along the shores. All the species of herons found in the Danube delta also live in this delta and in about the same proportions; thus the great white heron is rare in the Volga delta, too, although rather common in the nature reserve. In 1951, the number of fish-eating birds (cormorants, pelicans, herons, grebes) was estimated at about 600,000. Cormorants are captured in great numbers, sometimes even in the nature reserve. The graylag is the only goose breeding in the delta, but many mute swans and coots nest there. Formerly, during the spring and autumn

migrations many other geese visited the region, the lesser white-fronted goose *(Anser erythropus)* and the white-fronted goose *(A. albifrons)* appeared in great flocks, but now they no longer nest there since the shore meadows, where they used to graze, have disappeared. Many duck, especially mallards, pintails, gadwalls and shovelers, seem to use the Volga delta as a molting place. Banding them has revealed that many come from Siberia. White-tailed eagles glide high above the delta and the larger lakes.

Still more interesting than the many birds in the delta are the numerous fish, and their migration from the Caspian Sea into the delta, up the Volga and back again. Four species of sturgeon live in the Caspian Sea, and all but one migrate periodically into the river branches in the delta. This is also true of the two species of salmon in the Caspian Sea, all fifteen species of carp, and four species of herrings. In addition, the delta itself is rich in most of the species living in the Danube delta; it also has the razor-like fish, *Pelecus cultratus,* whose principal distribution is in Asia.

Two industries active in the Volga delta are fishing and the exploitation of reeds. Three-fourths of Russian caviar comes from delta sturgeon; but the fishing in the delta and the Caspian Sea, which dominates the economic life of the region,

can hardly be maintained. The most important commercial species have diminished greatly during recent decades. The extreme changes in the rivers and in the hydrography of the delta have so hurt the production of fish that efforts are now being made to counteract the loss by introducing foreign species of fish. Thus the Volga, the delta, and the Caspian Sea are becoming more and more artificial. By 1957 the catch in the Caspian Sea had dropped by sixty-five per cent compared with that of 1917. This great decline involves the most valuable commercial species, the herrings, vobla *(Benthophilus stellatus),* pike-perch, and sturgeon, the yield of the last named having dropped by half since 1913. On the other hand, the catches of a species of sprat, *Clupea phalerica,* have increased considerably, becoming the largest in the Caspian Sea with an annual volume more than three times that of the next largest catch, the vobla.

On the whole, one gets a strong impression that an extremely rich complex of living natural resources have here been exploited so intensively by man that the area is now turning against him and his interests. This serious situation is not due to over-fishing but to the fact that the natural hydrography, and consequently local climate and ground-water level, have been altered.

Seas of Grass

The Steppes of the U.S.S.R.

The greatest grass and bush steppes in the world extend in a 2500 mile-wide belt from the Ukraine in the west to Altai in the heart of Asia in the east. Of this vast area, about twelve hundred miles, that is, from the Carpathians to the Ural River (about as far as from the Carpathians to the Bay of Biscay) is located in Europe.

What we call steppe in Europe is the counterpart of prairie in North America—open, undulating grassy plains with wide horizons. No part of Europe changed so little during and after the last glaciation as this area north of the Black and Caspian seas. It consisted of steppes when the most extensive icecap covered the land and has remained steppe land until quite recently. During the glaciations the steppes bordered on the tundra extending south of the inland icecap. On the whole, they retained their character in spite of the change from an extremely hot to a very cold climate. But this is also the climatic cycle of the steppe—hot summers and very cold winters.

The immense European steppes of the past are today but a memory. Here and there fragments remain in the form of nature reserves, but the greater part of the Ukrainian steppes have been plowed and cultivated during recent decades. The same fate has overtaken the steppes north of the Caucasus Mountains and around the Volga and Ural rivers. I have flown over many of these mighty plains, and the same scene meets the eye everywhere—enormous cultivated fields. The variegated colors of the natural steppe no longer interrupt the pattern of the cultivated steppe.

A great part of Europe became steppe after the Ice Age, and herds of wild horses, saiga antilopes, European bison and other grass-eating animals roamed from one pasture to another. Gradually most of Europe became covered with forest, but southeastern Russia remained steppe, with typical steppe animals surviving there for a long time. As late as the nineteenth century, for example, a wild horse, the tarpan horse *(Equus caballus gmelini)*, was still living on the steppes of the Ukraine and Voronezh. Unfortunately, the species has since been exterminated—the last specimen died in captivity in 1918. Thus the last of the original race of wild horses, once a dominant animal on the plains of Europe, disappeared.

Since the transformation of the Russian steppe into cultivated land occurred only recently, not only were the regions studied carefully before their character was changed, but natural reserves are available for study.

As living space for plants and animals, both steppes and deserts demand great adaptability of their inhabitants. Sunshine and wind have free play over such vast expanses, and temperature and humidity vary enormously even from day to night. Animals on the treeless steppes have no shelter from the burning summer sun or the bitter winter cold. Small mammals, as well as reptiles, protect themselves from the cold and from enemies by going underground and living in extensive burrows. Some, among them the greater mole rat *(Spalax microphthalmus)*, spend practically all their lives underground. Hoofed animals, of which only the saiga has survived, have no other protection against the elements than their own layers of fat, and their habit of herding together. The latter provides some protection against winter storms, but it is more important as a collective security measure. The most effective protection hoofed animals have against beasts of prey, including man, is flight.

The topographical characteristics of the steppe have led to the evolution of a great many species of rodents and a relatively large number of ground birds such as bustards, larks, pipits, wheatears, gallinaceous birds and marsh harriers, while in the air such hunting birds as swallows, bee-eaters and insect-eating falcons predominate.

The factors that give rise to such diametrically different types of nature as steppe and forest are well known. In Europe and Asia the transformation from desert to forest, by way of steppe, takes place in gradual stages. The evidence is that soil and climatic conditions are the primary reasons for the differences between steppe and forest.

Obviously, the great steppes of southeastern Russia are not uniform throughout. There are roughly three main types. One very dry steppe, semidesert in character, extends around the Caspian Sea from the Caucasus Mountains to the Ural River and northward beyond latitude 50 degrees north. To the west, north and east it gives way to a grassy steppe covering a large part of the Ukraine. North of this grass steppe is a wide "forest steppe" belt running across the whole of Russia. Still farther north, it turns into deciduous and mixed forest. These three types of steppe thus form a transitional zone from south to north, from the deserts of Asia east of the Caspian Sea to the forest land of Central Europe.

The vegetation of the steppes change wherever there is a river or high land that has greater precipitation. In such places woods grow, providing shelter for the many forms of animal life; birds, in particular, haunt such environments, although their distribution in these wooded oases is limited.

DRY STEPPES AND SEMIDESERTS AROUND THE VOLGA

Around the lower reaches of the Volga are great plains of a semidesert character. Although vegetation covers the bare ground only in patches, the total area thus covered is still greater than the total area of bare soil. In summer one may travel for miles over a bleached and blinding landscape, the horizon extending on all sides and the air shimmering

Various species of feather grass and many flowering plants are conspicuous steppe flora where the soil has not been cultivated or grazed. (Kai Curry-Lindahl)

in the heat. The ground is scorching hot, both where the moving sand struggles for supremacy with stunted bushes and brave tufts of grass, and where the clay, formerly a sea bed, is covered with a crackling crust of salt. In winter, violent snowstorms rage with hurricane fury across the plain and far into the southeastern corner of Europe.

The whole of the Caspian lowland around the lower reaches of the Volga was, during the last glaciation, covered by the Caspian Sea, which was then eighty-five feet higher than now. In such flat country, such a change in level is immense. Practically the whole region east of the Volga northward to Saratov, or about latitude 52 degrees north, is semidesert. The vegetation is dominated by several species of wormwood *(Artemisia),* varying in density and number of species chiefly according to the dryness of the soil. At great intervals one sees the thin branches of a tamarisk bush. Over great areas the ground is patterned in black and white, where the sunbleached, cracked and salty clay is partly covered, at least in July, by a species of almost black wormwood, *Artemisia pauciflora.* This plant does a transformation act; when it rains, the leaves extend and look almost normal, but in time of drought they hide in black stalks, making the plant seem bare and dead.

In other places, where the soil is less salt, the sea wormwood *(A. maritima),* a paler species, dominates. It frequently forms communities together with a fescue *(Festuca sulcata),* crested hair grass *(Koeleria gracilis)* and other species of wormwood such as *Artemisia incana* and *A. terre-albae.* These plants spread out in irregular bands over the scorched, almost sterile soil; one must admire their persistence.

Numerous large and small salt lakes remain scattered over the semideserts—reminders of the former extent of the Caspian Sea—and are especially numerous between the Volga and the Ural rivers. The water in these lakes is so salt that practically no vegetation can live in it, but the shores have been colonized by a few plants. Around Lake Baskunchak, near the Volga and east of Volgograd (formerly Stalingrad), for example, one sees a bizarre, low-growing vegetation consisting of a halophyte *(Halochnemum strobilaceum),* which covers every inch of rising ground where the salt content is not too high. In other parts of the salty shores oraches *(Atriplex canum)* grow, but very sparsely. Where the shores are stony the vegetation is extremely poor, only occasional tufts of *Anabasis salsa* managing to survive.

It is only natural that the fauna should be very scarce on the dry steppes around the Volga and the Ural rivers. Never-

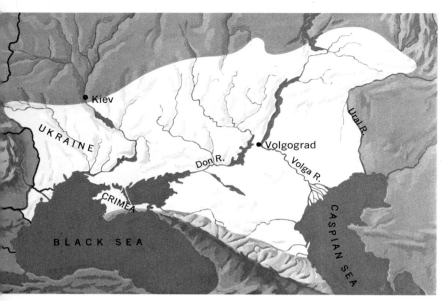

The steppe of southern Russia varies from south to north in three main belts: in the south, around the Volga River, it is a semidesert; to the west it is a transitional grass steppe, which is succeeded farther north by wooded steppe.

theless, as in true deserts, one is often astonished that this almost hopelessly poor land can shelter so many forms of animal life.

The animals of sand steppes are different from those of clay steppes. The former have more environmental problems than the latter, but still several species are found in the sand steppes, including the midday gerbil *(Meriones meridianus)* and the tamarisk gerbil *(M. tamarscinus),* the northern three-toed jerboa *(Dipus sagitta),* Eversmann's hamster *(Cricetulus eversmanni),* and the long-eared hedgehog *(Erinaceus auritus).* These small mammals are often specially adapted to a dry environment; many of them subsist on the underground parts of plants. The roots of many semidesert plants are very well developed, those of species of *Artemisia,* for instance, penetrating a yard or so below the surface, so it is easy to understand their importance for plant-eating animals.

These rodents have many enemies among the mammals— the corsac fox *(Vulpes corsac),* which is reddish-yellow in summer and grayish in winter, the wolf, steppe polecat and marbled polecat. Hardly any birds of prey are found in the sandy steppe region, but they are to be seen on the artemisia clay steppes and increase in frequency as the steppe vegetation becomes denser, for there the population of small mammals is greater.

One of the few birds on the sand steppe is the shore lark *(Eremophila alpestris brandti),* which in these torrid regions runs along the ground and chases insects. This bird has an astonishing environmental versatility, for it lives high up in the mountains as well as in semidesert regions—from arctic in the north to subtropics in the south. It is as much at home in northern Alaska and Siberia as in the northern Andes of South America and the Atlas Mountains of Africa. On the Caspian plain it is found in such extreme types of environments as the sparsely vegetated semidesert, and on steppes with a richer vegetation.

SUSLIKS AND SAIGAS

The wormwood-covered clay steppes give animals a better opportunity to find nourishment and protection than do the almost naked sand steppes. The most common mammal, the suslik, is represented by two species, the yellow suslik *(Citellus fulvus)* and the pygmy suslik *(C. pygmaeus).* They have similar habits but the pygmy suslik seems to be more dependent on clay soil. Both hibernate underground for eight months of the year, which is their way of surviving the dry autumn and the rigors of winter. They must therefore breed during spring and summer and lay up enough fat to last nine months of the year—a truly remarkable accomplishment for a mammal.

Susliks mate almost as soon as they awake from their winter sleep at the end of March or the beginning of April, and, twenty-five to twenty-eight days later, three to eleven young are born. They leave their nests about a month later. By the end of June the poor vegetation has become parched and the susliks go underground for their long hibernation. They then weigh about seventeen ounces; when they awake in spring they weigh only about four ounces. The period of activity is longer on the grassy and wooded steppes, where they hibernate for a much shorter time, so that their loss of weight in winter is not nearly so great. Susliks have only one litter a year. Considering that they are also the staple food of many predators, it is remarkable that they are so numerous. A population of pygmy susliks studied in spring had the following composition: seventy-five per cent of the young had been born that year, fifteen per cent were one-year-olds, seven per cent two-year-olds, and three per cent three-year-olds. Mortality during the first year was 68.5 per cent.

On the artemisia steppes there are many larks, mainly short-toed and calandra larks, but also lesser short-toed *(Calandrella rufescens)* and black larks *(Melanocorypha yeltoniensis).* Here one may also see the Pallas's sandgrouse *(Syrrhaptes paradoxus)* and the black-bellied sandgrouse *(Pterocles orientalis),* remarkable doves that have become adapted to dry steppes and desert-like sandy regions, where they live on seeds and young shoots of plants. Sandgrouse sometimes make migrations that take them as far as the British Isles in the west and the shores of the Arctic Ocean in the north.

The dry steppes of southern Russia often provide shelter for the houbara bustard *(Chlamydotis undulata),* which usually appears in flocks. It is a rather large bird, and lives on vegetable matter, insects, lizards and snails. The typical predatory bird of the artemisia steppes seems to be the tawny eagle. It is found on grassy steppes, too, where food is more plentiful; but there it is now persecuted by man. The tawny eagle is astonishingly numerous in dry steppe territory. A large dark-brown bird, it builds its nest on the ground, often on a little hill, and can be seen from great distances. Fortunately for this fine eagle, few hunters visit the sandy steppes. Its chief food is susliks.

The saiga, Europe's only antelope, lives on the dry steppe between the Volga and the Urals, and also farther east. In winter it wanders westward almost to the River Don. During the past hundred years, the saiga has had a very dramatic history. Around 1930 it was feared that it would become extinct because of a series of very severe winters, and, in spite of legal protection since 1919, because of hunting. At that time its whole distribution area, about 965 square miles in Europe and Asia, contained, according to Bannikov, only a few hundred specimens. During the mid-1930's the population began to increase, until, ten years later, the saiga was as common in Kazachstan as it had been a century earlier. In European Russia, too, the species increased rapidly in number, and occupied regions it had not inhabited since the beginning of the nineteenth century. In 1960 there were around 2,000,000 of them—an astonishing figure. About one quarter live between the Volga and the Ural rivers, where the population is about four times as dense as in Asia. In this region alone professional hunters kill between 150,000 and 200,000 saigas annually, representing about 6000 tons of excellent meat and more than 2,000,000 square feet of hides. In spite of this slaughter, their numbers are increasing. Considering the sparse vegetation of the dry steppe, this productivity is astonishingly high. As on the savannas of Africa, it is the wild hoofed animals that give a far greater economic yield than destructive domestic animals, and they do so without destroying the habitat on marginal lands by excess grazing or by trampling down young vegetation. This is only natural, for the wild hoofed animals have, through ages of selection and evolution, become adapted to their environment; on the other hand, tame domestic animals are newcomers and are not necessarily well suited to the area.

The saiga is polygamous. The stags may collect a harem of five to fifteen hinds, or even sometimes as many as forty to fifty. The hinds become sexually mature early, and they mate at the age of seven to eight months. Mating time is in December; and at the end of April the female gives birth to two young. It is clearly the breeding capacity of the saiga that accounts for its unexampled increase in the course of three decades.

The spotted suslik is one of the most common animals of the grassy steppes of southeastern Europe. (Wlodzimierz Puchalski)

GRASSY STEPPES OF THE UKRAINE

Before the steppes of southern Russia were converted into agricultural land they must have afforded a magnificent sight in June and July—mile after mile of flat country, with the long silvery plumes of grass swaying in the breeze as far as the eye could see. Now only a few fragments remain—large enough, however, to give some idea of what the steppe once looked like.

The dominant species of grass of the natural steppe belong to the *Stipa* family *(Stipa capillata, S. dasyphylla, S. lessingiana, S. tirsa)*. Some of these are as tall as a man, while others reach only up to one's knees. Numerous flowering plants grow there, too, their bright colors changing with the seasons. Red tulips *(Tulipa schrenki)*, anemones *(Anemone nigricans* and *A. patens)*, gageas *(Gagea bulbifera* and *G. pusilla)* and spring draba *(Draba verna)* bloom in April, followed in May by the adonis *(Adonis vernalis)*, dwarf iris *(Iris pumila)*, in bluish-violet and yellow, and great beds of dark red fernleaf peonies *(Paeonia tenuifolia)*. In June the steppe is decked out in charming colors, the silver of the grasses being, so to speak, accentuated by patches of blue sage *(Salvia nutans)*. Later, in the summer, when the grasses bloom, the steppe becomes a sea of silver.

But this is only a fraction of the plants that fill the steppe with color and scent. They are too numerous to mention individually, but some characteristic species must be pointed out, for they belong to communities dominated by feather grasses. Among them are the fescue, bulbous blue grass *(Poa bulbosa)*, and crested hair grass *(Koeleria gracilis)*. Bulbous blue grass ripens in summer when the feather grass has lost its plumes; the steppe then changes in color from silver to golden yellow.

We have pointed out that the steppe as an intermediary between semidesert and forest land is a product of soil and climate. But the role of animals must not be forgotten. It is difficult to say how much influence hoofed animals and rodents had on the vegetation of the steppes, for the most important of these animals are now extinct or have vanished from the area. Knowing the part played by hoofed animals in the formation of landscape on the African savannas, it is not difficult to imagine the symbiotic relationship that must have existed between animals and plants when the steppes were at their height. We know that the steppes were the haunt of many hoofed animals—aurochs, bison, roe and red deer, wild horses and saigas, most of them living in great herds. Their grazing and trampling on the vegetation must have been considerable, but each species exploited the vegetation in its own particular way; competition was avoided

Where the Volga crosses the semidesert of the Caspian lowland it flows between banks as much as seventy-five feet high. (Z. Z. Vinogradov: Institute of Geography, Moscow)

and the soil remained fertile and productive. The biological productivity of the virgin steppe was probably very high, as the present abundance of saigas in the poor semideserts of the Volga steppe testifies.

When modern Russia converts wild, productive steppes into cultivated land, using every up-to-date method, and is still faced with tremendous agricultural problems, one cannot help wondering whether the original steppes, with their characteristic vegetation and wealth of meat and hide-producing animals, did not yield higher returns than the harvests of today. One thing is certain: the high productivity of the wild steppe did not require enormous investments and artificial fertilizers.

When one wanders over the remaining steppes today—all in a few relatively small nature reserves—and ponders the importance of the former grassy plains for the large, hoofed animals living there until recent times, the pattern becomes clear. Aurochs and bison, wild horses, saigas and red deer probably moved in an annual cycle between grassy steppes on the one hand; and river valleys, wooded steppes and forests on the other. The grassy steppes were their summer habitat.

MARMOTS AND JERBOAS

The many rodents also left their mark on the steppes. These animals turn over the topsoil by their intensive burrowing. The bobak marmot *(Marmota bobak),* the marmot of the steppes, was the characteristic animal of the grassy plains. Its grass covered mounds, between two and three feet high, were so common that the plain seemed to be covered with small haycocks. That is what bobak marmot communities look like now on the steppes of Siberia, where between eighty and a hundred bobak burrows may be found in an acre of land. The bobak marmot has vanished even from most of the steppe reserves in Russia; and the large, hoofed animals have also disappeared. Thus the remaining reserves cannot give a true picture of the former condition of this very interesting type of habitat.

The suslik has survived, however, and is found in great numbers. Susliks are so numerous and live so close together in their burrows that they must be an important factor in the ecology of the grassy steppes. The way they break up the soil is amazing. It has been calculated that one suslik turns up about ninety-five cubic feet of soil per acre each year. About two hundred holes dug by spotted susliks *(Citellus suslicus)* have been counted in one acre of land.

It is interesting to note that the black kite, a bird which is

rather common on the steppes, seems to prefer susliks, though it also feeds on other rodents as well as carrion and insects. The black kite usually detects the suslik while soaring in the air, but it can also hover like a kestrel or fly very low, like a harrier, a yard or so above the ground, in order to take its prey by surprise. Sometimes the bird flies in pursuit of a running suslik, or sits in watch beside the burrows of these rodents.

The most interesting of all the large mammals that once roamed over the grassy plains is the tarpan horse. This wild horse was still rather common on the steppes west of the lower reaches of the Dnieper during the first half of the nineteenth century. The last wild tarpan was killed in 1876, in Askaniya Nova, north of the Black Sea, the region where nowadays African elands and zebras graze—strange substitutes for the original hoofed animals exterminated by man.

It is not known for certain how long man has lived on the steppes, but it took him thousands of years to drive away or exterminate all the hoofed animals of the plains. The red deer were driven into woods and mountains, while the bison, aurochs and the tarpan horse were exterminated. A few decades ago the saiga was in danger of sharing their fate, but was rescued at the last moment. Since then it has convincingly demonstrated its great economic value. The bison will prove just as valuable if it is given a chance to repopulate the

wooded steppes; but the tarpan horse and the aurochs are gone forever.

The grassy steppes provide a habitat for a fauna of rodents even richer than that of the semideserts. Many species found in the latter also live on the grassy steppes: for example, the spotted suslik. Several species of jumping rats, jerboas, which move like kangaroos, are also found there; jerboas' hind legs and feet are very long, and the forelegs very short. The outstanding jumping rat of the steppe is the great jerboa *(Allactaga major)*. It is a burrowing animal, like all steppe rodents, and hibernates in winter. In sandy regions the thick-tailed three-toed jerboa *(Stylodipus telum)* may be seen jumping along. The common hamster *(Cricetus cricetus)*, the gray hamster *(Cricetulus migratorius)* and several shrews and mice are common, but their frequency varies greatly from region to region. Foxes, stoats, and steppe polecats live largely on these rodents.

Larks and pipits are seen everywhere. All the year round, partridges and great bustards are found on the grassy steppe. The former have become adapted to the cultivated plain and are common everywhere, while the latter, owing to the cultivation of the steppes, have become rare. The same is true of the little bustard, which formerly had a wide distribution on the grassy steppes. On dry steppes and in damp valleys we find the decorative demoiselle crane *(Anthropoides virgo)*,

125

ashy bluish-gray with black head and white tufts of feathers behind the eyes. It lives on insects and snails, lizards and snakes. These cranes arrive at their nesting place in March and leave for northeastern Africa in September. They often migrate in snowplow formation, trumpeting as they fly. A demoiselle crane banded in the Crimea was found in the center of the Sudan. Rose-colored starlings *(Sturnus roseus),* of black and rose, fly in flocks over the steppe following the swarms of locusts.

Among reptiles, the sand lizard *(Lacerta agilis)* is most numerous. It is found on grassy land, where it hunts insects. Another characteristic lizard of the grassy steppe is the steppe lizard *(Eremias arguta),* which is found as far north as the wooded steppes of Voronezh. The steppe viper is the most common snake on both grassy and wooded steppes; some magnificent specimens of colubrid and elapid snakes *(Coluber jugolaris* and *Elaphe quatuorlineata)* also occur in this area.

Frogs are naturally neither numerous nor rich in species in these dry regions. The one frequently seen is the variegated toad *(Bufo viridis),* and sometimes it is found at a surprisingly long distance from the nearest water. Pools of water that remain all the year round are usually inhabited by edible frogs.

One of the most common insects is the migratory locust *(Locusta migratoria),* which appears at different periods, sometimes in great numbers. At such times, it is easy for lesser kestrels and other birds to find food. Large numbers congregate at the places where the locusts swarm, just as the same species do in winter in Africa. Indeed, the European steppes are similar in many ways to the African savannas.

WOODED STEPPES

Between the grassy steppes of the south and the deciduous and mixed woods of the north is a wide belt of wooded steppe extending right across Russia. A transitional zone between steppe and forest, it is perhaps the most charming type of country in European Russia. Most interesting is the dynamics of the region, manifested in the gradual conquest of the steppe by the forest, the expanded distribution of animals and plants, and their adaptation. Aesthetically the landscape, with its alternating steppe and forest, is very attractive. Many animals have found excellent habitats there; the grassy steppes provide summer grazing, and the adjacent woods food and protection in winter. Thus we meet animals of the steppe and forest simultaneously.

Generally speaking, the wooded steppes are of two types. One, dominant in the south, is a mighty steppe, usually with an unobstructed horizon, overgrown with grass (mostly feather grass, including the broad-leaved *Stipa joannis* and the tall *S. pennata)* and myriads of flowers in red, blue, yellow, and white. Here and there the steppe is broken by large or small groves of trees, sometimes virtually woods, composed mostly of oaks *(Quercus robur).* The other type of wooded steppe is more common in the north. It consists mainly of scattered, open oak woods in which flowering glades form a lovely mosaic-like pattern. In places the woods become very large and cover vast areas surrounded on all sides by open steppe. The woods may vary with topography and soil, and the number of deciduous trees may increase, but, in all the regions I have visited, the oak dominates. Smooth-leaved elms *(Ulmus carpinifolia),* hedge maples *(Acer campestre),* maples *(A. platanoides),* limes and aspens are sometimes seen among the oaks. Hazel and Tatarian maples *(A. tataricum)* may form dense thickets on the outskirts of the oak woods. These steppes are much more undulating than the grassy steppes and semideserts to the south, and thus favor the colonization by trees.

In some regions, especially around Poltava, the wooded steppes, whether overgrown with forest or not, are covered with large and small crater-like depressions, from three to six feet deep, with a diameter of thirty to one hundred and fifty feet. They are often smoothly rounded, and some of them are filled with water. They lie very close together there, forming a curious pattern on the steppe. These depressions were probably formed, at least in part, by water that accumulated there and depressed the loess. Great expanses of the wooded steppes consist of loess, borne to these regions by the wind over thousands of years. The depressions have often become colonized by aspens and sallow bushes, and sometimes by dewberries *(Rubus caesius).* These thickets are the forerunners of a future colonization by trees. Little by

The saiga, Europe's only antelope, manages to live on the poor vegetation of the arid steppes and semideserts between the Volga River and the Ural River as well as farther east. (R. Pucholt: Dilia)

The Sozj River in the basin of the Dnepr is one of the meandering waterways whose vegetation breaks the monotony of the steppes. (Z. Z. Vinogradov: Institute of Geography, Moscow)

little, elms, birches and limes will invade them, but the oak will not appear until later.

In the east, where the wooded steppe meets the foothills of the Ural Mountains, the birch has replaced the oak as the dominant tree, but the pattern of steppe-enclosed, isolated groves of trees and woods is the same.

The wooded steppes still contain some regions that are natural, in that the vegetation is virgin; but indirectly man has changed their character. The bobak marmot, for example, is no longer found there. The Streletsk steppe near Kursk is a specimen of such virgin steppe; the display of flowers on this steppe, which is wet in winter and dry in summer, is magnificent. There we can see, in the heart of Russia, what large areas of Europe looked like during part of the post-glacial era. Transported backward thousands of years, as it were, one can study the history of the earth and find for the hundredth time that there is nothing so beautiful on earth as the few patches man has left undisturbed.

The animal life on the great wooded steppes is roughly the same as on the grassy steppes; the spotted suslik is the most common mammal, but other animals leave the groves and woods, seasonally or occasionally, to visit the open areas. The wooded steppes do not shelter any vertebrates that are specially adapted to this type of habitat and are not found elsewhere.

Skylarks, calandra larks and whinchats are very common in the wooded steppes. The frequency of the whinchat on the great dry steppe is remarkable in view of the demands made by this species on environments in western Europe. In spring, multitudes of larks and pipits inhabit these steppes, but by July most of them have migrated. It is not yet known where these huge flocks spend their summers up to the time in autumn when they fly southward. The great bustard is now so uncommon that its breeding on the steppe in 1963 was considered very remarkable. This huge bird was once characteristic of the steppe. Montagu's harriers *(Circus pygargus)* and pallid harriers *(C. macrourus)* hunt in low flight, following the contours of the ground to catch small rodents unawares. The males are elegantly patterned in pale blue and white.

Many of the woods on the steppe may be characterized as "enclosed steppes," for large or small steppes open out almost like parks inside the woods. Foxes, badgers, and roe live there, the latter being represented by two races, *Capreolus capreolus capreolus,* common all over Europe, and the much larger *C. c. pygargus,* found mainly in Asia. On the European wooded steppes it lives around the Volga and eastward to the Ural Mountains. The small hills of the greater mole rat *(Spalax microphthalmus)* are seen everywhere, especially in glades in the woods. This animal must be very numerous. Among the small rodents are the bank vole *(Clethrionomys glareolus),* fieldmice *(Apodemus sylvaticus* and *A. flavicollis)* and the striped fieldmouse *(A. agrarius).* The dormouse *(Muscardinus avellanarius)* is typical of the groves. Among the birds, the yellowhammer *(Emberiza citrinella)* is a characteristic species in the "enclosed steppes," with their

127

The open steppe, clothed chiefly in broad-leaved and pinnate feather grasses, makes a sharp boundary with a dense forest of oaks. (Kai Curry-Lindahl)

During winter snowstorms the saiga is found on this sandy, wormwood-dotted Caspian steppe. (A. G. Bannikov)

mosaic of woods and glades. The beautiful, flutelike note of the golden oriole, the cooing of turtledoves, stock doves, and wood pigeons, the call of woodpeckers and the merry songs of the barred warbler *(Sylvia nisoria)* can be heard. The whitethroat has excellent hunting grounds, abounding with insects, at its disposal.

The transition of the enclosed steppes to woods proper is manifested in the increasing number of animal species. The ground vegetation is very dense and high in places. Raspberry thickets cover great areas, and in many places nettles *(Urtica dioeca)* grow to a height of six feet or so, so that one must protect one's face from them. Several other plants grow to the same height. In the sunlit glades grow plants that are as much at home as on the open steppes, covering the ground with variously colored flowers. The wealth of species is unique for Europe. As many as seventy species have been counted in a square yard of ground, and up to almost a hundred within a hundred square yards.

The moose is quite common in the woods, and sometimes wanders far out over the open steppe. In July we saw one on the steppe completely out of sight of woods. The stone marten, one of the most common predators in the steppe woods, makes occasional excursions over the open steppe. The deciduous woods also shelter many serins and black-

caps, hawfinches, great tits, blackbirds and mistle thrushes. In the glades, the miniature steppes surrounded by woodland, are many whinchats, goldfinches and linnets, while thrush nightingales haunt the dense thickets. The black kite is a common bird of prey in the woods, and the honey buzzard, sparrow hawk and hooded crow *(Corvus corone cornix)* also breed there. The kite and an occasional golden eagle may be seen in these steppe woodlands.

The fieldfare *(Turdus pilaris)* was observed in July as far south as Kursk. The tree sparrow *(Passer montanus)* breeds in great numbers in the oak woods, where it builds in the nests of larger birds. We found nests of tree sparrows, with eggs and young, built within the inhabited nests of magpies, rooks and buzzards. Serins and European robins are also common in the oak woods.

Reptiles and frogs are a feature of the animal life of the wooded steppes, both in the woods and in the open country. The sand lizard, steppe viper and variegated toad are very common there as they are on sandy steppes; on the wooded steppes, which are moister, one also finds the spadefoot toad *(Pelobates fuscus)*, the moor frog *(Rana arvalis)* and the slow-worm *(Anguis fragilis)*.

The beaver has long been an inhabitant of the wooded steppes around Voronezh. They are now commercially

128

On semideserts and arid steppes many lakes have a high concentration of soluble salts,which accumulate on the surface of the soil because of the dry climate. (A. G. Bannikov)

exploited and large-scale breeding is carried on. Still farther east, on the birchwood steppes of the Ural, flying squirrels *(Pteromys volans),* martens and bears are found.

THE GREAT RIVERS OF THE STEPPES

The great Russian rivers, the Dnieper, Don, Volga and Ural, wind from north to south through all types of steppe, from wooded steppes to semidesert land, breaking the monotony of the landscape. The valleys of these rivers form a world apart. Terrace woods, precipices of sand, brushwood, meadows, marshes and naked sandbanks characterize country along the rivers. Consequently, the river valleys often have a flora and fauna quite different from those of the surrounding steppe. The Volga is frequently bordered by steep banks of earth, one sometimes higher than the other.

The marshes are often very rich in bird life, representing species whose demands on environment cannot possibly be satisfied on the adjacent steppe. One can walk along the Volga and simultaneously study two entirely different animal worlds—the marshes and the steppe.

A Mountain Arc in East Europe

The Carpathians

9

The Carpathians are really an easterly offshoot of the Alps. Both mountain ranges were formed during the Tertiary, an era characterized by mighty foldings of the earth's crust, but since that time faults, volcanic activity, local glaciations and erosion have caused changes in both, and now the two ranges are different in a variety of ways. This is particularly true of the Carpathians, which usually have rounded contours; only the Tatra Mountains and parts of the Transylvanian Alps are alpine in character. Most of the Carpathian peaks reach heights between 5000 and 6650 feet. The highest, High Tatra, on the boundary between Poland and Czechoslovakia, attains 8743 feet. Several on the Czechoslovakian side are more than 8500 feet high, and Mt. Moldoveanu in Rumania, the highest in the South Carpathians, is 8346 feet.

The geology of the Carpathians is more complex than that of the Alps, and much still remains to be learned about the tectonic activity that has shaped this mountain range during millions of years.

The great arc of the Carpathians, 805 miles long, runs through Czechoslovakia, Poland, Russia, and Rumania. It begins on the plain of the Danube between Vienna and Budapest, runs northward to the province of Cracow in Poland, cuts through the western Ukraine in the east, and joins the Danube again between Belgrade and the Iron Gate. By far the greater part of the Carpathians is in Rumania, while Poland has the smallest part. The range lies between latitudes 45 degrees and 50 degrees north, so that the vertical limits of the vegetation zones are higher in the south than in the north. The mountains consist mainly of sandstone, which surrounds the range. The central part of the chain is built up of crystalline rocks and limestone; and signs of volcanic activity can be discerned in this sector.

The main reason that the Carpathians are so unlike the Alps is that they have few high alpine regions. Only the highest peaks are above the vegetation limit and, although they are covered with snow in summer, they are completely lacking in glaciers. The Carpathians thus form a green mountain range, with slopes covered right up to the top with woods or mountain meadows. This makes them far more accessible than the Alps to colonization by animals and plants. But,

nonetheless, the flora and fauna of the Carpathians and Alps have much in common.

The southern parts of the Carpathians are wholly in Rumania, on the same latitude as the Po Valley in Italy and the Crimea in Russia, but with a quite different climate. The warm winds of the Mediterranean hardly reach the Transylvanian Alps, which lie behind the Balkan mountains to the west and south. It is probable that the Black Sea has some influence on the climate of the Transylvanian Alps. In the Bucegi Mountains, in the southernmost parts of the Carpathians, just north of the plain of Valaki, the mean annual temperature in the Prahova Valley, the lowest part of the region, is 44.6° F at Sinaia (2600 feet above sea level) and 42.8° F at Predeal (3609 feet above sea level). These two places are at the southern and northern ends of the Prahova Valley. The difference in the temperature is not great, but at Cimpina—in the lowlands of the same valley, below the Carpathians—the mean temperature rises to 48.2° F. During a five-year period, 1955 to 1961, the maximum and minimum temperatures at Predeal were 82.4° F and −2.2° F. It snows all the year round on Mt. Omu (8238 feet), the highest peak in the Bucegi Mountains. From October to June the temperature is below 32° F, and the snow attains a depth of about twenty-two feet.

Meteorological data indicate that the climate in the northern part of the range is similar to this; for instance, the mean annual temperature at Zakopane, at the foot of High Tatra, 2949 feet above sea level, is 41° F. It snows there from September to May, and the mean annual precipitation is 37.5 inches.

A comparison of the vegetation limits in the Bucegi Mountains and in Tatra National Park is also interesting. The limits are consistently higher in the southern Carpathians than in the northern, a consequence, among other things, of a more favorable climate and a longer vegetation period. The depth of the snow in winter is also of great importance.

The upper vegetation limits, in various parts of the Carpathians, are as follows:

VEGETATION	Bucegi (Rumania)	Tatra (Czechoslovakia and Poland)
Beech or mixed forest	4600—5000 feet	4000—4150 feet
Coniferous forest	5250—6000	4250—5000
Brush vegetation (Pinus mughus)	7200	6000
Alpine vegetation	7200—8200	6000—7500

THE BUCEGI MOUNTAINS OF RUMANIA

At the point where the Carpathians, running from north to south through central Rumania, reach Valaki and turn westward, the Prahova Valley penetrates deep into the mountain range. The valley runs due north and is surrounded by the very high peaks of the Bucegi Mountains to the west and by the Girbova Mountains (up to 6309 feet) to the east.

Practically the whole of the Prahova Valley is populated,

The upper vegetation belt on Mt. Končistá in the Carpathians consists of shrublike mountain pines. (Ladislav Sitensky: Dilia)

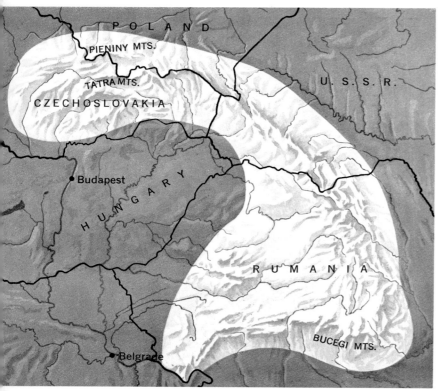

The Carpathians extend through Czechoslovakia, Poland, the U.S.S.R. and Rumania. The forests on their slopes are a refuge for mammals and birds from the plains below.

distributed widely in Europe, but which now grows as a relict in the Pyrenees, the Alps, and the Bucegi Mountains. Farther north in the Rumanian Carpathians is another very interesting relict, the dwarf birch *(Betula nana)*, which is far from its present distribution range, the southern boundary of which runs through Scotland, Scandinavia, and the Baltic states.

A rodent, the northern birch mouse *(Sicista betulina)*, found in association with the birch, was observed here in 1961 on a mountain meadow about 6500 feet above sea level, the most southerly and the highest occurrence of this species. The northern birch mouse is also found in the northern parts of the Carpathians up to a height of 5250 feet. Here, too, is the southern limit of the pine vole *(Pitymys subterraneus)*. Small rodents are plentiful, such species as the bank vole, the common vole *(Microtus arvalis)*, the dormouse, the forest dormouse *(Dryomys nitedula)*, the fat dormouse, the yellow-necked fieldmouse and the squirrel appearing on various levels.

Several of Europe's larger mammals, such as the red deer, roe, chamois, wild boar, bear, wolf and lynx, still live in the southern Carpathians. In some places quite large populations of wildcats are also found.

Several southern species of birds of prey may be observed here. Majestic black vultures, griffon vultures and imperial eagles are occasionally seen circling over hill and dale, and other large birds such as the buzzard and the raven are also seen there. Among the smaller species the wall creeper is worthy of mention. But northern birds, such as the nutcracker, three-toed woodpecker, Tengmalm's owl and the Ural owl *(Strix uralensis)*, may also be seen.

PYGMY OWLS

Every species of owl is a personality with its own peculiar habits. One of the most amusing, from the human point of view, is the pygmy owl *(Glaucidium passerinum)*, the smallest in Europe. In spite of its small size it is a true owl in every respect. When excited it jerks its tail sideways, and after alighting in a tree it usually cocks it upward in the manner of a wren. It is mainly diurnal but is most active at dawn and dusk. In spring and summer it lives in coniferous or mixed forests in both mountainous and lowland areas, but in winter it may be found in other habitats and may even come to man's parks, gardens or towns. Unlike certain other owls it does not feed mainly on rodents, and its numbers are therefore not so dependent on the abundance of small mammals. It takes not only voles, mice and shrews, but also small birds, lizards, and insects. It often eats its prey in the nest-hole, and in autumn and winter it tends to use the holes for storing large quantities of food.

The most common sound uttered by the pygmy owl is a whistling or fluty note, very much like that of a bullfinch; it is heard on autumn and winter evenings. On spring evenings, during mating time, these soft calls are produced in series and form a "song," with an interval of two seconds between each note. Because the owl turns its head in various directions as it calls, the sound seems to rise and fall. Sometimes the female answers, and the two birds give a long duet performance. The vocal activity starts at dusk and continues with much energy until darkness falls; then it is the turn of the nocturnal Tengmalm's owl, which is often found in the same

but the woods on the mountain slopes close in around Sinaia, in the southern part of the valley, only 325–500 feet above the bottom. This vertical distance between cultivated country and genuine mountain terrain is practically the same in the whole of the valley all the way up to the Predeal Pass and its continuation farther north toward Brasov.

The luxuriance of the beech woods is astonishing. In woods growing on slopes, the light penetrates through the treetops more easily than it can in woods on level ground, where the leaves often form a closed canopy. Consequently there is luxuriant ground vegetation on the Bucegi Mountains. Here an area of only about 325 square yards supports almost 1000 species of plants, about one-third of the flora of Rumania. A large number of the plants peculiar to the Carpathians grow in the Bucegi range and most of them are found above the timberline.

Beech woods dominate the lower slopes and become mixed with spruces *(Picea abies)* higher up. The yew is found here and there, and higher up the mountains (between 5750 and 6100 feet) are the stone pine *(Pinus cembra)* and the larch *(Larix europaea)*. The conifer zone forms the tree limit, and then comes a zone of low mountain pines *(Pinus mughus)* and mountain meadows of mat grass *(Nardus stricta)*. Low junipers and rhododendrons *(Rhododendron kotschyi)* and carpets of bilberries, cowberries and creeping mountain azaleas *(Loiseleuria procumbens)* also grow there.

It is on the plateaus of the Bucegi Mountains that the finest show of flowers is found. Many of the plants are similar to those in the Alps and the Scandinavian mountains, but many species—no fewer than thirty-five—are purely Carpathian. One interesting species is *Draba carinthiaca*, which was probably

habitat. At dawn the pygmy owl takes over again, sounding for all the world like a chiming clock.

Bucegi has seven species of reptiles, a large number for a European mountain. Lizards dominate, and it is interesting to note how the three *Lacerta* species are distributed ecologically. The wall lizard is found up to 3600 feet, the sand lizard up to 4600 feet, and the common lizard up to about 7200 feet. The latter endures cold better than any other European lizard and can live at the highest altitudes.

Trout *(Salmo trutta fario)* swim in the watercourses. But the most interesting fish in the Rumanian Carpathians is the Danube salmon *(Hucho hucho)*. This species was once found in the basin of the Danube, but water pollution and the building of hydroelectric power stations in the Danube River system have driven it from its former habitat; it is no longer found in the Danube itself. During recent years it has, however, been introduced into other rivers, even in North Africa. In Rumania, where it was once found in several watercourses, it is now restricted to the Bistrita and the Viseu rivers. Unlike other species of salmon, it makes no greater migration than about three miles and it does not spend any part of its life-cycle in lakes or the sea. This may be a recent adaptation to the special conditions in the Danube basin. This fish is much hunted and is undoubtedly of great economic value. It grows very quickly and can attain a weight of fifty-five pounds and a length of five feet.

The greater part of the Bucegi Mountains is now a nature reserve, and about 2500 acres of another and geologically interesting region of the Rumanian Carpathians, Retezat, is a national park. Situated in the massif of Banat it contains rich deposits and lakes of the Quaternary epoch.

THE RUSSIAN CARPATHIANS

The Carpathians meet the steppes of the Ukraine in the south-western corner of Russia. The plains and the mountains provide an interesting though undramatic encounter between two contrasting types of terrain. Many species are common to both of them, but the steppe does not seem to have influenced the composition of the fauna of the Carpathians to any great degree, for only a few of the species found in the Russian Carpathians are absent from the northern or southern parts of the mountain range. Exceptions are the moose, field vole, alpine chough, snow finch, scarlet grosbeak, and bearded vulture; the last named probably does not occur farther north. The snow finch and scarlet grosbeak occur in the Caucasus, too, living in the same elevation zone as in the Russian Carpathians.

The red-breasted flycatcher *(Ficedula parva)*, whose main distribution range is in Asia, is found here. Its song can be heard in the deciduous forests as well as in mixed woodlands up to about 3900 feet. But since the foliage in the canopy is dense, it is not easy to detect; sometimes one can hear its song as it moves from one branch to another, probably in search of insects. From listening to this species in various parts of Europe, I have found that the rhythm, melody and length of

A considerable number of chamois live in the Tatra Mountains, highest in the Carpathians. The Carpathian race is the largest subspecies of chamois. (Ladislav Sitensky: Dilia)

its notes vary not only from one male to another but also in the same bird. In all of its songs one can detect a resemblance to the songs of other species in pitch or rhythm, even though this bird does not imitate other birds in the way many warblers do.

The snow vole *(Microtus nivalis)* and the alpine shrew *(Sorex alpinus)* are two small mammals with a scattered distribution range in Europe. Both are found only in some parts of the Carpathians. The snow vole has a preference rare among rodents—it loves sunshine and can often be seen sunbathing on a tussock of grass in mountain meadows.

THE TATRA MOUNTAINS

The Tatra Mountains are the highest range in the Carpathians. They cover an area of more than three hundred square miles, with about one quarter in Poland, and the rest, including the highest peaks, in Czechoslovakia. The Tatras raise their impressive slopes and peaks almost directly from the surrounding alluvial plains, producing a striking contrast to them. As long ago as 1888 it was proposed in Poland that these mountains be made a national park, like Yellowstone National Park in the United States, but it was not until 1924 that Poland and Czechoslovakia decided to join in establishing such a park. This pioneering plan was not, however, realized until 1954—although a national park had been created on the Czechoslovakian side in 1948.

A general account of the vegetation zones in the Tatra Mountains has been given earlier in this chapter. In the central parts, that is the alpine High Tatra, consisting of granite, the mixed forest belt on the Polish side is dominated by stands of pure beech covering great areas of the lower mountain slopes. In some places firs *(Abies alba)* and birches *(Betula carpatica)* occur. Higher up a dense belt of spruce *(Picea abies)* climbs to a height of almost 4500 feet, where the dwarf pine *(Pinus mughus)* takes its place. At a few places around Lake Morskie Oko (4438 feet above sea level and about 165 feet deep), the largest lake in the Tatras, a surprising profusion of stone pine, mountain ash and birch, up to about 5000 feet above sea level, is found among these dwarf pines.

The flora in the Tatra Mountains is rich in species, with about twelve hundred flowering plants. Typical is a species of crocus *(Crocus scepusiensis)* which, when in flower, forms dense carpets. The edelweiss *(Leontopodium alpinum)* grows here, as elsewhere in the Carpathians. Four plants are endemic to the Tatra Mountains: *Cochlearia tatrae, Erigeron hungaricus, Erysium wahlenbergii,* and *Festuca aglochis.*

From the shores of the beautiful mountain lake and the slopes above one can get excellent views of the peaks of the Tatras, more than 6800 feet high. The chamois seems astonishingly numerous here, especially when one remembers that between 1957 and 1959 the total number in the Tatras was estimated at only 880 specimens. On a visit to the Polish Tatras (where there are said to be only one hundred specimens) in 1960, we saw these animals wandering over the

Left: In the Carpathians, dense forests generally grow on the slopes around streams and rivers. In the background is Mt. Muran. (Ladislav Sitensky: Dilia). Right: A young bear climbs a spruce in the Tatra Mountains. (V. J. Staněk: Dilia)

Virgin spruce forest on the slopes of Praděd in the Czecho-slovakian Carpathians. In the Tatra Mountains such woods reach a height of almost 4500 feet. (Jaroslav Holeček: Dilia)

Young foxes outside their den. The Carpathian Mountains are a haven for animal species exterminated in surrounding low-land countries. (Jaroslav Holeček: Dilia)

snow-covered slopes, grazing in the mountain meadows, or jumping from rock to rock. The Tatras are the most northerly distribution of this animal. The Carpathian chamois *(Rupicapra rupicapra carpatica)* is the largest race of the species, weighing up to 130 pounds. The red deer and the roe, too, are native to the Tatras and are found throughout the Carpathians.

The alpine marmot *(Marmota marmota),* a member of the same family as the bobak marmot of the steppes, occurs in the Tatra Mountains but belongs to a different race from the one in the Alps. It has been introduced into the Russian Carpathians. In the northernmost parts of the Carpathians there are also about thirty specimens of bears, from five to ten of lynx, and a few wolves. These three rare carnivores are thus distributed throughout the whole of the Carpathians. Of great interest is the isolated occurrence of a pine vole *(Pitymys tatricus)* on the Czechoslovakian side of the Tatra Mountains.

Among the large birds observed in the Tatra Mountains are the eagle owl, lesser spotted eagle, and black stork. The peregrine may be sighted in rapid flight, and the kestrel is to be seen flying over the mountain meadows hunting rodents. The most northerly breeding place of the alpine accentor is on High Tatra; the redpoll *(Carduelis flammea)* is also found.

THE PIENINY MOUNTAINS

Immediately northeast of the Tatra Mountains, the River Dunajec flows through the Pieniny range. This part of the Carpathians is composed of sedimentary rocks, most of them formed during the Jurassic and Cretaceous periods, 60 to 150 million years ago, though some were formed at earlier or later periods. The Dunajec broke through this heterogeneous material probably during the Miocene or Pliocene epochs, about ten to twenty million years ago. The result was a series of deep ravines and a winding river bed between steep mountain slopes, a geologically interesting terrain, now clad in luxuriant forests. From 1932 to the end of World War II Pieniny was a national park on both Polish and Czechoslovakian territory, for the Dunajec is a boundary river. The national park was the first international nature reserve, an admirable example of how valuable natural areas should be preserved. Unfortunately, the war put an end to this cooperation. Now the Polish part of Pieniny is a national park, while the Czechoslovakian side is a nature reserve. Efforts are being made to reestablish the international park.

The Pieniny Mountains are now one of Poland's outstanding areas of natural beauty. I floated down the Dunajec for

The Carpathians are one of the last strongholds of the lynx, which, like all the large carnivores of Europe, has for centuries been retreating before man. (Jaroslav Holeček: Dilia)

nearly a whole day on a kind of raft made of four boats fastened together. The trip provided an infinite variety of scenes: steep, narrow ravines, mighty precipices, wooded slopes, open farmland, and islands overgrown with sallows and the like. We saw white and black storks side by side, and little ringed plovers on the shores, while hoopoes flew with food in their beaks to a willow where they were probably nesting. We landed in Czechoslovakia and were cordially received by the reserve officials.

Several times during our trip on the river we could see the snow-covered peaks of the Tatra Mountains in the distance. This high mountain range protects Pieniny in such a way that its local climate differs from that of the rest of the Carpathians. The Pieniny area has a mean annual temperature of 44.6° F, that is, as high as at Sinaia in the southernmost Carpathians. This climate, unique for such a latitude, together with the soil and topography, has given rise to a remarkable flora. It has had a long development, for the Pieniny Mountains have never been covered with glacial ice, and elements of vegetation from the interglacial periods and even from the Tertiary can be discerned. Such relics as *Dryas octopetala,* an arctic plant, are found growing side by side with southern species. Alpine species and lowland plants grow close to each other, and plants preferring dry localities are found a stone's

throw from species most at home in wet ground. Pieniny has nine species of plants found nowhere else in the world. These mountains are botanically bewildering; they form an oasis where many plants have congregated during thousands of years, while surrounding regions have been confined in ice, which put an end to all life there.

The same variety of species, usually at home in other regions of Europe, is found among the insects of Pieniny. Two endemic beetles live there, but even more remarkable are the more than eighteen hundred species of butterflies and moths (equivalent to sixty-five per cent of all the species in Poland) representing Euro-Caucasian, Atlantic, Mediterranean, as well as alpine and arctic elements. This unique variety corresponds to that of the plants, which makes the area all the more interesting. Schreiber's bat *(Miniopterus schreibersi),* found chiefly in the Mediterranean region, has its most northerly outpost in the Pieniny Mountains, where it meets several of the northern animals mentioned in connection with the Tatras—the lynx, for example.

The long arc of the Carpathians that runs through Central Europe is everywhere rich in plants and animals, but curiously enough, nowhere is the wealth of species so great as at the extreme ends of the crescent—Bucegi in the south, and Pieniny in the north.

137

Mosaic of Lakes and Plains

The Hungarian Puszta

10

In the center of Europe, representing an isolated outpost of the great Russian steppe, is the Hungarian *puszta,* a word meaning plains; the greater part of Hungary consists of flat land encircled by mountains. In many ways the Hungarian puszta is a replica of the Russian steppe. Hungary has the typical continental climate, with cold winters and hot summers, despite the fact that the Carpathians separate the country from the great Russo-Asiatic steppes. The soil of the puszta is akin to that of southern Russia. The famous black earth *(tjernosem)* of southern Russia is also found on the puszta; a loose soil, rich in lime plant food, it is cultivated as intensively as in Russia. Since most of the puszta is agricultural land, very little of its original character—grass and deciduous forest—now remains. Here and there patches of the grassy steppe have escaped the plow, but these for the most part are trampled by grazing cattle.

The natural vegetation of the puszta is reminiscent of the steppes of the Ukraine, and several species of the flora and fauna found there are common both to Hungary and southern Russia.

A few major stages mark the geological history of the Hungarian plain. After being covered by the sea and later becoming a lowland full of lakes and marshes, the region was converted to dry land as a result of sedimentation by the rivers. Several large rivers cut right across Hungary: their courses have changed frequently—the Danube in particular—isolating lakes and creating enormous areas of wetland, and even today marshes and lakes are numerous. These provide an invaluable water supply for the puszta as well as for the surrounding country.

WHERE THE PUSZTA MEETS THE HIGHLAND

The largest unbroken areas of genuine steppe are in eastern Hungary, between Debrecen and Szeged. In northwestern and northern Hungary, the puszta gradually inclines upward, culminating in the Matra Mountains (3333 feet), northeast of Budapest. Isolated mountains interrupt the flat contours of the plain in other parts of Hungary. Northwest of Lake Balaton are the Bakony Mountains (2350 feet), and in the southwestern part of the country are the Mecsek Mountains (2250 feet). These isolated highlands, frequently covered with woods, on or near the puszta, make possible the survival of several species of animals that could not exist on the plain alone. The puszta is, therefore, richest in breeding animals where it is bordered by mountains.

Where the Matras slope toward the puszta the land is mostly cultivated, but here and there it is covered with oak and beech woods mixed with other deciduous trees and bushes. These are the home of red deer, roe deer and wild boars, and there can be heard most species of Central European birds. The birds of prey are also in general the same as those met with farther north in Europe, except for a few southern and eastern species on the edge of the puszta, which makes these regions ornithologically interesting.

One of these birds is the imperial eagle; there is a wide gap between the distribution range of the western race, which is found in Spain, and the eastern race, which breeds in Hungary, the Balkans and southern Russia. The mighty silhouette of this eagle is not an uncommon sight on the puszta, especially as it glides on outstretched wings down to its nest in woods on the slope. Once above the tree in which its nest is built, the bird folds its wings and drops rapidly. While it lives and breeds in the woods, it does its hunting for rodents on the plain.

Other birds of prey which are found in these regions are the lesser spotted eagle *(Aquila pomarina),* the booted eagle, and the saker falcon. All these species give a sense of life to the unbroken sky over the immense expanses of the puszta.

HAMSTERS AND OTHER ANIMALS OF THE PLAIN

Several animals of the puszta are characteristic of steppes, and are distributed eastward, in Russia and elsewhere in Asia. Among them is the hamster, which is constantly expanding its breeding grounds westward over the cultivated plains of Central Europe. The hamster, a rather large rodent, is well known for its habit of hoarding large quantities of food in its burrow. It lives on different kinds of vegetable matter, which it transports to the storage place in the large pouches inside its cheeks. In cultivated areas it hoards grain, beets, turnips, potatoes, beans, peas, carrots, cabbage and fruit. Curiously for a rodent, the hamster also eats meat, hunting shrews, rats and mice, and taking birds, reptiles, frogs and worms. Thus it is omnivorous, which has a bearing on its function on the cultivated steppe.

The habit of hoarding food is vital to the hamster, for it needs a store of easily accessible food during the winter. In winter it lies in a sort of coma, with a body temperature that falls from a normal 110° F to only 43° F. Its sleep is often

The little stint, an arctic wader, passes through Europe on its migration to tropical and southern Africa. On the way, it rests on lakes and seashores. (Ilse Makatsch)

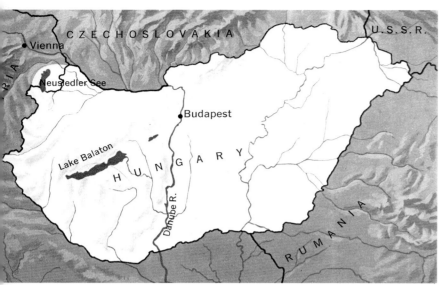

The grass plains of the Hungarian puszta are a continuation of the Russian steppes although separated from them by the Carpathians. The most famous lakes of the puszta are those west of the Danube: Neusiedler See in Austria and Hungary and Kisbalaton at the Hungarian end of Lake Balaton.

interrupted, however, and then—as in early spring—it needs food. Its hoard may amount to as much as twenty-five pounds, which is a great deal for an animal whose maximum weight is only about fourteen ounces.

The hamster is one of the few European rodents of economic value. The skins are sold, and in some years as many as 1,500,000 are marketed. The meat is eaten by domestic animals and by gypsies.

The suslik is also found on the puszta, but there it is the European suslik *(Citellus citellus),* not the species found on the Russian steppes. The westernmost reaches of another rodent, the steppe mouse, is on the puszta. And also very common on the plains are the field vole *(Microtus agrestis),* which has its southern limit in Hungary, and the common vole *(M. arvalis).*

FALCONS AND BUSTARDS

The grassy regions of the puszta are also rich in various species of insects, particularly grasshoppers and beetles. Consequently, rodent- and insect-hunting falcons are quite common there. They can often be observed hovering overhead, looking for prey. The most numerous is the kestrel, but the beautifully colored red-footed falcon is also found there. Even such a large species as the saker falcon, which is larger than the peregrine, is sometimes seen to catch insects on the puszta.

The red-footed falcon is somewhat smaller than the kestrel. The male is sooty-gray—sometimes the chestnut-colored feathers of the legs are visible—while the female has a rufous head and rust-colored underparts. Both sexes have red feet, and the features mentioned here are usually sufficient for recognition through field glasses. In the air the red-footed falcon resembles the kestrel, but it has a shorter tail and is generally more slender. It often hovers, but higher up than the kestrel, and it keeps its body more horizontal. With its claws

it catches and then eats insects in flight, particularly at dusk. Where large ground insects are abundant it hunts on the ground, moving about with rapidity: no European bird of prey except the honey buzzard has such a specialized insect diet as this falcon.

In places where the red-footed falcon is numerous, it is noticeably gregarious. In Hungary, in summer, small flocks congregate around trees in village streets and market places, and hunt there, especially at dusk. Sometimes they are joined by the hobby and the kestrel. Red-footed falcons are often seen perching on trees, telegraph poles or wires, carefully surveying the ground, and diving down now and then to catch some small creature, such as a frog, lizard, vole, and shrew. Vertebrate prey, however, is exceptional for this species, except when small rodents are abnormally common on the puszta.

At breeding time, too, the red-footed falcon displays its sociability. Before breeding begins, flocks of them perform aerial maneuvers. In the early morning they may fly back and forth for hours, high above the same spot, turning suddenly at certain points. As the day advances they fly lower and lower. In the display flight, which is performed immediately before mating, the male first flies back and forth above the female, which sits at the top of an oak about fifty feet high. Suddenly he glides away, gaining height in wide circles over a neighboring glade, until he rises to about 150 feet, whereupon he dives steeply and then climbs again with quick wingbeats. This maneuver is continued for about five minutes, after which the bird makes a long dive straight onto the female's back. The mating lasts for a few seconds. The bird makes no sound during the flight and mating.

The red-footed falcon breeds in colonies, and since, like other falcons, it does not build a nest of its own, it selects another bird's nest. Often all the nests in a rookery are occupied, so the falcons must wait until the last of the young rooks have left the nests. Sometimes, when the rooks have begun breeding late, the falcons may have to wait a long time, and not infrequently the females are compelled to lay eggs while flying or perching. During the last few hours of the rooks' occupation, the falcons watch the rookery from trees close by; no sooner have the last young rooks left the nests than the falcons move in.

This bird also takes over nests of crows, magpies, and even kites, and sometimes breeds in holes in trees. In Russia it has also been found breeding in bushes and holes in the ground, and thus not in colonies. It would seem that the falcon's sociability has grown out of its adaptation to the communal environment of rookeries.

The great bustard, one of the most remarkable birds of the plain, has three distribution areas in Europe: the puszta is the westernmost part of its eastern distribution area, which extends over the Russian steppe as far as Altai in Asia. It is, however, found only locally in Hungary where, because the few surviving pairs are subject to ruthless egg collectors, it has become very rare. To this hazard must be added the various handicaps of this bird, such as that it is the heaviest bird in Europe, weighing up to twenty-five pounds, it is coveted

The largest number of spoonbills nesting in colonies in reeds around lakes in Europe is found in Hungary and Austria. (George Kapocsy)

The surface of one of the many channels in Lake Kisbalaton is covered with aquatic plants and surrounded by reed beds and scattered willows. (Eric Hosking)

as food by man, and harvesting machines may crush its eggs or its young, for it has almost nowhere to breed but on arable fields.

The great bustard can fly very rapidly, considering its size. In flight the white wings with their dark tips are clearly visible; the head is stretched forward and the legs backward, so one can seldom mistake it as it passes overhead. Seen from a distance when they are grazing or hunting, great bustards look like a flock of sheep. Their display behavior is a bizarre sight. The male turns its plumage almost inside out and transforms itself into something that bears little resemblance to a bird. This extraordinary performance may still be seen on the steppes of southeastern Hungary, east of the River Tisza.

REALM OF THE WHITE-FRONTED GEESE

The area known as Puszta Hortobagy is an almost endless plain in eastern Hungary. Before World War II, grassy steppes stretched as far as the eye could see, and between Budapest and Debrecen one could travel for miles over this sea af grass. Birds were very numerous, geese congregating there in immense flocks in spring and autumn. The wet meadows and the marshes in the valley of the Hortobagy, transformed periodically into one gigantic swamp, were a paradise for various aquatic birds, but primarily for geese. They could be

counted in tens of thousands. When he visited this area in 1936, Peter Scott, the English artist—and zoologist—known for his work for conservation, estimated that he could see at least a hundred thousand specimens of the white-fronted goose at one time.

I was fortunate enough to see this country before most of it was converted into rice fields. There are still many birds there; in fact, the number of white-fronted geese has even increased in some places, but the indescribable charm of the wild puszta land has vanished. The mosaic of water and land, the virgin appearance of the landscape, and the few signs of former human activities, which, so to say, underlined the wild character of the country, combined to produce an atmosphere that is now gone. The geese, with their silhouettes and cries, were the most important feature of this view. Besides the white-fronted geese, there were graylag geese, bean geese, occasional lesser white-fronted geese, and red-breasted geese.

The white-fronted goose is probably the most beautiful species of all the European members of the genus *Anser*. This becomes especially evident when it takes wing. It can soar rapidly, rising almost vertically from the ground, and as it descends it often wheels quickly and with superb grace. White-fronted geese that are shot at or otherwise disturbed while in flight are said to be able to escape danger by soaring to great heights. It is not always possible to see the markings on the breasts of the geese when they fly past in regular mi-

Great white herons with two nestlings at Lake Velence in Hungary. Preening its wings, the adult shows its scapular feathers, famous for their softness. (Eric Hosking)

Little egret nestlings beg food from their parent. The older bird will soon regurgitate a meal which the young will pick from its throat. (Z. Tildy)

gratory formation, and it may therefore be difficult to determine whether the white-fronts are mixed with bean geese. These two species often congregate. In flight the white-fronted goose has slightly more slender and pointed wings. This is more easily seen when a few white-fronted geese are on the outskirts of or immediately behind a bean geese formation. The characteristic call of the white-fronted goose, consisting of shrill, rather melancholy notes, usually repeated at short intervals, is easily distinguishable from the call of the bean goose. It must be added, however, that the white-fronted goose has other notes, too, such as a more flutelike "viv," which are similar to those of the bean goose. Thus the calls of the two geese may sometimes be confused.

The white-fronted goose of the puszta has very regular habits. During the hour before sunrise the flocks of geese leave their night quarters, a lake, flooded ground, or a bank, to graze in the fields or, more often, the meadows. If not disturbed they usually stay there all day. About midday the geese adjourn to flooded hollows, ditches, or other patches of water to drink and take a siesta. At dusk they return to their night quarters, regularly following certain distinct routes. Knowing their timetable, one can enjoy the sight of them passing at a low level in the gathering dusk. Their gabbling can be heard far away in the still air over the open plain, the nasal "ka-ka-ka-kajack" of the bean goose mingling with the shriller "kao-

klee" of the white-fronted goose. As the blue dusk falls over the plain, the contours of the flocks of geese, silhouetted against a sky tinged with yellow, rose, and violet, become more and more diffuse.

The flocks coming from the west can be seen against the glowing sky for great distances. Those from the east, south, and north can be heard cackling and trumpeting before they even come into sight and, when they do appear, it is as if they have materialized magically out of the sky. The goal of all the thousands of birds is the still waters of the puszta. Once over the waters the great birds whirl, cackling and gabbling, and the orderly ranks dissolve into a frolicking bedlam. Reducing speed, they plane first to one side and then to the other, sometimes even turning somersaults as they descend to the water. As it alights, each bird makes bright silver tracks. While the geese on the lake settle down for the night, new contingents are heard arriving. At last the darkness is such that only their calls and the sound of their wings indicate their presence. Soon the last flocks come and silence reigns. At dawn the whole company returns to the fields and meadows.

East of the winding bed of the Danube and parallel to it is a series of lakes and marshes running across the puszta, many of them rich in animal and plant life. These wet meadows, inhabited by the lapwing and the black-tailed godwit, are shaded here and there by groves of trees which, in summer,

143

Above: About fifty pairs of spoonbills breed in this colony at Lake Kisbalaton in Hungary. (Eric Hosking)

Left, above: The reed warbler, one of the few passerine birds adapted to an aquatic habitat, suspends its nest in reeds. (Jaroslav Holeček: Dilia)

Left: Deep in the reed beds of Neusiedler See a male and female little bittern freeze in a posture of concealment. (Walter Fendrich)

provide breeding places for such colorful birds as rollers, golden orioles, turtledoves, and woodpeckers of various species. This combination of environment makes the region a show place for birds, with every marshy meadow and grove having a surprise in store. Nevertheless these regions are less abundant with birds than the three lake districts which lie farther west.

THE BIRDS OF VELENCE, KISBALATON, AND NEUSIEDLER SEE

The lakes on the plains of Europe are often rich in nutrients and have a high production of vegetable and animal organisms. Such lakes are not infrequently surrounded by fertile agricultural land, and this rural land is a dangerous neighbor for birds. The passion for draining in order to increase the amount of arable land has destroyed many lakes; it has also lessened the subsoil water, which has led to droughts and poorer crops on adjacent land. In recent years, moreover, the use of chemicals has poisoned the lakes. On the farmlands, spread over the cultivated fields, the chemicals have been washed into ditches and streams by rain and have then been carried into the lakes. There the poison has affected living organisms throughout the whole chain of nutrition; plankton,

The great bustard, Europe's heaviest bird and one of its rarest, is found on the Hungarian puszta, but it is rapidly disappearing as a result of man's persecution and the cultivation of the land. (Jaroslav Holeček: Dilia)

fish, birds, and mammals. In such ways the animal life in many of the shallow lakes of Europe has gradually been extinguished.

But there still remain a few lakes with a wealth of animal life. Among the most interesting of these are Velence and Balaton, on the Hungarian plain, and Neusiedler See in Austria and Hungary. These lakes belong to a type of steppe lake whose salinity is determined by the climate. Velence and Neusiedler See, luckily, are nature reserves, but Lake Balaton, once so plentiful with birds, has suffered from exploitation as a resort. Hotels and camping sites now fringe the lake. Balaton is the largest lake in Central Europe and one cannot help wishing that some parts of the shore had been preserved for the benefit of tourists and others seeking recreation in natural surroundings.

Fortunately, Kisbalaton, a small lake connected with Lake Balaton at its western end, has been preserved. This finely stocked bird sanctuary is now protected by a nature reserve of about eight thousand acres, which in turn is surrounded by marshy land covering an area approximately four times as large as the nature reserve.

By these lakes and their wide fringes of reed grass live most of the southern European marsh birds, described earlier in relation to the great south European deltas. There are, in addition, two species of birds, rare in Europe, which occur in greater numbers in Velence, Kisbalaton, and Neusiedler See than anywhere else on the Continent. They are the spoonbill and the great white heron. In Europe, around the turn of the century, the latter was almost exterminated, due to the vogue for trimming ladies' hats with egret plumes. Since then, this heron has been rare all over Europe, even in the deltas of the Volga and the Danube. The colony at Neusiedler See, of about three hundred pairs, is probably the largest in Europe, which is curious, for this lake is the western limit of the birds' occurrence in Europe. About twelve to fifteen pairs breed in Lake Velence, and about eight to ten pairs in Kisbalaton.

The situation of the spoonbill in Europe is somewhat brighter. It is more numerous than the great white heron and is, in addition, found in at least two areas of western Europe. In Neusiedler See there are about three hundred pairs.

Neusiedler See, approximately twenty-two miles long, is only about thirty miles from the center of Vienna. It is the largest shallow lake in Central Europe, its average depth being about five feet, though the depth varies greatly. Sometimes it dries up. To the south, west and east, Neusiedler See and its satellite marshes and meadows are surrounded partly by wooded hills, while the shores to the east merge into a flat, cultivated steppe, full of small lakes and salt ponds which offer an almost unique hydrochemical diversity in relation to their comparatively restricted area. Here the ground is often baked hard in summer, creating a genuine salt steppe in which a network of cracks gradually appears.

For the most part, Neusiedler See is surrounded by low-lying meadows, with sedge *(Carex)* growing in the wettest parts. These open shore meadows give way to a belt of reed grass, in places as much as three miles wide. Here and there on the open water are tussocks of club rush. Its surroundings offer a wide range of natural environment, and this gives rise to a rich fauna, especially of birds, which find important resting and feeding grounds during the migration periods and in winter. But there also are many breeding birds, such as the lesser gray shrike *(Lanius minor),* which is common there as

A female of the little crake (Porzana parva), *more often heard than seen, enters her nest in a dense "forest" of reeds at Hungary's Lake Velence. (Eric Hosking)*

One of the most common mammals found on the Hungarian puszta is the European suslik. It also occurs on the Russian steppes. (Charles Vaucher)

it is in most of Hungary. The aquatic warbler *(Acrocephalus paludicola),* found in four separate regions of Europe, is another species that breeds there. The mustached warbler reaches at Neusiedler See its northernmost range in Europe; and there, as on marshes and river banks, the bluethroat *(Luscinia svecica)* sings its charming song with great virtuosity. The black ibis, as also the pratincole and the gull-billed tern, are among the rare birds of the lake and of Europe; while the little tern is also worthy of notice.

Despite the fact that Neusiedler See is in the middle of the Continent, almost confined between the Alps and an offshoot of the Carpathians, it rivals the great deltas of southern Europe in its bird life. A botanical and zoological treasure trove, it represents Europe's most important interior wetland area.

Glaciers, Peaks and Chamois

The Alps

11

Flying over the Alps never loses its fascination. Whether one approaches from the north or south, the sight of that sea of mountains, that realm of snow, ice, and granite, makes a deep and lasting impression. One sits bewitched, looking out over that unearthly world with its rugged peaks, snow-covered domes, precipitous slopes and, far below, its toylike green valley and gray ribbon of a river. The range is 640 miles long

Right: The Dolomites, seen from Basso di Sella, form a spectacular zone of limestone mountains in the southeastern Alps. (Gerhard Klammet)   Below: The best known animal of Italy's northerly Parco Nazionale del Gran Paradiso is the ibex. In the nineteenth century the species was exterminated everywhere in the Alps except the Gran Paradiso massif. (Pepi Merisio)

Above: The edelweiss, the most celebrated alpine flower, grows on ledges at high levels. (L. Gensetter)   Below: A bellflower, Campanula cochleariifolia, *has found enough nourishment in a crevice of naked rock to grow and bloom. (Photo Klopfenstein)*

and up to 155 miles wide, covering an area of about 77,200 square miles. This is a large part of Europe, equivalent, for example, to two-thirds of the area of Italy. It is only from the air that the full grandeur of the Alps can be appreciated.

The Alps form one of Europe's youngest mountain ranges, which explains their "alpine" character, that is, their sharp peaks and jagged ridges. The ravages of time, in the form of weathering and erosion, have not yet worn them down the way they have the much older Caledonian and Armorican mountains of Central and northern Europe.

During the periods of glaciation the Alps played an important role as a generator of ice and as an influence on the climate of the surrounding area, in spite of the fact that they were south of the great inland icecap. These local glaciations also affected the present structure of the range. During the Ice Age most of the valleys in the central and eastern Alps were filled with mighty sheets of ice, which spread out beyond the limits of the mountains. This ice deepened and widened the valleys, gave them U-shaped contours and formed a number of basins, now filled with lakes; in addition, water from the melting ice rushed down the valleys with irresistible force, widening existing valleys and cutting new ones, and facilitating later colonization by plants, animals, and man. If the Alps are compared with the Pyrenees, formed at the same time (mostly during the Tertiary), and with the Caucasus Mountains, which were not exposed to Quarternary glaciation to the same degree, the very important role of ice in the formation of landscape will be understood. The valleys in the Pyrenees and the Caucasus range are usually much narrower and more V-shaped than those of the Alps. It is thus due mainly to the fact that they have been less influenced by ice that the Pyrenees and the Caucasus range have remained the most primeval tracts of southern Europe.

GLACIERS

The Alps extend into seven countries—Switzerland, Austria, Liechtenstein, France, Italy, Germany, and Yugoslavia—and almost entirely cover the first three of these. The Jura Mountains (which are more ancient than the Alps), together with their lower plateau stretch from the region of Geneva to the Rhine Valley near Schaffhouse.

Numerous glaciers are still found in the Alps, but, although very impressive, they are only remnants of their former greatness. Briefly, glaciers are formed by accumulated snow that is packed into a solid frozen mass. This mass of snow-ice moves by growing at the upper end and melting at the lower end. If the glacier terminates in a lake, huge chunks of ice break off and float away—a process called calving. Some glaciers are motionless and are referred to as dead ice. A glacier may move at the rate of an inch or so a day, thus adding up to about thirty feet a year. The rate of flow is usually greater in the middle of the glacier than at the sides.

In summer a glacier is often covered with water. Where the ice is smooth, water collects over the whole surface; where it is uneven or where the water has cut down into the ice,

In summer, herds of ibex are active mostly at night or in late afternoon; in winter they also move around by day. (Photo Klopfenstein)

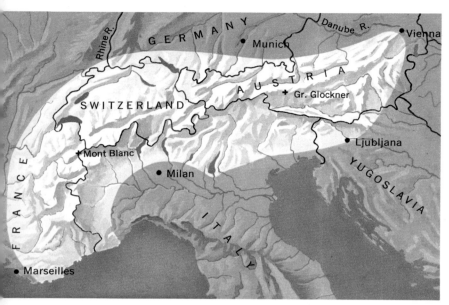

The Alps form a gigantic barrier between the plains of Central Europe and sun-washed Italy and southeastern France. The Alps also extend into Switzerland, Liechtenstein, Germany, Austria and Yugoslavia.

miniature brooks are formed. The many waterways give rise to a variety of sounds: disappearing into cracks and cavities, the water can be heard murmuring under the ice or bubbling deep down in crevasses; it pours out in miniature cascades from walls of ice; or it roars when boulders brought down by the water collide with each other. During recent years the majority of glaciers have been reduced considerably in volume, a sign that the climate is getting warmer.

In some countries the Alps are traditionally divided into the West and East Alps. Between them is the Rhine, the Splügen Pass and Lake Como. In Switzerland one also refers to a third, central area. The highest peaks are in the West Alps, with Mont Blanc (15,781 feet) between France and Italy, Monte Rosa (15,203 feet) in Italy, the Matterhorn (14,678 feet), the Finsteraarhorn (14,023 feet) and Jungfrau (13,642 feet) in Switzerland, Massif du Pelvoux (12,920 feet) in France, and Gran Paradiso (13,380 feet) in Italy. In the East Alps, Bernina (13,300 feet), on the boundary between Italy and Switzerland, is the highest peak, followed by Ortles (12,792 feet) in Italy, and Grossglockner (12,460 feet) and Wildspitze (12,382 feet) in Austria.

The Alps form Europe's most important watershed. Precipitation and melted ice are distributed by thousands of mountain brooks to the Rhine, Rhone, Po, and Danube rivers which, having drained large parts of the continent, flow into the North Sea, the Mediterranean and the Black Sea. The great deltas of the Rhone, Po, and Danube have been partly built up of sediment originating in the Alps. For millions of years, what has been broken down in the highlands has been building up the plains.

The Alps do not have the climatic characteristics of east and west Europe, for the varying altitudes in valleys and on slopes, the exposure and the angle of slope create different climates even at the same elevation. The climate on the shady side of a valley often differs greatly from that on the sunny side only a few hundred yards away. It must also be borne in mind that greater elevation does not always mean lower tem-

perature. Sometimes the warm and cold layers of air are reversed in winter, cold air accumulating at the bottoms of the valleys and making them colder than the slopes higher up. All these types of climate are found in other mountain ranges, but, owing to the well developed, wide longitudinal valleys, and deep transverse valleys, nowhere in Europe are they so marked as in the Alps. Contrasting climatic conditions on opposite sides of the valleys give rise to many kinds of vegetation. Mountain slopes facing south may form climatic oases, where the powerful rays of the sun soon melt the winter snow and allow the development of plants representative both of Central Europe and the Mediterranean zone. The soil, naturally, has much influence also on the vegetation.

ALPINE LAKES AND RIVERS

The Alps contain many lakes. Many of them, especially those in the Italian Alps, are very deep, Lake Como measuring 1345 feet, Lake Maggiore (1220 feet), and Lake Garda (1135 feet); then comes Lake Geneva (1017 feet).

In these mountain lakes and in several rivers live fish that thrive in cold water: the lake trout (*Salmo trutta lacustris*), char (*Salvelinus alpinus*), grayling (*Thymallus thymallus*), and various whitefish (*Coregonus*). Most of these fish, if not all of them, are glacial relics and have survived the subsequent cold in deep trenches in the lakes, after the distribution range of other such fish in Europe was reduced by the northward retreat of the inland icecap as the climate became warmer. Unfortunately, scientific study of the original distribution of these fish, especially whitefish, has been complicated during the past forty years by man's introduction of innumerable other fish.

Whitefish present so many problems because the different species often show environmental modifications. In Europe, more than a hundred species and subspecies have been described, a variability probably resulting from the fact that the whitefish, like other members of the salmon family, has had the number of its chromosomes doubled repeatedly in the course of its evolution and that different species have invaded the lakes at various times.

Practically all the large lakes in the Alps are surrounded by agricultural land, towns, or villages. They are frequently polluted by waste matter from industrial plants and towns, so that scarcely a lake remains unaffected. Yet, many still look very attractive. As always with beautiful lakes, it is primarily their shores that are responsible for their beauty—the surrounding mountain slopes, the reflections in the water, the play of light on the lake and on wooded shores.

The flight of birds over lakes and shores also plays a part. One notes, for example, the regal black kites that slowly patrol the shores of Lake Geneva. This bird need not hurry, for usually it does not have to take its prey unawares, living mostly on dead and half-dead fish, over which it quarrels with gulls. It breeds in large numbers on Mont Salève and in the Jura Alps on the French border. Of all birds of prey—kestrels, buzzards, sparrow hawks, honey buzzards, and short-toed

A Swiss glacier, Gornergletscher, as seen from Monte Rosa on the Italian border. In the background rises the famous Matterhorn. (Photo Klopfenstein)

eagles—this kite is the most common, or at least is seen most frequently. Immediately after its arrival in spring it starts its mating flight, which it repeats occasionally throughout the summer, until late August. The wedding flight usually consists of both birds flying side by side—but not always at the same height—with rapid wingbeats, following a curved, more or less horizontal course. Now and then they plane sideways toward each other. Sometimes the bird flying below turns over on its back with outstretched claws; at other times, one of the birds, probably the male, dives with folded wings from a considerable height down toward the other, whereupon the display flight begins again, accompanied by piercing cries from both birds. The spectacle is one of the most remarkable of the Alpine spring.

The black kite lives largely on carrion—especially of fish—and on other waste matter; in polluted lakes, dead fish are sometimes abundant and there is always refuse in populated areas, so that the kite is assured of a good living. Its prey includes mammals, birds, reptiles, frogs, live fish, insects, mollusks, crustaceans and worms. In Africa, where the bird winters, insects constitute a large part of its food. This probably explains its relatively late spring arrival in Europe. Insectivorous birds of prey usually return late to their breeding grounds, for in early spring there are few insects there.

Right: A gray heron, which can get its food only on open water, fishes in the nature reserve of Murnauer Moos in the Bavarian Alps. (Gerhard Klammet)   Below: Alpine hellebore (Helleborus niger) blooms amid snow. (Wilhelm Schacht)

Two young chamois race down a snow-covered Alpine slope. These ungulates climb on cliffs so sheer it seems almost impossible for a hoofed mammal to find a foothold there. (Charles Vaucher)

Living along rivers and streams, the dipper *(Cinclus cinclus)* is in some ways an astonishing bird. It dives and swims with the help of its wings—for its feet are not webbed—like the most skillful duck, and its nest is beautifully made. It is, moreover, the only passerine bird that gets all its food from water.

The dipper is also a charming little creature—very lively and nearly always on the move. Beside the water where it lives, an observer soon catches sight of a neat little bird in black and white, which flies away on short curved wings, uttering three or four short "zerrp-zerrp" cries. It flies just above the water and disappears around the nearest bend of the stream. If he follows the bird cautiously, he will find that it has not gone far. It has probably alighted on a stone amidst swiftly flowing water, and stands there, bobbing and curtseying, wagging its short tail and twitching its wings. Through field glasses one discovers that the bird is not only black and white, but also has brown on the head and nape. Soon it dives into the water, where it stays for five to eight seconds.

If the stream or river is not flowing too rapidly, one can watch the dipper under water, for it generally lives next to clear water. When it dives, it flashes like a fish—if the sun is shining—for bubbles of air form immediately on its oily

feathers. It can dive to the bottom, using its wings as oars, and can walk about among the stones with the help of its quite powerful claws. The ability of the dipper to run along a riverbed is unique and amazing. When it returns to the surface and makes for land, it swims with its feet alone. It may also walk about in shallow water looking for food like a wader. Sometimes it goes so far out that the water covers it entirely, and it is astonishing how it can press forward in strongly flowing water. It can also dive straight into the water from the air. It comes up again a little way off and then moves along the surface, its wings working like small paddles, until it dives again.

ALPINE VEGETATION

The deciduous forests in the Alps consist mainly of oak and beech, though these are mixed with many other leafy trees. The upper limit of the pure deciduous woods varies greatly in different parts of the range; it is nowhere very high, being usually about 1980 feet, though it rises in some places, such as the Jura Alps, to 2640 feet. In many valleys beech forests climb to about 5000 feet. Higher up is a mixed forest of beech and spruce *(Picea abies* and *Abies alba),* and, in some places, up to an altitude of about 3300 feet, pine grows *(Pinus silvestris* and *P. cembra).* The next belt consists of pure conifer woods, which are distributed throughout the Alps. Spruce, pine, or larch *(Larix europaea)* form the upper tree limit between five thousand and eight thousand feet. Man has frequently lowered the tree limit by clearing forests for grazing. The tree limit is highest in the central southern Alps: for example on Monte Rosa and Bernina and in the Dolomites. These vegetation zones naturally affect the vertical distribution of the animals, too. Species which belong to lowland in northern Europe go far up the mountain slopes in the Alps, sometimes to several thousand feet above sea level. The nutcracker, going up to 8000 feet, is one example of this, the red deer, going up to 9000 feet is another.

Alpine meadows open out here and there in the higher parts of the conifer forest, and in other places the woods merge into bush vegetation, while alders *(Alnus viridis)* climb along the streams high up into the mountains.

Avalanches play an important role as shapers of landscape in the Alps. In winter, masses of snow slide down the slopes, breaking off trees as if they were matches and sweeping the terrain clean. As a result, tongues of treeless land stretch far into the woods, not infrequently to the bottom of a valley. The vegetation soon begins to recolonize the land swept clean by such an avalanche; at first the light favors several species, but this homogeneity ends when the trees begin competing with each other. So the vegetation again passes through various stages of evolution until the forest has reconquered its former domain. But here, too, man influences the regrowth.

Although the Alps as an environment of woods and meadows largely confined between high mountain walls form a clearly limited area of Europe, the region has no terrestrial vertebrates that are not found elsewhere. The passes have facilitated invasion both by man and animals. While all the mammals, reptiles and frogs, except bats and some alpine

Clouds lie like lakes around Zugspitze (9089 feet) in the Alps on the German-Austrian border. (Heinrich Wolf)

Above: Growing on meadows and gentle slopes, rhododendrons cover vast areas of the Alps. (Gerhard Klammet). Right: A bouquet of alpine flowers: two species of primrose (Primula clusiana and P. farinosa), *one gentian* (Gentiana bavarica) *and one buttercup* (Ranunculus montanus). *(L. Gensetter)*

Right above: The mountain hare turns white or bluish white in winter. It occurs throughout northern and eastern Europe and occasionally in such mountain areas as the Alps. Right: The Alpine marmot, one of the most engaging mammals in the Alps, lives mostly on meadows above the timberline. (Both by R. P. Bille)

The pine marten, found not only in the Alps but in woods throughout most of Europe, is an excellent tree climber. (R. P. Bille)

species, have had to follow the passes in order to penetrate the mountain world, birds have been free to fly to practically any region that they could colonize.

Several species have, however, an isolated occurrence in the Alps. As with fish, some animals in the Alps, particularly birds, must be regarded as relics from late glacial times. To this group belong the redpoll *(Carduelis flammea),* the goosander *(Mergus merganser),* the ptarmigan *(Lagopus mutus),* and the dotterel *(Charadrius morinellus).* All these birds are now found chiefly in northern Europe; the ptarmigan is also found in the Pyrenees, and the dotterel in the Carpathians.

Among mammals, the alpine marmot *(Marmota marmota)* may be regarded as peculiar to the Alps, although it is found in a few places in the Carpathians. Of the large European beasts of prey—the bear, the wolf and the lynx—only the bear has survived, a score or so living in the Dolomites. Steep mountains and inaccessible valley forests with rich vegetation on the south slopes provide protection and food for this small population, but it is fighting a losing battle for survival. During the past decade or two, men with power saws and bulldozers, building hydroelectric dams, and tourists with all that follows in their wake, have destroyed most of this virgin region. It is tragic that no national park or nature reserve has been established in the Dolomites between Ada-

mello and Brenta. The magnificent scenery there, and the presence of the few surviving bears would justify such a step. Parco Nazionale dello Stelvio (about 235,000 acres) in Trentino, and Alto Adige, Italy's largest national park, could be extended to include the bear country.

The wolf, which once roamed over the whole of Europe, has been exterminated in the Alps, but occasionally, in 1948 and 1955 for instance, wolves have been killed in Switzerland. They probably came from the Apennines, or from the Balkans. The lynx *(Lynx lynx),* however, has now vanished.

ON THE WOODED SLOPES

One spring we followed the Rhone Valley from Lake Geneva up to Sion and the Diablerets range. We did not get higher than about 8200 feet, that is about 2300 feet from the summit, but it was high enough for us to find a large number of the charming spring flowers that color the slopes with violet, deep blue, rose, purple, golden yellow, and white, as well as birds announcing their presence with jubilant song.

In this part of the Valais canton one comes upon the Forêt de Derborence, one of the few surviving primeval forests in the Alps. Deciduous forests on the lower slopes of the Alps are idyllic places in the spring. Brooks chatter, the air is filled with the scents of newly opened leaves and damp earth. The renascence is almost total: many plants are in bloom, the display of bird plumage is at its most beautiful, snakes have just cast their skins and shine like jewels, insects flit from flower to flower, and ants rustle along their tiny paths with spruce needles and food. All is activity.

Though spring is similar throughout Europe, from its presence in the alpine world there emanates a special quality; for there variety is remarkable. A difference almost as great as between night and day may be observed between a sunlit glade and a shaded spot nearby. Besides this, each level on the slopes of the mountains presents a different stage in the progress of spring. Thus it may be full summer at the bottom of the valley when early spring flowers are just appearing a little higher up. Many of the flowers fascinate us with their singular shapes while others repel us by their unpleasant scent. But scents that repel us attract other creatures. Insects are drawn toward the evil smelling cuckoo-pint *(Arum maculatum).* On the other hand orchids, such as the early purple orchid *(Orchis mascula)* and the green-winged orchid *(O. morio),* do not advertise their presence by scent but by their bright colors—reddish-violet and purple. In other places fiery-red lilies *(Lilium bulbiferum)* light up like flames the shadows under their green canopies.

One of the most interesting birds in the lower alpine woods is the middle spotted woodpecker *(Dendrocopos medius).* It is found in many places in Central and southern Europe, although its distribution is very scattered, except in eastern Europe. This woodpecker lives in deciduous forests much more than its relatives. In the Alps it is found mainly on the slopes above Lake Geneva. There it haunts the leafy woods that have been allowed to grow freely, and, since very few such woods remain, the task of finding it is made all the easier. And there it lives in apparent harmony with the great spotted woodpecker. On the other hand, starlings sometimes drive the middle spotted woodpeckers from their nest holes.

I have observed this woodpecker in dense woods in

Sheathed cotton sedge (Eriophorum vaginatum) *and pines in a bog in Murnauer Moos, a nature reserve in the Bavarian Alps. (Gerhard Klammet)*

Sweden, Poland, France, Switzerland, and everywhere its habitats have a common denominator: old, somewhat neglected deciduous woods where dead branches are allowed to remain on the trees. Such woods provide an abundance of insects, both in rotting trunks and in the treetops. In Central Europe the beech usually dominates such woods. The woodpecker does not confine itself to large deciduous woods, but may nest in a well cultivated park, a garden, or a coppice where cattle graze.

Two of Europe's most beautiful woodpeckers, the green woodpecker and the gray-headed woodpecker *(Picus canus),* are common in some parts of the Alps. The green woodpecker lives in deciduous and mixed woods, particularly those with beech stands, in parks and gardens, and on wooded mountain slopes. In other words, Switzerland provides an infinite variety of habitats. The green woodpecker lives even in the mountains, ascending still higher than its gray-headed relative. It has been said that these two woodpeckers are hostile to each other when they live in the same neighborhood, and that the green woodpecker drives away its relative. In many regions of Central Europe, however, the two species tolerate each other, and this seems to be so in the Alps, too. Although the two species are closely related and have very similar habits, it is the ecological differences in these species that seem to make it possible for them to share the same wood.

A characteristic song heard in the woods of the Alps is that of Bonelli's warbler *(Phylloscopus bonelli).* It loves sunny slopes, and its quickly uttered song is usually heard from the fringes of woods and groves. It also inhabits bushes and is at home in pines and larches, perhaps because they, too, thrive in the sun. It may be found as high up in the mountains as 6600 feet.

NATIONAL PARKS

Not all the national parks in the Alps are worthy of the name, for in some of them much timber is cut. This is true, for example, of the Parc National du Pelvoux (about 8500 acres) in the French Alps, established in 1914 and thus the oldest national park in France. The most valuable animal there is the chamois. In spite of its name, this reserve is not a true national park, but in 1963 France established a strictly regulated nature reserve in the Alps—the Parc National de la Vanoise in Savoie.

Parco Nazionale del Gran Paradiso (about 245 square miles) in northwestern Italy is Europe's most alpine park. It is in the neighborhood of Mont Blanc and Monte Rosa, and it includes the majestic Gran Paradiso. This park has been of great importance as a reserve, for it was in this region, between the

Left above: Two young golden eagles nest on a ledge at Ayer in Zinal, Valais, Switzerland. Left: The sweet song and call notes of the snow finch contrast with the bare mountaintop where it makes its home. (Both by R. P. Bille)

Above: In some high areas of the Alps the vegetation belt is made up of bilberries, bogwortleberries, alpine rhododendrons, junipers and solitary stone pines. (R.P.Bille)
Left: Bird's-eye primroses (Primula minima) flowering on a lichen heath in the northern Tyrolean Alps. (Wilhelm Schacht)

Aosta Valley in the north and the Orco Valley in the south, that the last ibexes in the Alps dwelt. This remnant was saved from extermination only at the last moment.

The history of the ibex in the Alps is a dramatic one. During the sixteenth century it was distributed throughout the region, but three hundred years later only about sixty specimens remained, all of these in the Gran Paradiso range. In 1856 this region was proclaimed a royal hunting ground by Victor Emmanuel II, which in effect meant that the ibex was strictly protected, and in 1922 it became a national park. The ibex increased in number and spread from Gran Paradiso to the surrounding mountains, including the French side of the border. By 1938 about three thousand specimens were estimated to be living there. Then came World War II, and the ibex was hunted wantonly until in 1945 only 419 remained. But by 1954 the quantity had risen again to 2670 specimens.

The protection and consequent increase of the ibex in the Gran Paradiso made it possible to trap many animals and transport them to regions where the ibex had become extinct. Italian ibexes were taken to the mountains of Switzerland, Austria and Germany, and even as far away as the Carpathians. Thus a national park in one country can, by protecting animals, be of great benefit to many other countries.

Switzerland has only one national park, a genuine alpine region of 64 square miles, with mountains varying in height between about 5000 and 12,300 feet. Its original purpose, in 1914, to provide the alpine ibex with a sanctuary, has since been realized. The most important game animal of the national park is the chamois. About twelve hundred live there and the population is quite stable—in perfect equilibrium

An immature golden eagle with its victim, a hare; it will have difficulty bearing aloft so large a prey. (R. P. Bille)

with its environment. There is also a large population of red deer in the park. This species has increased rapidly in number, for all the predators that might have helped to keep down the number of deer have been exterminated. Furthermore, the administrators of the national park have, until recently, strictly forbidden the shooting of red deer, so that their present quantity does not reflect what the environment genuinely can support. This lack of realistic action is very risky, and the consequences of the unrestricted increase in the number of red deer (in spite of migration to surrounding country, where they are hunted) are that their grazing makes the forest meadows bare, at the expense of other grass-eating species, and prevents the regrowth of woods. The only factor that has caused a reduction of their numbers has been a series of severe winters with much snow and a shortage of food. The new decision to reduce them by hunting will only be enforced in winter, when most of the deer are beyond the boundaries of the national park.

The vegetation is also influenced by the dryness of the climate in the Swiss national park. As a result, the flora is rather poor in species, the woods grow slowly, and the fauna, with the exception of red deer, marmots, field voles, and an incredible number of ring ouzels, is astonishingly poor. When I was there one spring, I saw a beautiful golden eagle nesting on a ledge, and a wall creeper's charming coloration—ash-gray and wine red—but in some areas we walked for miles without seeing or hearing a single bird. Practically the only sign of life we saw were some Italians with their small pack-horses or mules, making their way along the ancient Roman track through the Livigno Valley, leading from Italy to Il Fuorn on the Swiss side, where, about thirteen miles from their village, they did their shopping. It was nearer to Il Fuorn than to the nearest Italian village! Only in Lapland have I found such trackless isolation in Europe.

The finest and most interesting parts of the Swiss national park are the high alpine regions, where the ibex, chamois, rock partridge, alpine swift, alpine chough and snow finches live.

Austria and Germany have several nature reserves in the Alps. The most valuable are those at Hohe Tauern and Gross Glockner. Austrian nature organizations have long been working to get these two reserves combined into a national park. One of the largest virgin forests of the Alps is situated in lower Austria, where an area is carrying mixed woods of beech and spruce *(Picea abies)* and silver fir *(Abies alba)*. This area is now partly protected by a reserve.

MARMOT, CHAMOIS AND IBEX

Three mammals are usually associated with alpine meadows above the tree limit and with the rocky country higher up: they are the alpine marmot, the chamois, and the ibex.

The alpine marmot is a large rodent, attaining a length of two feet or so. It is related to the bobak marmot of the steppe and the woodchuck *(Marmota monax)* of North America. Each of these species has become adapted to an entirely different environment, but their way of life has many features in common. Alpine marmots live on the open meadows which begin in the higher reaches of the conifer forests and continue up beyond the tree limit to the boulder fields and eternal snow. They live in colonies and are diurnal ani-

Ibex in their habitat in the highest Alpine zone. Once almost exterminated, ibex herds have now been restored in many parts of the Alps. (R. P. Bille)

mals, so it is easy to study their habits. Since they are very timid, it is best to observe them through field glasses. They spend the day eating grass and flowers, sitting upright on their hindlegs and holding food between their forepaws, or, preening their fur, playing and sunbathing. As soon as one of the animals scents danger it whistles shrilly, and all the marmots rush to take cover in holes or behind stones. If they are not in immediate danger the whole flock may sit upright to see what is wrong. They spend the winter, that is, six to eight months a year, hibernating in a comatose state with reduced temperature and metabolism. Their burrows may be ten feet deep and are reached by a passage up to thirty feet long.

The most frequently observed of larger animals is the chamois. A remarkably sure-footed climber, it can jump over crevices sixteen to twenty feet wide and land with incredible precision on a rocky surface no larger than a dinner-plate. It can bound up the face of a steep mountain slope as if the law of gravity were no longer in force, and it seems able to find a foothold in the tiniest crack in a mountain wall.

The great amounts of snow and the severe cold of winter drive the chamois down to conifer woods, where it takes the place of the red deer and roe deer, which in turn move down to the deciduous woods and the bottoms of the valleys. Winter in the Alps is often a difficult time for all these ungulates, and deathtraps in the form of avalanches, hunger and bad weather are in some years the order of the day. This is one of the ways that the populations of animals are kept at a level where they can be supported by the nutritional capacity of the habitat.

Birds which prefer higher altitudes dwell in the upper conifer belt. The citril finch *(Carduelis citrinella)* is found in the conifer woods, and becomes more numerous higher up in the mountains, where lone spruces or larches are scattered over the open country. At Zermatt in Valais, near the border of Italy, the bird is found up to a height of about 7200 feet. From the aspect of distribution range, the citril finch is one of the rarest birds in the world. In addition to the Alps and their neighborhood, it is found only in the northern parts of the Iberian peninsula and in Corsica and Sardinia. The reason for this limited distribution is not known.

Below the snow fields rock pipits *(Anthus spinoletta)* run

165

quickly over the alpine heaths hunting insects to feed their young. Their simple grass nests are hidden in crevices. This curious bird is an alpine species in the highest mountain ranges of southern and Central Europe, and a coast bird in northern Europe and the British Isles. It is found in the Alps, from the naked, damp land just below the snow down to alpine meadows where rhododendrons grow, while the meadow pipit, which lives in similar habitats in northern Europe, is found on marshes and fens in the Alps.

The blue rock thrush *(Monticola solitarius)* and the rock thrush *(M. saxatilis)* are two of the loveliest birds in the Alps. The former is a beautiful blue and the latter terracotta, blue, and white. Both live on slopes above the tree limit and remain much on the ground. They are difficult to detect, but in spring they sing or call quite frequently, which makes it fairly easy to discover the males.

In much the same kind of stony country lives the alpine accentor. Its song is confusingly similar to that of the skylark. The stone partridge is found there, too, for it is much attracted to dwarf pines and land overgrown with junipers. It nests high up among rocks under the flowers of the edelweiss but moves down to the woods in winter.

The snow finch is the ground bird that goes highest up the mountains. It flies quickly on flashing white wings in small flocks over deserts of stone and fields of snow. In Europe it is found only in the Pyrenees, the Alps, the Apennines, the Balkan mountains, and the Caucasus.

High above alpine valleys and slopes, choughs and alpine choughs fly to and fro, fetching food from lower altitudes to feed their hungry offspring. Flowering plants grow above 13,000 feet. The golden eagle circles with its magnificent wings around the summits and ridges of the mountains, and from the same summits alpine swifts dive to hunt the plankton of the air, and return to their young in nests high up in a crevice in the rocks, their beaks full of food.

Vegetation around the peaks of Wornerspitze and Tiefkar in the Karwendel Alps. In the foreground are mixed woods; beyond them conifer forests climb the slopes and form a timberline. (Toni Schneiders: Coleman and Hayward)

167

Beaches,
Dunes
and Fjords

The Atlantic Coast

12

The Atlantic coast of Europe extends for about 3500 miles—not counting innumerable bays and fjords—from the subtropical belt through temperate regions to the arctic zone. The climates of these regions are greatly influenced by the proximity of the ocean.

The sea is the most important climatic factor not only along the coast but over great parts of the interior of Europe. No other continent is, in fact, so much affected by maritime conditions as Europe. West winds prevail north of the Pyrenees and the Alps, so that low pressure systems often move from the Atlantic across Europe. Since most of the high mountain ranges run from west to east (with the exception of the Scandinavian range) they do not act as climatic boundaries for Atlantic winds.

Perhaps the most unexpected influence is that whereby the Gulf Stream, warmed up in the far-away Caribbean Sea, moves in a northeasterly curve thousands of miles across the North Atlantic to exert a decisive effect on the climate of western Europe. A comparison of conditions on both sides of the North Atlantic can quickly demonstrate the influence of the Gulf Stream on the climate of Europe. At the end of May and the beginning of June great fields of snow still remain in the woods and muskegs of eastern Canada in spite of the fact that Newfoundland and Nova Scotia are in the same latitudes as large parts of France. Hudson Bay, which is south of the Arctic Circle and is centered on the same latitude as Stockholm, is full of ice as late as midsummer. Yet the whole of the west coast of Europe, even far north of the Arctic Circle, is free from ice all the year round. In summer the effect of the Gulf Stream is felt as far northward as the European Arctic Ocean, and keeps vast expanses of water free from ice. The southern limit of the pack ice north of Norway is at Björnöya, 75° N; to the east, in Russia, it is at the mainland coast, 68—69° N, whereas in Davis Strait between Canada and Greenland it is at 61—65° N.

The chief features of the Atlantic type of climate in Europe are mild winters and cool summers; these prevail along the whole of the European coast. Compared with eastern Europe, which has a continental climate, the coastal regions are generally considered fortunate, although many people think there

is too much rain there. Annual differences between maximum and minimum temperatures in the coastal regions and western parts of Europe are much smaller than in eastern Europe, and become greater the farther east one goes.

Although the entire European coast is characterized as maritime, the vegetation range from the sunny coasts of Spain and Portugal, with their evergreen bushes and trees, to the tundra of northern Norway is a very wide one. Besides this, natural conditions tend to vary most where sea and land meet. No two coasts are alike and the sea is continually reshaping the land. Sometimes the sea is smooth, or only a swell rolls toward land; at other times the waves break violently against the coast. In addition to winds, there are the tides. These are a well known phenomenon, but the fact that they impinge on the coasts of Europe in various ways, depending on the topography of the sea beds, is not so well known. In some places the tide is measured in inches; in others, in feet and yards. Ebb and flood also vary as a result of the changing positions of sun, earth and moon. This greatly affects beach organisms, compelling plants and animals to adapt to a zone that keeps changing from sea to land and back again. The rhythm of the tides and the upper limit of waves determine the way of life of many creatures.

The coast that has been shaped by these forces ranges from stony shores and cliffs, flat beaches and beach meadows, and marshes and dunes, to fjords. At the mouths of some large rivers great deltas have been formed. In the south the coast is mainly even and smooth; in the north it is broken by fjords and archipelagos. The waves are the sculptors; the bedrock provides the material they shape. The work is still going on as it has been for thousands of years.

As a natural environment, the coast provides an infinite variety of habitats. Much of this has, however, been destroyed; the beaches and cliffs washed by the waves are relatively untouched, but man has left his mark a little higher up. It is only natural that the sea and coast should always have seemed an attractive area for people to live in. The climate, providing winter grazing, also surely helped to attract livestock farming to this area long ago. It has been claimed that the vast coastal heath, made up mostly of *Calluna vulgaris,* was the basis of an early western civilization, and was possibly more important than any other form of cultivation outside the Mediterranean region. In this way the coast of Europe long ago became farmland but remained natural. Only in the past hundred years has man invaded this region with towns, harbors, industrial plants and recreation centers, and in a comparatively short time has destroyed most of its natural aspects. Many plants and animals have adapted themselves to this development, and the play of light over sea and coast remains unchanged, but the beauty and harmony of the landscape has necessarily suffered.

THE COAST OF PORTUGAL

The largest part of Portugal's coast is in the Mediterranean vegetation and climate zone. Thus, from Algarve in the south to Minho in the north, the shore is similar to that of the

Sedimentary rocks on the Portuguese coast at Portimao show the effects of the ocean's erosive action. (Julius Behnke)

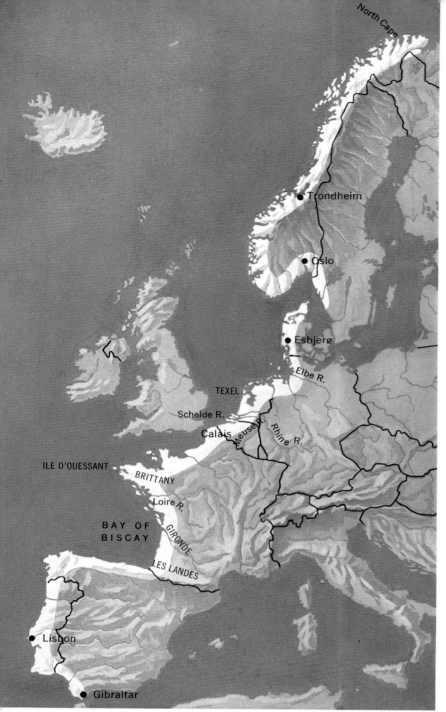

Europe's Atlantic coast extends from the subtropical belt through temperate regions to the arctic. From south to north the shore varies from sand beaches and rocky coasts to archipelagos and deep fjords.

troduction of exotic trees, shrubs and plants. Furthermore, the humid winds from the Atlantic have caused the native vegetation to grow more luxuriantly on the coastal mountains than does vegetation along the Mediterranean. This has to some extent prevented erosion; but, where the slopes of the Estremadura Mountains face the sea, sheep and goats have destroyed the vegetation and left the soil at the mercy of the elements. The interior of Portugal has suffered the same fate.

The most fascinating natural region of the Iberian peninsula, extending to the Atlantic in mighty sand dunes around the Guadalquivir River in Spain, has already been described in Chapter 3. This stretch, along the Gulf of Cadiz, is the most southerly part of the Atlantic coast of Europe. It begins as flat land along the Playa Castilla in Spain, but becomes highland on the Algarve coast of Portugal, where hills and sea meet to form magnificent scenery. The coastal mountains of Algarve display the most luxuriant vegetation along the Atlantic coast of the Iberian peninsula, with flowers hanging in clusters from crevices, and vegetation growing in every dell and ravine. Where fishing villages have occupied the cliffs, the soil has been scorched by the sun, and growth has of course ceased. But such villages have changed little since Phoenician times and the beaches between towns and villages still retain much of their original character.

Besides the eternal movement of the sea, a few birds give life to the beaches. Only a few species nest there, however, for most of the birds prefer to live in meadows, marshes, or rocky coastal country, where they can find suitable nesting sites as well as food. Thus very few birds are found on the sandy strips of coast. Occasionally a herring gull patrols the beaches, a common tern *(Sterna hirundo)* flies by, or a Kentish plover lays its eggs in the sand. The little tern flies playfully in the air, now and again searching the shallow water for small organisms. When it catches sight of prey, it dives into the water, sometimes keeping its beak closed in order to spear its quarry. Along the edge of gently sloping beaches or in small pools left by the tide oystercatchers and redshanks, avocets and black-winged stilts congregate. Pratincoles, Audouin's gull, and the gull-billed tern are among the other rare birds seen there.

The guillemot *(Uria aalge)* breeds on a rocky coast in central Portugal, the most southerly breeding site in the world for this species. The handsome shag *(Phalacrocorax aristotelis),* which sports an erect crest during its breeding season, also lives on the rocky coasts.

THE FRENCH COAST

Extending from the Cordillera Cantabrica in Spain north to Brittany is the great Bay of Biscay. Exposed to the full force of Atlantic waves, the bay is famous for its tidal currents and frequent storms. Practically the whole of the French coast from the Pyrenees to Brittany consists of flat beaches, over which the tide flows in great sweeps, exposing, at ebb, immense mudflats that stretch for miles out to sea.

Tides are a factor that vitally affect the fauna living within the area of ebb and flood. Many small marine animals do not move out with the ebb but simply burrow into the mud to await the next flood. This rich fauna thus becomes periodically more accessible to animals. In this way tides are of great significance to such birds as crows, waders and gulls.

Riviera. Most of the Portuguese coast is lowland declining gently toward the sea. The flatness of the beaches is occasionally interrupted by cliffs, particularly at Algarve, Minho, and around Lisbon, where the mountains extend down to the sea.

The vegetation on the sandy beaches is of a macchia type, with various shrubs and a few scattered trees. One of the colors most frequently seen along this coast is the evergreen of cypresses and junipers. In some places, principally in Alentejo, widespread woods of cork oak grow close to the sea. These trees are now cultivated by man and provide raw material for a large industry. Elsewhere the slopes are covered with olive trees. The landscape is thus very Mediterranean in appearance, but with one important difference—it remains more natural and has fortunately not been transformed by the in-

Tidal beaches are exploited by terrestrial as well as marine animals, but during ebb and flood it is chiefly marine animals such as mussels, mollusks, crustaceans and worms that remain there. Some mollusks, for instance the tiny *Hydrobia,* are present in immense numbers, investigators having counted as many as 5000 per square foot. It is easy to understand the importance of such concentrations to some birds.

The small marine animals in the tidal zone are distributed vertically from the surface downward into the deeper layers. Long-beaked waders can thus capture species that their short-beaked relatives cannot reach; this reduces competition between the various birds on the beaches during the migration period.

One of the most remarkable coastal regions of Europe is Les Landes, the almost straight beach of the Bay of Biscay that extends from the Pyrenees to the Gironde. A vast expanse of flat sand, covered partly with pines and rolling dunes, it has been built up by sand brought down by the River Garonne from the Pyrenees, Massif Central and the Cevennes. Some of the lagoons, isolated from the sea by the dunes, are periodically the haunt of many aquatic birds. On this wetland and on meadows farther inland live wild boars, red-legged partridges, Montagu's harriers, short-toed larks, little bustards and stone curlews.

WADERS AND GULLS

Throughout the year, waders and gulls, usually migrating or wintering birds, forage along the beaches of Les Landes, resting on the mudflats at ebb tide, or above high water level at flood tide. From March to June many waders on their way from their winter quarters to breeding grounds in northern Europe and Asia stay here for a while. By June the southward migration has begun, and continues until December. The avocet does not breed there, but is a winter visitor. It is at home on gently shoaling beaches, where sandbanks, small lagoons beyond high water level, muddy pools and waterlogged ground suit its habits perfectly.

Among arctic waders wintering at Les Landes are the gray plover *(Charadrius squatarola),* bar-tailed godwit *(Limosa lapponica),* knot *(Calidris canutus),* and the sanderling *(Crocethia alba).*

The sanderling in particular is a bird of the ocean waves. This small wader is scarcely larger than the larks that haunt the dunes, but it can take better advantage than many other waders of the minute animal life washed ashore. When a wave retreats, the sanderling hurries after it, driving its bill rapidly into the sand to pick up small crustaceans, mostly amphipods, before the next wave rolls in. It sticks its bill down into the sand so deeply that it may leave rows of small holes that disappear only after several waves have washed over them.

When sanderlings forage in flocks, the nature of their movements backward and forward in time with the waves assumes the visual patterns of a quaint ballet. It is a contest between giants and dwarfs, in which the latter just avoid being crushed. Every time the giants retreat the dwarfs pursue them; sometimes, when the sanderlings are caught by the waves they run and swim as best they can, bobbing up and down in the breakers like corks. Fortunately they can fly straight up from the water, and this often saves their lives. This curious pur-

suit of food, which seems to require so much energy, goes on for long periods.

Among the many waders resting at Les Landes, old male gray plovers are the aristocrats—stately birds flying on powerful wings just above the water. Bar-tailed godwits, knots, and the curlew sandpiper *(Calidris ferruginea)* with its copper-red breast, have much beauty; but a male gray plover's black, gray and white coloring is by far the most elegant. There is no doubt, too, which of these waders has the most appealing song. The gray plover's characteristic triad cannot surpass the whistle of such a master as the curlew, but it is very impressive. The melancholy, long-drawn-out note conjures up the desolate arctic tundra where this species nests and breeds.

No other European river has an estuary comparable to that of the Garonne. The Gironde, a wide, deep arm of the sea, penetrates far inland, separating Les Landes and Medoc from the coast to the north. This vast, funnel-like estuary receives not only the water of the river Garonne, but also that of the Dordogne.

From Gironde northward to the estuary of the Loire, the coast differs from that of Les Landes. The beaches are still flat, but are interrupted here and there by rocky promontories and islands. Long tongues of land as well as sand reefs have been created by marine currents depositing material transported by the rivers. The result is a coastal configuration entirely different from the almost perfectly straight coastline of Les Landes. In coastal regions both north and south of the Loire are numerous large and small marshes which are rich in food. The shallow bays and inlets from Gironde to Brittany also contain a great variety of plant and animal life. These regions are among the most interesting in Europe. Unfortunately, many shallow bays, lakes and marshes have been deliberately drained: there cannot be many coastal regions in Europe that have been changed by man as much as this one.

The costly and extensive drainage projects have not always accomplished their purpose; indeed, many have been total

A little tern at its nest on the beach. The chick is only about an hour old and its down has just dried. (S. C. Porter: Coleman and Hayward)

economic failures. Instead of providing the productive agricultural land anticipated, they have resulted in only a few poor pastures and large, almost useless areas. Vendée in particular has suffered gravely. Although great areas were drained there, after only a few years all cultivation ceased. This was because it was found to be unprofitable, with the result that in some parts no attempt whatever was made to cultivate the land. Such elimination and subsequent abandonment of nature's resources still continue. When the great Marais Vernier was drained, it was predicted that the region would be transformed into a granary, a "Ukraine in Normandy," but nothing worthwhile came of it. Marais Vernier was much more productive in its original state than after it was drained and plowed.

France is by no means the only country where the mania for draining has run rife. During the past 150 years many of Europe's bogs, marshes and lakes have disappeared—and with them the subsoil water in surrounding areas. Not until comparatively recently have people begun to understand that there is much in marshes that is valuable from the aspects of productivity, recreation and science.

The little that remains of the more or less natural marshland along the coast of France, south and north of the Loire, represents fragments of ancient Europe. The same is true of a few shallow salt-water regions such as Baie de l'Aiguillon in Vendée. This part of the French Atlantic coast, with wide mudflats covering an area of about 4500 acres, is one of the most important feeding grounds in Europe for migrating birds. Thousands of waders rest there. In spite of all the previous failures of such projects, it is now planned to isolate Baie de l'Aiguillon from the sea, in order to transform it into a series of freshwater ponds. This will cost vast sums of money, and it is difficult to understand what good will be accomplished by it.

The lower reaches of the Loire are surrounded by meadows, mires, marshes and lakes. One of these lakes, Lac de Grand Lieu, is among the largest in France, with an area of about 22,240 acres (measured in winter when the water level is highest). In the southwest this lake merges into marshland, which becomes a large marshy region at Machecoul, and gradually changes into a very shallow marine bay, Baie de Bourgneuf: the whole forms an interesting and varied series of aquatic regions and transitional zones. The open water of the lake is surrounded by a dense border of reed grass, where bitterns and little bitterns can be heard. In winter Grand Lieu is visited by Bewick's and whooper swans, graylag geese, teal, mallard, pochards, tufted ducks and great crested grebes. A large number of mallard, shovelers, garganeys, black-headed gulls, black terns and other birds breed there in summer.

Water lily leaves float close together on the patches of water, together with water plaintains (Alisma), a quillwort (Isoëtes echinospora) and water lobelia (Lobelia dortmanna). The last two species of aquatic plants may have spread to Grand Lieu with the help of birds. In the western part of Grand Lieu, before the lake becomes marshland, floating islands of reed grass, tree roots and other rotting vegetable matter are sometimes found. On these live Cetti's warblers, whose northern limit about 1955 was the Grand Lieu. Since then it has spread northward to the estuary of the Seine River. Sallows, dwarf willows, and other trees in and around Grand Lieu provide nesting places for a variety of herons, including purple herons, little egrets and night herons. These form one of the largest colonies of herons in France.

HERONS

The adult heron is one of Europe's most decorative birds. The young look just like small dragons, while the adults have many features usually associated with the flying reptiles of the Mesozoic era. When one has seen the bird, its spearlike feathers hanging down from around its gullet, stand motionless for hours with only its yellow eyes showing any sign of life, it is easy to imagine that it possesses cold reptilian blood. In flight it seems even more primeval. When the heron flies over with slow, stiff wingbeats, its head drawn back between its shoulders, its long black crest pressed backward like a comb, little imagination is needed to see in it a small version of a *Pteranodon,* a gigantic flying lizard that lived during the Cretaceous period and had a wing span of more than twenty-five feet.

The heron is an expert fisher. It looks for shallow water, preferably clear in which it usually stands with its head sunk between its shoulders. It sometimes fishes by wading slowly and soundlessly in the water near the shore, its neck always erect. Now and again it stands motionless, and then moves on. Occasionally its beak darts down into the water, a little fish is caught, and a faint splash followed by ripples are the only evidence of what has happened. With a little jerk, the heron turns the fish head-first in its beak and quickly swallows it; but if the fish is a large one, the heron must strike it time after time until its quarry is dead. It can also fish in the dark.

When herons hunt in water plentiful with vegetation, they are generally looking for frogs and water voles. They also hunt field voles. In Sweden a heron was seen flying to its nest with a leveret about eight inches long; and in England shrews, moles and field voles have been observed to be among its prey. Herons take small ducklings if they come within reach, but do not seem actively to hunt them. A report from England of a heron that caught a swallow as it flew past gives evidence of the incredible speed with which it can use its beak.

When a heron catches a terrestrial animal, it always rinses it in water before eating it; the reason for this is still unknown. All food is swallowed whole, which contradicts the common contention that herons prey on fully grown ducks and large young ones. Voles taken by herons are small, young ones.

Judging by the fish one sometimes finds on the ground around heron colonies, their prey consists chiefly of perch and roach, although tench, crucian carp, bleak, bream, pike and eels are also caught. Among marine fish are cod, several species of flatfish and the viviparous blenny. The size of the prey depends of course on the heron's swallowing capacity. Other small creatures, aquatic insects, larvae, snails, mussels, small crustaceans and crabs also form part of the bird's bill of fare. Balls of indigestible matter are disgorged. Studies of the heron's food in six habitats in England reveal that the fish that herons take depends on which species of fish are living in the various lakes. In two cases roach headed the list of prey; in two others, sticklebacks; in one habitat, bleak; and in another, eels.

Some coastal mountains at Algarve in Spain are luxuriant but others, such as those above, have been skeletonized by sun, wind, rains and the grazing of goats. (Julius Behnke)

The transitional zone between Lac de Grand Lieu and the wetlands to the west, Marais de Machecoul, is a mixture of marsh, arable land, and pastures. In spring, autumn and winter these are partly flooded; in summer they dry up. Tamarisk bushes, inhabited by singing bluethroats and other birds, are the only tall plants, except for trees around the farms. In spring, redshanks and lapwings can be heard both day and night from the wet meadows. Three waders have an isolated occurrence in the Vendée: the black-tailed godwit, which makes its most southerly appearance there; the black-winged stilt which makes the Vendée its most northerly permanent habitat in western Europe; and the avocet, which occurs only at that point along the French Atlantic coast. Waders and ducks are very numerous in the Machecoul marshes in autumn and winter, and snipe winter there in great numbers. Short-eared owls and hen harriers find good hunting in the area and remain there throughout the year.

Many of the birds—both ducks and waders—wintering in the marshes are found in Baie de Bourgneuf, where the shoaling beaches, exposed to the tides, provide a fertile supply of food.

North of the Loire, in a depression near the coast called Brière, is a region of fens and marshes which comprises about 17,300 acres. Brière is a relic of prehistoric Europe, for little of it has changed in thousands of years. A large part of the area ought to be made into a strict nature reserve. There, I have heard the jubilant song of the curlew, an uncommon sound in southwestern Europe. Vipers, too, are common on the bogs, where they sunbathe on tussocks surrounded by water.

THE COAST OF BRITTANY

The French coast changes as one moves north. Around the River Vilaine, north of the bogs in Brière, are wetlands of another kind. Beyond that, in the province of Brittany, the coast bends northwest. One of the most interesting areas on this coast is the Gulf of Morbihan. Like a large lagoon, it embraces many islands, and, although it is separated from the sea by two peninsulas, a waterway between these peninsulas connects it to the ocean. As the tides enter and leave the Gulf of Morbihan, they provide a magnificent aquatic spectacle. A network of channels causes the mud to retain water even at ebb, and numerous birds flock there for food. The gulf branches out into several narrow inlets that run for miles inland, and these are surrounded by salines, salt marshes and ponds. One of the most interesting of these inlets from the aspect of ornithology is Noyalo-Séné. Part of it has been isolated from the sea and tides by a causeway and it is developing a flora and fauna different from that of the rest of the region. More and more species of birds are finding their way to this part of Noyalo-Séné; cut off from the ebb and flow, it provides them with safe nesting sites with nearly constant water level, while the tide gives them food. An even more interesting part of the Gulf of Morbihan is the Baie de Sarzeau, where vast areas are covered by enormous beds of the small-leaved sea grass *Zostera nana,* which during the winter attracts thousands of brant geese *(Branta bernicla)* and thirty to forty thousand widgeons and pintails.

The coast of southern Brittany slopes gently toward the sea. Shore, meadows and flat sandy beaches are predominant here, but farther to the west the terrain becomes more rocky. In northern Brittany, as in Normandy, the cliffs along the coast act as enormous breakwaters. Nowhere is the meeting of land and sea so dramatic as along that coast, where the cliffs make a sheer descent into the sea. It would seem that animals living in such a vicinity, with the intemperate lash of waves ever present, would have a difficult fight for survival. But marine mammals and birds are able to solve such problems easily, some of the invertebrates attaching themselves to the substratum, while mollusks and mussels cling to the submarine cliffs or congregate in fissures.

The rocky coast of Brittany and Normandy attracts many marine birds, though it is isolated from their normal distribution range: for example the rock pipit, which is normally found in the Atlantic coast regions of the British Isles and by Scandinavian waters. Auks, such as the puffin *(Fratercula arctica),* razorbill *(Alca torda),* and guillemot, are all represented on this coast. The first two of these birds, as well as the gannet *(Sula bassana),* arctic tern *(Sterna paradisaea),* kittiwake *(Rissa tridactyla),* lesser black-backed gull *(Larus fuscus),* and great black-backed gull *(L. marinus)* have their most southerly breeding grounds here. Other marine birds that have an isolated occurrence on this rocky French coast are the Sandwich tern *(Sterna sandvicensis),* cormorant, and shag.

That all these birds should also be found along the Atlantic coasts of the British Isles is perhaps linked with the fact that those areas may be regarded as a natural continuation of the rocky coast of Normandy and Brittany.

THE PUFFINS OF THE SEPT-ILES

Off the west and north coasts of Brittany are a number of wind-swept islands, where low vegetation of grass, scentless mayweed, and sparse ferns in fissures provide nesting sites for many marine birds. The most important of these are Ile d'Ouessant, the westernmost outlier of France, and the group of islands called Sept-Iles. Most of the marine birds that are found in isolation in Brittany and Normandy breed there. Sept-Iles has been made into a nature reserve, primarily to protect its puffins. Its appearance alone sets the puffin's distinct individuality apart from other birds. It is a Scaramouch, with a white mask and comical gestures; moreover, it changes its nose periodically, its bill varying in size and color in the course of the year. In summer, its bill is its most colorful, and is then almost as high as it is long—a veritable caricature. To many people this bill looks like a parrot's, and in many countries the bird is in fact called a "sea parrot."

On Sept-Iles, as around the coasts of the British Isles and on bird mountains on the Atlantic coast, the puffin digs tunnels in grassy slopes. There it lays its single egg. It does not become sexually mature until it is several years old, and even then its rate of reproduction is not high. On the other hand it probably attains a considerable age.

The puffin lives on fish and mollusks and other marine organisms. It hunts out at sea, far from the breeding site, and returns with five, six, or more small fish, usually sand eels *(Ammodytidae),* held between the tongue and the lower mandible, and facing alternately left and right. In this way the bird can continue fishing until its beak is full.

The Sept-Iles is the southernmost limit of another remark-

Cascades of flowers on the Spanish coast south of Cadiz. (François Edmond-Blanc)

able marine bird, the gannet. In a short while it has increased from two pairs to a colony of fourteen hundred pairs. With a wing span of about six feet, it is one of the most beautiful sea birds. Diving for fish, gannets are an unforgettable sight; they dive from great heights, their wings folded, shooting like torpedoes into shoals of fish.

Storm petrels *(Hydrobates pelagicus),* kittiwakes and peregrines also breed on the Sept-Iles.

The rocky coasts of Brittany become lower above sea level in Normandy, and in the Gulf of St. Malo the beaches are flat. The whole of the Seine Bay is surrounded by low sandy beaches and tidal bogs. Most of the French coast as far as Flanders is of the same nature, but at Caux, north of the Seine, is a chalk plateau which, from a height of some three hundred feet, dips steeply down to the sea. This is the French counterpart of the famous white cliffs of Dover.

BELGIUM AND THE NETHERLANDS: A COAST BELOW SEA LEVEL

The flat coast of Flanders faces the North Sea, but it is dominated as much by tides as are the French beaches facing the Atlantic Ocean. At ebb tide the muddy shores are often exposed for two miles out to sea.

The Belgian littoral from the French boundary in the south to the border of Holland in the north is fringed with towns, recreation areas, villas and roads. It is only in the south, between France and La Panne, and in the north, between Le Zoute and the Dutch boundary, that the population is sparse. The result is that nearly all of this sandy beach, about forty miles long, is almost devoid of animal life. But the sea is teeming with life, as can be observed at low tide. Mussels, worms and various tiny organisms are plentiful, and attract quantities of gulls. But even the herring gull, with its powerful beak, cannot break through a mussel shell, so it takes the shell high up in the air and breaks it by dropping it on the wet, firm sand. When the sand is dry and powdery, the shell can withstand the shock, and the bird keeps dropping it time after time, apparently unable to understand why it does not break.

On the beach one often finds egg capsules of the beautiful lesser-spotted dogfish *(Scylliorhinus caniculus),* the thornback ray *(Raja clavata),* the flapper-skate *(R. batis),* and starry ray *(R. radiata).* The hairless, lesser-spotted dogfish, which appear in shoals along the Atlantic coast, are always present off the coast of Belgium.

The region between Knokke—Le Zoute and the Dutch border is the finest natural country on the Belgian coast. It is called Zwin, and is now a reserve where ducks, avocets and other

175

Gannets, among the larger sea birds, breed in colonies. The southernmost colonies in Europe are found in Brittany and Normandy. (Charles Vaucher)

waders breed. The Mayor of Knokke—Le Zoute, Count Léon Lippens, an enthusiastic ornithologist, has created this bird sanctuary which also provides recreation for human visitors. In addition to harboring breeding birds, the Zwin nature reserve, which extends to the other side of the border, is a resting place twice a year for multitudes of waders from northern Europe and Asia. In winter innumerable geese and ducks find a safe retreat there, and it is the only place in the world where I have seen five species of geese at the same time: graylag geese, bean geese, white-fronted geese, barnacle geese, and brant geese.

The dunes on the Belgian coast vary in height, the highest being about one hundred feet high, and in width, from a few hundred yards in the north to 1—1$^{1}/_{2}$ miles in the south. Inland, beyond the dunes, are miles of low-lying, partly water-logged flat land, where semi-aquatic vegetation alternates with cultivated land and groves of trees, and is crisscrossed by straight dykes. These areas are so-called polders, peculiar to Belgium and Holland. They lie below the sea level and water is pumped out of them into surrounding canals and thence to the sea.

The River Schelde penetrates far into Belgium and can accommodate ocean-going vessels as far as Antwerp. Because the river is sometimes hidden from sight, it is always astonishing, when watching the teeming bird life on the meadows

in the estuary delta, suddenly to see a giant liner, apparently driving right through the flat land.

The tide here is not to be despised, particularly in the labyrinthine delta land. I learned this on my first visit to the Schelde delta. When the tide came in, the innumerable arms of the river filled up rapidly, banks and promontories were flooded a moment after we had passed, and our casual retreat soon became a flight for life. We were repeatedly trapped by the water, and it was as much as we could do to force our way through it. The tide rolled past us like a spring flood in the mountains.

The heather-covered moor known as La Campine Anversoise provides an unusual landscape—a relic of the coastal heath that once stretched along most of the Atlantic coast of Europe. These heaths on sandy soil are indirectly the work of man, created by grazing sheep ever since the Stone Age. As elsewhere, the heath pastures of the Campine, some of which still remain, took the place of winter fodder, and were preserved for thousands of years. The permanent pastures are periodically burned.

About one-third of Holland is below sea level, so that, were the dams to burst during violent storms, almost half the country would be flooded. It has a broader coastal region than any other country in Europe, and, having the nature of a vast brackish marsh, it would also be at the mercy of the tides were it not for the protecting ridge of sand dunes and the man-made sea-walls. The tides still rush freely through the estuaries of the Schelde, Meuse, and Rhine, and it was due to the sediment transported by these rivers, since the last glaciation, that the Netherlands came to be created.

Above this low-lying country is a sand plateau, 15 to 150 feet above sea level, composed of older fluvial and glacial deposits. Once covered with *Calluna* heaths and bogs, most of this land—which forms the eastern part of the country— is now cultivated or planted with trees. The great stretches of land below sea level have been transformed from marshes into arable terrain, yielding rich crops, and pastures that support great herds of cattle. Besides this, man has reclaimed considerable territory from the sea, increasing the area of the country by about one-fifth, or 2700 square miles.

This reclamation is still going on. The former great marine bay called the "Zuider Zee," for instance, was separated from the North Sea by the construction in 1932 of the Wierengen-Friesland Barrage, and transformed into a lake—the IJsselmeer. Geologically, this has in a sense restored an ancient lake, called Flevo by the Romans, from which the Zuider Zee evolved some 1500 years ago. Most of the bottom of the IJsselmeer has now been converted into flat land, so extensive and desolate that a wilderness bird like the dotterel has nested there. One cannot help admiring the energy of the Dutch. It is easy to understand their desire to acquire more land: their country is the most densely populated in the world, with 894 inhabitants to the square mile. Fortunately, the great changes that have been made have not had a wholly negative effect on natural habitats. The Dutch landscape, with its damp meadows, innumerable canals and polders, as well as shallow lakes, still provides suitable habitats for many water loving animals. Conditions become less favorable for them, however, as the technique of drainage becomes more effective, and especially as water on low-lying land is rapidly drained with the help of great pumping stations.

The still considerable areas of wetland in the coastal regions of Holland have their characteristic fauna. Birds are, of course, the first living creatures one sees on the meadows and polders, and, of the 180 species of birds, forty per cent are aquatic or semiaquatic.

TOURNAMENT OF THE RUFFS

In the meadows there are great numbers of lapwings and black-tailed godwits. On similar land along the coast, one can also see curlews, redshanks and ruffs.

The courting behavior of ruffs in the spring is fascinating. They behave like knights in a tournament, an effect which is emphasized by their having quite individual colors. They reveal their presence in the meadows by jumping above the surrounding grass; from immemorial use of the same areas flocks of males have worn away miniature arenas.

In courting, the birds advance toward each other with crests erect like battle helmets, and ruffs spread out like shields. Suddenly the posturing may cease, as if by command, and all the birds stand motionless; moments later the tournament begins again. Each male has its own place in the arena.

These antics are of course sexual in nature; a preliminary to mating. Now they flap their wings, rise like helicopters just above the ground, or with feathers on end and body bent forward run round and round, tilting at the air like so many small, feathered Don Quixotes. Occasionally, birds collide and for a moment pretense becomes reality and they fight in earnest. If a reeve should stray into the arena, the males, with wings half-open, crests erect and ruffs spread out, display their plumage and invite the reeve to choose her mate. Ruffs may remain in this courting attitude up to twenty minutes. The reeve trips among her suitors and, after much deliberation, chooses one of them; mating takes place at once, either in the arena or outside it.

Hundreds of thousands of aquatic birds come to Holland during their winter migration. Some of them remain; others continue on their way after resting in tidal zones, salty marshes, freshwater pools, fields and meadows. At Waddenzee in northern Holland, between the mainland and the Frisian Islands, it is not unusual to find up to 600,000 birds at the same time. Many geese winter there, including 30,000 to 40,000 white-fronted geese and 15,000 to 20,000 barnacle geese.

Two mammals are very common in Dutch marshes and polders: the brown rat *(Rattus norvegicus)*, and the vole-rat *(Arvicola terrestris)*. Both of these rodents have made themselves at home in water-logged ground. Another historically and ecologically interesting mammal is the root vole *(Microtus oeconomus arenicola)*, a late glacial relict that has become isolated in the Netherlands. It lives in a wide variety of environments, both wet and dry, but when it meets with competition from the common vole, it leaves the dry habitats and takes to marsh vegetation. It is also found in deltas flooded by tides; at high water it escapes drowning by taking refuge on floating plants.

Holland is one of the few countries that has reserves for frogs. Small sanctuaries have been established to protect species threatened with extinction by pollution of water and draining. At present these sanctuaries protect the tree frog, yellow-bellied toad *(Bombina variegata),* spade-foot toad, mid-

On the rocky coast of Brittany at Ile de Croiz, the cliffs, acting as breakwaters, are sculptured by the waves. (Klaus Eschen)

wife toad *(Alytes obstetricans),* palmate newt *(Triturus helveticus),* alpine newt *(T. alpestris),* and the spotted salamander *(Salamandra salamandra).*

One of Europe's finest marsh bird reserves is Naardermeer (1845 acres) near IJsselmeer. In spite of its northerly location, Naardermeer gives the impression of being almost as rich in plants and animals as lakes and deltas in southern Europe. Here there are colonies of spoonbills (about 300 pairs) and purple herons (about 150 pairs). The isolated occurrence of these two species in Holland may be related to their long association with this part of Europe; at one time, they had a wide European distribution.

Another rare bird in Naardermeer is the bearded tit. But it is the cormorants that predominate near this lake and in winter they are joined by thousands of ducks and coots.

Texel (seventy square miles) is the largest and most southerly of the eleven Frisian Islands which protect the coast of Holland from the North Sea. This chain is continued eastward in the East Frisian Islands in Germany, and the North Frisian Islands in Denmark. This girdle of islands is all that the sea has left of a former coastline. During postglacial times the level of the sea rose and repeatedly invaded the land. Texel consists of sand and mud and is fringed by beaches. Moving inland from the beach, we come first to dunes with marram grass, then *Calluna* heaths, grassy bushland with sea-buckthorn *(Hippophaë rhamnoides)*, brambles *(Rubus)*, elder *(Sambucus nigra)*, and creeping willow *(Salix repens)*, small reedy lakes surrounded by dunes, planted pine woods, plains grazed by sheep, and groves of deciduous trees, chiefly alder and maple.

The dune lakes are the most interesting environments of all, for they are the haunt of spoonbills, which nest in elder bushes, as well as herons, mallard and teal. Montagu's harriers and marsh harriers also breed in the vicinity.

Among the varied animal life on the beaches at Texel is the common seal *(Phoca vitulina)*, which sometimes creeps up onto the sand reefs. This seal is greatly in need of protection and the Dutch have thoughtfully provided several reserves for it. The three European species of sandpipers—ringed plover, little ringed plover, and Kentish plover—make rather different demands on a habitat, but at least two of them, and sometimes all three, at times share the same stretch of flats as a breeding ground. In such cases a rivalry arises between the species, for they are continually trespassing on each other's domain. Even when the territory is defended against the two related species, avocets and other waders are allowed to pass freely. The maintenance of territory boundaries probably also acts as a safeguard for keeping the ringed plover and the little ringed plover apart during the mating period—a practice made necessary by the close similarity of their display ceremonies preceding copulation.

THE MATING OF OYSTERCATCHERS

The black and white oystercatchers and avocets are to be seen everywhere; and the sound of oystercatchers, among the more garrulous birds on the beaches, can be heard on all sides. During the breeding season the oystercatchers search for food or rest, sitting on stones in the water. After a while they become more lively and begin to take an interest in each other. At times two of them, probably males, start fighting; but they soon tire, and then the two rivals may stand side by side preening their feathers.

The display behavior of oystercatchers is difficult to understand. Their postures and calls are always very similar, though the reaction of birds not taking part in the display varies greatly. For instance, long after the mating season one or more birds—including young ones—may be seen posturing exactly as if they were courting. The females, moreover, exhibit the same behavior as the males. It seems, perhaps, that when the oystercatcher's posturing is unrelated to sexuality it is indicative of general uneasiness, or restlessness.

When posturing, the oystercatcher humps up its shoulders, turns its neck stiffly downward, as if it were out of joint, and points its open bill groundward. Meanwhile, it utters a series of piping trills, at times so slowly that the notes seem to issue one at a time. At first the song is usually high, clear, and rapid, but it gradually decreases both in volume and pace, the hen sometimes giving voice to a long, sustained "cheiii." While singing, the oystercatcher runs forward in a stiff, crouching position, and when several birds perform this ceremony at once and in the same direction, the effect is very ludicrous.

THE NORTH SEA COASTS
OF GERMANY AND DENMARK

The German North Sea coast is, topographically, a continuation of the Dutch coast. Sand islands and beaches stretch along the coast to Esbjerg in Denmark. The Frisian Islands, lying like a gigantic string of beads along the coast, are the remains of an ancient barrier of dunes, and still protect the mainland from the North Sea. When storms rage in the North Sea, the water between the islands and the mainland may be almost as smooth as a lagoon.

The entire North Sea coast of Germany has shores of sand, either in the form of crescents in the wide bays or of straight beaches along flat-fronted coasts. This amazing quantity of sand is the result of forces that have been at work ever since the land rose from the sea. Materials deposited by the former icecap have been collected and stratified by the waves. Great rivers have, in addition, transported sediment from the interior and deposited it on the coast where it has been worn down and crushed by waves.

The waves not only break down and intermix the mineral sediment, but also move it laterally, depending on the direction of surface current and tides as well as of water flowing from the rivers. These aquatic motions constantly change the size and shape of sandy promontories, reefs and islands off the mainland. Above the high-water level on the beaches, where waves and spray have no effect, the wind sculptures the sand, forming mobile sand dunes stretching for miles along the coast. Buildings and other man-made structures have, however, robbed them of much of their former extent and beauty.

The characteristic plants of the sand dunes along the coast of the North Sea are sea lyme grass *(Elymus arenarius)* and

Left: Migrating dunlins rest on a sandy shore. These waders will find food in seaweed thrown up by the waves. (Arthur Christiansen) Right: In few places does nature display a broader spectrum of colors than along coasts where rocks, beaches and the sea are exposed to strong light. (Michel Terrasse)

Ruffs displaying. During the spring mating period, the plumage, bill and legs of each bird is differently colored, an almost unique characteristic in the bird world. (Arthur Christiansen)

marram grass *(Ammophila arenaria)*. It is astonishing that these graceful plants can colonize such an unstable environment as a sand dune. Both sea lyme grass and marram grass always keep their leaves above the sand, thanks to rootstocks that grow rapidly when covered with it.

The shelduck *(Tadorna tadorna)*, a colorful duck almost as large as a goose, is common on the sandy coasts. The North Sea coast environment satisfies its need for shallow water, generous supplies of mollusks of the genus *Hydrobia,* and sandbanks where it can make a hole for its nest. It keeps its eggs well hidden, which may afford one explanation for the fact that the female, unlike nearly all other ducks and geese, which lay their eggs in rather exposed situations, has evolved as colorfully as the male.

The common tern is one of the birds that lay eggs on the flat beaches or among the sand dunes. It flies with supreme grace, lifting itself slightly with every wingbeat, then settling downward obliquely. Occasionally, without warning, it dives headfirst into the water to catch a small fish, often disappearing under the water, then reappearing almost immediately. It rises easily from the surface, shaking the water from its plumage, and continues patroling.

One bird which has increased in numbers along the coasts of the North Sea during recent decades is the herring gull *(Larus argentatus)*. It is a highly competitive species that has been favored by the fact that in many places along the beaches the rubbish dumped from towns provides an inexhaustible supply of food. The tidal zone also suits the herring

gull; at ebb tide the gulls can be seen parading along the mudflats and investigating what the sea has left behind.

Of all the waders breeding along the coast none is heard as often as the redshank, an elegant bird whose habit of holding its wings stretched upward for a second after landing is a beautiful sight to watch. Some describe it as a nervous bird, for it continually gives its warning cry as it flies to and fro over its nesting site. However, this is its natural instinct, from which other birds profit.

At one place in Germany the redshank has been studied for three years. It was found that a very large proportion (seventy per cent) of the breeding birds returned to the same site the following year. When pairs of redshanks breeding together returned to the same site, most of them had the same partners. On beaches the redshank usually eats crustaceans and mollusks, on the shores of lakes it takes insect larvae, on meadows and wetlands earthworms, beetles and other insects and their larvae, as well as spiders. It also eats vegetable matter and, in exceptional cases, small fish and frogs.

Along the Danish North Sea coast there are many narrow sandy peninsulas which separate lagoons and lakes from the sea. These completely or partly isolated expanses of water are surrounded by low-lying meadows. On the southwest coast of Jutland tides affect these meadows and constantly change the contours of the coast. Within the wave-washed fringe of the shore and of the salty marshes there are frequent borders of dunes, with vegetation unique in Scandinavia.

Everything in nature changes, but often so gradually as to be hardly perceptible. Along the North Sea coast of Jutland, however, the wind and waves, together with the tides, may change the landscape from one day to the next. The small island of Jordsand, off the extreme south coast of Denmark, provides an example of this. In many places in the tidal zone there are great banks of mussels, layer upon layer of which seem securely anchored. When storms break over them, however, they are shifted and rearranged, such that the aspect of the beaches can be transfigured. Where perhaps lay an almost endless mudflat, full of miniature craters made by sandworms, there may later be found nothing but water. The marshy meadows are intersected by small channels through which water flows, both inland and to the sea. Numerous pools, which increase or decrease in size daily, dot the meadows.

The grassy meadows out of reach of tides provide breeding sites for many birds that feed on the beaches; the two environments complement each other for the benefit of the birds.

The bird fauna of northern Europe is here mainly represented by the same species as are found on the rocky Atlantic coasts. The flashing white wings of terns and gulls, the musical cry of waders, and the silhouettes of ducks in flight are much the same from Denmark to the north of Norway. But there are some species whose distribution range is limited to Scandinavia.

On the west coast of Jutland, Denmark has some storehouses of ornithological treasure: Tipperne on the southernmost part of Ringkjobing fjord, the most famous of Danish bird sanctuaries; Nissum fjord farther north; and Vejlerne east of Hanstholm, between the sea and Limfjorden. Characteristic of all these are flat beach meadows adjoining the sea. Bird life is found there throughout the year. Geese, ducks and waders stay there in winter, and there too, during the autumn and spring migrations, great flocks, mostly of waders, find a resting place. At Tipperne as many as thirty to forty thousand ducks can be counted in a single day. Many species breed there in spring and summer; several of them, such as the black-tailed godwit and the gull-billed tern are rare in northern Europe.

THE ROCKY COAST OF NORWAY

Most of the north and west coasts of Scandinavia consists of mountains meeting the sea. The grayish-green waves are dashed to spray on the massive rocks, a grand finale to their long journey over the open ocean.

The Norwegian mountains meet the sea in many ways. High and inaccessible the cliffs rise vertically from the sea. Channels, some wide, some narrow, lead the Atlantic into long narrow fjords; these fjords, cut by glaciers during the Ice Age, run far inland, several of them more than a hundred miles into mountainous country, where they divide into branches. Some of these fjords are very deep; Sognefjord, for example, is more than 4,000 feet deep, but the entrance is blocked by a threshold that prevents the deep-water organisms of the Atlantic from communicating directly with it. A multitude of islands, islets and sugar-loaf-shaped pillars—as many as 150,000 of them—split almost the entire coast into archipelagos. Innumerable waterfalls dash down from high cliffs into the fjords or the ocean itself.

Many marine birds live on the stark, often bare cliffs. Common gulls and great black-backed gulls occupy the outer islands, but their realm extends across the whole of Scandinavia. The sharp-winged common tern flies screaming over the fjords. Gulls sometimes build their nests on the smooth cliffs, but seem to prefer the small patches of vegetation in fissures and crevices, where eiders also build their downy nests.

In spring, sea birds often congregate here in large colonies, clothing the rocks in white. Activity in such a colony reaches its height when the young have been hatched; then there is a seething of life which persists practically all day and night. Terns and gulls have to work hard to feed their young. When arctic skuas (Stercorarius parasiticus) see these birds passing with well filled gullets or with quarry in their beaks, the skuas fly after them at breakneck speed and the hunt is on. A remarkable aerial combat begins, a kind of cat-and-mouse game in which the skuas harry the gulls until the latter drop or disgorge their food, which the skuas catch in mid air. Not even the fastest tern can escape, and a skua is evidently able to tell at a glance whether a bird has food in its gullet or not.

Granite and gneiss cliffs, the flutter of white wings over rocky islets, impressive mountains crowded by sea birds—these are what remain in one's memory after a visit to the Atlantic coast of Scandinavia. Besides gulls and terns, there are eiders and red-breasted mergansers (Mergus serrator), tending their armadas of ducklings around islets where they nest in low vegetation. Black guillemots (Cepphus grylle) hurry back and forth to their nests under boulders on the rocky shores. On the rocks, oystercatchers are searching for snails and mussels at the water's edge and in fields of seaweed. The ringed plover runs over the rocks, stops, curtseys and cries "tu-i." The variegated turnstone (Arenaria interpres) butts the heaps of seaweed cast up by the waves, makes a breach and turns over a piece of seaweed to feed on the small animals it finds underneath. A closer study of the cliffs reveals that wheatears and rock pipits, as well as wagtails and robins, live there too. One does not associate robins with treeless cliffs by the sea, but they do in fact build willingly in the meagre windswept ground vegetation to be found there.

When red-breasted mergansers foregather in small flocks they may fish cooperatively. They form a line and, by beating the water, drive shoals of small fish to a suitable spot near the shore, where the fishing begins in earnest. The birds peer into the water, diving as rapidly as they can in order to catch as many fish as possible. Some of the mergansers hastily turn the fish headfirst before swallowing them. While the feast is going on the mergansers break ranks and the rest of the fish soon escape to deeper water.

The islets and rocks on the Atlantic coast of Norway are only the first line of defense against the sea. The islands closer to the coast are larger, as are their shrubs and trees. There are also genuine archipelagos with islands of various sizes.

None of the waders breeding in Scandinavia is more international than the turnstone. In northern latitudes it lives on the shores of Europe, Asia and America. During migration and in winter quarters it is seen almost everywhere. This little bird sees a great deal of the world, annually covering about 18,000 miles on its journey to and from its breeding site in Scandinavia. Not long ago a turnstone was found in Portugal;

nine weeks earlier it had been banded in its nest, before it was fledged, in northwestern Greenland. It had evidently crossed the Atlantic at a very early period in its life.

The most interesting characteristic of the turnstone is the way it finds its food, which consists of insects and their larvae, small crustaceans, mussels and mollusks, spiders, and sometimes small fish washed up by the waves. It does most of its foraging in seaweed on the shore and under small stones that it turns over with its beak—hence its name. Like other waders it also searches for food in the surface layers of the beach when the tide goes out. For moments it peers about, then runs to a stone or piece of wood, sticks its bill under it and quickly turns it over.

Common terns, the majority of which are to be found along the Scandinavian coast, migrate very long distances, flying from the coasts of Europe as far as Cape Town. One bird from Sweden, no more than six months old, was found in Australia. The flight may also be a very fast one. A common tern, only a few months old, that had been banded in Norway on July 12, 1959, was found in Ghana on September 3. It could not have been fledged before the first week in August, which means that it had flown about 5000 miles along the coasts of Europe and Africa in one month.

The mountains of the Atlantic and the Arctic Ocean, together with the ledges in their steep cliffs, provide good nesting places for myriads of auks, razorbills and guillemots, as well as kittiwakes. It would be impossible to calculate their quantity. When the ledges are crowded with these birds, the dark face of the cliffs becomes streaked with white patches. And when thousands of kittiwakes fly out from a precipice, it is soon hidden by a cloud of fluttering, grayish-white wings.

In Norway the kittiwakes have begun during recent years to build nests on the roofs and ledges of houses. This practice may have originated in their habit of waiting in such places for the daily cleaning of fish when the fishing boats return with their catch.

Certain marine birds found on the Norwegian coast do not breed anywhere else in Scandinavia. Two of them are the fulmar *(Fulmarus glacialis)* and the gannet. Norway is the gannet's most easterly locality in the North Atlantic area. The arctic skua is distributed along the whole of the Norwegian coast. There are two phases of this species—a dark one, and a paler one which is more common farther north. In May, when skuas are demonstrating what is probably their mating flight, they give an unsurpassed exhibition of the beauty of bird flight, indulging in extraordinarily rapid maneuvers.

If one sails along the Atlantic coast of Norway in summer, the visible wildlife becomes richer the farther north one goes. One catches sight of multitudes of birds on cliffs, and in the archipelagos of Lofoten and Vesteralen the colonies of kittiwakes and auks become more and more frequent. The explanation of this is not that the rocky coast provides better habitats than those found farther south, but rather that the food supply is more plentiful. In this respect, the Arctic Ocean, during its brief summer, is a region of climax. This is con-

The maritime climate contributes to vegetation density on the slopes surrounding Norway's fjords. Speckled alders, mountain ash, ferns and junipers crowd together at Geirangerfjord in Romsdal. (Gerhard Klammet)

Left: In the Norwegian mountains such fjords as Nordfjord, near Olden, penetrate deep inland. The Jostedalsbre glacier is in the background. (Toni Schneiders: Coleman and Hayward) Right: An arctic skua chases a kittiwake to make it regurgitate the food it has just swallowed. (Wlodzimierz Puchalski)

firmed by the presence of whales, in addition to millions of such marine birds as gulls, terns and auks. These birds often live on the same kind of small organisms as the huge whales.

During the years 1957–1961, 344 pairs of the white-tailed eagle, which has become rare throughout Europe, bred along the coast of Norway, nesting on cliffs. And, in spite of much persecution along the coast, the Norwegian population of the white-tailed eagle is still one of the most important in Europe, all of whose territories it once frequented. It remains there in winter, because the ocean, from which it gains its livelihood, does not freeze over. The golden eagle also breeds along this coast, and occasionally competes successfully with the white-tailed eagle for breeding sites. Both species eat carrion and offal, but they seek their prey in different domains. The white-tailed eagle hunts fish and sea birds and looks for carcasses between the islands and out at sea, while the golden eagle flies up into the mountains in search of mountain hares *(Lepus timidus)* and grouse.

THE DWINDLING SEALS

Three species of seals live around the coasts of Scandinavia: the common seal, the ringed seal *(Phoca hispida),* and the gray seal *(Halichoerus grypus).* Of these, the common seal goes farthest south, although it is also found on Arctic coasts. While decreasing in number, it is the most predominant seal along the coasts of Norway. It seems to be most at home in archipelagos, where it has a gift for staying out of sight of man; but if one keeps a sharp lookout, ultimately these seals betray their presence, by creeping up on rocks just above the water. Even then, it is not easy to sight them in the rocky archipelagos, for they are about the same color as the rocks; however, on the low sandy islets off the south coast, their round contours contrast with the flat surface of the islets, and they are easily detected, particularly when they adopt their favorite posture—on their bellies, with head and hindquarters raised. Common seals may be observed quite frequently in the fjords, often in those parts farthest from the sea.

The number of common seals has diminished greatly throughout the southern part of their habitats. This has been attributed to persecution: the fact that they cannot find enough sites along the coast for undisturbed rest and breeding. And young common seals are born in summer, when human traffic in the archipelagos and along the coasts is at

its height. Luckily the young can take to the water one to eight hours after birth; but even during that brief period, the young seals may meet with a fatal accident from disturbance by man. The first time they dive, young common seals can stay underwater for several minutes; this ability has probably saved the lives of many of them. Furthermore, the common seal is the only Scandinavian species that is wholly dependent on land during its breeding season. The ringed seal, however, rears its young on ice, as do gray seals in the Baltic region, whereas the Atlantic population of this species is restricted by the same habits as the common seal.

As for the gray seals, there has been a catastrophic reduction in their number along the Norwegian coast, even in the animal's ancient habitats outside the Trondheim fjord. It migrates as far as the coast of the Arctic Ocean. Many young seals from Farne Island and the Orkneys in Great Britain have traveled to the Norwegian coast, where some of them have been found only six or seven weeks after they had been marked. Young seals from Britain have also reached the coasts of Sweden and Denmark.

We conclude our survey of the Atlantic coast of Europe at its most northerly point, North Cape, 71 degrees north. There the coast turns eastward to face the Arctic Ocean.

Islands of a Thousand Landscapes

The British Isles and Ireland

13 Many and rich are the associations aroused by the name British Isles. Geographically they comprise two large islands, Great Britain and Ireland, surrounded by a large number of smaller islands, particularly in the north, where the Hebrides, Orkneys and Shetlands are, as it were, British outliers in the sea. From the aspect of natural history, each of the major cultural areas of Great Britain—England, Scotland and Wales —has its own individual features.

Great Britain is Europe's largest island, but until recent geological times it was part of the continental mainland. The English Channel is a relatively new development. The great changes in sea level during and after the Ice Age, and the resulting encroachment by the sea are the chief forces that made Great Britain an island. The former connection with the Continent can be recognized in many ways even today: for example, the chalk cliffs on both sides of the Channel, or the fact that the geological structure of the English lowlands is about the same as that of nearby parts of the European continent, such as the Paris and Munster basins.

One of the most remarkable characteristics of the British Isles is the great variety of its landscapes; archipelagos, sandy and rocky shores, plains, heaths, woods, mountains and lakes abound. In spite of cultivation and the ever-increasing industrial development since the nineteenth century, much natural beauty has been preserved. Genuine wild country can still be found in many areas, and although there are traces of human activity everywhere, one can travel for miles across the English countryside without seeing many people, considering that there are some fifty-five million inhabitants in 120,592 square miles. This impression results mainly from the fact that most of the inhabitants have gradually moved from the country into towns. Although the pressure on nature is great, it is apparently not having the same grave consequences as in many other parts of Europe. My theory is that the British have a deeper feeling for and interest in nature than any other people in Europe. This has long manifested itself in many ways and has helped to protect the countryside.

The geological history of the British Isles has been the main factor in the creation of the variety of landscape. For millions of years folding and faults, glaciations and marine invasions have affected the topography. Bedrock and soil have determined the vegetation, which in turn has influenced the fauna.

There are two main types of topography in Britain: lowland in the south and east, and highland in the west and north. In southeastern England, limestone meets sandstone, and high ridges surround valleys and plains. To the southwest the lowland rises up to the mountains and hills of Cornwall and Wales, which continue, on the western side of the Irish Sea, in southern Ireland. The dominant chain of mountains in England is the Pennine Range, which rises to a maximum height of about three thousand feet above sea level and extends for 140 miles. Scotland is mainly a mountainous country, with the highest peak, Ben Nevis, reaching an altitude of 4406 feet. The mountain ranges were created during different epochs: roughly speaking, the greater part of Scotland, Wales and Northern Ireland belongs to the Caledonian mountain range, one of the oldest formations in Europe, which continues in Scandinavia, while the Pennine Range and other highlands in England and Ireland are remains of the Armorican formation, and belong to a more recent era. The lowland consists of Mesozoic and Tertiary sedimentary rocks.

The varying structure of the soil explains the great variety of vegetation in the British Isles. The flora comprises more than two thousand species. Many of them are favored by the mild Atlantic climate which, together with fertile soils and hitherto lenient methods of cultivation, explain why so much of the British Isles leaves one with the impression of a "green and pleasant land."

The British Isles are within the European deciduous forest belt. Before the appearance of man, most of the country was covered with hardwood forests—chiefly beech, oak and ash. Pines grew on some of the low mountains, and in the northern highlands birch and pine covered large areas. Today very little is left of these forests, though in Scotland there are some remnants of the original pine forests *(Pinus silvestris)*. In spite of the transformation from primeval forest to park landscape during the past two thousand years, a surprisingly large number of animal species is still found there.

THE ENGLISH COUNTRYSIDE

Southernmost England has open, pleasant country, with more sunshine, and, in parts, lush vegetation than any other section of the British Isles. The country from Cornwall and Devon in the west to Sussex and Kent in the east varies from county to county. The granite cliffs of Cornwall in the southwest extend far out into the Atlantic. The steeper cliffs are either naked or are covered with lichens of many colors. In other places grass grows in the fissures, and in summer great expanses of common heath *(Erica cinerea)* carpet the slopes with purple. The plateaus above, such as those in Dorset, may be flat or undulating. Wide heaths, on a substratum of coarse sandstone, stretch over large parts of Devon. They are covered with heather and gorse *(Ulex europaeus)*, but merge into grassland and, further south, into groves and trees. There red deer graze, as they have grazed for thousands of years,

Castellated and lichen-covered granite cliffs at Land's End in Cornwall extend far out into the Atlantic. (D. P. Wilson)

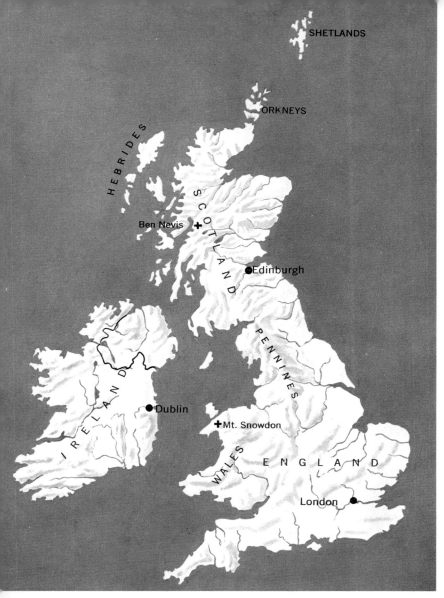

The British Isles and Ireland exhibit almost all the natural features of the Continent although on a smaller scale: sandy and rocky shores, moors and woods, lakes and mountains, subalpine and alpine vegetation belts. Despite intense cultivation, much of living nature still persists.

and Dartford warblers sing. These warblers, among the rarest birds in the British Isles, have here their most northerly European breeding grounds.

Contrasting with the open heaths are the luxuriant woods of the valleys. The rivers, on their way from the plateau to the sea, have cut down into the limestone, and there, protected from the wind, woods have grown up into a vegetation of a richness seldom equalled in the British Isles. Such wooded valleys enclose the famous New Forest in southern Hampshire. This forest consists mainly of conifers, beech, and oak *(Quercus robur),* often covered with ivy, which form as it were a closed canopy over large areas. Trees have been cut for centuries, so the New Forest is by no means virgin territory. It is probably not unlike the Stone Age woods on the same site, although pines have been planted there in recent years. Large areas, too, are covered with dense carpets of heather and bilberry *(Vaccinium myrtillus).*

In the New Forest, as in many other deciduous woods in Europe, one can hear the cry of the green woodpecker, a loud, triumphant "klee-klee-klee." Woodpeckers occupy individual territories that they jealously defend against intrusion by other green woodpeckers, sending out warnings from certain favorite trees that they return to year after year. When threatening a trespasser of its own species, a male green woodpecker strikes a curious pose: with wings and tail half-outstretched it sits on a tree trunk, swinging its head and neck from side to side with its bill thrust stiffly upward. When it has driven a rival away it repeats the pose—as though proclaiming its triumph.

Beautifully colored butterflies flit above the glades in the New Forest and the whir and glitter of many other insects is constant. This of course attracts numerous birds: in spring the leafy arches ring with their song. Indeed, this land of parks, gardens, groves, fields, meadows, dense hedges, wooded river banks and bushy, rolling hills is a paradise for birds. There are many mammals, too, and their tracks in wet or soft soil betray their natural prowlings. Foxes, badgers and stoats are among the beasts of prey whose tracks are seen most frequently.

STOATS, BATS AND SQUIRRELS

The stoat is at home both in cultivated and wild areas. It seems to avoid large forests, but is not otherwise selective in its choice of abode, frequenting fields, meadows, stony banks, fringes of woods and clearings, and leafy groves. It makes its home in heaps of stones, among the roots of trees, in holes in banks and fields, under the floors of barns, in hollow trees and the like. It is mainly nocturnal in habit, but in the autumn and when it has young it is active in the daytime and is often seen hunting. It usually moves at a kind of gallop, often along the edge of a ditch. Sometimes it sits up on its hind legs, with its forepaws on its chest. It is a good swimmer, and occasionally climbs trees. Both sexes change hunting grounds at intervals of a few days.

A stoat hunts mainly by sight but it will also follow a scent until it catches sight of its quarry, which it takes by surprise with a series of rapid jumps. Its prey consists chiefly of voles and mice, but it also eats shrews, hares, rabbits, birds and their eggs (although it cannot bite a hole in a hen's egg), and sometimes frogs, fish, insects and berries. Along with the fox, it is probably the mammalian predator that preys most on the smallest of rodents. It can even store food but it is not, as many believe, a bloodsucker.

When mating, the male stoat jumps about in front of the female, flashing its white underparts like a signal. If food is abundant the stoat may have two litters. The gestation period is about nine months, but the fetus does not start to develop until a rather late stage. Another oestral period, which may lead to pregnancy (and from five to eight weeks' gestation), is usually without result.

Although most human beings dislike bats, these tiny, flying mammals, which are generally seen around towns, parks and gardens, are very interesting. They may often be seen flying about quickly and erratically in their hunt for insects or heard calling to each other at mating time in autumn.

In flying, bats use their forelimbs as wings, and since they generally fly about in pitch darkness, they find their way by means of a system of echo-sounding. They emit high-frequency sounds, inaudible to the human ear, at the rate of thirty to sixty a second, and with a frequency of 25,000 to

70,000 cycles a second, which are reflected by objects they approach. The bat gauges its distance from the object by the time it takes for the sound to reach the object and return.

The common bat *(Pipistrellus pipistrellus)* rests in the daytime in buildings, boxes, hollow trees and the like, and also hibernates in such places, often in large colonies. Contrary to popular conceptions, it does not always hang upside down from a wall, but may lie buried in straw on a floor. A sudden fall in temperature in autumn or winter sometimes causes the common bat to seek warmth in a house. When temperatures are very low in winter (below 14° F) bats often leave their original winter quarters in search of a new dwelling place. Regular seasonal migrations of bats, sometimes for great distances, have been observed in Russia, with 715 miles as the longest flight so far recorded.

The common bat often hunts in small flocks close to houses and cliffs and around treetops. It has two periods of activity, one beginning just before sunset and the other ending just after sunrise. It generally covers the same territory night after night; but it may make a change, depending on the supply of food, which consists of insects, flies and moths. The prey is caught and usually consumed in flight, but large insects may be taken to the nest and killed and eaten there. When common bats drink, they hover over water, wings stretched upward, and dip their noses carefully into it.

The red squirrel *(Sciurus vulgaris)* is not so widely distributed in the British Isles as in the rest of Europe. This may be largely the result of the decrease in forests, but it is also claimed that it has been displaced by the North American gray squirrel *(S. carolinensis)*, originally introduced in 1876. Although the larger gray squirrel has been observed killing its red relative, a British biologist, Monica Shorten, has cast doubt on the theory that there is a genuine antagonism between the two species.

LITTLE OWLS, ROBIN REDBREASTS AND WOOD PIGEONS

The English landscape is eminently suitable for the little owl since it prefers open areas, such as parks, gardens, avenues of trees (particularly of willows), even in towns, where it can move about all day long. It hunts mostly at dusk and dawn, but when it has young in its nest it will also seek food in the daytime. It often sits on wires or isolated trees, or, in the middle of the day, half hidden on the ground under a shrub. It can run surprisingly fast and undoubtedly catches mice and beetles in this way. Usually it perches on a bough and dives down on its quarry. Like the kestrel it patrols fields and meadows, and it is swift enough to catch flying quarry. Like a woodpecker, it sometimes pecks insects from trees. In general, insects form the main part of the little owl's diet, but it also takes small rodents and shrews and occasionally small birds, reptiles and frogs. First introduced, like many other owls, to control rodents, the little owl acquired an unflattering reputation as a slayer of birds. A comprehensive study, however, has shown that only about five per cent of this owl's diet consists of birds.

The gently winding Thames runs from the Cotswold Hills in the west, across country that has been cultivated for thousands of years, through London to its estuary in the east. Since man first penetrated far up the Thames Valley, where he found an abundance of wild animals, he has exerted increasing urban influence on the valley; but much of the region is still green and rich in flowers and animals. The peacefulness around such a town as Lechlade, where meadows and groves surround the Thames, is extraordinary. This acreage of rich pastures, arable land, gardens and groups of deciduous trees seems to be something of a paradox in so industrialized an area.

The robin redbreast, Britain's national bird, is found in many parts of the country. A lively, cheerful bird, the cock robin is active all day long, helping the hen to build its nest and at the same time collecting food. It also keeps a keen watch at the nest, for the robin has a well developed territorial sense and responds aggressively when other robins approach. When the eggs are laid, only the female sits on them. In the British Isles hen and cock robins have separate territories in autumn and winter.

In spring and summer robins live on insects and their larvae, as well as on worms and other small creatures found on the ground or on low branches. Favorite hunting grounds are wooded valleys, where the soil is often damp and overgrown with rich vegetation. It is interesting to watch a robin in search of prey. The instant it catches sight of a larva it stands perfectly still, as if preparing itself for a decisive attack; it is thus easy to tell when it has detected a tidbit. In late summer and autumn the robins eat berries and disgorge the pips, thereby helping to spread seed. Most of their food is taken on the ground, however, and they are quick to take advantage of what other creatures, as well as gardeners, dig up, particularly when snow covers the ground. When a fox scratches through the snow in search of voles or rabbits, he soon attracts the attention of robins.

After the young robins have left the nest the cock robin stops singing until autumn. The birds hop around in families, under shrubs and trees, the young ones uttering warning cries. In characteristic robin fashion they bob and curtsey, peer inquisitively about with their bright, buttonlike eyes, and fly rapidly hither and thither. They are soon able to fend for themselves.

In England, the wood pigeon has become adapted to farm country and has greatly increased in number in recent years. Great flocks of them may now be seen feeding in fields. These birds are especially active at sunrise. Their quick wingbeats resound as they settle in trees, and their muffled, staccato calls echo in the woods. Sometimes a bird rises high in the air on flashing wings and makes a few wide circles and quickly returns to the branch it has left. During the hottest hours of the day wood pigeons keep out of the open; they are correspondingly active in rainy weather, even at midday.

Beginning as early as February or March, a wood pigeon's breeding season may continue until far into autumn, and may result in several broods a year. The courting behavior of the male, which often takes place on a branch, is reminiscent of an eighteenth-century minuet. With tripping steps and tail elevated and spread, he postures for the female, which now and then responds with a bob. To and fro he struts, feathers erect and throat puffed up, uttering a cooing sound, quite different from his usual song. At times he interjects a rapid, muffled "go-go-go," then bows deeply, almost standing on his head, with his breast on the branch and his tail thrust straight up. Meanwhile the female, with head on one side, appears to be watching him with the greatest interest.

Above: Recalling their past glory, oaks and beeches in the New Forest form a closed canopy. (Noel Habgood: Coleman and Hayward) Left: The little owl is the owl most often observed in southern England, although the nocturnal tawny owl is probably more common. (Walter Higham)

Right: The spotted flycatcher, distributed over almost the whole of Europe, is a common bird of woods and parks. Left, below: The whitethroat is found among bushes and thickets in woods and open fields. Its young will be fledged in about eleven days. Right, below: Like the female, the male nightingale keeps busy feeding the nestlings. (Photographs by Eric Hosking)

A GYRATION FLIGHT

The rook *(Corvus frugilegus)* is also common in England, and is often seen in fields together with carrion crows *(C. corone).* One day, near Windsor, I was fortunate enough to catch sight of rooks and carrion crows engaged in what is known as a gyration flight. In this maneuver the birds make use of rising currents of warm air. It was a hot day, with a blue sky and a few scattered cumulus clouds. As the crows and rooks came into the field of rising air, they were drawn into the spiral, and as they reached the center of the current they rose in small circles with astonishing rapidity. High in the air they turned in a northeasterly direction, and glided quickly on still wings until they were out of sight.

The rooks came from a rookery in the neighborhood; as they passed in casual flight over a field, the majority of them were drawn into the gyration. There were, naturally, interruptions in the stream of rooks entering the living spiral, but not for long. Wood pigeons were unaffected by the rising current: when a rook and a wood pigeon flying at the same height reached the rising current, the rook seemed to glide automatically into the spiral and up, while the wood pigeon continued on its way. Usually from three to ten birds took part in the gyration, but on various occasions I counted from seventeen to twenty-two participants. My impression was that

The weasel, widely distributed in the British Isles but not found in Ireland, feeds mainly on small rodents. (Jane Burton: Coleman and Hayward)

the birds flew into the current of air in order to gain a high altitude as quickly as possible and that they then glided to some distant feeding place. I first saw the rooks in gyration flight at 1:10 p.m. It was still going on when I went on my way at 3:15 p.m.

Another variation of English landscape is the stony heaths around Oxford. In keeping with the desolate wildness of the heath is the shrill, plaintive cry of the long-legged stone curlew.

GOOSE COUNTRY

In the Bristol Channel and the Severn estuary, on the east side of the river, are wide expanses of flat land called the New Grounds. The tides in the estuary affect an area about a mile wide. Beyond is a belt of salty marshland, and still farther inland a wide stretch of meadow, which is sometimes flooded, called The Dumbles. This region is ideal for the arctic geese that winter here. In September and October pink-footed geese *(Anser fabalis brachyrhynchus)* arrive from Greenland, Iceland and Spitsbergen, occasionally accompanied by brant geese *(Branta bernicla).* Thousands of white-fronted geese also arrive in October and soon become the most numerous species. More than half of the white-fronted geese wintering in Great Britain stay on the New Grounds. The Canada goose *(Branta canadensis)* also comes to The Dumbles in winter. It was introduced into Great Britain in the seventeenth century, and, according to a census in 1953, there were then between 2200 and 4000 of these birds there.

The bean goose also appears along the Severn in winter; and in the course of the years, so have all the other geese that winter regularly in Europe. Many species of duck visit the region in great numbers. It is only natural that the English, with their great interest in ornithology, should have taken advantage of the many geese in the New Grounds to establish the Wildfowl Trust there; under the leadership of Peter Scott, the Trust performs an important function in its field.

Although East Anglia is intensively cultivated, there is much marshland along the coasts of Suffolk and Norfolk; the most famous marsh is Minsmere. Such birds as the bittern, marsh harrier and bearded tit, all rare in the British Isles, breed there. Havergate Island, in the estuary of the River Ore, is the only place in Britain where the avocet breeds. Farther north, on the sandy reefs of the Wash, one comes on a favorite haunt of the common seal; this species prefers the east coasts around the British Isles because of wide river mouths, sandbanks, and rocks that are left dry at low tide. The gray seal prefers the rocky shores and is therefore found chiefly along the west coast of Great Britain.

In the highly industrialized north of England, the sandstone and limestone mountains of the Pennine Range lend great variety to the countryside. They stand out strikingly in a landscape marked by mills and factories. In Derbyshire, with its richly wooded valleys, the steep limestone cliffs are inhabited by the ring ouzel *(Turdus torquatus)* and kestrel. Still higher up, the hills are covered with vast heaths, where only the cries of the curlew and golden plover *(Charadrius apricarius)* break the silence. The heather gives the whole countryside its seasonal color scheme: brown in winter, green in spring and early summer, and purple in late summer.

From Derbyshire the Pennines run northward between the

sizable coal fields of Lancashire and Yorkshire, Westmorland and Durham, Cumberland and Northumberland, culminating in striking formations such as those at Ingleborough and Cross Fell. The Pennines ultimately merge into the Cheviot Hills on the border of Scotland; grazed by sheep, these are now almost treeless. From Cross Fell (2930 feet) one gets a magnificent view of the fertile valley of the Eden, with the river shining like a silver band on its way to the Solway Firth. To the west, the Cumbrian Mountains, with numerous valleys and beautiful lakes, form part of the spectacular region known as the Lake District. In some lakes, such as Windermere, anglers still fish for char—a relict of late glacial times.

THE FARNE ISLANDS

The Farne Islands, off Northumberland on the east coast of England, are remarkable because they form the only archipelago along this coast. This group, a bird sanctuary since 1923, consists of about twenty-five rocky, basalt islands and islets, half of which are under water at high tide. Thousands of birds breed on those islands not periodically covered with water, and far more—mostly marine species—land on them during flights over the North Sea or along the coast. The water around the islands is quite shallow, and at ebb tide several of the islands are connected with each other by land. The sea bed exposed at low water is an important source of food for the gulls that haunt the islands all year round.

Open sea with an unbroken horizon is impressive, but the sight of giant waves crashing against the isolated cliffs of these islands is overwhelming. But birds are masters of this world of wind and water; their life goes on whether the sea is smooth as glass or a storm is whipping foam from the crests of great waves.

The calls of seabirds are an integral part of the mighty symphony of nature around such islands, the voices of gulls blending with the melodious notes of kittiwakes and terns, and with the harsh cries of guillemots.

The Farne Islands offer a variety of habitats to breeding birds, and certain preferences can be discerned. Some islands such as Megstone and North Wamses are occupied by hundreds of cormorants and shags, their guano discoloring the whiteness of the cliffs. The smell of semidigested fish reaches the visitor even at a distance. The shag is the most marine of European cormorants. Its nest, made chiefly of seaweed, is built either on a narrow shelf of a steep cliff among nests of kittiwakes, or in a cave, whereas cormorants prefer plateau ledges where their nests can be grouped. Great colonies of kittiwakes also breed on shelves in the cliffs. Their nests are enlarged from year to year with seaweed, lichens and straw, and are held together with excrement and sometimes with clay. In such breeding places the young kittiwakes, unlike gulls hatched on the ground, do not have need of protective coloration, and in this respect they are different from their relatives.

Guillemots breed on ledges, showing marked preference for the flat tops of pillar-like rocks called stacks. The basalt cliffs of the Farne Islands, rising vertically to a height of 150 feet or so, are ideally suited for this purpose. While some guillemots sit on their eggs, others stand along the edge of the cliff, comically nodding and bowing. In spite of the crowding on the ledges, guillemots usually live in harmony; occasion-

A female badger (right) with three nearly full-grown cubs. The badger is nocturnal and omnivorous. (Ernest G. Neal: Coleman and Hayward)

ally, however, quarrels do occur, when the birds croak harshly and fence with their bills. Some such displays may be a ceremony between two mates and have some sexual significance. First, the female pecks the male, and then turns away so that his answering stroke will hit the side or back of her head. Then he begins to pluck gently at the feathers on her head. Sometimes two quarreling birds tumble from a cliff, and may even hold onto each other for a few seconds as they fall. There is a continual flutter of wings, with some birds taking off and others landing, often on the backs of their companions. The eggs are pear-shaped and relatively large; if they are jostled they roll in a circle, which usually prevents them from falling off the ledge. The eggs vary in color from bluish-green to white, and are spotted; it has been assumed that the differences in color make it easier for each parent bird to recognize its own eggs.

Of the approximately five thousand pairs of birds breeding on the Farne Islands, the most common is the puffin, and the rarest is the roseate tern *(Sterna dougallii)*. The latter is mainly an American bird and is found in only a few places in Europe.

It is impossible to give here a comprehensive account of the bird life of the Farne Islands. Some mention must, however, be made of the fact that these cliffs in the sea provide shelter for the only large breeding colony of gray seals *(Halichoerus grypus)* along the east coast of Britain.

WALES

Wales is highland country, covered by the Cambrian Mountains, remains of the ancient Caledonian folds. Their highest peak here is 3571 feet, that of Mt. Snowdon.

Since mountains and coasts are such dominant features, the scenery of Wales is by no means as varied as that of England. A variety of vegetation belts, innumerable mountain streams, rivers, waterfalls, lakes and peaks give the inland country its character, while cliffs, promontories and islands give the coast its special features. Compared with those in the English and Scottish highlands, the woods of Wales are in many places surprisingly well preserved. North Wales in particular has arresting scenery, with light deciduous woods covering the mountain slopes, and a very fertile ground vegetation extending right down to the edge of the swiftly flowing streams and the numerous waterfalls. After brief showers on hot summer days, these deciduous woods are almost subtropical in appearance; damp heat rises from humus-rich soil, myriad drops of water glisten in the sunshine, and a chorus of bird song rises from the trees.

Gray wagtails *(Motacilla cinerea)* are a feature of the watercourses of Wales, for these beautiful yellow and gray birds have a predilection for shaded mountain brooks, whose stony banks provide them with food and nest holes.

THE SHEARWATERS OF SKOKHOLM

Perhaps the greatest natural attractions of Wales, apart from the magnificent scenery, are certain rare plants and a few bird islands, Skokholm, Skomer and Grassholm, off the coast of Pembrokeshire. It is on Skomer that one can find certain true marine birds—birds which live on land only when breeding. Skokholm, which has been described so vividly by R.M.

Gray seals on a skerry in the Farne Islands, their only large colony on Britain's east coast. (Charles Vaucher)

Lockley, is the breeding place of the Manx shearwater *(Puffinus puffinus),* on which some interesting experiments have been performed. A number of these shearwaters, hatched on Skokholm, were caught and taken by boat or air to other places, and then released. The birds quickly found their way back to Skokholm from such places as the Faeroe Islands, Cambridge, Birmingham, Manchester, and Surrey. Two birds were even flown to Venice and released near a lagoon. A fortnight later one of them was back at its nesting site on Skokholm; the following spring, in the breeding season, the other returned. A third bird, released in Boston, across the Atlantic, returned to Skokholm after twelve days.

The Manx shearwater breeds in dense colonies, there being as many as ten thousand of this species on Skokholm alone. It lays its single egg in a hole in the ground or in shallow depressions in grass. The male and female take turns at sitting on the egg for periods of from two to five days; at night, the bird that is not sitting feeds its partner. Another remarkable characteristic of the Manx shearwater is its ability to fly in from the sea after dark and find its way, among many thousands of nesting holes, straight to its own nest. The incoming bird announces its arrival by yodeling cries. Its mate, incubating underground, answers by calls which guide its partner right down to the nest. Carried out in total darkness, this is a truly amazing performance. The storm petrel *(Hydrobates pelagicus),* another strictly pelagic species, also breeds on Skokholm.

On Grassholm the gannet dominates. At the beginning of the nineteenth century, the gannets on this island were reduced to about a hundred pairs by man's persecution. But the island was later made into a nature reserve and the gannet has so increased in numbers that its colonies now contain between eight and nine thousand birds. The nests are so close together there that the sitting birds brush against each other, and at a distance they look like vast fields of snow.

SCOTTISH MOORS AND HIGHLANDS

The Highlands of Scotland differ in many ways from other parts of the British Isles. This is the result not only of the elevation of the country, but also its northern location. The mainland of Scotland is situated between latitudes fifty-five degrees and fifty-nine degrees north, the same as southern Norway and Sweden; the Shetland Isles are farther north than the southernmost point of Greenland. The scenery is thus reminiscent of the Scandinavian mountain range above the tree limit, and northerly plants and animals become more common the farther north one travels, while southern species become less common or are altogether absent.

Fortunately, the Atlantic climate, warmed by the water of the Gulf Stream, has neutralized the effect of Scotland's northern location, and the climate has allowed people to live in and cultivate the land for thousands of years. But nowadays Scotland is almost devoid of trees, the celebrated moors resulting chiefly, on their lower reaches, from the felling of trees, and from fires, and to a lesser extent from the check given to the growth of trees by grazing sheep. For centuries the tree limit has been pressed downward into the valleys, so that, along with the mountains, moorland has become the dominant feature of the Scottish landscape.

Reforestation has been carried out in places, but the area of forest land is only a fraction of what it once was. The largest deciduous woods are in the southern parts of the country, whereas in the north the woods are coniferous, mixed here and there with birches and alders. In their natural condition the Scottish Highlands were wooded, with oaks in the valleys, alders along the rivers, and pines and birches on the slopes up to about 2500 feet.

The former forests account for the many plants and animals in Scotland today. The wildcat has survived and even increased in number during recent years. Red deer, which once inhabited the woods, have successfully adapted themselves to the open moors and now number about 150,000. The pine marten, after being on the verge of extinction, is found there too. The capercaillie *(Tetrao urogallus)* was exterminated, but has been reintroduced and is now firmly established. On the other hand, several species have been favored by the expansion of the moors at the expense of the woods. That is one of the reasons why the willow grouse is so common in Scotland. The abundance of the mountain hare *(Lepus timidus)* is probably due to the same cause, for its ecological range has been extended greatly. Like the red deer, it has adapted itself to a new environment. The relative frequency of the golden eagle in Scotland is probably a consequence of the dense population of the mountain hare, as well as moorland game in general, and carrion of sheep and deer, and is therefore indirectly due to the expansion of the moors.

Rivers, long narrow lakes and deep narrow fjords, beach meadows and steep shores, great archipelagos, cultivated land with groves of trees and parklike scenery, valleys and lowlands are all aspects of the wild beauty of Scotland that man's ever-present influence has not diminished. There are even, in the Scottish mountains, at least eight fairly primeval pine woods as well as many small ones. Several of these environments accommodate an astonishingly large number of animals, as well as a profusion of flora and fauna.

A colony of guillemots breeds on top of the Pinnacles, on the Farne Islands of England's east coast; kittiwakes nest on the lower ledges. (Eric Hosking)

BIRD LIFE IN THE LOWLANDS

The Lowlands of Scotland, around and between the Solway Firth and the Firth of Clyde on the west coast and around the Firth of Forth and northward along the east coast, provide resting and wintering places for many geese. Immense flocks of pink-footed geese and graylag geese fly back and forth between their night quarters and feeding places, creating scenes of singular beauty.

The Scottish shore of the Solway Firth consists partly of wide grassy banks and salt marshes. Because much of the region is in the Caerlaverock National Nature Reserve, and the human population is sparse, geese and duck find an abundance of food and shelter there. One of the most important bird sanctuaries in Great Britain, in winter it harbors astonishing numbers of oystercatchers. They decorate the shore in black and white, and barnacle geese do the same higher up on the beach meadows. They need not move beyond the boundaries of the reserve, for there they can find everything they need—suitable sleeping quarters and feeding grounds. Between 2500 and 3000 barnacle geese spend most of the year on these shores, arriving in September or early October and remaining until March or the first week in April. Banding some birds has shown that these geese come from Spitsbergen, and that they comprise the greater part, perhaps the whole,

of the population breeding there. They also winter on the Western Isles of Scotland and in Ireland. In the winter of 1961-62 their number was estimated at between thirteen to fourteen thousand specimens. Barnacle geese from Novaya Zemlya migrate to Germany and Holland, where about twenty thousand of them spend the winter. These figures do not cover the entire population of these geese, but they show how important it is to protect a species in its winter quarters—especially when it is as relatively rare as the barnacle goose.

The most magnificent spectacle on the beach meadows around the Solway Firth is the pink-footed geese flying over in thousands. At times, the whole sky seems to be full of geese strung out in bands. Gradually they congregate on the meadows. In the fall, up to fifteen thousand of them have been observed there, comprising about one quarter of the pink-footed geese wintering in the British Isles. The species breeds on Spitsbergen, Iceland and Greenland, those wintering in Great Britain coming mainly from Iceland and Greenland. This goose seeks its food on fallow fields and arable land, where it is often seen together with graylag geese. At dawn it leaves its sleeping quarters on the sandbanks in the mouths of rivers to fly to its grazing grounds inland, following the same route year after year. Peter Scott and Hugh Boyd, Great Britain's leading experts on geese, took me over the goose country by the Firth of Tay, to witness this spectacle. It was still dark when we set out. As soon as the sky began to lighten, the first geese came flying straight over our heads, following their traditional flyways, and were soon followed by successive flocks.

Besides geese, many duck congregate in the fall and in winter in shallow lakes and on flooded meadows along the rivers; and from October to March whooper swans are surprisingly numerous.

THE WILDCAT OF THE SCOTTISH WOODLANDS

Although very little of the former forests remain, Scotland has one remarkable woodland animal: the wildcat. The only wild feline species in the British Isles, its distribution is restricted to Scotland, which is its northernmost range in Europe. It inhabits wooded slopes and moorlands and is almost common in the Grampian Mountains.

In appearance the wildcat is very similar to the domestic cat, although there is no genetic relation between them. The cat was originally domesticated in North Africa; it is probable that interbreeding between wild and domesticated cats of northern Europe and the British Isles occurred there later than elsewhere. Due to its wariness, the wildcat is seldom seen, but, as far as is known, it is active both at night and in the daytime. It creeps along, pressed close to the ground, until it is close to its quarry, and then, in a series of amazingly quick leaps, takes its victim by surprise; it can kill a rabbit in a few seconds. When its prey, chiefly mammals and birds, are feeding on the ground, they have only a restricted view over the ground vegetation, which is often heather. Even if the victim does look up, the wildcat's habit of freezing, coupled with the excellent camouflage provided by its striped fur, makes it a deadly stalker of prey. In addition to rabbits,

The stone curlew makes its home on hills with chalky soil, or on sandy or stony heaths. (Eric Hosking)

it eats hares, squirrels, mice and voles, willow grouse, black grouse and other ground birds. It is a good climber, but seldom hunts in trees, since they do not provide enough concealment.

At breeding time the wildcat, like its tame relative, gives nocturnal concerts. But its voice is quite different from that of the domestic cat and it has a larger repertoire: melodious, gentle "miaows" may give way to hoarse, harsh sounds.

Much has been written about the fierceness and bad temper of the wildcat, but such accounts refer almost exclusively to captive animals or those threatened by man. From a human point of view, such behavior may appear to be vicious; from the animal's viewpoint it is simply a matter of self-defense.

SAGA OF THE SALMON

Lakes and rivers are numerous in both the Highlands and Lowlands of Scotland. Many of them are well suited to the needs of the salmon and its relatives, the salmon living in the rivers, and the char, a survivor of arctic times, in deep lakes. Trout live in virtually all the lakes and watercourses in the Highlands.

The salmon is hatched in spring on the gravel beds of rivers. For a time the fry, alevins, remain in the gravel, where they subsist on the yolk sac. When this is empty they work their way to the surface of the gravel and begin their lives as free-swimming fish. The young salmon, called parr, have "territories" in the river, where they remain for two or three years. During that time they grow larger, but usually only from April to October, because the young salmon in these rivers become passive when the water temperature falls below 44° F (7° C). Most young salmon in Scotland migrate to the sea when they are two years old. At this stage the parr become smolts. The migration down the rivers is made individually; the smolts living farthest from the sea start first, and perhaps stimulate those living nearer to the sea to begin their travels.

During their first stage as free-living fish the young salmon eat mollusks, amphipods, fish roe and insects in the water and the air. When they reach the mouths of rivers their main food is crustaceans and shrimps, though they also take small fish. The salmon migrate far out into the Atlantic Ocean. We know very little about their migration routes, but a Scottish salmon has been caught off Greenland eleven months after being marked, and a salmon from western Sweden has also been caught off the west coast of Greenland. The salmon becomes a glutton when it reaches the sea, and grows very rapidly; by the time it returns to its Scottish river after a year or two in the sea, it is a very sizable fish. Salmon come up the east coast rivers in spring (sometimes as early as January), but they do not return to the west coast rivers until July or, in some rivers, as early as April. In spite of their long absence, they always find their way back to the river in which they were hatched. Nothing certain is known about how they do so, but it is supposed that the chemical composition of the water in the river is of great significance, the salmon recognizing the water from their "home" rivers by means of their highly developed sense of smell.

Salmon spawn from September to January in the streams and rivers of Scotland. In good seasons, some rivers in the Highlands are thick with salmon in October and November. They congregate in places where the bed is suitable for dig-

With its rolling hills and grassy moors, Snowdonia in the Cambrian Mountains is typical Welsh highland country. (Noel Habgood: Coleman and Hayward)

ging spawning beds. As the female works she is courted by one or several males. Young males that have not been in the sea, but are sexually mature, may gather around a female and even contribute to fertilization. The digging of spawning beds takes much time, for the female digs from ten to thirty beds or troughs, each requiring from one to four hours' work. From fifty to one hundred eggs are deposited in each bed and simultaneously fertilized. Then the female, by movements of her body and with the help of the current, covers the eggs with gravel. The whole procedure is spread over a period of two to three weeks. The male's capacity lasts somewhat longer.

Most of the males in the rivers of eastern Scotland die during the winter following spawning, but the western populations manage to spawn several times. There is also evidence of salmon wandering up the rivers during four or five spawning seasons. If the exhausted males, which drift backward down the river, reach the sea, they usually recover and again make long migrations. Although they have never been in the sea, the young male parr that take part in the spawning always die afterward, provided they have delivered milt.

MOORLANDS

The most striking features of the Highlands are the moors. They roll over the wide plateaus, the mountain slopes and higher valleys, often climbing to summits of more than three thousand feet. Very few sheep graze at such high altitudes, and these regions are the only areas, except for parts of the rocky shores, that have escaped alteration by man. It is impossible to generalize about the vegetation limit, for it varies greatly. On mountains exposed to strong, humid winds from the Atlantic, many plants do not grow as high as they do on the drier eastern side of the country. Mountain peaks and ridges in the Scottish Highlands are among the wettest places in the country.

Although the vegetation of the moors varies locally, it is usually characterized by such plants as heather—except in the southwest and parts of the west, where the heather has been destroyed by burning and grazing. Among the common plants on some moors are purple bell heather, cross-leaved heath, purple moor grass *(Molinia caerulea)* and other grasses. Many species of sedge fill damp depressions in the moors; these depressions are often large enough to form marshes.

STAGS AND HINDS

The most magnificent animal on the moors and hills is the red deer; it is common in Scotland and has lived there longer than man. Red deer, particularly hinds, are sociable animals; hinds and calves up to two years old form great herds in which social relations are highly developed. Each of these herds is under the leadership of a hind and has a well defined territory. The hinds live apart from the stags for about ten and a half months a year. The stags live in herds, too—sometimes as many as six hundred together—but do not usually have such close-knit groups.

Besides the vertical migrations, mating and calving are the most interesting events in the red deer's life. The calves are dropped in June and mating begins around the middle or end of September. Then the antlers of the stags have reached the peak of their seasonal development. The antlers are shed each year and, during the growing period, the blood vessels in the skin, which is called velvet, bring nourishment to the horn. As long as the antlers are covered with velvet the stags remain in herds, but when the velvet has peeled, the herds scatter, and each stag goes off alone. His aim is to get as large a harem of hinds as possible. He breaks into the herds of hinds, trying to collect as many as possible and, at the same time, trying to ward off rivals.

I remember particularly one day toward the end of October as I sat on a slope on the Grampian Mountains, looking out over a magnificent vista of valleys, moors, and mountain ridges. The almost unceasing bellow of the red deer could be heard for miles; it blended with the laughing call of the willow grouse and the hoarse cries of ravens. This wild concert seemed to have been composed specially for the grand, open moorland. Several herds of hinds were in sight, with the stags so busily engaged in keeping their harems together and driving rivals away that they hardly had time to eat and sleep. The hinds, on the other hand, were relaxed; they grazed and rested, or sometimes succumbed to a young stag while the old master of the harem was busy expelling his other rivals.

Everyone has seen pictures of battles between stags, but in reality such contests are not very common. The stag with his harem on his own territory seems usually to be in full command of the situation. He bellows and shows off, confronts trespassers threateningly, and sometimes goes through the motions of attacking, whereupon the intruder usually retreats. Sometimes a fight does take place, whereupon the stags lock antlers. This is indeed a dramatic spectacle and may end in death, with a new stag taking over the harem. As a rule, however, such fights are bloodless and seem to be little more than exercises.

Although the social order of the herds of hinds may be upset during the mating season, with the stag seemingly becoming the leader, the old order actually remains undisturbed—with a single hind still reigning over the others. The stag's function amidst the group of hinds is of course purely sexual. The stag has a difficult task for about six weeks, but it is very rare for one stag to attend a bunch of hinds throughout the mating season; usually the stags replace each other every few days. Dr. F. Fraser Darling, whose study of the red deer of Scotland is a classic, found that exhausted red deer congregate on high mountain plateaus, where, with no signs of rivalry and without bellowing, they recuperate, feeding on club moss *(Lycopodium)* and other mosses, as well as lichens.

WILLOW GROUSE

The moors provide very suitable habitats for the willow grouse *(Lagopus lagopus)*, and the expansion of the moors

at the expense of woodland accounts for the frequency of this bird in Scotland. As mentioned above, the pleasant call of the willow grouse can often be heard along with the hoarse roar of the red deer. The reason for this is that the willow grouse establish their individual territory in autumn mornings, but gather in flocks in the afternoon and are very active during the same period as the red deer.

Along with three British scientists, David Jenkins, Adam Watson and G. R. Miller, who have studied the willow grouse in the Highlands for several years, I set off for the moorland one October morning. At dawn the willow grouse came to life, and one cock after another came flying to take up its position on a tussock, stone, or other high point. Soon a large area of the moor was occupied by the males, which now and again flew back and forth, policing the boundaries of their territories. Throughout, they sang their peculiar song, "kowk-ok-ok, go-bak-bak-bak." Occasionally a hen joined the company, and although it was late in the fall, some of the cocks showed signs of excitement; but the hens seemed quite indifferent to the males.

The object of the cock willow grouse during the fall is to establish a territory for itself as a prelude to successful breeding the following spring. This nuptial preparation continues during the early winter, but only in the mornings. The rest of the day the birds wander about in flocks. Later in winter, when the moors are covered with snow, the grouse flock together all the time, but toward the end of the winter they reoccupy their chosen territories and defend them all day long until the breeding season. Old cocks return year after year to their same territories, while young ones occupy deserted territories or try to create new ones between two occupied sites.

TWITES AND HEN HARRIERS

Another bird of some Scottish moors in the west is the twite *(Carduelis flavirostris)*, which is also found in Norway, the Kola peninsula, Caucasus, and a few isolated spots in central Russia. In Scandinavia it inhabits remote mountain wildernesses, but in the Shetland Islands it can be seen hopping about in farmyards.

The most beautiful bird on the Scottish moors is the hen harrier, which is quite common in some localities. With its pale blue and white plumage, the male makes a striking picture as it glides over the purple or brown moors.

Other birds live on the moors at higher altitudes, but they are rare as far as the British Isles are concerned, their chief distribution being in Scandinavia or northeastern Europe. Among these species is the greenshank *(Tringa nebularia)*, which is quite common in the northwest Highlands, where it adds a decorative and musical element to the scene. The dotterel is another wader met with on the high mountain plateaus. In Highland lakes at various altitudes one finds the common scoter *(Melanitta nigra)*, horned grebe *(Podiceps auritus)*, red-throated diver *(Gavia stellata)*, and black-throated diver *(G. arctica)*, all of which have isolated ranges

The Lancashire countryside consists of cultivated landscape with meadows, bare hills and scattered woods of conifers and deciduous trees. (Noel Habgood: Coleman and Hayward)

Left, above: Young hedge-hogs are weaned and begin a solitary existence at the age of six weeks. Left, below: The water vole (Arvicola amphibia) is found in France, Spain and the British Isles. (Photographs by Geoffrey Kinns: A.F.L.)

Above: A deciduous forest near the river Glen in Argyll, Scotland, (Geoffrey Kinns: A.F.L.). Left: Primroses (Primula vulgaris) in sheltered woods (D. P. Wilson). Right: Crossleaved heath (Erica tetralix) is a characteristic plant of the Scottish bogs, as are sedges and Sphagnum mosses. (D. P. Wilson)

in this part of Europe. The ptarmigan and snow bunting *(Plectrophenax nivalis),* requiring an alpine environment, live on the highest peaks. There, too, one may see such a lowland species as the pygmy shrew *(Sorex minutus)* moving rapidly over the snow and looking quite out of place at such an altitude. White-coated mountain hares also live on the mountain tops; they can turn white in Scotland as early as the end of October.

There are few places in Europe that provide such opportunities for seeing golden eagles over moors and mountains as Scotland. This eagle breeds on a ledge in a cliff or in a tree; there it builds its nest, repairing and enlarging it year after year.

BASS ROCK

Although much has already been said about various European coasts, a word must be added about the coasts of Scotland. They vary greatly, ranging from the mudflats of the Solway Firth, covered periodically by the tide, to the rocky coasts of the northwest, with fjords penetrating far inland, and those of the innumerable islands. One of the most remarkable is Bass Rock in the Firth of Forth. A strangely shaped rocky islet about 350 feet high, it stands at the mouth of a wide firth. In some places its cliffs fall almost vertically to the sea, in others the slope is more gentle. Bass Rock is a volcanic dome made of basalt; millions of years of exposure to the elements have destroyed the crater walls and the slopes of the ancient volcano. The upper parts of the island present a pattern of green grass and white birds. About nine thousand gannets breed there among fulmars, kittiwakes, herring gulls, cormorants, guillemots, razorbills and puffins—about the same species as those inhabiting the Farne Islands.

Another type of coast, with other birds, surrounds the mouth of the Ythan River north of Aberdeen. Sandy shores and sand banks with incredible quantities of mollusks, and, farther inland, dunes, calluna heaths and meadows, form a paradise for eiders and shelducks. About eight hundred pairs of eiders breed there, the largest colony in the British Isles. *Hydrobia,* almost microscopically small snails, are the staple food of the shelduck. It has been found that British populations of shelducks migrate to the waters in the Bristol Channel and around Helgoland, off the coast of Germany, just after midsummer, and usually complete their migration by the end of July. The return of the shelducks is more of an irregular vagabondage, gradually bringing the birds nearer to the breeding grounds, than a true migration.

THE ORKNEYS, SHETLANDS AND OUTER HEBRIDES

North of Caithness, the most northerly mainland county of Scotland, are the Orkneys, a group of ninety-nine islands and many skerries. Still farther north in the Atlantic lie the Shetland Isles, a rocky archipelago of 117 islands. Whereas the Orkneys are quite flat, and have extensive moors, many lakes, an occasional marsh, and even some woods on the principal island, the Shetland landscape is more irregular, with steep, rocky coasts on the western side. Great areas consist of desolate stony land, very similar to the mountainous plateaus of

Scandinavia. Only on the southern part of the main island are there sandy beaches and dunes. The interior is covered with moors where Shetland ponies, sheep and cattle graze.

Almost everything on the Orkneys and the Shetlands is connected with or dependent on the sea, including the fauna. Among mammals, seals are fairly common. The common seal is most numerous, and may be seen in hundreds on the Shetlands; the gray seal is found there too. The number of seabirds is considerable, whereas the species of land and freshwater birds decrease as one goes farther north. While there are eighty-nine species of land and freshwater birds breeding in Caithness, sixty-seven species are found on the Orkneys, thirty-five on the Shetlands, and only nineteen on the Faeroes. But other interesting species are found to the north: on the Orkneys the red-necked phalarope *(Phalaropus lobatus),* arctic skua *(Stercorarius parasiticus)* and great skua *(S. skua)* are to be seen. They also live on the Shetlands, as does the whimbrel *(Numenius phaeopus).* The arctic skua is also found in small numbers on the mainland. The rock dove *(Columba livia)* has its most northerly breeding site on the Shetlands.

Halfway between the Orkneys and Shetlands, the waves of the Atlantic and North Sea break against Fair Isle, a rocky island little more than a square mile in area, rising about eighty-two feet above sea level. Long famous for its migrating birds, it was bought by a Scottish ornithologist, George Waterston, to be used as a station for the study of bird migration. The island seems to have become a port of call for birds migrating over the sea, and more than three hundred species have been observed there. It is surrounded by jagged rocks, which often make it inaccessible to seafarers.

Far away in the Atlantic, west of the Orkneys and north of the Hebrides is North Rona, inhabited by hundreds of Leach's petrels *(Oceanodroma leucorrhoa)* and other marine birds, including about five hundred pairs of great black-backed gulls. This island has an area of three hundred acres and is forty-seven miles from the northernmost point of the Hebrides. It is still farther from the Orkneys, and therefore very isolated. The absence of human beings may explain why North Rona sometimes shelters and provides breeding sites for about fifteen per cent of the world population of gray seals. The puffin is very numerous there, its population numbering about a hundred thousand; still others live on the Flannan Isles west of the Outer Hebrides.

The Outer Hebrides, a chain of islands about 140 miles long, is the oldest mountain formation in Scotland, and consists of gneiss. To the east the coast is rocky, with many inlets and fjords, but the west coast is less rugged, consisting of rocks alternating with rounded, shell sand beaches. On the landward side of the beaches are dunes, now bounded by beautiful green grass extending far inland. In winter, barnacle geese and white-fronted geese graze there. The islanders believe that the manuring of the meadows by grazing geese is important for regrowth.

The inland regions of the Hebrides contain vast areas of uncultivated land, where the wetter parts are covered with *Sphagnum* mosses and sedge, and the dry land by crossleaved heath. In summer the white patches of cotton sedge *(Eriophorum)* lighten up an otherwise darkish landscape, where brown is the prevailing color. There are thousands of small lakes and tarns in the marshlands, and most of these are also brown. The very timid graylag goose, which cannot be approached at close quarters, breeds there. Mallard and teal are

The red deer finds few woods in much of its habitat in Scotland. In mild winters it may stay on the highest hills through the winter. (J. Allan Cash)

also found there, and red-necked phalaropes swim on the small tarns. Shovelers and tufted ducks breed in the Outer Hebrides.

The Outer Hebrides were probably once covered with woods or scrub, but the trees have disappeared, probably through the agency of man. Around Stornoway Castle on Lewis, the largest island, a fairly large area was planted with trees, mainly conifers, about one hundred years ago. Other small regions of the Outer Hebrides have also been planted with trees and have attracted several birds that could not otherwise live there. At Stornoway Castle, for example, there is a colony of rooks. Small red deer also live in some of the wooded area.

ISLAND OF BIRDS

Forty miles west of North Uist, one of the larger islands of the Outer Hebrides, is a group of islands called St. Kilda, uninhabited since 1930, and famous for the number of its birds. One of the islands, Hirta, is quite large, being 1575 acres in area, whereas others are only stacklike cliffs rising straight out of the sea. The vegetation on the larger islands is dominated by purple bell-heather, heather, fescue, bilberry and cowberry *(Vaccinium vitis-idaea)*. On high cliffs grows the dwarf willow *(Salix herbacea)*, which is also found in arctic regions. An even more surprising sight is the spotted orchid *(Orchis maculata)*.

Birds overwhelm St. Kilda. The colonies of gannets there are the largest in the world, no fewer than 17,035 breeding pairs having been counted in 1951. But this is small compared with the number of puffins—at least one million of which inhabit the islands. In addition, there are colonies of guillemots, razorbills and gulls. Another exceptional characteristic of the St. Kilda group is its four species of petrels and shearwaters—the storm petrel, Leach's petrel, Manx shearwater and fulmar. They are all marine birds that visit land only during the breeding season. Of these birds, the history of the fulmar is the most interesting, and also the best known, as a result of James Fisher's study.

During the last two hundred years the fulmar has multiplied surprisingly, especially when one considers that it usually lays only one egg a year. A large colony (about forty thousand nests as of 1949) has been known on St. Kilda since 1697, and up to 1878 it was the only part of the British Isles where the bird was known to exist. It was in 1878 that the species arrived in the Shetlands, where there are now about 43,000 pairs. Since then they have colonized the British Isles at such a rapid rate that in 1949 there were at least 120,000 of them. This enormous increase in numbers has been attributed by some zoologists to the activities of man in the North Atlantic, the waste matter from whaling and fishing providing the bird—so it is claimed—with new sources of food.

The twite and wren are among St. Kilda's land birds. The latter is larger than and different in color from the usual form, which has caused it to be regarded as a separate race *(Troglodytes troglodytes hirtensis)*. The same is true of two

Tralee Bay and Dingle peninsula in southwestern Ireland illustrate the broken outline of Ireland's Atlantic coast. (W. Suschitzky)

small rodents on St. Kilda, the house mouse *(Mus musculus muralis)* and the long-tailed field mouse *(Apodemus sylvaticus hirtensis)*. The house mouse may have become extinct since human beings left the islands in 1930, but the long-tailed field mouse has increased in number. Lately a warden and soldiers have been stationed on St. Kilda.

The most famous animal on St. Kilda is the Soay sheep, which was probably brought to Soay a thousand or more years ago. It has adapted itself to the barren environment of these lonely isles, and is now unlike any of its brethren.

Though they are isolated, North Rona, Sula Sgeir and St. Kilda are not the outermost of the British Isles; that distinction belongs to Rockall, a rock that rises, like the head of a gigantic monster, seventy feet above the sea 184 miles west of St. Kilda. Rockall is assumed to be about forty million years old, which, geologically speaking, is comparatively young. Its composition of various kinds of granite is, however, considered geologically unique. An interesting botanical feature is that its vegetation consists only of algae, which, so far as is known, represent twenty-one species and form five distinct vertical vegetation zones.

The number of marine invertebrates is also astonishingly small: only six species are known—a mollusk *(Littorina rudis)*, an amphipod *(Hyale nilssoni),* and four microscopic species, two mites, a rotifer and a fluke. It is interesting to note that both the mollusk and the amphipod are viviparous, which has probably helped them to survive.

Twenty-three birds have been observed on or around this island rock, but no species has yet been found breeding there.

IRELAND

After Great Britain and Iceland, Ireland is the third largest island of Europe. Most of it is lowland rimmed by coastal mountains. Some of these mountains, with their offshoots, extend into the central lowlands; the highest, those of Kerry in the southwestern corner of the country, rise to 3414 feet. The coast is broken, particularly in the west, by wide or wedge-shaped fjords that run far inland. There are many lakes, both in the interior and within the girdle of mountains, and a profusion of peat bogs.

The appearance of the Irish landscape today is largely the result of glacial action. The topography of the island is the result of ice that deposited layers of boulder clay, the fertility of which is one of Ireland's few natural resources. Everywhere there are gravel hills left by the melting ice on the plains, as well as low hills of glacial moraine; they can be counted in thousands. These ridges, called eskers, run in the same direction as did the glaciers that deposited them. About one-eighth of the lowland country is said to consist of such eskers.

Green is the prevailing color of the "emerald isle" in lowlands and highlands, plateaus and on slopes down to the sea. The meadows and pastures, which comprise the greater part of the land, are green all the year round, for the Atlantic influence is stronger in this country than in any other part of Europe, which means that the climate is mild and the rainfall heavy. In the southwest the mean temperature in January, the coldest month, is 44.6° F (7° C), and in July, the warmest month, it reaches no more than 60.8° F (16° C). Owing to the varying geology and topography, the Irish landscape differs from county to county. Some counties, such as Connemara, are rough and very poor, others are fertile plains, and still others are marked by remarkably wild and lonely mountains and fjords. The areas of grassland, which are considerable, provide food for large numbers of cattle and sheep, the island's principal source of income.

The flora and fauna of Ireland are more insular than those of Great Britain. The probable explanation for this, borne out by botanical and zoological evidence, is that Ireland seems to have become isolated earlier and more completely from Great Britain than did Great Britain from the Continent. Among the large number of terrestrial vertebrates widely distributed in Great Britain but lacking in Ireland are the weasel *(Mustela nivalis)*, the yellow-necked field mouse *(Apodemus flavicollis)*, harvest mouse *(Mycromys minutus)*, field vole *(Microtus agrestis)*, vole rat *(Arvicola amphibia)*, bank vole *(Clethrionomys glareolus)*, dormouse *(Muscardiunus avellanarius)*, great bat *(Nyctalus noctula)*, barbastelle *(Barbastella barbastellus)*, mole, common shrew and water shrew *(Neomys fodiens)*. Only one of Great Britain's six reptiles, the viviparous lizard, is found in Ireland. The island is devoid of snakes, which is of course the source of the legend that Saint Patrick, the patron saint of Ireland, expelled these creatures from the country. Only two amphibians live there—the natterjack toad and the smooth newt *(Triturus vulgaris)*—whereas Great Britain has six, not counting two introduced species.

Ten species of freshwater fish, now living only in freshwater, are found there, whereas Great Britain has twenty-two. Did these species colonize Ireland while the island was joined to England and the Continent, or did they reach Ireland by way of the channels or the Irish Sea, which probably had a lower concentration of salt during the last phase of the melting glacial ice? Nearly all ten species of Irish freshwater fish have proved themselves able to live in brackish water in other parts of Europe. The char *(Salvelinus)*, is found in various forms in several Irish lakes.

Only fifty-seven per cent of Great Britain's approximately 2300 plants are found in Ireland, but it must be borne in mind that Great Britain is much larger and covers more climatic regions than Ireland. The island is, nevertheless, very interesting, for many of its species have an Atlantic distribution while some have Mediterranean, Iberian, or even, in a few cases, American affinities.

About one quarter of the country consists of marshes, mountains and lakes that look wild but have in fact been modified by man for thousands of years through deforestation, burning, grazing, and the cutting of peat for fuel. Arable land occupies about twenty-five per cent of the country; the rest is meadowland. Man has destroyed the forests that once grew there. Heaths occur everywhere, the blossoms of gorse *(Ulex)* coloring them yellow in early spring. The surviving woods consist of elm, oak, ash, birch and alder trees. The pine became extinct in Neolithic times, not because of man, but because the change of climate did not favor its growth; in historic times it has been reintroduced, making the region much more suitable for squirrels and pine martens.

The climate of Ireland encourages the formation of peat, and peat bogs cover about eight per cent of the surface of the island, the largest proportion in Europe outside of Scandinavia and northern Russia. Like those on the Outer Hebrides, the bogs are a mixture of mosses, sedge and heather scattered over both wet and dry parts of the bog. In the mountainous western region they cover hilltops and slopes as well as the lower plains. The formation of peat is a complex process, that takes place only under special climatic and soil conditions. High precipitation is important because the bog is often waterlogged, and this almost constant flooding greatly hinders soil bacteria from breaking down dead vegetation and converting it to humus. The decomposition of the vegetation therefore proceeds much more slowly than the production of organic matter. The accumulation of plant organisms is also favored by the impoverished soil itself, because its organic substance is highly acid and without lime, factors that work against bacterial activity.

Peat bogs are formed during thousands of years. Peat deposits in the British Isles have been estimated to have begun at the end of the Boreal period, about nine thousand years ago. Ever since then, the development has been alternately slow or rapid, according to the shifting of climate during the Atlantic, sub-Boreal and sub-Atlantic climatic periods. Since the latter period still prevails, peat bogs are still being formed not only in the British Isles but also in large areas of Europe, especially in the northern regions.

One ornithological feature that distinguishes the coasts of Ireland is that some species of arctic and subarctic waders rest there in great numbers during migration. Some also winter there. Two of these species, the bar-tailed godwit *(Limosa lapponica)* and knot *(Calidris canutus)*, are particularly numerous. On few other European shores can these two species be seen in such magnificent flocks. The knot is an especially faraway guest, breeding on the Siberian tundra, Spitsbergen and Greenland.

Plains and
Green Woods

Deciduous Forests from
the Atlantic to the Urals

14

Much of Central Europe is a plain that was once covered with vast deciduous forests extending from the Atlantic to the Ural Mountains. The country abounded in marshes and bogs surrounded by thick forests, and was dotted with steppes. Great rivers wound through dense woods of sallows and willows. They rose in the mountains of the interior and transported tremendous amounts of sediment, especially during spring floods, to the valleys below. Thus many of the depressions in the low-lying land were gradually built up into magnificent meadows; in other places the marshes remained and with them a jungle-like ground vegetation that covered much of the dark water with a green blanket. On the dry ground round about was a dense forest of oaks, maples, ash trees, lime trees, beeches and hornbeams. These were the principal trees in the virgin deciduous forests of the temperate areas of ancient Europe. Sun and warmth in conjunction with high humidity created such forests, which in density and luxuriance are without parallel in Europe today. During the period from about 6000 to 1000 B.C. the mean temperature was higher than at present, so that plants and animals thrived much farther north than they do now.

Very little remains of this natural abundance. Most of the forests have disappeared. When man ceased to live on the roots, seeds, fruit and wild animals he found in woods and water, and began tilling the earth, forests became a hindrance to him; he cut clearings in them to make way for arable land and pastures, transforming the countryside beyond recognition. Most of the woods of Europe are now cultivated, with man determining the site, height, and life span of the trees. Unlike the trees of antiquity, they are held in check.

In speaking of the deciduous forest belt of Europe today, we mean those regions where such forests grow spontaneously, despite cultivation of the area. Geographically, the deciduous forest region covers Central Europe from the northern part of the Iberian peninsula, France, the British Isles and Denmark and southernmost Norway and Sweden in the west, to the Ural Mountains in Russia in the east. From a wide expanse on the Atlantic coast, the forest region narrows inland to form a triangle with its apex in the Urals; it is bounded to

the north by taiga, and to the south by steppe. In southwestern Europe the Mediterranean zone forms the boundary. Thus the great mountain ranges, the Pyrenees, Alps and Carpathians, are in the deciduous forest area of Europe, but their altitude encourages the growth of coniferous forests. Similarly, many other European mountain ranges provide coniferous forest enclaves in the deciduous forest region; these are particularly common in Germany.

Going by road and rail across Europe—from the Hague to Warsaw, for instance—a traveler may find it difficult to believe he is passing through a deciduous forest zone. Surrounding him will be open fields; all that remains of forest are a few groves of trees or an occasional conifer-clad ridge. The transformation has given rise to completely new environments for flora and fauna. Some plants and animals have become adapted to the new conditions, others have been driven to the few remaining patches of woodland, while a third group has been wiped out. The disappearance of the forests has also affected the climate, the hydrography of the land, and the soil. In other words, the whole ecology of Central Europe has been altered.

So far the disappearance of deciduous forests from Europe has not proved catastrophic to man; on the contrary, the results have been greatly advantageous. The cultivated land has for centuries supported a growing population, without, miraculously enough, much impairing the fertility of the soil. A comparison with the Mediterranean zone emphasizes the fertility of Central Europe, due mainly to its temperate climate.

There are, however, many signs that the productive life of the plain of Europe is slowly being exhausted through misuse. Spring floods, which were once distributed over the countryside in an endless network of rivers and streams, and which at times flooded the meadows and were stored in marshes or in the soil, have been canalized, and the soil is no longer enriched by them. The groundwater level has sunk, in many places catastrophically, and desiccation has set in.

A CULTIVATED WORLD

As has been indicated, arable land, the open cultivated plain, is today the dominant type of landscape in the deciduous forest area of Europe. The vegetation is without variety and the fauna limited. Some animals have, however, been favored by these conditions. Among them are the brown hare, the common hamster, such voles as *Microtus arvalis* and *M. agrestis* the harvest mouse *(Micromys minutus)*, the partridge, the rook, buzzard, kestrel, larks, finches and buntings *(Emberiza citrinella* and *E. calandra)*. Regrettably, during recent years the use of toxic chemicals in agriculture has almost eliminated certain species of birds from large areas. This is a dangerous development, and man, as a dependant, may suffer from it.

Arable land is among the most artificial and unstable habitats for plants and animals, for it is always subject to drastic change. Periodic plowing, sowing and harvesting disrupt both the microflora and microfauna, preventing the stabilization and natural development of the biocommunity.

In easternmost Austria between the Leitha Mountains and the "Little Carpathians" the Danube has worn a narrow passage through steep cliffs. (Otto Kraus)

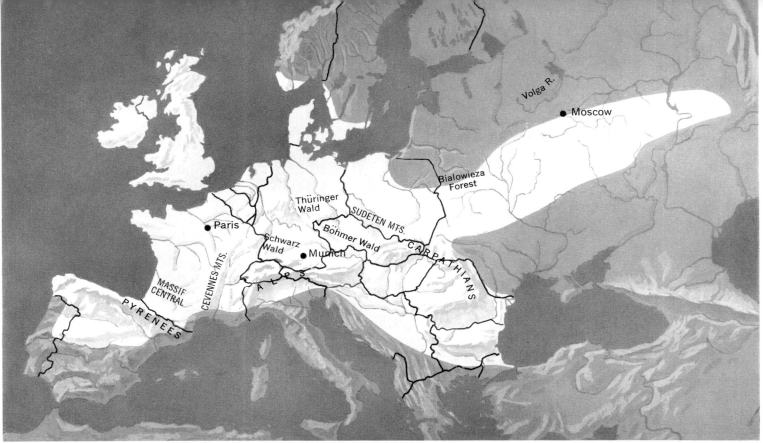

Although cultivated plains characterize most of Central Europe, scattered woods and parklike country, marshes, and mountain forests lend much variety to the landscape.

THE PARTRIDGE

Of the larger ground birds on the plain one notices the partridge most frequently. Most people know it as a pigeon-sized bird that, when disturbed, flies up with a hoarse "kirr-ick, kirr-ick" and clattering wings.

Partridges live in flocks for most of the year, and families often remain in such flocks far into the winter. The partridge is a true ground bird, taking to flight only when necessary. It can run quickly and for long distances, takes nearly all its food on the ground, where, unlike the roosting pheasant, it spends the night. Like many other birds living in flocks, partridges have very regular habits. In the early dawn they leave their night quarters and fly by stages to their feeding places, at midday they quench their thirst in a ditch or stream, dipping their bills and holding them up to allow the water to run down their throats. They then remain inactive until later in the afternoon, when they feed again.

Certain animals demand only a few shrubs around the fields they inhabit. Thickets along ditches, gardens, groves or avenues of trees and small woods attract shrews, moles, weasels, stoats, badgers, foxes, roe deer, stock doves, little owls, tawny owls, long-eared owls, the whitethroat *(Sylvia communis)*, linnets, and many others to cultivated regions. A building or two on the plain may provide nesting places for bats, swallows, house martins, barn owls and white storks. White storks are also still common in the agricultural regions of eastern Europe, but are becoming rare in the west.

Few birds come into such close contact with man as the swallow. It makes its home in stables, barns, and outbuildings, flying through open doors, broken windows, and even holes in walls. Once indoors it flies straight to its nest. Thereafter, a soft, melodious twittering can often be heard from where it sits on a beam in some dark corner.

THE SURVIVING FORESTS

The surviving deciduous forests of Europe represent the maximum productive capacity of the soil on this continent, but they are surpassed by tropical rain forests. These forests also accommodate many more species of animals than do farmed plains. Where deciduous woods have been allowed to grow freely, forest scenery in the ancient European tradition may still be found: mighty oaks spread their gnarled crowns; huge maple leaves, shaking in the wind, create strange shadow patterns; elms strive upward, and the trailing branches of lime trees form thick curtains. Sometimes the trees grow up straight and thin, branching out only when they reach the light. In these regions there also grow beeches and ash trees; ivy winds around the tree trunks, clothing them in dark green; hazel bushes grow in bouquets, sometimes yielding large crops of nuts, which form an important part of the diet of many animals; and there are dense thickets of elder, hawthorn *(Crataegus)*, currants, raspberries and dog-rose *(Rosa canina)*. On and around hills and banks the blackthorn *(Prunus spinosa)* forms a prickly, almost impenetrable wall; hope *(Humulus lupulus)* and honeysuckle *(Lonicera periclymenum)*, the lianas of the European woods, twine through bushes and high up into trees; yellow, white, red, blue and purple flowers grow on meadows in the glades; the exotic shapes of orchids glow like dark flames; the poisonous yellow kingcup *(Caltha palustris)* grows around still tarns covered with the leaves of aquatic plants and, in the water itself, stand stately yellow irises *(Iris pseudacorus)*. The smell of the warm damp earth, enriched by decayed leaves and the work of bacteria, blends with the secretions of living plants and fungi to form a world of mysterious scents.

Each layer of the woodland teems with life; the soil, the surface of the earth, shrubs, the treetops, the air above and below the canopy of trees. Insects and other invertebrates are by far the most numerous. Their significance to the life cycle of the forest cannot be exaggerated. Lizards rustle over last year's dry leaves; grass snakes, their sensitive forked tongues extended and quivering, glide along the banks of the marshes hunting frogs; a tiny field mouse nibbles a root. Here and there can be seen signs of wild boars rooting for acorns, or of red deer that have rolled in muddy tarns; numerous birds call from the trees, while buzzards and kites glide above.

The most common type of forest in these temperate regions is comprised of beeches. Beech forests are not so rich in plant and animal species as mixed deciduous forests, but in spring, when the leaves are just budding, they afford one of the most beautiful sights in Europe. At that time the pale green foliage does not shade the ground and the sun can reach the young flowers. Wood anemones *(Anemone nemorosa)* form a delightful green and white carpet.

The oak, ash, lime and other trees sometimes form woods, too, but they are much less dense than the beech woods. Here and there they open into glades, which may be crowded with flowering plants and bushes. Some such glades are natural; others have been created by grazing cattle or cultivation.

Climate is very important for forests, but forests also influence climate. There is of course less light in wooded regions than in open fields. The temperature in the forest is usually lower in summer and higher in winter than on the surrounding plains, and the daily temperature curve often shows smaller fluctuations. Changes in temperature, too, take place more slowly in forests than in open fields because the foliage prevents the direct warming of the soil by sunlight. The air and the moisture below the canopy are in general not blown away by strong winds, and this also contributes to the stability of the climate. When the air over meadows and rocky ground vibrates in the heat of the sun, it is usually cooler in the woods; at night the woods are often warmer.

No terrestrial habitat offers such a diversity of conditions

Mistletoe in France. Since this parasitic plant remains green in winter, it becomes conspicuous on the leafless trees. (J. Allan Cash)

Left above: The moor hen, distributed across most of Europe, breeds in a variety of aquatic habitats. (Julius Behnke) Left: The kingfisher is found along many streams in deciduous forests. It lives on small fishes and invertebrates it catches in running water. (Eric Hosking)

Above: In the limestone Alps of southern Bavaria a narrow gorge cut by the river Tiroler Ache is now a nature reserve. (Otto Kraus)   Right: Whereas man's works usually destroy the natural landscape, a dam such as the one in Nord-Rhein-Westfalen creates a new natural environment. (Laenderpress, Dusseldorf)

Cultivated landscape with grazed meadows and woods dominated by spruce at Hofsgrund in the Schwarzwald, Germany. (Lichtbild-Archiv)

favorable to animal and bird life as deciduous forests. Hiding places and living quarters can be found everywhere—in the soft soil, under tree roots, in thickets, in hollow trees and many other places. The woods also provide food for vegetarian, carnivorous, and insectivorous species alike. The supply of food varies from year to year, and this causes a chain reaction throughout the nutritional cycle—from plants to vegetarians and carnivores, the number of animals fluctuating more or less with the supply. This phenomenon is even more pronounced in coniferous forests; and it also occurs on the tundra.

Nor does any other manifestation of nature reflect the seasonal changes so distinctly as woodland. The account we have just given is of woodland in spring, when the trees are covered with pale green leaves, and flowers and animals are most conspicuous. In summer, fruit and berries ripen, and many animals born in spring then set forth on their journeys of discovery. The drought of summer often changes the aspect of woodlands: the water in brooks and tarns dries up, the green of the leaves becomes deeper, and the birds fall silent. Autumn transforms the deciduous woods into a fire of red and gold, the foliage of each tree changing color as the chlorophyll becomes exhausted. Then the leaves fall, a process

very important for later rebirth; by the time winter comes the trees are bare except for a few dry leaves.

The climatic variations in the forest belt from the Atlantic to the Urals, and from southern France to southern Sweden provide a variety of distinct ecological conditions. In the western part, with its mild Atlantic climate, the growing season is longer than in the east with its long, severe winters; and latitude has of course a similar effect. Thus no wood is exactly the same as another.

THE FORESTS OF FRANCE

After the Soviet Union, France is the largest country of Europe; within its boundaries are represented all the types of natural environment found on the Continent—Atlantic and Mediterranean coasts, plains, forests, mountains and high alps. As is evident in countless works of art, the variety of countryside is, as it were, an old French tradition; it is maintained today. Most of the land, however, is a plain; few forests have survived. Nevertheless, France remains a country of indescribably charming natural woodland. If farming had not taken over, forests would still thrive throughout the country; they have diminished to about twenty per cent of the total acreage. An attempt to explain why the cultivated plain of France is so different from the agricultural regions of other Central European countries would take us too far back in time, but we may mention in passing such factors as methods of cultivating and dividing the land and, not least, the individuality of the inhabitants.

Most of the deciduous woods grow on the slopes of the Massif Central, the Cevennes, the Vosges and other mountain chains, while the most magnificient forest in France is Fontainebleau, covering some 42,500 acres thirty-five miles southeast of Paris. Part of it is at present a nature reserve. Although the vicinity of a growing city is a precarious one for such a reserve, the city does increase the recreational value of the reserve and may save it from encroachment. Magnificent beech woods stretch over undulating country of rocky hills and gently rounded dells; old oaks, ash trees and hornbeams form mighty vaults. But of course no primeval forests have survived in the lowlands of France.

The mountain woods of France are comparatively abundant in fauna. From the plain of southern France, the Massif Central rises to a maximum height of 6188 feet. In southeastern France, the Cevennes, reaching 5755 feet, are even more interesting, for they are so far south that their deciduous woods are influenced in places by the Mediterranean climate zone. In northeast France are the Vosges (high point 4695 feet), separated from the Black Forest by the Rhine.

On the lower slopes of all these isolated mountains grow deciduous forests; higher up the woods are coniferous forests. Nowhere have these woods escaped the attention of man. Cutting and planting for hundreds of years have transformed them into cultivated land, with conifers often favored at the expense of hardwood trees. This has also caused changes in the fauna: birds typical of coniferous forests, the crested tit *(Parus cristatus)*, firecrest *(Regulus ignicapillus)* and goldcrest *(R. regulus)*, for example, have been forced to extend their ranges elsewhere.

Between wooded mountains, enclosed by arms of the Saone and Rhone, is a large stretch of marshland—la Dombes. Woods grow there, too, but of a quite different type from those already mentioned. In the maze of small lakes and bogs, channels and brooks, the marsh forest is in places very dense. Willows, sallows and alders fringe the water, and farther inland on islands and the mainland are thickets of brambles, above which elms, poplars, ash trees and oaks raise their leafy crowns. Although la Dombes is a world of water and marsh birds, many birds that build in trees inhabit its woods; for example, six species of woodpecker and five of owls. La Dombes is undoubtedly one of Europe's most valuable and interesting natural areas, despite the fact that it has been intensively exploited by man.

In the spring, frogs and toads congregate and spawn around the tarns and lakes of the deciduous forests. Waking from their winter coma, their fast unbroken, toads *(Bufo bufo)*, set out for their spawning waters, with the small males often riding the females. For about a fortnight in April, May or June, depending on the latitude, the chorus of toads can be heard from dusk to dawn. The male clings to the female's side with its forelegs, both on and beneath the surface of the water. The eggs are joined together by a jelly-like substance, forming two long strings, which the female, with the help of the male, twines round plants after the eggs have been fertilized. These strings may be from ten to fifteen feet long, and contain from two to seven thousand eggs.

The tree frog, often a beautiful green and only about an inch and a half long, may be found around pools rich in vegetation, but it also inhabits deciduous forests far from water, concealing itself in leaves. It can modify its color to conform to its surroundings, varying it from yellow and green to gray and black. When spawning time is over, the frogs sit sunning themselves along the edge of the water or on water lily leaves, but at the first sign of danger they dive into the water and hide at the bottom. Male and female frogs alike usually winter in the mud at the bottom of the spawning pool, hibernation lasting from September to April or May.

With many hiding places and an abundance of food, deciduous woods provide excellent habitats for lizards and snakes. The smooth snake *(Coronella austriaca)* prefers dry, rather sunny and stony sites, but it may also be found among plants in coppices. It leaves its underground winter quarters quite late in the spring, and mates in May. At this time the males fight each other, but the battle is bloodless. The smooth snake is a skillful climber and is very strong. When picked up by its tail, it can lift its head to the level of the hand holding it, a feat that no other European snake can equal. It is sometimes killed in mistake for the venomous adder *(Vipera berus)*. When taken by surprise and unable to hide or retreat, it curls up. It may bite if it is touched, for it has a quick temper, but its bite is harmless to man. Lizards and snakes are its principal items of food, but it also eats frogs, mice and voles. It can wind itself around its prey and devour it alive.

In autumn the red deer stag loudly announces mating time. A hind stands partly hidden by young spruce in the Hunsrück Mountains of western Germany. (Julius Behnke)

The aesculapian snake *(Elaphe longissima),* since antiquity symbol of the medical profession, is found on stony ground among shrub vegetation. Its northern limit runs through France, central Germany, Poland and southern Russia.

Among the lizards in deciduous forests is the legless blindworm or slowworm *(Anguis fragilis).* It winds in stiff convolutions and, when caught, makes only a half-hearted attempt to escape. Its method of defense is self-amputation: if caught by the tail, for example, it can, like many other lizards, detach part of its tail and thus escape. This is probably a mechanical process caused by the contraction of muscles. These muscles act on vertebrae that have "breaking points" and on surrounding tissues that are perforated. There is no loss of blood and a new segment of tail is regenerated in a few weeks or months; but it never attains the length or mobility of the original. Blindworms should therefore be handled carefully. The new tail has no vertebrae, but consists wholly of cartilage. If the blindworm is again caught by the tail it must detach it higher up, at another vertebra, and so the tail becomes still shorter.

The water snake *(Natrix natrix)* is common in deciduous forests in the neighborhood of water and in damp lowlands having many frogs. It is an excellent swimmer, both on and beneath the water. It spends the winter under heaps of stones or in underground cavities. Large numbers of these snakes may occupy such winter quarters. When spring comes they make a regular migration back to their respective territories, which may be some distance away.

A cross spider, Argiope bruennichi, *captures a victim in its large web. (Erich Sochurek) Below: Two scops owls hiding in a spruce. Common in southern Europe, this species occurs mainly in deciduous woods, gardens and parks, often close to buildings. (Oscar Schmid)*

NATURAL OASES IN BELGIUM

The Belgian landscape is the result not only of its geological past but also of its national history. Devastated by wars, subjected to an extremely high population density as well as intensive farming and industrialization, it is astonishing that there are any natural areas in Belgium at all. But even though over nine million people live in an area of no more than 11,775 square miles, there still remains much natural beauty.

The area Belgium now occupies was originally at the bottom of the sea, but about 250 million years ago foldings occurred and the region became a veritable alpine tract, probably with peaks of up to fifteen thousand feet and with deep valleys below. In the course of millenia the mountains were eroded and the sea flooded the land again, even covering what we now know as the Ardennes. In the epoch that followed, the sea advanced and retreated in a thousand-year cycle, again radically changing the land.

For long periods, millions of years ago, large sections of the marshy parts of Belgium were covered with tropical vegetation and swarmed with animals. The nearness of the sea enabled marine fish to invade the marshes; some of these fish gradually evolved into froglike creatures, whose cries were among the first to be heard on the earth's surface. Reptiles slowly came into being and several lizards grew to a gigantic size. Eventually mammals appeared. All of this can be traced in the soil of Belgium, where the strata of sediment

The roe deer is the most common wild ungulate in Central Europe. It adapts to cultivated landscape but is also spreading northward into more natural forests. (Helmut Ctverak)

from various epochs are a storehouse of information on the plants and animals of Europe. Much of this prehistoric evidence can now be seen in Belgian museums.

Only a shadow of this wealth of flora and fauna remains today. The prehistoric period has, however, left traces in the topography, which gives the country its great variety of scenery. One notes immediately three main types of country: the flat coast with many polders on the inland side of the line of dunes; the fertile plain with wide expanses of cultivated land covering gently undulating hills and dales, and with groves of trees and parks around towns, villages and chateaux; and finally woodland, which rises toward the east to culminate in the Ardennes.

There is virtually no genuine virgin nature left in Belgium. Villages and towns are sprinkled all over the countryside and, as one motors along the main roads, houses stand like a screen on both sides. But Belgium has many oases, often astonishingly abundant in wildlife. It seems a paradox that this country should produce more game—red deer, brown hares, pheasants and partridges, for example—than does Sweden, and that a small Belgian park in the middle of a town should harbor more birds and a much greater number of species than an area in Sweden about fifty times as large.

Everywhere, the plain of Belgium is broken by groves, parks,

and small woods, in most of which the beech is dominant. The most famous of these is the Forêt de Soignes, near Brussels. It boasts ravines, dales, small lakes, gentle slopes and plateaus, all of which contain many rare and beautiful plants. Roe deer graze there, badgers shuffle along their paths, and birds such as the golden oriole and the blackcap sing jubilantly from the treetops. The rippling notes of the wrens rise in a chorus, and the voice of the chiffchaff provides a continuous accompaniment. The hawfinch, with its great caricature of a beak, may be seen, but it is seldom heard; turtle-doves and stock doves fly over the glades; woodpeckers drum, and at dusk nightingales sing from bushes to the thorough bass of little owls, long-eared owls and tawny owls. A walk through the Forêt de Soignes in spring is indeed an exhilarating experience.

Among the small mammals here is the common European white-throated shrew *(Crocidura russula)*. Here, too, the pine vole, which seldom leaves its underground haunts, as well as the garden dormouse, find one of their most northerly sites.

Another inhabitant of these woods is the golden oriole *(Oriolus oriolus),* one of Europe's most striking birds. Few species surpass it in song, color and vigorous temperament. The male rapidly repeats his flutelike call, a melodious "kock-lo-kyo." His vivid yellow plumage flashes in the sun as he flies over a glade. An aggressive creature, he bullies larger birds when they trespass on his territory.

The golden oriole is a genuine southerner, the only European representative of a tropical family. Several species live in Africa, others in India and on the islands of Indonesia. In spite of its conspicuous colors, lively manner, and distinctive song, it is not easy to descry: the contrasting colors of its plumage are excellent camouflage in the crowns of sunlit trees. And the female, with her quieter colors, may elude one even in open country.

For many years I have periodically studied two pairs of golden orioles in a private park in Belgium. The park is full of tall forest trees—beeches, chestnuts, lime, oak, elms birches and poplars––and fruit trees, mostly cherries, to which orioles seem partial. The courting flight of these orioles is spectacular. The male and female fly at high speed among the trees, the male so close behind the female and following her acrobatics so exactly that one gets the impression that it is a performance by one bird with two pairs of wings.

A CULTIVATED WILDERNESS

The Ardennes in the southeastern part of Belgium and in Luxembourg is a cultivated wilderness in the heart of western Europe. The deciduous woods there have often belonged to the same families for centuries and have in many cases been cared for devotedly. The hills of the Ardennes are undulating (the highest point is 2225 feet above sea level) but draped with woods almost everywhere, regardless of altitude. At many points, however, hardwood trees have been replaced by culti-

Left: The roe deer has been greatly favored by the cultivated landscape with its alternation of fields and small woods. (Erich Angenendt) Right: Winter in the Schwarzwald, Germany. A thin layer of snow covers the ground under dense growths of spruce. (Photo Stober)

vated spruce. Trout inhabit the rivers, nowadays in competition with the introduced and rapidly spreading rainbow trout *(Salmo gairdneri)*.

Few regions in western Europe are so rich in game as the Ardennes. The slopes of the valleys are in general covered with deciduous woods, where, under luxuriant summer foliage, many red deer, roe deer and wild boars live. The wildcat occurs there, too. In the bogs of the mountain plateau black grouse may be heard, the grasshopper warbler *(Locustella naevia)* sings its quaint buzzing song, and woodcocks perform their display flight around the treetops. Caves are numerous in these hills, and are often very deep.

The Ardennes lies athwart a bird migration route and is a welcome foraging place for forest birds; in the spring redwings, bramblings and many others from the forests of Lapland and the taiga of Siberia mix with songsters from Europe's deciduous forests. The effect is like a choir singing in many languages, but somehow harmonious and melodious.

Parc National de Lesse et Lhomme, with some twenty-five hundred acres, contains some of the finest natural scenery in the Ardennes. Conspicuous are the green bouquets of vegetation decorating the pale limestone cliffs. At the foot of the cliffs grow lime-thriving plants that flower in spring, among them the dwarf orchid *(Orchis ustulata)*, helleborines *(Cephalanthera)*, and the fly orchid *(Ophrys insectifera)*. The last has curious flowers, velvety, black and purple in color, and placed one above the other like a row of insects on the yellowish-green stalk. Insects are attracted to the flowers, not so much because of their appearance, as their scent; this exerts a sexual appeal on the males of two species of the genus *Gorytes,* causing them to attempt copulation with the flower. Such a mating gesture is not without significance, for only these insects can pollinate the orchid and carry its pollen to the next flower.

GERMANY: MOSAIC OF PLAINS, WOODS AND MOUNTAINS

Germany may be divided roughly into a northern plain and a southern plateau wherein mountain peaks and river valleys are striking features of the landscape. The whole area is within the deciduous forest belt, but this country too has been cultivated and industrialized to such an extent that the deciduous forests have been much reduced. Mountain ranges—the Taunus (with the highest peak about 3000 feet), the Schwarzwald (4900 feet), the Harz (2745 feet) and the Thüringerwald (3000 feet)—are scattered across the southern part of Germany, and the Erzgebirge (4122 feet) and the Böhmerwald (4784 feet) on the boundary of Czechoslovakia have some deciduous woods on their slopes, but most of the trees are conifers. Not all the areas of Germany that were formerly covered with woods have been transformed into arable land, for coniferous forests have, with the help of man, replaced the hardwood forests. About twenty-eight per cent of Germany is wooded, and seventy per cent of the woods is coniferous forest.

In spite of the intensive cultivation of the Rhine Valley, tree-clad mountains, rising steeply from the arable land in the valley, as well as terraced vineyards, are dominant. The luxuriant foliage of the trees suggests how the region must have looked when the river wound through a virgin landscape where deciduous woods grew on both slopes of the valley up to the mountain tops.

Lüneburger Heide (that is, heath), in northwestern Germany on the plain south of Hamburg, has a completely different type of nature. About fifty thousand acres of the heath is a nature reserve. It is an Atlantic type of man-made heath, mainly of heather, with some woods, marshes, fens and bogs.

The pattern of nature in Germany, with forest-clothed mountains and lowland woods scattered here and there in highly cultivated areas, creates faunal "islands" everywhere. Animals move to and fro between the wooded slopes of the mountains and the patches of forests on the plains, so that many species are dispersed over large parts of the country despite the fact that it is highly industrialized. Game animals are favored and for a long time the country has had very high standards in the regulation of hunting and conservation as well as a sound approach to wildlife.

The roe deer *(Capreolus capreolus)* is found all over the deciduous belt of Europe, in most of the Mediterranean countries, and in Scotland and Sweden, where it has multiplied greatly in recent decades. But its primary environment is deciduous forests. It is particularly at home where woods and groves alternate with open plains and cultivated fields, as they do now in many parts of Europe.

No European mammal can match this deer in grace. To escape danger it flees with high leaps, even when the terrain is flat. It is an animal of the dusk, but may frequently be seen in the daytime, particularly in neighborhoods where it is not hunted. Its day quarters are usually in places concealed by vegetation. When several roe deer are resting together they lie with their heads facing in different directions in order to detect an enemy approaching from any side.

The oestral period of this deer is in July and August, although mating has been observed several times in Germany as late as November and December. The buck is polygamous and probably mates with two to four does. Before her period of heat culminates, the doe provokes the buck to wild gallops across the countryside. Although the buck seems to be pursuing the doe, the demonstration may stop as suddenly as it started, and mating does not occur until several days later.

Another familiar mammal of such areas, the wild boar, favors damp, low-lying places in deciduous and mixed woods, but may sometimes be found in coniferous forests. It ranges throughout the deciduous forest belt and the Mediterranean zone. It is mainly nocturnal, sleeping away the days in a thicket or a depression. Wild boars usually live in small herds or family groups, and wander from place to place in the woods, sometimes making long migrations when food is scarce. They are omnivorous, generally grubbing for food in the ground, but also eating acorns, nuts, fruit, fungi, grain, roots, and almost all animal food: carrion, sick mammals, birds, eggs, reptiles, insects and snails. It is thought that their grubbing in beech woods spreads the beechnuts, thus assisting in seeding new trees.

Among ground-living vertebrates in deciduous forests, small rodents such as voles and mice are the main food of several other vertebrates. Any alteration in their condition is therefore likely to cause chain reactions in various directions. Also

Fox cubs at the entrance to their den. They are almost omnivorous, but their staple food is small rodents. (Oscar Schmid)

218

important in the forest economy is the food consumption of the small rodents themselves and their influence on the vegetation. But the relationship between the food intake of animals and the cycles of vegetation is very complex and has for the most part not yet been clarified.

The environmental requirements of various species of rodents in the deciduous forests differ greatly. Of the commoner voles and mice living in European woodlands, the bank vole (Clethrionomys glareolus) seems to be least adaptable, while the field vole, in almost the same range, can adapt itself to a wide variety of habitats.

Both long-tailed and yellow-necked field mice prefer deciduous and mixed woods with shrubs and luxuriant undergrowth, although they can survive in a pure coniferous forest. Sometimes they may also be found in more open grass fields or in ditches. The field mice are extremely clever at finding food, and they will, if need be, move their headquarters several times a year.

When settled in a habitat, these small rodents generally abide by a quite rigid daily routine. Excursions outside the home territory are undertaken only to seek food, follow an almost fixed schedule, and are made on definite, usually well protected routes. Only during the mating and migration season do their movements seem to become more irregular; then the animals rush about in many directions, venture across open areas, and engage in apparently irrational activity.

The fox, perhaps the most celebrated European animal, prefers small woods alternating with open country, but it is found almost everywhere, even in built-up areas. Since it easily adapts itself to cultivated country and the neighborhood of human beings, it is common in many parts of Europe. Although it is an omnivore, it prefers mice and voles, which it hunts in fields and meadows around dawn. But it is also a scavenger, eating carrion from rubbish heaps; and it fills out

The brown trout was for a time widely distributed in Europe but increasing water pollution has restricted its range. It now occurs chiefly in streams in such mountainous country as Bohemia, Czechoslovakia. (Ladislav Sitensky: Dilia)

its diet with berries, fish, frogs, birds, hares and rabbits. Studies made in Germany reveal that 42.6 per cent of the fox's food consists of small rodents, while as much as 18.3 per cent is vegetable material or berries.

As far as we know, the fox is, by human standards, one of the most intelligent of European mammals. Thorough analyses of its behavior when hunted have shown that it has an astonishing ability to extricate itself from the most complicated and seemingly hopeless situations. Its judgment at critical moments is evidently based on an amazing knowledge of local topography, memory of previous experiences, and an ability to make an instantaneous decision. Natural selection has also helped: hundreds of generations of "wily Reynards" have had to face man and his hounds; we may perhaps assume that those who survive the longest are the fittest and that the dullards are generally eliminated.

Once such large beasts of prey as the wolf, the lynx and the bear had disappeared from most of the deciduous forest areas of Europe, the badger became the largest predator there, although a rather mild one. Although it is classified as a carnivore, and is actually omnivorous, its diet consists largely of roots, grass and berries, and other vegetable material. On its nocturnal excursions it also eats worms, insects, small rodents, shrews, frogs, toads, and birds' eggs. In most parts of Europe it seems to prefer country where woods and fields alternate, but it is also found, although more rarely, on wide plains and in large forests. It is active at night and regular in its habits. Many of its burrows are probably centuries old, becoming larger and more labyrinthine with time.

Though the badger usually flees when disturbed by man, it can fight back fiercely when cornered by dogs or human beings. It is in many ways a most engaging animal and deserves to be better understood. In several countries it is cruelly persecuted and there are even organizations of hunters that have special badger-killing services because, it is claimed, these animals prey too freely on pheasants and partridges.

OWLS AND CUCKOOS

Owls, even more than foxes, live on small rodents. Two of the most common owls in deciduous forests are the long-eared owl (Asio otus) and the tawny owl (Strix aluco). The former likes open country, for it hunts in fields and meadows but nests in groves and woods, so that Europe today, with its varied terrain, is well suited to its needs. Studies made in Holland, Germany, Denmark, Sweden and Norway have all shown that the field vole is the staple food of long-eared owls. Winter is therefore a difficult season for them: long spells of very cold weather and a lack of small rodents in early winter are often fatal to them.

Long-eared owls have very sharp hearing and hunt small rodents by listening for their movements under the snow. In winter many of them flock to places where food is abundant and where trees will provide shelter. The ground beneath such trees may soon be covered with pellets of fur, bones and other indigestible material disgorged by the birds.

The most common owl in the deciduous forest belt is the tawny owl; it is found in most parts of Europe south of latitude 60° N. During the day it has regular resting and sleeping quarters in leafy trees and dense conifers. It is the most musical of all European owls. Its mating call may be heard in late autumn, but becomes more frequent in January and February. The well known "oo ... who-who-ooo" is heard most often; but the sound that distinguishes it from other European species is a drawn-out, tremulous "oo-oo-oo-oo" which it repeats for about fifteen minutes, and which has been compared to a rapid "roll" on a xylophone. Although it is part of the male bird's courting behavior, it may be heard all year round. The female replies with a shrill "kiwitt." This duet may continue for a long time, increasing in speed and ending abruptly, or it may become a squeaking sound, probably uttered during copulation. When pursuing the female, the male utters a series of horrendous sounds—screeches, groans and rattles—which have understandably caused the bird to be traditionally associated with ghosts and sundry horrors.

The owl's reputation for wisdom is doubtless based on the fact that its huge round eyes are, like those of man, set in the front of its face and directed forward. In reality, owls show no higher intelligence than other birds and are indeed much inferior in this respect to such corvids as ravens and crows.

When the cuckoo comes to Europe, its familiar call is heard everywhere in the countryside. Of all European birds it has probably been the most interesting to human beings. Curiously, neither town nor country people know much more about it than its call and the fact that it lays its eggs in other birds' nests. For most people its appearance and curious habits are wrapped in mystery.

Its most remarkable characteristic is of course its parasitic relationship to other birds. It is one of the two European birds that does not sit on its own eggs and take care of its young. Unique among the birds of Europe is the young cuckoo's practice of throwing its foster brothers and sisters out of the nest. The "craftiness" of the female cuckoo in setting about laying is proverbial. Laying her eggs at intervals of two days, she must make sure that the nest of the host bird is available and contains newly laid eggs, so that incubation periods will be synchronized. The hen cuckoo must therefore observe closely the host bird's nesting and laying habits. If necessary she may compel a bird to lay a new clutch of eggs by destroying the first clutch or even the nest itself.

Many of the practices of the cuckoo still remain to be explained. One of these is how the female can lay her eggs in nests which other birds have built in holes in trees. It has been suggested that she lays her eggs on the ground, picks them up in her bill and transports them to such nests; but there has been no proof of this. Cuckoos on other continents and of other species have shown some skill in "shooting" their eggs at short range into otherwise inaccessible nests. Cuckoo eggs have thick shells, but in most cases it is most unlikely that they could be shot into the holes in which they are found. An adult cuckoo was observed to force its way through a hole roughly one by two inches wide. Another in Estonia was found hanging by its head in the hole of a nest box; a fresh cuckoo's egg was found in the box, but the dead cuckoo was not necessarily the one that laid the egg. So we must wait for further evidence before accepting the idea that the cuckoo can place its eggs in such a way.

Many people are familiar with the ludicrous sight of a tiny foster or host parent feeding a young cuckoo twice its size. It does of course seem surprising that a small passerine should feed a huge nestling like the young cuckoo. Apparently its bright reddish mouth and begging cries release feeding activity

The hedgehog's method of defending itself by rolling up into a spiny ball is effective against other animals but pathetic against automobiles on a highway. (W. Suschitzky)

of the foster parent. It has even happened that a young cuckoo, reared in a hollow tree, has grown so fat that it was unable to leave the nest and starved to death when the foster parents migrated southward.

WOODCOCKS

The best known wader in European woods is the woodcock *(Scolopax rusticola)*; wet coniferous or deciduous forests are its favorite haunts. The courting flight of the male woodcock in spring has made the bird famous, and it is one of the most rewarding attractions in the forests. It is at its best on damp, slightly misty evenings when fine rain is falling. Toward sunset, when the wind drops, it is time to go to the woodcock pass. When dusk comes, the first woodcocks may be expected. In calm, slow flight the male, silhouetted against the pale evening sky, passes overhead just above the treetops. As it flies, it utters its call at regular intervals—"knorrt-knorrt-knorrt-pisp." The first notes of this sound can be heard at a distance, but then comes the high pitched "pisp," which can be heard only when the bird is close overhead. A male usually makes two or three such tours an evening. In April, the last evening flight of the woodcock usually coincides with the beginning of frog concerts; in May it occurs at the very time the nightjar is in full song.

DENMARK: FOUR HUNDRED AND EIGHTY-FOUR ISLANDS

The whole of Denmark as well as the southernmost parts of Norway and Sweden are within the deciduous forest belt. Ex-

cept for Bornholm, almost all of Denmark consists of limestone, sandstone and layers of boulder clay, for the inland icecap of the Ice Age covered the entire region. During the last glaciation, however, a large part of southwestern Jutland was not affected by the ice, as can be seen clearly today: low hills rise between plains, and the landscape is gently rolling—the result of sedimentation by ice rivers and erosion by water, wind, and frost.

All of Denmark is a plain, with the highest point only 570 feet above sea level—in terms of vegetation a direct continuation of the Central European deciduous forest belt. At the same time, Denmark may be considered an archipelago, although many of its islands are so large that they lose their island character. The largest unbroken territory of Denmark is Jutland, the mainland, with an area of 9586 square miles, but the 483 islands have an over-all area almost as great— 7390 square miles. Denmark has a coastline of 4600 miles.

Seventy-five per cent of the country is cultivated, and deciduous forest, the natural vegetation of this corner of Europe, has virtually disappeared. The woods of Denmark, most of them planted coniferous forest, cover about nine per cent of the land. Dunes, heaths and marshes occupy eight per cent. Deciduous woods may be found everywhere, however, which means that forest animals are common. Most of the woods are of beech, but oaks, ash, elms and lime trees grow in many places. A few oaks a thousand years old grow at Jaegerspris on Zealand, representing perhaps the only remains of the primeval forests.

After the Ice Age there were land connections between south Sweden, Denmark, and continental Europe. In its plant geography, south Sweden belongs to the same region as Denmark; and Scania is related to Zealand geologically. The southernmost parts of Norway may also be included in the deciduous forest region, although beech does not grow there, or is very rare, its place being occupied by other hardwood trees, mostly oaks *(Quercus robur)*.

Wild boar sow with her litter. It likes swampy, mixed or deciduous woods with open fields and glades nearby. (François Edmond-Blanc) Below: Many badger warrens have been in use for centuries and are often much older than neighboring human settlements. (R. P. Bille)

THE RIVER VALLEYS OF AUSTRIA AND CZECHOSLOVAKIA

Most of Austria is alpine country. It is only in the northeast, around the Danube and Neusiedler See, that plains are found; there arable land dominates, but lakes and fens, pine and hardwood forests may also be seen. Enchanting woods flourish around Vienna and, farther west along the Danube where the river flows between the Alps and the foothills of the Böhmerwald chain, deciduous woods have been allowed to grow densely on the slopes, as in the Wachau Valley between Melk and Krems. But these woods show traces of cultivation everywhere. The beech is the most common deciduous tree, but the spruce, which grows at higher altitudes, is extending its territory downward as a result of planting.

Few places in Europe are so rich in wildlife as Czechoslovakia, largely because it has so much forest land. The mountains around the plateaus of Bohemia and Moravia are covered with woods and, in spite of cutting and reforestation,

In beech woods the ground is shaded by the canopy and the vegetation is not dense. In June, last year's leaves still cover the ground. (Ingmar Holmåsen)

they shelter many wild animals. This is also true of the many peaks scattered over the intensively cultivated plain. Coniferous forests account for fifty per cent of these forests, mixed woods for twenty per cent, and pure deciduous woods for thirty per cent.

The mountains of Czechoslovakia are also remarkable geologically. The Böhmerwald range and the Sudeten Mountains, although different in structure, are remains of the Armorican epoch, but later formations have left their mark on them, turning them into a mosaic of volcanic and sedimentary rocks from various epochs. In several places, bizarre pillar-shaped rock formations have been created by the solidification of an extrusive rock, basalt. These pillars stand close together, forming steep walls and looking from a distance like organ pipes. Such multisided pillars are found in other parts of Europe— on the coast of Northern Ireland and in Fingal's Cave on the Island of Staffa in the Inner Hebrides.

One of the most interesting woods in Czechoslovakia is in the far south, where the Danube runs in two arms between Bratislava and Komarno, enclosing an area, Zitny Ostrov, about 125 miles long and ten to sixteen miles wide, built up of sediment deposited by the river. The shores change continuously, for the river gives and takes unceasingly. This river island is intersected by a large number of natural channels, sometimes widening into lagoons and meres. The water of the Danube floods great areas there at least once a year; at that time the ground water level rises, sometimes to the surface.

This remarkable country of land and water has not remained untouched by man. There are cultivated fields and pastures, and a man-made reservoir. The wood has obviously changed greatly since prehistoric times, judging from several species of exotic trees found there, and there are still traces of the original swamp forest.

Great oak, old walnut, ash and elm, slender alder and aspen grow there, as well as gnarled maple whose crowns are adorned with hops and traveler's joy. Willow thickets fringe all the watercourses, indicating that they grow almost everywhere. Elsewhere, dewberry *(Rubus caesius)* and other shrubs combine to make a veritable jungle.

In small ponds in deciduous forests one may find several species of newts, Europe's most amphibious batrachians. The crested newt *(Triturus cristatus)* has the widest distribution. At breeding time the male of this species finds its way to pools or ponds and marks its territory with scent deposits; these stimulate the female, which then attracts the male. During mating, the male displays in front of the female, lashing his tail to show off his colors. Display activity may continue for several days. Gradually the male stimulates the female's sex organs by movements of his head and by arching his back, and finally the female responds by tapping the male's sex opening with her nose, which causes the excretion of sperm enclosed in a jelly capsule, which is called a spermatophore. This capsule is attached to a stone or other firm base, and the female takes it from there with the lips of her cloaca. The capsule then bursts and the sperm enters the cloaca, where it may remain, capable of fertilization, for two years. Fertilization occurs when the female's eggs pass out.

European bison in a spruce forest. After having been exterminated in the wild, free-living animals once again roam the Bialowieza forest in Poland and the U.S.S.R. (B. Gippenreiter)

The tawny owl is one of the commonest of its kind in Europe. (Ingmar Holmåsen)

THE PLAINS OF POLAND

Most of Poland is located within the great plain extending from the North Sea across Central Europe into Russia. Seldom does this plain rise higher than one thousand feet. Its topography is mainly the result of the inland icecap, river deposits, and man. Man has destroyed the great forests that grew in Poland after the Ice Age. Today about one fourth of Poland is wooded, while more than half is cultivated. Thus the country still contains much woodland, though only a modest part of this is deciduous forest.

The boundary between the deciduous forest zone and the mixed forest of deciduous trees and conifers—or the southern coniferous forest region—runs through Poland, but it is difficult to pinpoint, since man, by planting pines, has obliterated the natural vegetation boundaries. Roughly speaking, Poland west of the River Wistula and south of latitude 51° N belongs to the deciduous forest region, while the northeastern part is in the mixed forest region. Since the deciduous woods occupy a considerable part of the Polish mixed forest region, they are discussed simultaneously.

The Polish plain consists of typical European cultivated steppe. The fields are cultivated, and divided into strips running parallel to each other, whether the country is hilly or flat. Drainage ditches are rare, and their absence is marked in the fields and around farms by the presence of white storks, a common sight in Poland; these birds prefer wet or moist meadows. That part of Poland lay under ice during the last glaciation and is reminiscent of the southern Scandinavian moraine landscape, with lakes and marshes, eskers (sinuous ridges of gravel left by the land-ice) and woods. The vegeta-

tion is roughly the same, and so is the fauna. A quite different picture meets the eye south of the farthest extension of the former icecap.

Not far from Kracow in southern Poland is a remarkable mountainous region, the Ojcow National Park. To reach it from Kracow one crosses a wide cultivated plateau, a relic of the Jura epoch, with no sign of the woods one is approaching. Suddenly and dramatically the land opens into a fissure valley, and there, below the plain, is another world, wooded, and with cliffs almost two hundred feet high. To the uninitiated the abrupt change of scenery seems almost magical.

Evidence of the climatic changes in this region during recent geological times can be seen in numerous caves containing the remains of tundra and steppe animals—mammoth, reindeer, saiga antelope, giant deer, cave-bear, cave-hyena and cave-lion. Stone Age people also took refuge in these caves, which are now inhabited by large numbers of bats. Wind, water and frost have sculptured the mountains into curious rock formations. The bedrock is limestone, which means that the flora is rich—luxuriant deciduous woods growing everywhere, and brightly colored flowers shining in the glades. And some steppe plants such as *Stipa pennata, Inula ensifolia* and *Veronica austriaca* may still be found there.

The black redstart is typical of Ojcow. Since the altitude is only about 1350 feet, one is astonished, too, to find an occasional rock thrush. The turtledove, stonechat and red-breasted flycatcher are among the birds of this area whose song remains in one's memory.

The most interesting plant in Ojcow is a birch, *Betula oycoviensis,* which is unique; after studying it for thirty years, Polish botanists have decided that it is a separate species.

In many parts of Poland one is impressed by the density of the woods—whether they are coniferous or mixed—and by the size of the trees. The fauna is astonishingly varied. Red deer and wild boars are typical of the woods; no one here has complained of their damaging woods and crops, but that may be because their numbers are kept fixed.

The famous Bialowieza Forest, the largest on the Central European plains, occupying about 485 square miles, includes the Bialowieza National Park and is well known for two reasons: the European bison, and what is probably the last remains of lowland primeval forest in Central Europe. The bison lived wild in Bialowieza until it was exterminated during recent years, but it has been reintroduced and now roams about in complete freedom.

Twelve distinct forest communities can be distinguished in Bialowieza, most of them dominated by deciduous trees. The most remarkable trees are the limes, which have tall trunks, no branches, and a small crown—looking altogether like long-handled brooms.

The Bialowieza Forest is, in size, age and virginal condition, unique in Europe. In it one can see how the primeval forest formed different communities on different kinds of soil. The forest consists of twelve species of trees: hornbeam, ash, alder *(Alnus glutinosa),* oak *(Quercus robur),* lime, maple *(Acer platanoides),* birch *(Betula verrucosa* and *B. pubescens),* aspen *(Populus tremula),* elm *(Ulmus scabra* and *U. campestris),* wild apple *(Malus silvestris),* pine *(Pinus silvestris)* and spruce *(Picea abies).* Thus, there are no beeches, for the northern limit of this tree in east Europe is at low latitudes. It is found in northern Poland, but in Russia it does not extend farther north than latitude 50° N.

Generally speaking, the Bialowieza Forest is a replica of the ancient forests of east Europe. It is therefore interesting to observe that the hornbeam is a dominant species. In no less than thirty-five per cent of this primeval forest it forms a distinct community; in addition, it has, together with the oak, occupied another ten per cent of the national park. Finally, a considerable area of a type of primeval forest in Bialowieza consists of three kinds of trees—ash, alder, and pine.

THE REVIVAL OF THE EUROPEAN BISON

That most interesting animal in the Bialowieza Forest, the European bison, was formerly widely distributed in the deciduous forests of Europe as far north as southern Sweden. No doubt this creature, with its enormous mass of flesh, was a much coveted animal, and perhaps also feared, and this, together with the reduction of the forests, led to its general extermination. Since its distribution range also diminished rapidly, by the Middle Ages it had disappeared from most of Europe, and by the beginning of the present century it was found only in the Bialowieza Forest and the Caucasus. The populations in these two habitats—one a plain forest, the other a mountain forest—belonged to different races.

For a long time, Bialowieza was a Polish and Russian hunting reserve, and bison were protected there. During the Napoleonic War, however, the bison suffered greatly, and was reduced to about three hundred specimens. By 1857 there were about nineteen hundred animals left, with about 500,000 acres at their disposal. At the same time there were about seven thousand red deer, seven thousand fallow deer and five thousand roe deer competing with them for food. Human hunters and beasts of prey were evidently too few to regulate their numbers, and the animals became too numerous for the natural food supply. Feeding was resorted to, which helped the animals but led to fatal illnesses, particularly among the bison; also, this had the effect of diminishing their fear of human proximity, which eventually was to have deleterious consequences.

About seven hundred European bison were living in Bialowieza at the outbreak of the World War I. Since many of them were tame, they became easy prey for invading troops, who reduced the population to about 150. The animals were then left in peace for a few years, and increased to about two hundred specimens. But the aftermath of the war and the Russian Revolution brought an end to the bison: the last free specimens were shot in Bialowieza in 1921 and in the Caucasus in 1925.

Luckily the species was not completely exterminated, for a few zoological gardens had specimens. In 1923, an international society was established to rescue the European bison. A report in 1925 showed that sixty-six bison existed in various zoological gardens but that they were not all thoroughbred; by 1930, the number had dropped to thirty. In 1929, the Nordiska Museet and Skansen in Sweden sent two cow bison to Poland; later joined by a bull, they lived in an enclosure in Bialowieza. When World War II broke out, the number of bison in Poland had risen to thirty specimens; at the end of the war there were forty-four, in spite of the fact that a number had been killed or taken away by the invaders. The Polish bison population continued to grow, and in 1952 a few animals were set free in the forest of Bialowieza. In 1960 the

Russians freed several animals in their section of the forest, and by 1964 sixty-three European bison were roaming in Bialowieza, at least thirty-six of them born free. Some bison still live in enclosures, and there are now ninety-nine animals in Bialowieza.

Thus, the most remarkable member of the European fauna has been restored to one of its ancient habitats.

THE DECIDUOUS WOODS OF THE U.S.S.R.

Virtually all of Russia between the Caucasus, the Carpathians and the Urals may be characterized as lowland. Thus the distribution pattern of the vegetation in this area is not broken by mountain regions; it provides an excellent example of how vegetation regions succeed each other uninterruptedly from north to south: desert, semidesert, steppe, wooded steppe, deciduous forest, mixed forest, coniferous forest and tundra.

It is difficult to determine the boundary of the deciduous forest in the south because the steppe there is overgrown with trees. Its northern boundary is also in doubt, for deciduous and mixed forests often mingle. It seems best to include the whole of the wooded steppe in the deciduous forest region, although it is really a transitional zone. The mixed forest belt north of the deciduous forest zone represents the meeting of two worlds: after the glaciations, deciduous trees invaded Russia from the west, while conifers came in from the east.

Oaks *(Quercus robur),* lime trees, hornbeams, maples and elms dominate the pure deciduous forests. Due partly to the climate, the number of species is small in comparison with that in more westerly localities. The continental climate, with hot dry summers and long, cold winters makes eastern Europe an inhospitable region for many species of deciduous trees. The closer one approaches the Ural Mountains, the fewer such trees one sees. The hornbeam does not grow beyond longitude 36° E, the ash stops at about longitude 48° E, and the oak at the Urals. Hazel is often the ground cover in oak woods, where it sometimes grows so thick that it forms a continuous canopy of leaves under the oaks.

The easternmost deciduous forests of Europe are on the south slopes of the Urals, the threshold of Siberia. One corner of the triangular deciduous forest zone reaches the foot of the Ural Mountains near Ufa. As the land rises and humidity increases, a forest of lime trees and elms *(Ulmus scabra)* climbs the slopes, covering a large area of the mountain chain at an altitude of about two thousand feet. The forest continues upward, with lovely maples growing here and there. Plants such as the Easter-bell starwort *(Stellaria holostea),* the European wild ginger *(Asarum europaeum),* sweet woodruff *(Galium odoratum)* and male fern *(Dryopteris filix-mas)* adorn the fissures. The birds are similar to those heard farther west in Europe; among these are the chiffchaff, the greenish warbler *(Phylloscopus trochiloides),* the icterine warbler, the blackcap, and the cuckoo. The deciduous forest thins out between 3000 and 3500 feet, and is replaced by the fir *(Abies sibirica)* and the spruce *(Picea abies),* which in turn give way higher up to the stone pine *(Pinus cembra),* the larch *(Larix sibirica)* and an occasional birch *(Betula tortuosa).* Stunted spruce may also occasionally be seen there. The forest limit occurs at an altitude of about 5000 feet, although dwarfed spruce sometimes grow still higher, climbing almost to the stony plateau at the summit, 5430 feet high.

Sea Birds and Green Archipelagos

The Baltic Sea and Its Islands

15

The Baltic Sea penetrates far into the great coniferous forest region of northern Europe. While other factors contribute to the special nature of the area, the meeting of sea and coniferous forest gives its shores a character that is unique in Europe. The post-glacial upthrust of the land is changing the contours of the coasts, new skerries are rising from the sea and sounds are becoming shallower. This upward movement of the land has been going on ever since the ice receded and the pressure of the ice on the land was removed. It is taking place at the rate of about three feet a century in the northern parts of the Gulf of Bothnia and seventeen inches around Stockholm, although in Scania and Denmark it seems to have stopped completely.

The basin of the Baltic has changed several times since the great glaciations; at some periods it has been a sea, at others a lake. The present sea phase has now lasted about seven thousand years, from the time when land connections between Denmark and Sweden were severed.

The climate of the Baltic region is mild compared with those parts of Asia and America on the same latitude. Stockholm is as far north as northern Kamchatka, southern Alaska, the Ungava peninsula, and the southernmost point of Greenland, but its mean temperature in January is 27.5° F (−2.5°C), and in July 62.4° F (16.9° C). And yet, for the most part, the northern parts of the Gulf of Bothnia are usually icebound for at least half of the year.

Salt water from the Atlantic flows through the Sound into the Baltic Sea; thus salinity decreases in the northern Baltic, and the water in the far north of the Gulf of Bothnia is all but fresh. This is due to the great volume of fresh water flowing into the Baltic from west and east, that is, from the great rivers draining the Scandinavian mountain range and the forests of Sweden and Finland. This has made the Baltic a sea of brackish water, which also affects the shores. These shores vary greatly, from steep cliffs to flat sandy beaches. Two main types, however, predominate: sandy shores in the far south, rocks and moraine in the other parts, each roughly corresponding with the deciduous and coniferous forest regions.

THE SANDY COAST

The waves of the southernmost parts of the Baltic Sea usually wash over shores of soft sand or clay. Almost all of the coasts of Poland, Germany and Denmark consist of such materials, although in places chalk cliffs rise steeply from the water. At the German island of Rügen, for instance, and at Mön in Denmark, they rise 472 feet out of the sea. The dunes along the Baltic coast of Poland are characterized in many places by narrow tongues of sand, partly or completely separating lagoons and lakes from the sea. West winds and moving sand have been responsible for these phenomena. The dunes at Leba west of the Gulf of Danzig (Gdansk) are the largest in Europe; that is why this region has been called the Sahara of Poland. The dunes move quickly at Leba, twenty to thirty-five feet a year, and in one instance as much as sixty-five feet. In the eighteenth century an entire village was buried in the sand; part of the old village church is still visible. One after another, the woods along the beach meet with the same fate. These mobile dunes reach impressive heights, some rising to 130 feet. One dune, now stabilized by plants, is more than 180 feet high.

A storm was blowing when I visited the dunes at Leba, which gave me an excellent opportunity to study their movement. The sand was blown from the ridge of each dune in unbroken, parallel clouds and was swept along the ground until it was stopped by the next dune. On the land side of the border of dunes are pine and mixed forests, marshes and lakes. The forests have overcome the dunes in places and go all the way to the sea. In other places along this unusual coast the shores are steep and covered with deciduous forest; one of these is at Rosewie, where a beautiful beech wood meets the sea—just as it does in southeastern Sweden on the opposite side of the Baltic. Icterine warblers and wrens sing there to the accompaniment of roaring waves.

The fact that all of the south coast of the Baltic was covered with ice during the last glaciation has left its mark on the entire coastal landscape. Ice from the north carried down great masses of soil and deposited them in north Germany and Poland. This can be seen very clearly in Mecklenburg between the Oder and the Elbe where a series of eskers runs parallel to the Baltic coast. Thick layers of soil were also deposited on Scania, the Danish islands and eastern Jutland, covering the mosaic-like sandstone and limestone strata, which in turn rest on Precambrian granite and gneiss bedrock.

The vegetation on these sandy coasts of the Baltic differs but little from that on the North Sea coasts. Cushions of prickly saltwort (Salsola kali) and sea rocket (Cakile maritima) grow on the pale sand, contrasting with emerald-green carpets of sea purslane (Minuartia peploides).

THE BIRD MIGRATION AT FALSTERBO

In late summer and autumn, thousands of birds of passage fly south and southwest over the Falsterbo Peninsula in Sweden.

Islands on the inner archipelago east of Stockholm are covered by conifer woods. On islands farther out to sea the conifers give way to birch, after that, to shrubs, and, finally, to barren skerries. (Rune Bollvik)

In most parts of Scandinavia birds migrate individually or in small groups, but over Falsterbo they appear in immense flocks. The flights culminate in September and October; in inclement weather, an incredible number of birds may then congregate in groves of trees and shrubs around Falsterbo. When the weather improves, warblers and thrushes set out at night, whereas other small birds, as well as sparrow hawks *(Accipiter nisus)* and falcons, wait until dawn. As the morning sun warms the air, buzzards and kites take advantage of rising currents of air to sail away over land and sea.

For many species of birds the migration at Falsterbo is unique in Europe The Falsterbo Peninsula forms the last outpost of Sweden to the southwest and since the sea between Falsterbo and Denmark is quite narrow, birds can see the Danish coast as they leave Sweden. Few land birds will fly over wide expanses of water if they can avoid it. When they set out on their autumn migrations from northern Sweden and other regions in the northeast, they make for Scania, whose coasts guide them down to Falsterbo. Some birds cross the sound at Hälsingborg, which is even nearer to Denmark. Once over the sound, the front formed by the birds widens, and it becomes more difficult to observe the migration flight.

Some waders migrate southward as early as June. They are accompanied by young starlings, which in that month can pass Falsterbo at the rate of ten thousand a day. The migrating waders increase in July, when swifts may also appear in great numbers. And in August terns and gulls begin their long migration.

The prelude to the incomparable spectacle that takes place in September begins a month earlier. Swallows, kestrels, sparrow hawks and stock doves start out early in August, and by the middle of the month a continuous stream of birds is passing over Nabben, the utmost point of the Falsterbo Peninsula. Tree pipits *(Anthus trivialis)* and yellow wagtails, honey buzzards and ospreys are among the August migrants, the two passerines arriving in flocks of from thirty to fifty birds a minute. On calm sunny days honey buzzards *(Pernis apivorus)* may sail slowly by in the hundreds, often from 2000 to 2700 feet up. There are usually far fewer ospreys than other common birds of prey, for, unlike buzzards and sparrow hawks, they do not fear wide stretches of water, and will cross the sea from any point along the coast of south Sweden.

The most spectacular of all migrants at Falsterbo are the buzzards *(Buteo buteo),* of which up to fourteen thousand may pass by on a fine day.

So the migration flight of birds over Falsterbo continues week after week, and month after month. In September the graceful flocks of house martins and swallows pass on their long journey to Africa; up to twenty or thirty thousand of them may fly over in a day. Their flight seems almost playful because they go out of their way to hunt insects, which they consume while in the air.

The chaffinch dominates the flocks of small birds flying over at the end of September. One day in the autumn of 1943, about 145,000 of this species flew over Falsterbo, and the total number that year was about 463,000. The peak migration period at Falsterbo lasts from the middle of September to the

Chalk cliffs, rich in fossils of marine invertebrates, at the Jasmund nature reserve on the island of Rügen off Germany's Baltic coast. (Herbert Ecke)

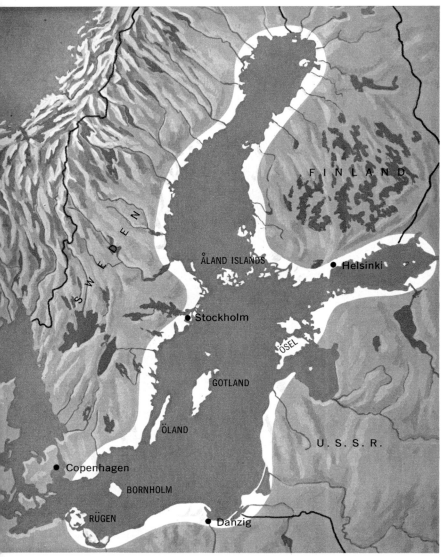

The Baltic Sea, along with the gulfs of Finland and Bothnia is a huge arm of the Atlantic Ocean but with its salinity reduced by great rivers from the Scandinavian mountains. Along the coasts of Sweden and Finland are vast archipelagos, including such geologically interesting islands as Öland, Gotland, Ösel and Dagö.

middle of October. Passerines, birds of prey, pigeons, ducks and waders hurry over, alone or in flocks, silent or noisy. Although the stream of birds diminishes in November, crows, jackdaws and diving ducks are still migrating at that time; and as late as December an occasional buzzard or small flock of siskins may cross over to Denmark. Soon the birds begin to return from the south and spread out over Scandinavia.

Great numbers of eiders winter around the Danish islands. Many and perhaps all of the eiders living in the Baltic area move to the southwest corner of the sea for the winter. A Danish biologist, Dr. Knud Paludan, has calculated that at least 600,000 eiders winter in Denmark, whereas the breeding population there is only about 3000. These birds fly northward in spring, often in single file, just above the water, to their breeding quarters in the outer parts of the archipelago. There they pair off, the camouflaged female choosing a nest site and ringing it with down—the commercially famous eiderdown—plucked from her breast. She lays from four to eight eggs in it. During the twenty-five to twenty-nine days the female eider incubates the eggs, she does not seem to eat anything. Occasionally she leaves her nest to drink, always carefully covering the eggs with down before leaving them. When the young are hatched and dry, the mother escorts them to the water's edge for their first meal.

THE BALTIC ISLANDS

The large islands in the Baltic provide good examples of a variety of natural environments. The chalk cliffs of Rügen have already been mentioned. Of the other islands, Bornholm is an island of granite, the only surface of this kind in Denmark. Öland, Gotland, Ösel and Dagö are of limestone, sandstone and slate; while Åland is mainly granite. Thus two of these large islands belong to the Scandinavian bedrock region. This is especially noticeable at Bornholm, where the sea has carved the rocky coast into rugged, monumental formations: in some places the waves break on precipices 250 feet high.

Although Öland is very close to Sweden, it is quite different from the mainland. Its landscape is largely coastal, the island consisting chiefly of a limestone cliff rising steeply in the west and declining gently eastward till it meets the sea. The beach varies greatly; stony shores, pillars of rock, beach meadows, and sandy beaches with dark fringes of seaweed encircle the island. The seaweed beds extend like carpets a foot or two thick, providing breeding places for myriads of tiny organisms, which in turn become food for numerous waders and other birds. One has only to lift a small stone in the seaweed for multitudes of isopods and other creatures to appear. The larvae of water flies also swim about in the seaweed or in the rotting layer at the bottom of the carpet.

THE ALVAR HEATH

The most remarkable habitat on Öland is a kind of heath or steppe, unique in Scandinavia, called alvar, on a mighty limestone plateau that rises above the coast and woods of the island. The alvar is perhaps a remnant of the steppe that covered most of Europe about four thousand years ago. A thin layer of soil on a limestone substratum, little drainage, considerable frost action in winter, and scant snow are some of the conditions necessary for the creation of this type of landscape. Similar alvar are found on Gotland, in Estonia and, on a small scale, in Västergötland in western Sweden. The Great Alvar on Öland the largest of its kind, reminds one of similar heaths in southeast Europe and Asia.

Singular plants from many countries and epochs grow on the Great Alvar. The shrubby cinquefoil *(Potentilla fruticosa)* —whose center of distribution is in Siberia—is covered with yellow flowers throughout the dry summer. Among other plants are the early purple orchid *(Orchis mascula)*, which has an odor quite out of keeping with its beauty, the Öland rockrose *(Helianthemum oelandicum)*, which is found only here, and several other rockroses, some of which are not found any nearer than Central Europe, Austria and the Balkans. Also found here are such typical flowers of mountain heaths as the red alpine catchfly *(Viscaria alpina)* and several other arctic plants that are, like the rockroses, relicts of late

Sand dunes at Kuskiy Zaliv (Kurische Nehrung) along the coast of the U.S.S.R. on the southeastern Baltic Sea. (Alfred Ehrhardt)

glacial times. Now they grow side by side with species that invaded the island in postglacial times.

In sharp contrast to the heath is one of the largest deciduous forests in Sweden, growing on the plateau north of the Great Alvar. It contains nearly all species of deciduous trees that grow in Scandinavia except the beech—just as did the forests of five thousand years ago. The white elm *(Ulmus laevis),* which does not occur on the Swedish mainland, is also found here.

These woods provide habitats for many animals, including a variety of birds, such as flycatchers, finches and warblers. Various insects have made Öland famous: for example, the great long-horn beetles *(Cerambyx cerdo)*—glossy black, with immense antennae—and the scarlet red *Cucujus* that live in the rotting wood of gigantic oaks at Halltorp. The badger finds its favorite insects, larvae and worms in the soft soil here. Common shrews snuff around looking for the same quarry, but if the two mammals meet, the badger usually makes short work of the shrew.

The grass snake has warm, wet ground at its disposal, and many holes in which it can hide. It lives on moor frogs *(Rana arvalis)* and jumping frogs *(R. dalmatina).* When a snake, gliding slowly through the grass catches sight of a jumping

frog, it seems to explode at its quarry. Even so, the frog may escape, for it can jump as much as six feet.

To be in a wood on Öland on a fine June night is an enchanting experience. Insects buzz high in the crowns of trees, nightingales sing in almost every shrub, and whiskered bats flit erratically between gnarled branches. Strange scents rise from a soft mold alive with thousands of tiny sounds and even lights from glowworms *(Lampyris noctiluca),* and a gentle breeze sifts through the mighty trees.

GOTLAND AND OTHER ISLANDS

Gotland, the largest Baltic island, is in many ways a world apart. It is farther from the mainland than any other of the larger Baltic islands and, although it is about as far north as Labrador, it has the mildest climate in Scandinavia, much warmer and more uniform than that of the mainland. Gotland is made up of limestone, marl, and sandstone. Here, as nowhere else in Scandinavia, the sea has dictated the character of the shore. In every inch of the long coast one can see how the sea has shaped, and is still shaping, the limestone walls, carving out caves and isolating stacks.

233

Among the rock pillars and boulders at the foot of the limestone cliffs one may study not only the animals of today but also those of hundreds of millions of years ago, in the epoch of the Silurian Sea. The waters then covering what is now Gotland, was no misty primeval ocean, but a sunny tropical sea with corals, hydrozoa, graptolites, sea lilies, worms, sea stars, mollusks, trilobites and many other forms of life. All these have been preserved in fossils for no less than 500 million years.

Off the west coast of Gotland two islands rise like monuments to the ancient past: Stora and Lilla Karlsö. The strata of these limestone cliffs can be traced back millions of years: each stratum represents a former bottom of the sea and contains fossils of animals that lived during various epochs. And on the beach stand curious pillars, called *raukar* in Swedish— remains of the coral reef that once surrounded these islands.

But it is not only the geologic past that attracts our attention when we land on the Karlsö Islands. During spring and summer life seethes on the ledges of these ancient cliffs. A ceaseless murmur of bird voices, along with the acrid smell of guano, rises from every side. For thousands of years the harsh cries of guillemots and the shrill calls of gulls have been the music of these two small islands. Guillemots and razorbills occupy shelf after shelf, while great colonies of black guillemots inhabit the caves.

Right: In early summer, masses of rock roses brighten the Great Alvar heath on the island of Öland in the Swedish sector of the Baltic Sea. (Ingmar Holmåsen) Below: Many of the Baltic islands are rich in orchids. One of the most beautiful is the lady's-slipper orchid (Cypripedium calceolus). *(Wilhelm Schacht)*

The constantly rising land causes skerries to emerge from the sea in the outermost parts of the Stockholm archipelago. Soon after the rise, vegetation starts to colonize the rocks. (Sven Gillsater: Tio)

Young guillemots quit the ledges before they can fly. During a single night at the beginning of August, most of the many thousand guillemots leave their nesting sites on the Karlsö Islands. The parent birds call up to their young from the water. Soon the nestlings begin throwing themselves headlong from the high shelves, and, often bouncing off cliffs and boulders, fall to the shore below. There they lie, seemingly lifeless; but soon they recover, hurry to the water, and immediately begin swimming and diving. The whole colony then swims out to sea. Their winter quarters are in the Sound and in Kattegat.

The islands of Ösel and Dagö off the coast of Estonia are also made up of limestone. The west and north coasts of Ösel consist of steep cliffs, but no guillemots breed there. The western part of Ösel is nonetheless most interesting because this is the area of the Vaikas skerries, with one national park, famous for its bird life, and another, in Viidumae, known for its vegetation. Most of Ösel is lowland, with a few oak woods and some quite large marshes.

The deciduous forests on the island of Abruka, off the south coast of Ösel, are unusually rich in birds. The many meteor craters at Kaali, covering an area of almost thirteen acres in the middle of Ösel, are also noteworthy. Dagö, immediately north of Ösel, is partly cultivated, but it also has a varied landscape, wooded eskers and low hills alternating with bogs, marshes, and sandy flats. In some places, blocks of rock embedded in the inland icecap have striated large areas of the limestone; these have yielded valuable information concerning the movement of ice during the various glaciations.

ROCK AND MORAINE COASTS

Most of the Baltic coast consists of the Fenno-Scandian bedrock, a formation of granites and gneiss dating from the early periods of the earth—about 1800 million years ago. This coast is much older than the parts of Europe around it; the waves of the Cretaceous sea washed against it some 100 million years ago. Long before these coasts were formed, the sea extended, with boundless horizons, all the way to Africa.

Today almost all the Baltic coast north of latitude 56° N is the meeting place of the Scandinavian coniferous forest belt and the sea. There are many deciduous trees in this coastal forest of spruce and pine, and on some islands they may dominate, but they are never numerous enough to form more than light colored patches in the dark coniferous region as a whole.

236

The dunes at Leba on the Baltic coast of Poland often move as much as twenty to thirty-five feet a year, inexorably burying the wooded land in their path. (Wladyslaw Strojny)

Almost all lands around the Baltic Sea are covered by moraines, that is, glacial deposits. But, during the glaciation, the coastal moraines were below sea level and developed into a distinct type. The moraine coast ranges from gravel and boulder-strewn shores, reedy inlets and bare cliffs washed by the waves, to grassy meadows and bush, and mixed and coniferous forests. On both sides of the northern Baltic the shore is fringed in places with sea buckthorn *(Hippophaë rhamnoides)* which, like a silvery wall, separates the sterile gravel and boulders of the shore from the fertile mineral soil farther inland. This is really the only striking contrast in an otherwise rather monotonous coast.

Even from the mainland, one may sometimes see, on clear summer days, small shoals of porpoises rolling and diving in the water. The porpoise is the whale of the Baltic and is found along all its coasts. In winter, however, it leaves the Baltic in order to avoid being trapped under the ice.

The rocky coasts of the Baltic are nowhere so spectacular as in Ångermanland in Sweden. Nordingrå, on the east coast, is outstanding in this respect. There the mountains are marked by dizzying precipices and deep inlets. This remarkable landscape is evidently of volcanic origin, and its creation was undoubtedly one of the most dramatic of primordial developments.

VAST ARCHIPELAGOS

The largest archipelagos of the inland seas of Europe are in the Baltic and the Mediterranean. The archipelagos between Sweden and Finland, and between Greece and Turkey, consist of thousands of islands; but that is all they have in common. A variety of factors have made them very different—at least from the aspect of natural history. Whereas archipelagos in the open Atlantic, such as those around Scotland, are most often rugged cliffs or bare rocks, those of the Baltic and the Mediterranean have gentler contours and often are, or have been, wooded.

The archipelagos of the Baltic differ according to their latitude. In the south, off the southeast coast of Sweden, the coasts and islands of Blekinge are clothed in deciduous woods. The pale green of beeches, hornbeams, oaks, limes and ash trees trails right down to the beach; hidden on the land side of the fringe of trees are meadows and glades full of flowers.

The boundary between the remarkable coastal deciduous forest of southeast Sweden and the less luxuriant landscape of the outer archipelago is not determined only by its geological past, by altitude, or the effects of wind and sea; it is due also to the history of cultivation or, more exactly, the distribution of the land between great estates and farming communi-

237

Granitic rocks, created about a billion years ago, sculptured by the Ice Age's glacial shields and polished by the sea, are common in the Baltic archipelagos. (Sven Gillsater: Tio)

ties during the past five or six hundred years. Along the coast and on the islands of eastern Blekinge, it is obvious that lush deciduous forests have usually been preserved only in places where the woods have been taken care of and the grazing restricted.

The great archipelagos farther north along the Södermanland and Uppland coasts of Sweden, usually called the Stockholm archipelago, and around Åland and the southwest coast of Finland are quite different from the southern deciduous forest archipelago. The vegetation zones there are very similar to those on the mountains. Conifers grow on the islands nearest the mainland; the next belt consists of birches and other deciduous trees; this is followed by shrubs and low ground vegetation, and finally the lichen-covered or barren skerries.

It is only natural that the fauna of such a heterogeneous region should be versatile. Mute swans, mallard, and great crested grebes *(Podiceps cristatus)* swim in the coastal waters, just as they do in inland lakes. Farther out are velvet

scoters *(Melanitta fusca)*, tufted ducks, goosanders *(Mergus merganser)* and red-breasted mergansers *(M. serrator)*. White-tailed eagles build their large nests in the tops of lonely pines. Still farther out to sea is the domain of eiders, black guillemots, and razorbills. Multitudes of gulls and terns dominate the archipelago from Stockholm to the outermost skerries. Common gulls *(Larus canus)*, lesser black-backed gulls, herring gulls, and common terns are found everywhere. Black-headed gulls are most common near the mainland, while great black-backed gulls, arctic terns, Caspian terns *(Hydroprogne tschegrava)* and arctic skuas prefer the outer islands. The graylag goose inhabits a few places in the Stockholm archipelago.

The flight of a white-tailed eagle is a sight to be remembered. Its huge nest, high up in a pine tree, is improved and enlarged year after year, so that a nest six feet across and equally deep is not exceptional. When these eagles wish to break off dry branches for their nests, they dive on them from above, grabbing them and snapping them off with their talons.

238

If that fails, they hang upside-down for a second and break off the branches with the weight of their bodies.

The Stockholm archipelago is an extraordinary sight from the air. It consists of no fewer than 24,000 islands in all possible phases of development, depending on the length of time since they rose from the sea. In May and June, before summer has darkened the foliage of the trees and the flames of the orchids have been extinguished, the whole region is a paradise. Behind the polished rocks, protected from the wind, are flowering meadows, over which the bird cherry *(Prunus padus)* spreads it sweet scent and butterflies dance from flower to flower. Exotically colored orchids bloom in the grass; *Orchis sambucina* and lady's slipper orchids *(Cypripedium calceolus)* are to be seen alongside pale Nordic helleborines *(Cephalantera longifolia)*. At sunset the air is heavy with the scent of lilies-of-the-valley *(Convallaria majalis)* growing in dense carpets under the canopy of mountain ash *(Sorbus aucuparia)* and hazel; thrushes and robin redbreasts sing, and the woodcock performs its courting flight over wooded hills and over marshes of *Ledum palustre,* a European relative of the Labrador tea. And at dawn, after the brief northern night, the same birds hail the rising sun. Then other birds join the choir: chaffinches, willow warblers, wood warblers, icterine warblers, garden warblers *(Sylvia borin),* and whitethroats. By the middle of June, the birds have fallen silent, and most flowers have faded.

Far out to sea, where the islands are rocky and treeless, the cliffs still flower around midsummer, when the sun barely sinks below the horizon. It seems incredible that plants can find enough nourishment in the rocks to keep them erect, or that they can defy the most violent storms. At Gillöga skerries, in the Stockholm archipelago, both flora and fauna are astonishingly abundant. No fewer than thirty-two species of birds, including the whitethroat, were counted there one midsummer day. Hares and toads were also observed; this is especially remarkable, for Gillöga lacks fresh water.

In some parts of the archipelago the common gull is the most numerous of the gulls; in others, the lesser black-backed gull and, during recent years, the herring gull, have become almost as common. The Caspian tern is a remarkable visitor on some of the islands. This species breeds in Europe only in the archipelagos along the coasts of Sweden, Finland and Estonia, on the coasts of the Black Sea and the Caspian Sea, and in a few places in south Russia. The Caspian tern is in fact at home on all five continents.

ÅLAND

The sprawling archipelago of Åland lies between the Baltic Sea and the Gulf of Bothnia, and between Sweden and Finland. It consists of 6544 islands and islets, with a total land area of 572 square miles. These figures are only approximate, for the lowering of the land level here, as in the Stockholm archipelago, is continually adding to the number of skerries above water and, consequently, the land area. If this continues, Sweden and Finland will, at some very far distant date, be united, and the Gulf of Bothnia will become a lake.

The Åland archipelago extends about fifty miles from north to south, and about sixty-five miles from east to west; on the east side is the Åbo archipelago, about forty miles wide. Åland belongs to the Scandinavian bedrock region and is

The common tern is frequently seen among the vast archipelagos of the Baltic Sea. (Ilkka Virkkunen)

therefore related geologically to the Stockholm archipelago. Naked rocks are a common feature of Åland. After being planed down by ice and washed by the waves, the many islands of Åland have risen slowly from the sea—first, as the level of the sea dropped, and then as the land rose. As recently as four thousand years ago most of Åland was below sea level. Plants have had five thousand years in which to colonize this world of islands as it rose from the sea.

Pine and spruce trees are dominant, and go right down to the sea, tall and straight if they are rooted in fertile soil, but gnarled and bowed down by the winds on the more meager land of the hilltops.

In many places the darkness of the conifers is relieved by light, inviting coppices of mixed deciduous forest—the result of cultivation. Indeed, some islands have leafy glades reminiscent of Central Europe. In the south, on the Sottunga Islands, they become a coppice landscape, with birch and alder, ash and maple, bird cherry and mountain ash, and occasional oaks. Hazel is also common on many of the islands, while these coppices and groves are not infrequently bounded on the beach side by a dense wall of sea buckthorn.

The fauna of the beaches of Åland is similar to that of surrounding regions. Eiders are very common, as are razorbills and black guillemots. The black guillemot finds excellent conditions on Åland in spite of its rigorous demands on a habitat: it prefers rocky beaches both on inner and outer skerries with a nest usually protected and hidden by cliffs or large boulders. The velvet scoter and the goosander are common in parts of the inner archipelago. The goosander is at home around islands in clear water, with good fishing and plenty of nest holes, which are usually provided by hollow trees within easy reach of the shore.

Second only to the eider in numbers that is, among the diving ducks, are the velvet scoters. After arriving at their breeding places in April or May, they wait a month or more before they begin to lay. During this time they perform their mating flight, usually in the evening and early in the morning. A female, followed closely by one or more males, flies in wide circles up over the land and then back over the water. Sometimes, when the nests lie very close together, female velvet scoters steal eggs from each other. Eggs of other species, the red-breasted merganser, for example, have also been found in scoters' nests. The female velvet scoter may also increase her brood by coaxing the young of other female scoters to join her. Thus an abnormally large brood may sometimes be observed around one female.

While the nature of the archipelago itself affects the wildlife, other factors also play a part. One of these is the declining salinity of the water. This does not influence the birds directly, but it has some effect on the submarine flora and small fauna, which become less abundant as one goes northward. The bladder-wrack *(Fucus vesiculosus)*, the northern boundary of which is, in Finland, around latitude 63° N, is a particularly important environmental factor for mollusks and crustaceans, which in turn are food for many sea birds. Many species, such as ducks and gulls, often search for food in or near the submarine meadows of bladder-wrack. For example, the sand flea *(Gammarus)*, which is not a flea but a crustacean, is often part of the diet of diving ducks. The eider is very partial to mussels *(Mytilus edulis)*, and it is possible that the scarcity of this bird in the northernmost part of the Baltic Sea is due to lack of food in the near freshwater of the Gulf of Bothnia and the Gulf of Finland.

The archipelagos in the most northerly parts of the Gulf of Bothnia are unique. Many of them consist wholly of sand carried down to the sea by the great rivers, whose deltas have risen above the sea to form reefs, dunes covered with sea lyme grass *(Elymus arenarius)*, and wooded islands; on some of the latter, mobile dunes are smothering and burying the woods. Occasional sand islands are found farther south, too.

Little terns nest on the northern Luleå archipelago, far away from their sandy beaches in the south Baltic. The scaup *(Aythya marila)* builds its nest on sea lyme grass tussocks, and the Temminck's stint *(Calidris temminckii)* hovers in its display flight on uplifted, trembling wings.

In the spring, flocks of migrating birds rest there, waiting for the snow and ice to melt in the forests and mountains. Such old acquaintances from the south as mallard, teal, and goosanders swim in the open water around the ice floes, and courting widgeon, goldeneyes *(Bucephala clangula)*, and flocks of bean geese land on the ice after having flown the whole length of Sweden. The birds stay there for a few days, or sometimes weeks, and then fan out in pairs to meet the spring in forest and marshland. Somewhat later the lesser white-fronted goose comes from the north or east, faithful to its age-old route around or across the Gulf of Bothnia.

The most remarkable island in the archipelagos in the Gulf of Bothnia is Haparanda Sandskär. It is about twenty miles out to sea, as measured from the mouth of the Torne River. This island has a great range of landscapes: beaches of sand and stones; dunes on which grow sea lyme grass and Bothnian wormwood *(Artemisia borealis* spp. *bottnica);* hard sterile sand plateaus alternating with sandy plains covered with sea pea *(Lathyrus maritimus)* and other species; sand ridges on which grow rowans and clusters of wind-cut pines; a luxuriant virgin forest of aspens, with huge beds of ferns; thin birch woods with a few bird cherries and a ground cover of *Calamagrostis* as tall as a man; and meadows with butterfly orchids *(Platanthera bifolia)* and other plants. The beach vegetation between the water line and the curtain of sea buckthorn consists of rushes and sedge, with occasional patches of marsh pea *(Lathyrus palustris)*; a promontory of sand, thrusting several miles into the sea, is overgrown with crowberry.

Haparanda Sandskär has about 170 flowering plants and an interesting fauna. In the lagoon vegetation and in the thickets of the transitional zone between the beach meadows and the deciduous trees one finds garden warblers, whitethroats and sedge warblers—three species one hardly expects to see so far out to sea. The most remarkable vertebrate on Sandskär, however, is the moor frog, which is here far from its normal range.

THE RINGED SEALS

The ringed seal *(Phoca hispida)* is native to the Gulf of Bothnia. The smallest of all seals, it is a relict from the time when the Baltic Sea and the Gulf of Bothnia were an Ice Sea.

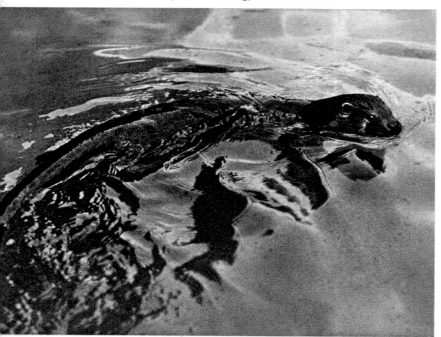

The otter is found along the coast of the Baltic Sea as well as in inland lakes. (Eric Hosking)

Barnacle geese grazing on the Rone Ytterholme on the eastern coast of Gotland in the Baltic Sea. Each spring these geese spend one to two months here on their way from western Europe to their arctic haunts. (Arthur Christiansen)

The Baltic population has been separated from that of the Arctic Ocean for thousands of years, ever since it became isolated in the Ancylus Sea, the predecessor to the Baltic. (Its relatives in the Atlantic could wander northward to an arctic climate more suitable to them.) Thus there are now two separate races—the ringed seal of the Arctic Ocean, *Phoca hispida hispida,* and the Baltic ringed seal, *P.h. botnica.* The two races seldom or never meet, in spite of the fact that the ringed seal comes down from the Arctic Ocean into the Skagerak nearly every winter.

Unlike the gray seal, the ringed seal is not dependent on ice-free water in the winter, for even during the coldest winters it can make holes in the ice—a large one by which it leaves the water, and smaller holes for breathing; the latter are about two inches in diameter and are sometimes covered with a cupola of ice that has a tiny opening at the top.

In winter the ringed seal lives among ice floes in the dark world below the ice. Males and females sleep separately on the ice or in snow or ice caves. In March and April, as the sun climbs the sky above the arctic inland sea, ringed seals mate and give birth to young on the ice—a suitable environment for this relict of the Ice Age.

Birch Forests, Eagles and Lemmings

The Scandinavian Mountain Chain

16

The Scandinavian mountain chain, running about 1100 miles from the southwest coast of Norway to the northernmost mainland of Europe on the Arctic Ocean, was formed more than three hundred million years ago while the Cambro-Silurian Sea still rolled over what is now Scandinavia. This range belongs to the Caledonian mountain system, branches of which extend to Scotland and Greenland.

The dramatic events that characterized the process of creation were continually counteracted by destructive forces, weathering, wind and water erosion, which cut deep fissures and ravines in the enormous mountains. At that time the Scandinavian mountains must have been more alpine in appearance, with sharper contours than today. During the millions of years that followed, the mountain range was slowly worn down, eventually to disappear completely. But at the beginning of the Tertiary, that is about fifty million years ago, a new epoch in the development of the mountains began: the North Atlantic region sank and the smooth land was thrust thousands of feet above its former and present level. Thus, new mountains with alpine features were formed. At that time, Scandinavia was probably much larger than it is now, while the Baltic was only a fjord in the south and had probably disappeared before the Tertiary elevation had ceased. Doubtless the valleys were filled with plants requiring high temperatures, for traces of such vegetation have been found in south Sweden and on Spitsbergen.

Then, about 1,500,000 years ago, the present geological period, the Quaternary, began. The bedrock of the mountains was then concealed under layers of erosion gravel, and the Cambro-Silurian formation occupied a greater area than it does now. The bold formations were gradually neutralized by erosion, which is still going on, and other forces helped to give the mountains rounded contours. As the climate became colder, icecaps were formed in the mountains; glaciers increased in number and size, spreading over valleys and plateaus until they became linked together. The sheet of ice thus formed moved southward along an ever widening front. The brief, cold summers could not check the advance of the ice, which eventually covered the whole land area. This was the

first Quaternary Ice Age, which has probably had most significance for the formation of the topography as we know it today. The mountains were cleared of gravel from erosion, and whereas some contours were rounded off others were chiseled out. After tens of thousands of years, the ice began to retreat, a process that, after yet further thousands of years, was followed by new glaciations, most of which lasted much longer than the interglacial periods. It is believed that the mountains were striated at least three or four times by Quaternary ice, and each time they were cleared of the erosion debris that had accumulated during the interglacial period. The ice receded from the region of Stockholm only about ten thousand years ago, but it was not until several thousand years later that the whole range was freed from ice.

Succeeding the retreating ice came plants and animals. At first the flora and fauna were arctic in character; but as the climate warmed, these species were driven into the highest mountains. The warm period came during the Stone Age and persisted through the Bronze Age, after which the formation of glaciers recommenced and the warmth-loving fauna and flora died out or retreated. It was then that the mountains reached essentially their present form. During recent times the mean temperature has risen again, the glaciers are slowly melting, and some plants and animals are extending their distribution.

The mountain range acts as a neutralizing force between two climatic regions—the oceanic and the continental. The former makes for cool, damp summers; the latter for hot, dry summers and cold winters. The mountains form more or less a barrier to the oceanic climate east of the range and to the continental climate on the western side—except in passes running from east to west. Currents of air over the mountains usually rise, whether they come from east or west. One result of this is a drop in temperature, formation of clouds and, usually, precipitation. On the lee side of the range the air moves in descending currents, which become warmer as they descend. This usually makes for less precipitation and fine weather. The currents of air may be very powerful, sweeping over the mountains and down the slopes at a fearful speed. In a moment the wind force may increase from five to sixty-five miles an hour. Curiously, in a storm, the wind force is greater on the lee side for there the wind is forced down at a high speed, while on the other side it slows down because it is rising.

Although the mountain range acts as a climatic boundary, the Scandinavian mountain region has a higher mean temperature than many other places in the same latitude. The mean temperature in January in the high Scandinavian mountains at latitude 65° N is −4° to −11° F (−20° to −24° C), while in Canada it is −22° to −31° F (−30° to −35° C), and in Siberia −31° to −40° F (−35° to −40° C).

THE INVASION OF PLANTS

The distribution of mountain plants is fascinating. It has often, moreover, suggested the solution of many problems pertaining to the extent of the inland icecap during the last glacia-

In the mountains near Grotli, northwest of Jotunheimen, Norway, where birch forests form the timberline. (Torrey Jackson)

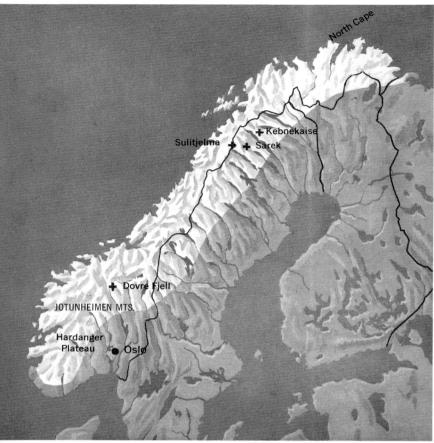

The Scandinavian mountain chain is distinguished by light birch forests, a threshold between the prevailing dark conifer forests and the treeless arctic regions of the upper mountain slopes. In Norway, the encounter between mountains and the oceans is spectacular. North Cape is Europe's northernmost point.

tion. The distribution of the rarer alpine plants in particular provides much useful evidence on conditions in the Scandinavian mountains and elsewhere tens of thousands of years ago. The more common mountain plants have less to tell us regarding immigration routes because their distribution is so wide.

As we have seen, the arctic plants followed in the wake of the retreating ice, appearing south and east of the Baltic and in Denmark. Finds of alpine fossils of such plants have been made in southern Sweden, on Öland, Gotland, and elsewhere. Thirteen or fourteen thousand years ago mountain avens *(Dryas octopetala)* and black bearberry *(Arcostaphylos alpina)* grew there among polar willow *(Salix polaris)* and dwarf birches *(Betula nana)*. Remains of alpine flora can be seen even today. The alpine lady's mantle *(Alchemilla alpina)* still grows in south Sweden; but the insect-devouring alpine butterwort *(Pinguicula alpina)* is found (apart from the Scandinavian mountain range) only on Gotland.

It is therefore evident that arctic flora invaded Sweden from the south at the end of or during the last phases of the Ice Age. This invasion was facilitated by land connections between Sweden and Denmark and the Continent. But this type of flora cannot be traced all the way up to the mountains either as fossils or relicts. The northernmost finds of arctic-alpine plants in south Sweden have been made at about

60° N. No signs of an earlier arctic flora have been found north of the mighty moraines along the lakes of central Sweden. This most northerly of the terminal moraines, formed during a pause in the recession of the ice, shows the location of the edge of the ice when the climate became warmer again. This time the climate grew warm so rapidly that woods took possession of the land quickly. This prevented the alpine flora from spreading northward; central Sweden, consequently, had no arctic flora after the last glaciation. An arm of the Yoldia Sea (that is, the Baltic in about 7000 B.C.), which divided Sweden in two parts at the end of the last glaciation, also hindered the immigration of alpine plants coming up from the south.

The plants now existing in the Scandinavian mountains could not, therefore, have come only from the south, but must also have come from the west and east, and perhaps from the north. In the west the highest peaks in the mountains were the first to become free of ice, which melted eastward, with the result that a number of ice-logged lakes were formed. The remains of an alpine flora have been found in sediment at the bottom of the deepest of these lakes. These plants must have come from the west by way of the passes. When the ice barrier in the east finally disappeared, opening the way for southern and eastern species, a regrouping of the flora took place: pines and birches, together with several species of plants, advanced along the valleys and up the mountain slopes, while the genuine alpine flora retreated higher up the mountains to where it is still found. Colonization of the northernmost mountains took place much later, for the most part by plants from the west, although an invasion from the northeast cannot be excluded and in certain cases seems probable.

How can the claim that the present flora of the Scandinavian mountains came from the west be justified? The view held by many biogeographers is that most of the alpine flora survived the last glaciation on refuges free from ice on the Atlantic and the Arctic Ocean coasts of Norway. There is much evidence to support this theory. Very significant is the occurrence of many "west arctic" plants, found nowhere else in Europe or western Asia. The bicentric distribution of many alpine plants in Scandinavia, and only in areas believed to have been free from ice during the last glaciation, is difficult to explain in any other way.

The distribution and immigration of animals in the mountains also provide evidence of ice-free refuges in Norway during the last glaciation. In fact the present distribution of many species of plants and animals is extremely curious and difficult to explain if no such refuges existed. As yet, however, no conclusive geological evidence of the existence of such ice-free areas is available, but that may be because such evidence is at the bottom of the Atlantic Ocean.

MOUNTAIN BIRCH FORESTS

The Scandinavian birch forest *(Betula tortuosa)* is a subarctic (or subalpine) belt, occurring as a vertical transitional region

Trolltinderne in Romsdal, Norway, in the Scandinavian mountains. This range is part of the Caledonian formation extending from Scotland to Greenland. (Toni Schneiders: Coleman and Hayward)

Above: Late June in virgin birch forest in the Sarek National Park of Swedish Lapland. The snow has melted but the leaves have not yet come out. (Kai Curry-Lindahl) Right: The Norwegian lemming is famous for its population fluctuations, a sudden great abundance being followed by a sharp decline. (Teuvo Suominen)

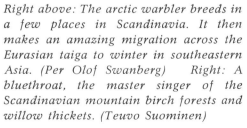

Right above: The arctic warbler breeds in a few places in Scandinavia. It then makes an amazing migration across the Eurasian taiga to winter in southeastern Asia. (Per Olof Swanberg)   Right: A bluethroat, the master singer of the Scandinavian mountain birch forests and willow thickets. (Teuvo Suominen)

Two whooper swans over a bog in the mountains of Swedish Lapland. As a breeding bird it is one of the rarest species in Scandinavia. (Ingmar Holmåsen)

between the lower coniferous forest zone and the higher, treeless arctic (or alpine) region. The Scandinavian mountain chain is the southernmost outpost of the subarctic and arctic vegetation zones in Europe.

In nearly all the mountain ranges of Europe, the coniferous belt forms the tree limit bordering on the alpine vegetation belt. But in the Scandinavian chain and eastward to the Kola peninsula (and in Iceland, in the northern Urals, and in parts of Scotland) the birch extends highest up the mountains.

The Scandinavian birch forests and the vegetation belts still higher up are stable communities, environments in balance, almost unique in Europe. They have passed through a natural course of evolution and vast areas are still untouched by man. Perhaps this helps explain why the mountains reflect the seasons of the year more apparently than any other parts of the Scandinavian landscape. The long winter, the short spring, the brief productive period of the summer, and the brilliant colors in autumn are evidence of the extremes of climate found in Scandinavia. In summer some birch forest valleys have luxuriant vegetation almost unequalled elsewhere in that region. It seems strange to find such a wealth of flowering plants and animals high up in subarctic regions, only a few hundred yards below the barren rocks and "eternal snow." The explanation is not far to seek. Some mountain valleys are transformed into veritable hothouses in summer. The south slopes of these valleys are made up in places of rocks rich in mineral nutriment; they erode easily and the

fragments, washed down by melting snow, accumulate in the lower parts of the valleys, where the soil is often calcareous, fertile, and damp. When the heat of the sun concentrates on the south slopes the plants grow at an amazing speed.

These splendid birch forests may extend for miles into the mountain valleys. The birches are locally tall and strong, often perfectly straight and not gnarled as elsewhere in the mountains. Scattered amongst them grow mountain ash, alders, aspens, bird cherries *(Prunus padus),* willow shrubs, and thickets of bramble and juniper bushes. The grass meadows are crowded with great beds of globe flowers *(Trollius),* buttercups *(Ranunculus acer),* and still smaller violets *(Viola biflora),* all with the same clear yellow color. Alpine lettuce *(Lactuca alpina),* of which bears are so fond, can be seen everywhere swaying on long stalks. One of the most conspicuous plants is the tall—sometimes six feet or more high—angelica *(Angelica archangelica),* a plant favored not only by bears but also by man. It is the giant of alpine plants. Another species, also growing as tall as a man, is the northern monkshood *(Aconitum septentrionale).* There are quite a number of plants in these meadow birch woods that grow to impressive heights. The melancholy thistle *(Cirsium heterophyllum)* and the baneberry *(Actaea spicata)* thrive there. The rosebay willow herb *(Epilobium angustifolium),* the meadowsweet *(Filipendula ulmaria),* and the great valerian *(Valeriana sambucifolia)* are other tall plants. Among the more conspicuous inhabitants of this plant community are the red campion *(Melandrium rubrum),* the wood cranebill *(Geranium sylvaticum),* which sometimes has a white flower in these tracts, the goldenrod *(Solidago virgaurea),* a stitchwort, *Stellaria nemorum,* and others. There are many grasses there, including the broad-leaved *Calamagrostis purpurea* and the spreading millet *(Milium effusum),* as well as some strikingly tall ferns in different shades of green. The aristocrat among the plants of wet meadow birch forests is, however, the tall, elegant King Charles's scepter *(Pedicularis sceptrum-carolinum),* which rises proudly above its relatives such as the Lapland lousewort *(P. lapponica).* Fragrant orchids *(Gymnadenia conopsea),* together with alpine bartsia *(Bartsia alpina)* and several species of sedge grow in places with more calcareous soil.

Heath birch forests, where birches grow far apart in carpets of bilberry, crowberry, and a few herbs, occupy a far greater area than the luxuriant meadow birch forests. Lichen heath birch forests are found principally in the northeastern parts of the mountain range and become more and more common eastward in northern Russia.

Birds are naturally the most conspicuous of the animals living in the birch forests. Except for "rodent" years, when the presence of great numbers of lemmings and voles stimulates other mammals and birds to breed more prolifically, mammals seem to be rare in the mountain valleys. Of course they are there in lean years, but are more difficult to detect.

Although the birch forest differs greatly as an environment from the coniferous forest zone, a surprisingly large proportion of the animals of the coniferous forest is also found in the birch region. If the vertical distribution of vertebrates is analyzed, it will be found that the timberline, that is the upper boundary of the birch forest, is an important ecological barrier for many species.

Space does not allow for a description of the many birds in the mountain birch forests. Quite a large number are species also found far away in southern Europe: for example, the willow warbler *(Phylloscopus trochilus),* the most common bird in Scandinavia from Scania to the coast of the Arctic Ocean, and from deciduous forests to the willow thickets. The recurrent song of the brambling *(Fringilla montifringilla),* as of the redwing *(Turdus iliacus),* reveals that these birds are characteristic of the birch forest belt. The brambling has a simple, oft-repeated call, whereas the notes of the redwing are very melodious, particularly when hundreds of birds are heard in the evening or early in the morning. The song of the redwing varies greatly from place to place, often within a few miles. One of the sweetest songsters of the mountains is the bluethroat.

Rough-legged buzzards, crying their plaintive "peeaa," sail over the valleys from their breeding places on the cliffs. Some of them build far down in the valleys, as well as in inaccessible shelves in precipices. They may also breed high up on the barren heaths.

Just below the edge of the precipice, where a very beautiful white saxifrage *(Saxifraga cotyledon,* called Bride of the Mountain in Sweden) grows in trickles of water, the ring ouzel's triad is heard. This bird may live on all levels, from the birch belt to the lichen zone. It fetches material for its nest from the bottoms of valleys, and hunts small creatures both there and on the mountain plateaus, but it moves so quickly that it is difficult to catch sight of. Other birds, such as the raven *(Corvus corax),* can be seen among the boulders higher up in the mountains. Like the ring ouzel, the raven may be found at all altitudes, but it often breeds above the upper limit of the birch forest. The merlin *(Falco columbarius)* and the kestrel may also be found there. Both species take over nests abandoned by buzzards; in fact these small, quick birds usually drive away the much larger but meeker buzzards from their nests.

Farther down the valley a woodcock may be seen performing its mating flight in broad daylight; a stoat peeps from its hiding place in a heap of stones and the shrill squeak of a shrew can be heard, while over a mountain stream by which orange-yellow saxifrages *(Saxifraga aizoides)* grow, a dipper comes flying swiftly just above the water, utters a sharp "zerrp" and disappears round a bend in the stream. Common lizards *(Lacerta vivipara)* move about in the ground cover. A female willow grouse, made almost invisible by its protective coloring, is sometimes to be found sitting on her eggs although the hens are seldom observed at this time of the year. One may flush a merlin, which flies up and around with a high-pitched "gree-gree-gree." Its nest can then soon be found, perhaps in a birch tree and in the remains of a nest built originally by crows—for although crows prefer cultivated regions, they may roam far into the mountain valleys.

GOLDEN EAGLES AND WILD BEARS

Two of Scandinavia's noblest and also rarest birds, the gyr falcon *(Falco rusticolus)* and the golden eagle, still breed in the mountains, both above and below the birch belt. The gyr falcon is probably the rarest of the two, nesting in only a few isolated localities. Although protected by law in Sweden, the golden eagle is still persecuted ruthlessly by man. In Norway it has no protection at all. About a hundred pairs of golden eagles remain in Sweden. They live mainly on carrion;

Streams running from glaciers through subarctic birch forests down to the Rapa Valley in the Sarek National Park form a characteristic scene in the mountains of Swedish Lapland. (Åke Wallentin Engman: Coleman and Hayward)

thousands of reindeer die of starvation or illness or in railway accidents, and, in the early spring, beasts of prey and golden eagles can feast off carcasses scattered over the mountains and in the forests. The golden eagle is a heavy, rather clumsy bird and therefore prefers such a diet. In folklore, eagles are often depicted stealing babies, but a golden eagle can in fact hardly lift a hare and, if it must carry carrion any distance, it tears it to pieces. Nor have golden eagles—or most birds of prey—the gluttonous appetite often attributed to them. In Lapland, for instance, a female golden eagle with two young were recorded as having lived for two days and nights on half a hare and bits of a stoat. The frequent claim that golden eagles attack people is also untrue; their long experience of man's persecution has made them wary, if not timid, and they tend to fly away when people approach their nests.

The bear is another creature whose reputation has unjustifiably been blackened. The bear rarely preys on domestic animals or attacks human beings. Although hunters and newspapers are apt to describe every bear as being fierce, only a minute percentage of the bears in Sweden are killers

Overleaf: Lake Breidal, near Geiranger in central Norway, showing the birches, willows, junipers, heather and sedge characteristic of the Scandinavian mountains above the conifer level. (Gerhard Klammet)

249

of cattle or goats. Bears are mainly vegetarians. They may eat carrion, the carcasses of reindeer that have died during the winter, but as soon as plants begin to grow they return to their vegetable diet, with the addition perhaps of some voles, other small rodents, and ants. In the autumn this huge animal prefers a diet of berries—cowberries, bilberries, cloudberries and the like. Bears are omnivorous, but their anatomy and biology show that they are adapted chiefly to a diet of plants and berries.

Just about the time of the first autumn snow, the bear goes into a den for the winter. The den, which it often uses year after year, may be a mountain cave, a hole dug in a slope, an ant hill or under the roots of a fallen tree. There the bear sleeps on a bed of earth and moss. It does not, like some animals, go into a coma with a sharp drop in body temperature, but rather into a deep sleep, from which it can awaken immediately and completely if danger threatens. The female gives birth to young during the winter period. At birth, a bear cub is no bigger than a rat, but it grows quickly; it is a remarkable fact that although the mother does not eat for half the year, she can suckle her young for about four months. By the time it leaves the den in April a cub is as large as a medium-sized dog.

The common sandpiper is a familiar bird along mountain watercourses; there it can be heard all day and night in the summer. Small islets covered with willow, and reefs in deltas, make ideal nesting sites for these birds. There the birds chase one another about or fly on regular routes over the islands and along the channels. Constantly they utter eager cries, and not even when dark clouds roll down from the peaks and thunder echoes along the valleys do they grow quiet.

ABOVE THE TIMBERLINE

The birch forest becomes progressively less dense higher in the mountains, but solitary trees, including occasional spruce and pine as well as birch, grow above this forest limit.

A magnificent panorama meets the eye on the mountain heath; one stands amazed at the immensity of everything. In front are heaths rolling like huge waves higher and higher, covered with lichens and low shrubs; in the distance massive mountain peaks gleam dazzlingly white; far down in the valley are lakes at various levels, while down the opposite slope there plunge innumerable streams and at the bottom of the valley a wide river winds like a silver ribbon.

From a distance the vegetation looks uniform, but as one gets closer one is often astonished at the variety of plants. The length of time the snow lasts, the lime content of the soil and the supply of running water determine the composition of the plant communities in the willow region. The poor heath, with crowberry dominant in wind-exposed places, and bilberry on slopes that are snow-covered in winter, occupies most of the non-calcareous ground. These plant communities are at their best in autumn when cascades of reddish color enliven the mountain slopes. But even in spring and summer bright-colored flowers light up the heath—the snow-white bells of the polar heath *(Cassiope tetragona),* the violet of the Lapp heath *(Phyllodoce coerulea)* and the red flowers of the mountain azalea *(Loiseleuria procumbens).* But they still cannot compare with the glorious autumn colors.

The tallest vegetation above the timberline is willow, form-ing more or less dense thickets, particularly in wet, sloping country over which trickles water from the melting snow. The upper boundary of this willow shrub belt marks the limit of the vertical distribution of many animals.

In the highest zone the ground is firm, not spongy as among the tussocks in the willow region, although when the snow melts in the spring it is generally soft and water-logged. Lichen-covered stones lie scattered all over the heath. Short grass and budding shrubs appear in the shelter of large boulders. But even here, high in the mountains, spring flowers bloom and birds sing. There are yellow and white ranunculuses, reddish-violet Lapland rosebays *(Rhododendron lapponicum)* an abundance of white, yellow and purple saxifrages and, on some mountains, yellow poppies. One can hear overhead the raven's harsh cry; the ring ouzel sings from a precipice; rough-legged buzzards sail over the vast expanse of heath; the black-throated diver calls from tarns; and there Temminck's stints hover, while from afar comes the bark of the arctic fox. With few exceptions, all the plants and animals met with on the higher mountain wastes are purely arctic species.

LEMMINGS: FACT AND FABLE

The most celebrated animal of the Scandinavian mountains is the Norwegian lemming *(Lemmus lemmus).* For centuries, stories about this small rodent have been told around the world. In 1532, a Strasbourg scholar published a treatise on the animal, based on information from two Norwegian bishops. He declared that in stormy weather lemmings fell from the sky in great numbers, that their bite was venomous, and that they perished by thousands when the grass began to grow in the spring. In his chronicles on the march of King Charles XII's soldiers over the mountains between Sweden and Norway in August, 1718, Joran Norberg wrote: "People maintain that clouds passing over the mountains leave behind a vermin called mountain mice or lemmings; they are as big as a fist, furry like the guinea-pig, and poisonous." A similar legend of the lemming's cosmic origin has been perpetuated by Eskimos, whose name for one Alaskan species means "the creature from space."

The Norwegian lemming is found in all high parts of the Scandinavian mountain range, as well as in the highlands of northeastern Swedish Lapland, in Finland, and on the Kola Peninsula. In some years their numbers increase prodigiously; in intervening periods the population is much diminished.

During a "normal" spring in most parts of the mountains, the lemmings do not migrate great distances toward lower altitudes; their winter and summer quarters are generally close to each other, usually in the high alpine belt of vegetation above the upper limit of the willows. Thus, above an altitude of about three thousand feet, the migration is generally in a horizontal direction.

In summer, lemmings seek shelter in depressions and cavities in the ground, or make tunnels in ground vegetation. Such refuges, often no larger than the animal itself, are used regularly, and the lemmings's well marked paths can sometimes be discerned in a carpet of lichen. From May to August,

Reindeer, excellent swimmers, cross a fjord in Finnmark, northernmost Norway. (Pierre Marc)

they prefer to inhabit moist, stony ground partly covered by sedges, willow shrubs, and dwarf birch. Such habitats provide them with food and the hiding places so vital in an area of many predators—consisting of stoats or ermines, weasels, rough-legged buzzards, common ravens, and the long-tailed skua *(Stercorarius longicaudus)* and snowy owl. Since its fur is water resistant, water does not seem to inconvenience the lemming; rather it behaves almost as if it were aquatic. However, it needs dry holes for reproduction, as the newborn are sensitive to moisture and cold. In autumn, a pronounced move starts toward drier places, away from damp ground and severe cold that can prove fatal to them. Usually the lemmings can live in comparative safety under the snow, which protects them from both cold and enemies. If rain and frost should blanket the vegetation with ice before the snow cover is established, however, the difficulty in gathering food may prove fatal.

Although many summer predators are absent in winter, the stoat and weasel remain and hunt under the snow. But even they are relatively rare in the lichen region during winter. Thus, the lemmings above the timberline are almost free from predation until early spring, when they first venture above the snow. Beneath the snow, lemmings burrow extensive passages and build round grass nests that are sometimes attached to willow shrubs and may be seen hanging on twigs after the snow melts.

During an ordinary winter, these rodents take advantage of their protected situation under the snow cover to breed there.

The wolverine is the king of beasts in the Scandinavian mountains. Even bears, wolves and lynxes retreat from it when they occasionally come together around a carcass. (Sven Gillsater: Tio)

The lemming is so prolific in some years, as in the population explosions of 1960 and 1961, that only vigorous winter breeding can explain it. This seems to be a unique situation among rodents, although it is known that some voles may occasionally breed in winter.

For centuries men have speculated on the reasons for sudden increases in the number of lemmings. The explanation is probably that this species, hidden from autumn to spring, can create several generations in a single season. But how is it that the lemming shows such extraordinary increases in certain years? In addition to a high breeding potential, certain environmental factors contribute to these increases: (1) Generally favorable climatic conditions, which in turn affect both the food supply and the animal's ability to take advantage of them during most of the year. Early spring and late autumn would therefore be propitious. (2) A stable climate during the winter periods when the newborn young are in the nest. Mild weather and thaws, as much as sudden severe cold, may then be fatal. (3) The almost complete lack of interference from predators in winter.

But if, as indicated above, the long winter and the snow are so advantageous, how can the early spring and late autumn also be favorable? The fact is that the food supply beneath the snow is limited, so that the winter idyl may prove to be a trap if prolonged unduly, particularly during years when lemmings are most numerous. It seems very probable that the prolongation of winter conditions is a quite common occurrence.

The seasonal migrations of lemmings should not be confused with the dramatic marches that have made them so famous. In the light of the 1960-1961 population expansion, the lemming populations seem to move from their natural habitats, that is from the mountain heaths in the lichen belt down to willow, birch, and conifer zones, whence they disperse overland. The impression created by their movements is of a gradual flowing down the mountain slopes, though individually the animals seem to move at random, simply straying in various directions. Breeding continues during these territorial wanderings, but females in an advanced stage of pregnancy settle at any level, even if far from the most favored and densely populated habitats which lie high on the mountain heaths.

The major concentrations, on the other hand, seem to occur only in certain locations: when a large lake stops the rodents' slow, almost imperceptible progress, or when two rivers meet and the lemmings are, so to say, caught in a funnel. In these situations, the concentration of animals becomes so great that panic ensues and they take to reckless flight—uphill or downhill, over rivers and lakes, and sometimes to the sea, particularly in Norway where the mountains are close to the shore. Leaving the mountain heaths, they may also wander over the glaciers.

There is much evidence to suggest that such mass migrations stem from a kind of psychosis, possibly due to competition with other individuals for shelter holes and territory. So far as is known, food is not an important factor even when lemmings are most numerous, since enough food appears to be available in the vicinity. It is quite possible, however, that the diet of the Norwegian lemming is on occasion far more specialized than has hitherto been thought; if this is so, lack of certain food requirements may be of decisive importance. Diseases have also been advanced as an explanation of the phenomenon, but it is significant that migrating populations have not been too ill to resettle and breed in new territories; and it should also be added that many animals do not join in the exodus but remain in their original habitat. The idea that lemming migrations always end in a kind of mass suicide is nonsense, as is the story that they form a veritable stream of moving bodies during the migration.

A drastic decline of the lemming population almost always follows a peak year. There is no doubt that predation is often influential in keeping populations of small rodents in check, but, on the whole, the quantity of animals seems to be ordered by a complex of factors in combination with their self-regulating habits. The Norwegian lemming is a striking example.

If neither predators nor food plays a decisive role in the population explosions of lemmings—which is almost without parallel in the vertebrate world—what is the cause of their wholesale deaths? Of course, lemmings die within the four-year life cycle of their species. But this hardly explains the death of hordes of the animals following population explosions. The truth is that we do not yet know what mechanisms are involved in the fascinating population dynamics of this unusual rodent.

THE CHAR—FISH OF THE MOUNTAINS

The range of the char *(Salvelinus alpinus)* in northern Scandinavia covers lakes and rivers in the upper coniferous forest, and the mountain region throughout the zoologically most important vegetation belts, i.e. the *Betula, Salix* and lichen zones. It is also found in small, swift-running rills high up in the cloud-wrapped mountains. Sometimes it is found to inhabit lakes into which migration appears to be impossible. There is also evidence from prehistoric time that chars were introduced into lakes by Lapps, as living food storage during their seasonal exodus through the mountains.

The vertical distribution pattern of the trout *(Salmo trutta)* is the opposite to that of the char: while the char gradually increases in number at higher altitudes, the trout becomes rarer, and finally, in the upper alpine zone, the char is usually unaccompanied by other fish. Coordinated with this geographical distribution is an ecological relationship between the char and the trout. Where one species is solitary, it spreads and occupies various habitats, but wherever it is joined by the other, there is competition, and the two species confine themselves to limited ranges offering various conditions for each. In higher altitudes the char is favored by its arctic adaptation; it also seems to compete successfully with the trout in running waters in arctic and subarctic areas but seldom or never in lower regions where the trout dominates.

Very striking is the frequency with which the char penetrates up rivulets that are often so shallow that one can easily catch the fish by hand. In spite of the difficulty of swimming in such waters, however, the char is not deterred from its progress upstream.

Chars living more or less permanently in running mountain waters in northern Lapland may also spawn in such habitats. A fish living in such a habitat as a fast-running and very shallow rill high up on a mountain slope must have special attributes. We know that the char is an arctic species, and thus well qualified to survive in cold-water environments, but this does not explain how it thrives in small rills. The char

The wolf, here shown in northern Swedish Lapland, is now ruthlessly hunted from helicopters and snow scooters. Only about twenty to forty of these animals remain in Sweden. (Sven Ivar Svensson)

has, however, a particular quality that I have often observed in Lapland: when trout and chars have been caught with nets in lakes or rivers, chars survive longer than trout. This suggests that the char is tougher than the trout and better equipped for the restrictions of a small stream.

Apparently fish cannot survive in upper montane rills during the winter, and therefore chars found there in summer are not permanent residents. Why in any case do they migrate upward? I believe spawning may be excluded as an answer, because such habitats are not suitable for this purpose. More likely reasons are such ecological factors as the search for the best feeding waters, the drive of an arctic species to reach colder waters, or the hazard of competition on lower levels. Chemical or hydrographic changes in the environment—for instance, heavy rainfalls—are known to incite upstream and downstream migration in several marine and freshwater fish. The electrical conductivity of running waters, especially in their downstream reaches, generally increases with heavy rainfalls; perhaps this may stimulate certain fish, causing them to wander. We know that this is true in tropical Africa.

The Great Taiga

Northern Europe's Coniferous Forests

17

The Eurasian conifer forest, extending across the temperate land areas from the Scandinavian mountains in the west to the Pacific Ocean in the east, is the largest forest in the world. Though only a small part of this vast belt is in Europe, it forms the greatest forest complex on the European continent, covering about 1430 miles of lowland between the Scandinavian highlands and the Ural Mountains.

In the south, the European conifer forest is bounded by deciduous forests, and in the north by tundra. Nowhere on the forest plains is there territory high enough to challenge the visual dominance of the conifers.

MIXED FORESTS

The southern part of the European conifer region is a mixed forest in which conifers dominate; but in certain areas deciduous trees play an important role. The northern limit of mixed forest is marked by the oak *(Quercus robur)*, found up to latitudes 56° and 61° N. The mixed forest extends farthest north in Sweden and Finland, while in Norway (where it should not be confused with the coastal forests) it reaches approximately latitude 59° N. In Russia, the northern limit of the mixed forest lies west of Ladoga, at 60° N; it descends eastward until, at the Urals, it lies at 56° N. Birch *(Betula pubescens* and *B. verrucosa)* is the foremost deciduous tree of the mixed forest—which also contains oak, maple, linden (basswood), alder *(Alnus glutinosa* and *A. incana)*, mountain ash, hazel, and aspen *(Populus tremula)*. Large parts of the southern conifer forest region are cultivated, especially in the loamy areas around lakes and in river valleys.

Apart from the Scandinavian countries, the Baltic region and Russia, only northeast Poland lies within the European mixed forest zone. That region is a glacier-carved lowland, filled with lakes, swamps, marshes, ridges, and hills. The Mazury lakes in Poland and the Pripet marshes in Russia are the largest swamplands in the European interior. These lakes and marshes were formed when the glaciers melted. At first they were blocked by ice, and ice-filled rivers filled them with mud, sand, and gravel. Although the forest-encircled lakes and marshes abound in everything that beavers, otters *(Lutra lutra)*, and various water birds need for survival, many of them support very little wildlife. This seems due partly to their meager aquatic vegetation and partly to merciless hunting. The beaver was once exterminated but has been reintroduced in a number of reserves. There are now no fewer than fifty-three nature sanctuaries in the Mazury lakes: birds abound principally in these areas.

For bird life the foremost lake is Luknyany, a stretch of shallow water between thirty and sixty miles long, alongside Lake Sniardwys, one of Poland's largest lakes. Before being silted up, Luknyany may once have been a bay of its huge neighbor; its bed is now covered with aquatic plants, chiefly *Chara* and *Nitella,* that provide food for vast flocks of birds and swarms of fish. The lake's surface is dotted white and black with swans and coots, interspersed with mallard, gadwalls, pintails, widgeon, shovelers, pochard and tufted ducks. Luknyany is perhaps the principal nesting area of the mute swan *(Cygnus olor)*. In 1960 about 250 pairs nested there side by side.

Around Luknyany the male swan's well known territorial aggressiveness has been modified, it seems, by collective agreement. Also squeezed in among the white shapes of the swans are black cormorants, which have begun to build their nests on the ground—a new departure for this tree-nesting bird. In the reeds, bearded tits nest and the great reed warblers rasp. Marsh and hen harriers, lesser spotted eagles and ospreys patrol the lake. When I visited Luknyany, a number of black kites were living in the middle of a heron community in pine woods along the shore; a kestrel had also attached himself to this company and a golden oriole sang nearby. Above them circled a sea eagle.

The Mazury lakes lie on a flyway, and migratory geese and duck rest there in spring and the fall. The importance of such protected areas is apparent at Lake Jezioro Siedmiu Wysp, in the northeast part of Mazury. This area, made a reserve in 1948, had never been visited by bean geese before 1949; that year flocks of bean geese lingered there and ever since have visited the tract in increasing numbers.

Southeast of the Mazury lakes, like a monument to the Ice Age, an immense bog covers an area about 300 miles long by 220 miles wide—the Pripet marshes. This is a wonderful land of swamp forests, marsh, moss, lakes, and tilled fields. Brooks and rivers wind everywhere, all making their way to the swamp's main artery, the Pripyat River, which empties into the Dnieper River north of Kiev. North of the Pripyat a mixed forest of spruce and deciduous trees has grown up on solid ground a few inches above the water; south of the river, spruce is found only in isolated clumps, while leafy trees hang like curtains on river banks and

Right above: Stages of vegetation on the Swedish island of Gotland. Lichens are the pioneers; in the foreground are swallowworts (Cynanchum vincetoxicum), *and in the background junipers and pines. (Ingmar Holmåsen)   Right: Because it is one of the earliest spring flowers, the liverleaf* (Anemone hepatica) *has been collected commercially and has thus disappeared in many areas. (Pepi Merisio)   Far right: A carpet of lichens and mosses in a conifer forest in Finland. (Teuvo Suominen)*

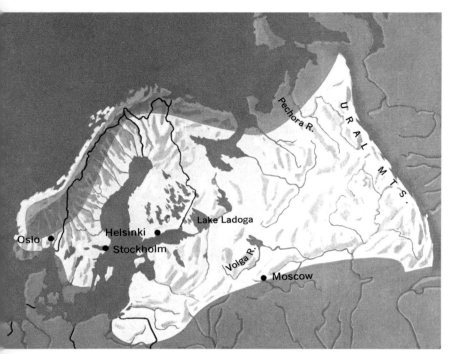

The great conifer forest of Europe includes both deciduous and conifer trees and abounds in lakes, bogs and rivers. Extending over Norway, Sweden, Finland, the Baltic countries, a corner of Poland and an immense section of Russia, it is part of the world's largest forest. East of the Urals it continues to the Pacific Ocean and then across North America.

around lakes and marshes. There are also vast expanses of sand, left in the wake of the glacial flow. Dunes were formed here, but they were tamed by vegetation and now support a pine forest.

THE AMAZING BEAVER

This land of water and forest is a paradise for beavers. Food is plentiful, and countless streams serve them well by transporting materials for dam and home construction. Few mammals provide such conspicuous evidence of their presence as the beaver: everywhere there are the telltale stumps, the efficient dams, the canals leading to the logging grounds, and the impressive dwellings of turf and branches. Its engineering, lumbering, and transportation skills are remarkable, and in fact its ability at performing technically complex tasks is only surpassed by man.

Beaver cabins vary greatly both in shape and size. They usually consist of three compartments: a "dining room" with water basin, a "living room," and a "bedroom." The beaver's purpose in making a dam—constructed of branches, twigs, earth and clay—is to maintain and regulate a constant supply and level of water in its territory. This is vital to beavers, since they are greatly dependent on water for the tunnel approaches to their cabins, their feeding areas, and for the dead-end canals where they transport felled logs.

The beaver family in a single cabin consists of the parents and the last two litters—that is, six to eight animals. Each family has its own territory, though several families use the same feeding grounds and have unrestricted passage along the waterways. Their nightly operations provide both food and building materials. In winter the beaver depends on the food it has gathered in late summer and autumn. Supplies of deciduous tree stems, branches and twigs are stored in their cabins and in the water; working like engineers on the bottom of the dam, they fasten and anchor together bunches of branches and twigs.

Beavers are now found in many places and are valuable for their pelts. The beaver population in Poland and Russia, which was once badly stricken, has been restored. In Sweden and Finland the beaver was exterminated in 1868 and 1871 respectively, but fortunately the species survived in Norway. Reintroduced into Sweden, the present population there is probably several thousand. In some places, however, the beaver has again been reduced through man's regulation of the waters; in those areas all the mammal's building skill and industry have been in vain, especially since short-period regulation for hydroelectric purposes occurs mostly during the winter and washes away the beavers' food and dwellings.

BLACKBIRDS AND JAYS

Scandinavia was the last part of the European mainland freed from the glaciers of the Ice Age, almost nine thousand years ago. The transformation from arctic tundra to deep deciduous forests, mighty peat bogs and huge spruce forests, has taken thousands of years; but only in the last 150 years has man decisively remolded the landscape.

At the start of the nineteenth century the Scandinavian countryside was still so varied that it could cater to the needs of both men and animals in widespread areas. It is true that man had fought the advancing forest for thousands of years, but until the nineteenth century man's influence was not sufficient to alter the general aspects of the animal world. Then, with the gradual expansion of industry, the draining of marshes, the exploitation of rivers for hydroelectric power, and because of the increasing market value of coniferous forests, the nature of Scandinavia became violently transformed. Only parts of the mountain ranges and the seas have since remained unchanged. Man has not only drastically altered habitats, but he has also interfered directly with animal life by hunting, by the random destruction of predators, by polluting lakes and rivers, by introducing foreign species, and by his use of insecticides and other lethal properties. All of these activities have started chain reactions whose ultimate consequences are unpredictable.

In comparison with other European countries Scandinavia is a sparsely populated area, because of which the transformation of the countryside has been more gradual. The hardest pressed creatures are the large carnivores that man either fears or dislikes. Of the birds of the deciduous forest there are only a few species that human beings come to know relatively well. Among these is the pied flycatcher, which lives in holes in trees or in nesting boxes. Hardly any other European bird has been studied in such detail. Thus, in southern Finland's mixed forest region, Lars von Haartman has observed this bird for twenty years. Among other things he has discovered that the pied flycatcher seems to be "polyterritorial," occupying during the mating season several territories other than its eventual nesting area. This is apparently related to the male's tendency to take two mates, sometimes simultaneously and sometimes in succession.

All northern thrushes, except the ring ouzel, appear to have become adapted to urban habitats. This development has proceeded furthest with the blackbird, apparently starting in England where this bird's urban, or suburban, habits are of ancient origin. The movement of blackbirds into the cities of Holland began about 1820, in Denmark about 1890, in Sweden about 1900, in Finland about 1924, and in Königsberg (now Kaliningrad) about 1933. Since then, blackbirds have occupied more and more cities and villages and their numbers have increased tremendously.

In the forest the blackbird is unsociable, living either alone or with its family. In cities and gardens, on the other hand, one may see several blackbirds at their listening posts or running about lawns and fields searching for worms and other nourishment. The blackbird obviously has collective feeding grounds, where the males tolerate each other; yet each family has quite separate territorial boundaries, sometimes only a hundred feet or so apart, and the appearance of a trespassing male bird triggers off an immediate protest or attack from whichever male claims right of ownership.

Two of the mixed forest's most interesting birds are the jay *(Garrulus glandarius)* and the nutcracker *(Nucifraga caryocatactes)*. The former nests in deciduous, mixed, and coniferous forests over large parts of Europe. Within the mixed forest areas the westernmost race of the latter *(N. c. caryocatactes)* keeps to deep spruce woods, with trees ranging from bearded oldsters to scrawny saplings, and preferably with some dense, moist thicket nearby. An abundance of hazel not too far away is an essential requirement of this thick-billed race. Nesting places of the eastern race *(N. c. macrorhynchus)* are found in the Siberian stone pine forests.

Because of its fondness for spruce forests the nutcracker frequents several widely separated areas, from Scandinavia to Bulgaria. The only European habitats of the eastern race of this species are in northeast Russia and the Urals. In late summer and autumn the jay gathers such food as acorns, and the nutcracker hazelnuts for consumption during the winter. These birds bury their winter stocks of food in the forest, and it is remarkable how they manage later to find their caches even when the woods are deep in snow. Several of the forest tits, such as the coal tit *(Parus ater)*, crested tit, willow tit *(P. montanus)* and Siberian tit *(P. cinctus)* also lay up a winter food supply, but these are stored in trees and are for communal consumption by the members of each species.

NIGHT IN THE FOREST

Compared with the almost incessant nocturnal chatter of animals in the tropics, night in a northern forest seems muted and subdued. But in late winter, spring, and in early summer, countless voices can be heard, bearing witness to the richness of life in these areas. Changes of season and weather greatly influence the sounds uttered by creatures of the night. On late fall and winter nights only a few owls can be heard calling before they leave for their hunting grounds. Otherwise it is still, except when storms rage. But under the snow small mammals are active, and in the morning one can read in the snow what foxes, weasels, hares and other creatures have been up to during the night. The mountain hare's prints, two abreast and two trailing, tell of its nocturnal quest for food; night after night the fox follows the same trail. Occasionally mice,

An osprey, the only fishing expert among the raptors of Europe, catches a bream. (Siœten Jonsson)

voles and shrews make nocturnal excursions above the snow, leaving faint prints here and there. But brief as their exposure may be, the ermine and weasels catch them. These agile creatures go down into the grass tunnels of voles and push the nests to the surface from underneath; whereupon the fox, which has been listening for sounds from the nests, digs them up from above. The pattern of these deeds is written in the snow.

As early as March the northern night starts responding to spring. Mountain hares range restlessly about, for this is their mating time, and one hears the cry of the courting fox. But above all it is the owls that animate the March nights. In April the sounds that accompany spring are most notable at dawn and dusk: the migratory birds begin to arrive, led by the various thrushes, and the fragile, silvery notes of the European robin are heard briefly before dawn and after dusk. In April, too, the woodcock makes his evening and dawn rounds; on the moors and in the fields the black grouse *(Lyrurus tetrix)* begins his display, making a sort of bubbling murmur; and in the deep woods the capercaillie plays.

Each night, overhead, waves of migratory birds spread out over the land. Then, even the wings of ducks seem to sing, the widgeon whistle; the teal sound like flutes; the wings of the goldeneyes make a musical noise. The scoters' annual flight is marked by a rhythmic, monotonous, "pjy, pjy, pjy." And in April bats, too, resume their nocturnal aerial acrobatics in earnest.

Of the most remarkable of sounds heard on spring nights are those of frogs and toads: when darkness closes over the tarns and ponds, the air is filled with the noise made by these small creatures.

Northern wildlife is most active during May. At this time the hours of darkness are so few or, as in northern Scandinavia and Russia, almost nonexistent. From the lakes comes the continuous clamor of ducks; and the water voles *(Arvicola*

259

The jay, a familiar bird in many kinds of woodlands, occurs in deciduous forests as well as the taiga, where it is spreading northward.   Below: A fox with its prey, a hazel hen. As its tracks in the snow reveal, the fox is active mainly during the night. (Both by R. P. Bille)

terrestris), munching at reed stems, are audible from a distance. The bream (Abramis brama), thrusting among the lush growth of the bottom mud in search of food, stands almost upright. While testing various organisms for their edibility, this fish sometimes makes a loud smack and throws up a small spout of water among the lilies and other aquatic plants.

Late summer and autumn nights bring flights of migratory birds. Of the passerines, one hears mostly thrushes; and on certain wet October and November nights the air seems filled with the charming redwing's dainty "tsyyb." The cries of waders in the night sky are even more fascinating: the common sandpiper is often heard, as are the ringed plover, the curlew and the whimbrel (Numenius phaeopus). Frequently one can hear the greenshank, and the green sandpiper (Tringa ochropus), returning south, is heard as early as July, almost always alone, for one rarely hears the call of more than one of these birds at a time.

Bird flights through the night skies of autumn are best heard in cities or villages, where the lights are believed to stimulate bird cries.

CONIFER FORESTS

The northern conifer forest occupies much of Scandinavia and Finland. This is the taiga—mentioned at the beginning of this chapter—a Siberian name for the immense lowland forest of northern Eurasia.

Compared with deciduous forests, the taiga has relatively few species of trees. There are more kinds of conifers in the east, because the conifer invasion after the Ice Age came chiefly from that direction. The leafy trees, on the other hand, moved in from the west. Since the ice lingered longest in Scandinavia below the polar regions, the forestation of northwest Europe took place only at a relatively late stage.

In Scandinavia, Finland, and westernmost Russia, the conifer forests consist of spruce (Picea abies) and pine (Pinus silvestris), but at approximately longitude 39° E there is larch (Larix sibirica); at longitude 42° E, Siberian fir (Abies sibirica); and at latitude 53° E, Siberian stone pine (Pinus cembra); while everywhere in the northern conifer area there are intrusions of birch and aspen, but these are found chiefly on land influenced by cultivation: thus they occur very rarely to the east, since the Russian taiga is sparsely populated. Far to the north, however, at the edge of the tundra, the birch embraces vast areas because the climate, despite the low altitude, is like that of the mountain birch belt. Thus only in Scandinavia and on the Kola peninsula does the birch form the northernmost forests, while spruce forests abound near the tundra from the White Sea to the Urals.

The immense taiga as a natural habitat does not vary much and therefore supports fewer species than any other type of European forest. However it displays an amazing amount of vegetation for a region with such a harsh climate. It seems incredible, for example, that the dry gravel between Petjora and the Urals should have produced such an immense forest.

Spring at Porkkala in southern Finland. The snow is melting, and birches, spruces and pines are temporarily surrounded by water. (Teuvo Suominen)

The great gray owl is a bird of the taiga forests. Despite its size, man does not yet know much about its habits. (Goran Hansson)

Especially on dry ground where the pines parade in sparse clusters, the taiga seems monotonous; but if one views the woodlands as a whole there is much variety. The scene ranges from glittering forest tarns to piney lichen heath; from wide moors and marshes adorned with white balls of cotton sedge to spruce forests with dense carpets of bilberry; from leafy river banks to scrawny birch groves. The forest spreads out like a tumultuous sea, with shimmering blue ridges, broad moors and river channels marking the crests and troughs of the waves.

A stroll in the spruce forest, a boggy place with slender, lichen-crusted trunks mingling with white birch, is always exciting. Moving quietly over the cushions of bear moss, one surprises wild creatures again and again. In the denser parts bilberries are seen everywhere. One clambers over ancient tree trunks, admires the huge ant hills, which sometimes provide winter quarters for the bear, listens to the chiffchaff *(Phylloscopus collybita)* and the redwing thrush, is startled by the capercaillie's explosive take-off, finds the spoor of a moose or a fox, and pauses at a suitable place to watch for the northern red-backed vole *(Clethrionomys rutilus)* and the bank vole, both busy in the ground cover. Soon one stops again: the ground now is more moist, the spruce darker, the

willows thicker, the view more limited; these are some of the warnings that one has reached the domain of a forest stream.

A stream seldom runs far in a conifer forest before losing itself in a bog; and there are hundreds of thousands of bogs in the taiga. Although they look much alike, each bog is different from the next. On one there may be many waders, on another perhaps a lone wood sandpiper; a short-eared owl patrols one bog, a hen harrier another; and on yet another these two species keep company. While a bog seems empty and lifeless, a tarn may hold myriads of creatures such as the newly hatched tadpoles of the grass frog, *Rana temporaria*. There are always a few meadow pipits on the bog, and sometimes, too, a pair of red-throated divers *(Gavia stellata)* may be seen rising from a tiny tarn—an aquatic take-off strip just adequate for them.

In winter when northern areas are deep in snow and it is not possible to tell whether bog or lake borders the forest, the first impression is often of a total absence of life, with creatures neither of the air nor ground in evidence. Actually, many creatures live beneath the snow.

The northern conifer forests in Europe are less amenable to cultivation than those of the south. Dominating the landscape from Sweden to the Urals, the taiga is essentially a forest. This is made obvious when it is seen from the air. Once one has passed the boundary of the northern conifer area, the brownish surfaces of bogs are more in evidence and cultivated clearings are the exception. The taiga's colors form a mosaic: in summer, of green and brown; in winter, of dark green and white. It is the same all the way east to the Urals.

The Fenno-Scandian bedrock, chiefly granite and gneiss, is succeeded east of the White Sea and Karelia by geologically younger rock forms. Almost all of the conifer forest area is covered by moraine and glacial river deposits. The mixture of sand, gravel and boulders in the moraines was produced by the land ice, while the peat of the bogs is composed of the organic remains of marshy vegetation from various postglacial periods.

Next to the dominant soil types—moraine and peat—sand and loam are most widespread. In some tracts, ice rivers left tremendous amounts of gravel in the form of ridges, hogbacks and glacial deltas; but some of the ancient lakes were filled with sediment composed mostly of sandy soil.

The taiga forms what the Russians call *podzol*, a soil identified by its three distinctively colored layers; ash-colored surface humus, near-white sand in the middle layer, and golden brown loam at the bottom.

Though the conifer forests from Scandinavia to the Urals are markedly uniform, there are forest complexes that deviate from the prevalent type. For instance the world's northernmost pine forest lies in the Stabbur Valley, near Porsangerfjord, Norway, at latitude 70° N, and the birch grows tall and the willow dense on the valley floor alongside the Stabbur River. The birch persists on the valley slopes, but is there accompanied by aged pines that have sometimes formed proud forests of giant trees, many of them several hundred years old. The mighty forest at the edge of the Arctic is an astonishing sight. When I wandered there one summer day, wondering just what creatures of the conifer forest could possibly exist in this northern outlier of the taiga, the only mammal I encountered was a red squirrel; among the birds, I noted the Siberian jay *(Perisoreus infaustus)*, the Siberian tit, and the song thrush.

The size of the pines at the taiga's outer edges is most impressive compared with those of alpine or subalpine zones. This is of course due largely to the fact that these are virgin forests and the trees are nature's own. In the conifer forests the oldest trees are almost always pines because, unlike the spruce, they can withstand fire. The most magnificent virgin pine forest I have ever seen in Europe is in northern Swedish Lapland, in Vietasvagge, in the Great Lake Falls National Park, at an altitude of from 1485 to 1700 feet above sea level. There, pines form the conifer forest's highest ramparts at the edge of the birch belt, one huge pine after another rising from a dense moss mattress, which in turn is hidden by crowberry *(Empetrum hermaphroditum)* and lingon *(Vaccinium vitis-idaea)* foliage. Unhappily this old forest is being shredded by a huge hydroelectric project.

Botanically and zoologically spruce forests are always richer than pine forests. The clearings often support a wealth of plant life, with bilberry usually the dominant species, and mosses outnumbering lichens—again in contrast to the pine forest. Spruce forests have a greater range than pine forests because they can colonize varied terrain, from relatively dry slopes and ridges to watery hollows and moist valley basins. As a result, we recognize several kinds of spruce forest.

The conifer landscape in Norway, Sweden, Finland and Russia west of the White Sea and Lake Onega is much more varied than in eastern Russia. This is largely due to the many lakes in Fenno-Scandia, on the Kola Peninsula, in Karelia, and around Lake Onega. Finland, especially, has so many lakes—55,000—bays, and islands that it is like a vast archipelago. This in fact is what it was when sea covered much of the country in the postglacial period. The total length of shoreline of the Finnish lakes is immense: it is estimated that there are 110 yards of lakeshore to each of Finland's 4,500,000 inhabitants.

The northernmost spruce forests are often dwarfed and form sparse scrubland. But they change character from east to west. In Finnmark (northernmost Norway), on the Kola Peninsula, and in northern Karelia, birch and pine generally form a horizontal belt between the conifer forest and the tundra, while on the Kanin Peninsula and in the Timan area birch and spruce alternate. Between Petjora and the Urals spruce alone usually builds a fence against the tundra. East of the Urals, the larch is the northernmost species of tree.

ANIMALS OF THE TAIGA

Geologically the taiga is a recent development. During the colonization period since the ice receded, vegetation and animal life have varied with the climate, but have remained relatively stable during the past few thousand years. Because the taiga in Russia reclaimed its present area relatively soon after the land ice and tundra retreated to the north, the vegetation and wildlife there are older than those of the Fenno-Scandian conifer forest region. Recently man has wrought disruptive changes, transforming virgin forests into tree farms and thereby drastically altering the natural community.

Although the conifer forest may seem impoverished it supports a myriad fauna, filling every nook from the ground up to the treetops. For example, one Swedish conifer forest contains at least two million insects and spiders per square yard, not to speak of other invertebrates.

During the winter, when the snow cover creates a microclimate of amazingly high temperature beneath it, many invertebrates are active; this explains how such restless insecteaters as the shrew, as well as small vegetarian rodents, manage so well during the long winter.

The birds of these forests, such as the tits, woodpeckers and owls, are primarily hole-nesters and must have access to trees suitable for nesting. But the forest also provides cover and food for many other bird groups that nest on the ground, in shrubs and trees.

Characteristic mammals of the conifer forest are the rodents, predators and hoofed animals; there are relatively few insect-eaters or bats. Most of the hoofed animals of tropical forests are small and have insignificant horns; but those of the temperate forests are often large and have good-sized antlers which, from the evolutionary viewpoint, is regarded as acceptable evidence of their relatively recent arrival in the forests.

THE MOOSE

The moose *(Alces alces)* is Europe's largest land mammal, although the bison is heavier. It is found everywhere in the conifer forest region and its numbers are increasing. Considering its size, Sweden has relatively the largest moose population in the world. This is no ancient inheritance; the

A crane beside its nest in a conifer forest. Because it migrates in spectacular formations and with much trumpeting, this species has been a well-known migratory bird since antiquity. (Arthur Christiansen)

abundance of moose in Sweden has, in fact, varied significantly. Although it was found throughout the forested areas of Sweden at the start of the nineteenth century, it was then near extinction in southern Sweden. It was given full protection between 1808–1817 and between 1826–1835, and since then it has steadily increased in numbers. In 1961–1962 Sweden had about 118,000 head, Europe's densest population of moose. It is interesting to note that the tremendous increase in the past twenty years has taken place despite an astonishing rise in the number of moose killed by hunters (about twenty to thirty thousand head annually) and the rapid conversion of land in southern and central Sweden for lumbering, agricultural and industrial uses, and the extension of highways and of human communities. The moose has shown a similar adaptability in northern Russia. Moose seem to thrive in the neighborhood of cultivated lands; but most moose, of course, prefer the deep forests.

This thriving of the moose is a remarkable phenomenon. It can hardly be attributed solely to the character of the surroundings, since in the northern United States and Canada, where the habitat is strikingly similar to that of the northern European conifer areas, the moose retreats as man moves north. The American moose has obviously not discovered the advantages of cultivated landscape, since it clings stubbornly to the wilderness.

LYNXES AND WOLVERINES

Like that of so many other large European carnivores, the story of the lynx during the past century is mostly a tale of one long retreat. It has been driven to the most inaccessible parts of the Continent, mainly to mountainous regions. Yet the lynx is a typical forest creature and once inhabited the woods of Europe from Scandinavia to the north coast of the Mediterranean. But ever since ancient times the lynx has been hunted all over Europe, partly because of its valuable pelt and partly because it was considered destructive. In more recent times, when the number of lynxes had shrunk to a minimum, the limited ability of the species to reproduce itself may even have been jeopardized.

In Europe the lynx now occurs most abundantly in Russia's vast forests, but even there the species is declining because of hunters, forest "farming," and increasing construction in forest areas.

Although the lynx is a creature of the forest, it now seems to prefer mountain tracts or terrain marked by stone outcroppings and ravines. It can also adapt itself to cultivated areas if they offer an adequate supply of wild creatures for food, since in general it seems not to prey on domestic animals except reindeer. The lynx is most active at night, but in winter it also hunts by day. During daylight hours the lynx usually keeps to a rocky ledge, where it can survey the surroundings or beat a hasty retreat if threatened. It is an individualist, though for most of their first year of life the young are dependent on their mother. If a young lynx loses its mother before or during the winter it is usually doomed. Even in February, when almost nine months old, it still has its milk teeth and its claws are so undeveloped that it can hardly kill a mountain hare. Since most small rodents are beyond its reach, frequently under more than three feet of snow, an inexperienced young lynx will have great difficulty in finding

food just when its capacity for survival is critical. Lynxes feed principally on hares, but they will take small rodents, foxes, badgers, roe deer, gallinaceous birds, fish, and insects. In certain areas during winter lynxes will also ravage reindeer as well as dogs and cats.

Only partially a creature of the taiga, the wolverine is also found in more northerly areas. It is a great wanderer, moving over an extensive territory. In winter its trail usually leads deep into the conifer forest, but in Scandinavia the belt above the timberline is now its main habitat.

The wolverine has shown a remarkable ability to survive in its old haunts in the Scandinavian mountains, though its numbers have been greatly reduced in the forests. Here, too, persecution by man has been the decisive factor. Though primarily a mountain species in Scandinavia, it is also found in the forests.

The wolverine often feeds on carrion, and it is in competition for such food that it demonstrates a remarkable domination over other animals. It will brazenly challenge a larger animal feeding on a carcass and force it to abandon its meal without a fight. In one case two full-grown bears retired from their feast when a wolverine approached. In similar situations, observers have seen a lynx, two pumas, and three prairie wolves retreat from lone American wolverines although the latter were in each case smaller. But this is not a matter of threat or bluff alone; in one known battle between a wolverine and a lynx in Finland, the wolverine killed the lynx.

THE VANISHING BEAR

Once found everywhere in Europe, the bear has become almost a legendary animal there. It is now limited to isolated regions in the Pyrenees, Apennines, Carpathians, Caucasus, Italian Alps, Balkans, Scandinavia, and in areas on both sides of the border of Finland and Russia. The largest tribe is found in Russia. Most bears are found in the taiga despite the fact that deciduous woods seem much more suitable for them. Once again, as man has extended his domain, a large predator has retreated into inaccessible mountain areas and deep forests.

In the Baltic countries the bear now appears only in Estonia. In Russia, it is found not only in the Carpathians but has spread as far west and south as White Russia along the Oka River; to Rjazan, near Moscow; and farther east, in Mordov and Mari, to the Urals. Thus it occurs farther south in western Russia than in the east.

The bear is a forest animal, preferring the rich vegetation of spruce and birch woods. If left in peace, it will stay within a certain large territory; if often disturbed, it may roam over tremendous areas. Usually it lives alone, although the females remain with their young up to a year and a half and generally give birth only every other year. Despite the fact that the bear is Europe's largest predator, it feeds chiefly on plants: it is nevertheless considered omnivorous. In summer it feeds mostly on grass, herbs, fruit, berries, and roots, but it also relishes ants, honey, beeswax, insect larvae, small rodents, fish, and the carrion of reindeer and other animals. Only exceptionally do bears acquire a taste for fresh meat and attack larger mammals such as moose, reindeer and domestic cattle. The bear is not dangerous to man unless it is attacked and wounded or its young are threatened.

Most of Scandinavia is in the coniferous forest zone, a part of the great taiga. Even in the southern half of Sweden, as here in Dalecarlia, such forests dominate the landscape. (Gösta Tysk)

SABLES, SQUIRRELS AND BATS

Two characteristic predators of the taiga are the marten and the sable *(Martes zibellina)*. The latter is found chiefly in Siberia; it appears in Europe only on the slopes of the Urals near Kama and Petjora. The marten, however, occurs over the greater part of the European conifer area, though in many tracts it has become rare or extinct due to intensive hunting. The sable's distribution in Europe coincides with that of the Siberian stone pine. It is not clear why this is so except that in the autumn both animals eat the seeds of stone pine cones. The sable gets a good part of its nourishment from such fruits as bilberries, and the berries of the mountain ash, but it also catches small rodents and smaller birds. The marten's diet includes berries but, being a much better climber of trees than the sable, it takes squirrels, pursuing them through the trees at an astonishing speed or surprising them in their nests. In some areas it depends heavily on other rodents such as mice and voles. The marten also steals birds' eggs and hides them in moss, where they remain fresh for several months.

In the taiga, as in the mixed and deciduous forests, the ermine and weasel are among the most common predators. Voles and mice are the chief foods of both species, but in the true conifer forest of the taiga only the voles and the lemming of the two rodent groups, *Murinae* and *Microtidae,* are found. Six species of voles are found in the conifer forests of Euro-

pean Russia: namely, the root vole, common vole, field vole, bank vole, large-toothed red-backed vole *(Clethrionomys rufocanus)* and the red-backed vole *(C. rutilus)*. The first four are to be seen over vast areas of Europe—the reader has met them earlier in this book—but the last two are of the extreme north, occurring only in Scandinavia, Finland, and Russia. The vole rat also ranges far north, but it cannot be said to belong to the true taiga. The wood lemming *(Myopus schisticolor)* is a resident of the moss cover and its way of life is still largely a mystery. It inhabits parts of Scandinavia, Finland, Karelia, the Kola peninsula and the mixed forests of central Russia.

The red squirrel, a typical forest creature and valuable because of its pelt, is found everywhere in the taiga. In Finland and Russia there is also the flying squirrel *(Sciuropterus russicus)* which, unlike the red squirrel, is a nocturnal animal. A broad skin flap joining front and back legs on both sides of its body enables it to sail up to sixty-five yards through the air. In the eastern parts of the European taiga we find the ground squirrel *(Tamias sibiricus),* a hibernating rodent which feeds largely on Siberian stone pine seed. This is the nearest European relative of the North American chipmunk.

It was said earlier that among mammals the insect-eaters *(Insectivora)* and bats are rather sparsely represented in the conifer forest. The mole, however, does occur in the taiga up to approximately latitude 65° N. The Scandinavian shrews, *Sorex araneus, S. minutus, S. caecutiens* and *Neomys fodiens,* all occur throughout the European taiga. All of these species live farther north in Scandinavia and on the Kola peninsula than in northern Russia.

The northern bat *(Eptesicus nilssonii)* is the only bat found more or less everywhere in the taiga region. The whiskered bat *(Myotis mystacinus)* is found in Sweden at the Arctic Circle, in Finland at Kuhmo and Kajana, and in Russia north of Archangel, but it has not been reported in the eastern taiga region.

CAPERCAILLIES AND GOSHAWKS

It is the birds, far more than the mammals, that catch the eye of the wanderer in the taiga's dense conifers and sparse pine heath. Many are associated with conifer forests and almost all of them appear chiefly in northern Asia. Here we can mention only a few.

Birds like the black grouse, capercaillie, hazel hen *(Tetrastes bonasia),* and willow grouse are spread throughout the European taiga; but they seek out different habitats. The hazel hen keeps to deciduous trees mixed with spruce; the capercaillie prefers old, mossy depths of spruce and pine; the black grouse likes more open, thinner mixed woods, preferably with bogs nearby; while the willow grouse inhabits various kinds of forest and heath, occurring both farther north than the others and at higher levels in the Urals and Scandinavian mountains.

Several forest birds present extraordinary performances late in the winter and spring. The capercaillie males develop "spring fever" while snow is still deep; individual birds may perform almost anywhere in the forest, but usually all the cock birds from a large area assemble at a traditional place. Just before dusk the male flies to his playground and settles for the night in a spruce or pine. The performance begins with the first hint of dawn: a few introductory rappings, then silence. But the sound is repeated, now more confidently, in an accelerating, two-toned "pell-oep," until it explodes in a clucking gurgle. This is followed by a peculiar hissing noise that gives the impression that he is breathless. But he is still vigorous and the game continues as darkness fades. Gradually the cock bird becomes visible on his branch: a magnificent figure, with outstretched throat feathers, bill pointed skyward, wings downthrust and tail extended to form a fan, welcoming the dawn.

In Scandinavia and Finland the number of capercaillie fluctuates greatly. One hypothesis is that the fertility of the bird is related to the availability of food, especially for the egg-laying hen. Other investigations show that during the first weeks the thermo-control of capercaillie chicks, as of the young of many other birds, is imperfect, and that they need the added warmth of the hen during inclement weather. If the surrounding temperature remains low over too long a period, the chicks cannot find enough food for their bodily needs. Apparently they then either freeze or starve to death.

The goshawk *(Accipiter gentilis)* is probably the taiga's most typical bird of prey, but it is a shy bird and is not often observed. Only near the start of the nesting period, in March, does it reveal its presence in the forest. Then it circles high over the nesting area, tail feathers spread ostentatiously, uttering its loud call. A few wingbeats give it enough momentum to glide a hundred feet or more; and it can develop great speed in its hunting flights through the trees in pursuit of a jay or squirrel. It hurls itself like a projectile through thick brush or dense woods, making such sharp turns that one wing points straight up and the other down. If it meets a human it emits a characteristic whistle and accelerates at an astonishing rate.

Many owls inhabit the great conifer forests. Of Europe's thirteen species, nine are found in the taiga conifer forest region—though only three may be said to belong almost exclusively to the taiga. These are the hawk owl *(Surnia ulula),* Ural owl *(Strix uralensis),* and great gray owl *(S. nebulosa).* The eagle owl *(Bubo bubo),* short-eared owl, Tengmalm's owl *(Aegolius funereus)* and the pygmy owl are fairly common in the taiga although they are also found elsewhere.

THE REPUTATION OF EAGLE OWLS

The eagle owl, largest of all European owls, was formerly distributed over most of Europe. Today its numbers are greatly diminished and are still decreasing in most countries of western and Central Europe. In eastern Europe the population is shrinking, but more slowly. The principal cause of this bird's decline is man's relentless pursuit of it through the centuries; year after year eggs have been destroyed by hunters or taken by collectors, nestlings have been caught or killed and the adults shot or constantly disturbed. The fact that hunters and gamekeepers have always regarded it as very destructive of game partly explains this harsh treatment. Another reason is of course the advance of cultivation. Though it seems able to tolerate human neighbors and changes in the forests where it breeds, it cannot stand disturbance during its

Left: The great crested grebe on its floating nest of reed stems and other aquatic debris. (Ilkka Virkkunen)   Right: The black-headed gull is the most characteristic species in the so-called "bird lakes" of Europe. (Ingmar Holmåsen)

A beaver and its cub inside their hut. This rodent has contributed amazingly to the landscape formations found in many bogs and wooded swamps in the taiga. (Lars Wilsson)

The pygmy shrew, which has a wide range in the conifer forest region, daily consumes at least half of its own weight in food. (U. A. P. Skaren)

breeding season. If frequently disturbed near its nest, it abandons eggs and nestlings.

A Swedish investigation into the feeding habits of the eagle owl shows clearly that small rodents comprise forty-two per cent of its diet and are its main food. First among its food items was the brown rat *(Rattus norvegicus),* then the hooded crow *(Corvus corone)* and the vole-rat *(Arvicola terrestris).* It is surprising that brown rats are caught so often by eagle owls, since these rodents usually appear only around human habitations. In fact in northern Sweden they can as a rule be caught only close to buildings. The brown rat may extend its range during summer, but such movements probably occur only in southern areas. The food of the eagle owl, according to the Swedish figures, consists of fifty-five per cent mammals, thirty-five per cent birds, eleven per cent fish, and one per cent reptiles and amphibians. Insects and crustaceans were not found significant in the Swedish samples.

Though individual birds may specialize in certain prey, in general this owl has a catholic taste in food. In Germany an eagle owl killed a roe deer weighing nearly thirty pounds. At the other end of the scale, 2397 bones of the grass frog were found in pellets from one eagle owl's territory in Switzerland. Generally speaking, however, small rodents are the main food of the eagle owl.

In Sweden, eagle owls generally do not start calling before February or March, although I myself have heard them call in every month of the year. The male's display before mating is seldom seen, but loud calls advertise his sexual activities.

THE GREAT GRAY OWL AND OTHER OWLS

The great gray owl is the taiga's rarest owl. It thrives best in pure conifer forests with huge trees, but is also found occa-

sionally in sparse mixed woods near bogs, as well as in forests of pure spruce or pine. With its garb of dense feathers, enormous head and long tail, it seems just as large as the massive eagle owl. But when "undressed," or when its feather coat is clasped close to its body, it is seen to be much smaller.

One winter night in Lapland I heard time and again from the darkness a series of muffled hoots. Wearing skis, I moved softly over the snow crust toward the sound. As the deep, low-pitched tones came closer and closer, I suspected it might be a great gray owl. It was, and I was able, to my surprise, to approach quite close to it. The great gray owl seems no more shy when "singing" at its nesting site than when hunting in winter.

The Ural owl is a larger, lighter edition of the tawny owl of the more southerly forests. The boggy virgin forest areas of the taiga, with conifer giants providing abundant nesting sites, constitute its preferred habitat. It is primarily a nocturnal bird, but during the season of brief northern summer nights it must hunt by day too. It hunts either from a perch in a dry fir or lone bog pine, watching the ground for passing voles, or it flies about, patrolling clearings, mossy banks and pine swamps.

Tengmalm's owl is distinctly a nocturnal bird which, even during the long, light days of the northern summer, stirs only at midnight. It remains very secluded the year round, but, when spring approaches and the nights get shorter, reveals its whereabouts with a soft, flutelike murmur. This sound may be transcribed as a rapid quaver, "ho-oh-oh-oh-oh-oh," repeated after a pause of about three seconds but differing from the sound of a tawny owl in that it always has the same number of syllables and equal pauses. Hour after hour this sound, probably the most musical owl call in the forest, continues, interrupted only at long intervals by a more hollow, less resonant "poh-poh-poh-poh." This xylophone-like song usually means the female is nearby. It should be added that even before the eggs are laid the male delivers freshly killed mice or voles to the nest, either to prove his claim to it or to please his mate.

Of all the taiga owls, the hawk owl is truly unusual. When first glimpsed in rapid flight during the day, it might be mistaken for a sparrow hawk *(Accipiter nisus)*. This owl is distinguished by its absolute fearlessness of man and its habit of seeking an exposed perch at the top of a tree, often a dead one, preferably at the edge of a clearing in a burned-over forest meadow or in an open forest glade. This kind of area is also the hawk owl's habitat. In hunting, the hawk owl plunges from its treetop observatory to seize a vole, or monotonously patrols over the forest clearings, sometimes hovering like a kestrel. But it can also travel swiftly, and it is in fact considered to be the fastest-flying owl of the taiga. It flies a straight, undulating course like a woodpecker, and can capture birds in flight. No other northern bird can match these birds in dive-bombing attacks on intruders near their nests. They attack from different directions, delivering slashing blows with their talons and uttering burst after burst of shrieks. Even foxes and larger birds of prey have been known to flee before such blistering attacks.

WOODPECKERS AND CROSSBILLS

Since woodpeckers depend on tree cavities for nesting, they are bound to the forest. Of the ten European woodpecker species, four belong chiefly to the conifer forest region, namely the black woodpecker *(Dryocopus martius)*, the three-toed, the lesser and the great spotted woodpecker.

The black woodpecker, Europe's largest, is coal black and has a red crown—a resplendent color combination. During the winter months one sees and hears little of this bird, but its lively drumming starts as early as March, especially at sunrise. It is easy to distinguish its drumming, since each outburst lasts about twice as long as that of other woodpeckers.

Throughout the year the black woodpecker finds most of its food in decayed stumps, chiefly of pines. It feeds on all insects and their larvae and on spiders, but mainly on such species of ants as *Camponotus herculeanus* and *Formica rufa*. In winter it seeks out the former in buried stumps where these insects then lie dormant. Similarly it usually eats *Formica rufa* ants late in winter, when they are still concealed in their ant hills.

In connection with this last habit, this woodpecker has an uncanny ability to locate small ant hills buried as much as three feet in the snow. How does it achieve this? Does it simply recall the location of stumps with ants in them, or is it able to hear the miniscule sounds made by hibernating ants? Doubtless it has, like most woodpeckers, an amazing sense of hearing, which normally helps it locate ants in decayed trunks. But it may also rely to some extent on its remarkable memory, which is probably the case in wintertime.

Among the passerines, many species frequent the conifer forest, especially among seed-eaters. For such birds the conifer cone crop is of great importance. Variations in the crop from year to year may well account for fluctuations in the number of seed-eating finches in these forests. This is true for example of the specialists of the conifer forest, the crossbills. In the taiga there are three species of these: the common

crossbill *(Loxia curvirostra)*, the parrot crossbill *(L. pytyopsittacus)*, and the two-barred crossbill *(L. leucoptera)*. The first of these likes spruce cones, the parrot crossbill prefers pine cones, and the two-barred crossbill takes to the Siberian stone pine.

One factor in the adaptability of crossbills to the conifer cone crop is their early nesting. In midwinter crossbills build their nests, hatch their eggs, and then nourish their naked newborn with a kind of seed porridge. The walls of the nest are well insulated against the cruel cold. This unique habit of winter nesting coincides perfectly with the ripening of spruce and pine cone seeds.

WAXWINGS, JAYS AND TITS

The pine grosbeak *(Pinicola enucleator)* is a large finch that, despite its name, prefers spruce forests. In winter it feeds on the flowers and buds of the spruce as well as cones that have dropped on the snow. Surprisingly, during a winter visit to Lapland, I observed the pine grosbeak feeding on these instead of on the abundant mountain ash berries, which it seems to prefer in the years when, as is its custom, it wanders south.

The redpoll *(Carduelis flammea)* and the siskin *(C. spinus)* also belong to the seed-eating birds of the conifer forest, though the redpoll occurs much farther north than its relatives, and the siskin is found in mixed woods.

The chaffinch, brambling, and bullfinch *(Pyrrhula pyrrhula)* are among the taiga's most common birds. The song of the first two is often heard in the northern conifer forests.

One of the most beautiful birds of the wilderness is the waxwing *(Bombycilla garrulus)*. In the summer it feeds on insects and in autumn and winter on berries, with a marked preference for the red fruit of the mountain ash. The latter is a very important food resource for these birds, which is why they seldom linger on their enforced winter visits to western Europe. Later, one can admire this bird from the Siberian taiga in the parks of European cities. It is distinguished not only for its hues but for its music: the notes issuing from a flock of waxwings sound like the tinkling of a thousand tiny ice fragments at the water's edge.

The great gray shrike, which first we met in sun-drenched Spain, is also found on the edges of the conifer forest along the taiga. This interesting passerine is like a small bird of prey in its habits as well as appearance. Not only does it hunt small rodents and birds, but insects as well. Like its relative, the red-backed shrike, the great gray shrike impales its victims on thorns, apparently to facilitate butchering.

The most common members of the crow family found in the taiga are the raven, the hooded crow, and the Siberian jay. Of these, the Siberian jay is especially identified with the conifer forest. If one ventures into the taiga, sooner or later one becomes familiar with this species. Fearless and curious, it flits among the branches, seeking to discover what the forest larder holds. In the Lapland forest, in winter, when sometimes I have settled on a fallen tree for lunch, these charming birds have hopped around my feet snatching crumbs that have fallen to the ground; or they have perched alongside me on a log, intently watching my movements.

The Siberian jay's discreet brown hue blends remarkably well with the bark of trees and with lichens, but in the conifer gloom its tail flashes like a redstart's. In flight and while fluttering about the spruces, Siberian jays move silently; but they have an impressive repertoire of lusty calls, and it is chiefly through these that we know how common they are.

The Siberian jay feeds on insects and berries. In the winter it gathers whatever leftovers it can, but its principal nourishment is the fodder it has stored during the seasons of plenty. Thus it provides an example of harvesting, a basic necessity for most passerines that remain in northernmost Europe over winter. During the dark period temperatures can be very low, increasing the energy requirements of warm-blooded creatures active in winter. The Siberian jay is thus a hoarder like the jay, the nutcracker, the Siberian tit, and many other tits.

Most tits are forest birds and many are found in the conifer woods, but there are three species in particular in the taiga—the willow tit, Siberian tit, and crested tit. Of this trio, the willow is the most common, but the Siberian tit is best suited to the conifers. In the spring it lives a shy existence in the deep conifer forest. Almost always an encounter with this species is a surprise, since, unlike the willow tit, it does not announce its presence everywhere. One hears a few delicate calls from among lichen-covered spruces, glances up, and there is the Siberian tit.

During winter the Siberian tit travels about the snow-laden woods in small groups of six to eight. Often these groups join forces with great tits and willow tits. These mixed flocks follow the same course through the forest day after day, and, beginning late in February, twice daily. For months on end they visit selected trees methodically, even though, we may assume, they have stored food during the summer months. A comparable phenomenon can be observed in tropical forests, but there the bird processions include species that do not store food.

It is impossible to mention all the species of taiga birds here, but we should note that sparrows belonging to the *Emberiza* family are represented by seven species, and that many warblers such as the willow warbler *(Phylloscopus trochilus)*, chiffchaff and arctic warbler *(P. borealis)*, as well as the redstart, redwing, fieldfare and song thrush, go far to the north.

BOGS AND LAKES

Bogs (or muskegs) and lakes cover a large part of the conifer area of northern Europe. There are fewer lakes east of the White Sea, but bogs and fens occur constantly all the way to the Urals, and beyond that to the Yenisey in Siberia.

Thus the bog is a characteristic element of the northern European landscape. There are many different kinds of peat bogs, but we can distinguish two main types: acid bogs in the proper sense, and marshes or fens. The former consist to a variable extent of fairly dry hummocks, built up chiefly by certain mosses and covered by dwarf birch, heather, and crowberry. The plant life is therefore very meager, due mainly to lack of nutrients, for bogs get most or all of their water from rain and snow.

Peat land that gets most of its moisture from mineral soil water, which is more nutritional and has less acidity, has of course a richer and more varied marsh or fen vegetation. Bog hummocks and areas of marsh can even occur in a complex—

a mixed bog—where the dried "ridges" or "islands" consist of bog moss, and the wetter areas of marsh or even shallow pools, in an arrangement that may often resemble a terraced rice field. Numerous species of sedge *(Carex)* are found in most marshes, together with purple moor-grass *(Molinia caerulea)*, the water horsetail *(Equisetum fluviatile)*, cotton grass *(Eriophorum angustifolium)* and bog bean *(Menyanthes trifoliata)*, in addition to numerous mosses—such as "brown mosses" and *Sphagnum*. All these plants are lacking on the true bogs where the flora is in fact very different.

Bogs and marshes comprise the taiga's most difficult terrain as far as inquisitive humans are concerned. But after braving jungles of willow or vast quagmires and fighting millions of mosquitoes, one may occasionally reap such rewarding sights as a whooper swan *(Cygnus cygnus)* on its nest, or a spotted redshank *(Tringa erythropus)* rocketing into the sky, or come upon a moose.

The bog's tentacles spread for mile after mile among the swamp woodland, pine moors, and the arctic or alpine barrens in the taiga's northern border zone. As dominating as is the silence over the bog in winter, so is the buzzing of the mosquitoes on summer nights. But if one crosses the water-logged bogs in May there are no mosquitoes; by then birds have arrived.

At such a time, moving precariously over the half-frozen tussocks edging the willow thickets along the lakes, streams and ponds, one occasionally sees a wading bird take off. It is a great distance to the haunts of the next one; then suddenly one comes upon several pairs relatively close together. Greenshanks *(Tringa nebularia)* prefer smaller bogs; the spotted redshank places its eggs high and dry on a wooded ridge, though it still feeds in the water. Wood sandpipers are found almost everywhere on the marshlands and are the most common waders of the bogs. The common sandpiper is also widespread, but chooses the shores of lakes and streams.

Among ducks, the teal and the goldeneye *(Bucephala clangula)* are usually the most common. The sedge warbler sings energetically in the willow vegetation along the bog streams, its song mingling with that of the bluethroat. The yellow wagtail is also found here as well as on small patches of bog adjoining the swamp woodland. The reed bunting *(Emberiza schoeniclus)* keeps primarily to the willows screening the brooks and marshes, and the winchat most often inhabits the birch-covered promontories on boggy reaches.

The hen harrier is the north European bogland's outstanding bird of prey: it subsists mainly on small rodents. The bean goose nests in the dwarf-pine bogs. The short-eared owl's leisurely wingbeats are a quite common sight, especially where rodents are abundant. During the nesting period, the crane lives a secret existence on the conifer forest bogs. The taiga's mosaic of forests and bogs also provides a perfect habitat for the crane; now and then its cry reverberates over bog and forest. The small tarns of the bog are usually inhabited by red-throated divers: they fly daily to the larger lakes to fish.

The black grouse is partly a bog bird, too, since it is on

The stoat is an amazingly nimble carnivore. To get a better view or scent, it often rises on its hind legs as shown in this photograph. (Gustav Hansson)

Spotted redshank in Swedish Lapland. It breeds in open areas and on dry ridges in the taiga but feeds in bogs and swamps. (Goran Hansson)

waters, from moorland ponds to forest encircled lakes. Often the latter have rocky shorelines with little vegetation at the water's edge; but some lakes support reeds, sedge, and rushes. Although only a few species of fish have succeeded in colonizing some of the conifer forest waters, others are found throughout most of the taiga. These include the perch, pope *(Acerina cernua)*, pike, several species of whitefish *(Coregonus)*, grayling *(Thymallus thymallus)*, brown trout and burbot *(Lota lota)*.

Only one European bird of prey, the osprey, is wholly dependent on fish for food. It inhabits those parts of the taiga wherever there are lakes, but is of course most abundant in the lake-dotted western region. The osprey usually nests in high pines in a forest or on a bog, often far from a lake. Nonetheless, lakes provide the best opportunities for observing this remarkable fisherman at work. In fishing, the osprey follows a rigid routine. During its flight patrol it abruptly stops and hovers, legs lowered, scouting the water. Then suddenly, wings folded, it plunges to the water, shattering the surface. It often misses its prey but sooner or later it rises with a fish in its talons, shaking the water from its feathers as it gains altitude. The osprey holds its prey head forward, its talons gripping both sides of the fish. As the bird is about to alight in a treetop on the shore or on its nest in the tallest pine on a bog, it frees one claw in order to make a landing. Then it gorges its catch itself or divides it among its young.

Certain breeding ducks of the conifer forest are dependent on holes in trees for nesting sites, not infrequently those hollowed out by the black woodpecker. These include the goldeneye and the smew *(Mergus albellus)*, two typical taiga ducks. A third hole-nester is the goosander *(M. merganser)*. However, since most of the ducks of the conifer forest lakes nest on the ground, they are also found on lakes with bogs around them. The tufted duck *(Aythya fuligula)*, common on many lakes of the Central European plains, is found also on lakes of the taiga, as are the red-breasted merganser *(Mergus serrator)*, shoveler, pintail, widgeon and mallard. Some of these species are also found on the tundra lakes.

THE NORTH URAL MOUNTAINS

Like a wall between Europe and Asia, the Ural Mountains extend from about 2000 miles north of the Arctic Circle to the Kirghiz steppes. Toward the west the slopes of the Urals are gentle, covered with broad belts of vegetation; but to the east they drop sharply down to the Siberian conifer forests and steppes.

The Ural Mountains were formed some 200 to 500 million years ago. They have survived many invasions by the sea; over the ages they were worn down to a plateau but rose again as a new mountain chain, which once again is being demolished by erosion, frost, water and wind. The highest peak, Marodnaya (6183 feet), is in the northern part of the chain. Opinion is divided as to whether the few small glaciers in the Urals are the remains of the land ice or they are of more recent origin. The chain is very rich in minerals, including iron and copper, which means that large parts of it have been exploited and now present an industrial landscape.

The upper limits of the vegetation on the western slopes of the northern and central Urals are very different because of the chain's vast territorial extent from south to north. The

the bog that the males give their mating performance as spring approaches. Before daybreak a bubbling, cooing sound from the bog indicates that the cock birds have assembled and begun to perform: rising and falling, their chorus is of an exceptionally beautiful tone. As day breaks the performance gains volume until, on a quiet morning, it can be heard for up to half a mile. Gradually, round, white objects can be distinguished moving back and forth on the bog: these are discs formed by the cock birds' outstretched undertail feathers. When the sun illuminates the battleground, the blue-black combatants advance in all their splendor, their red "eyebrows" distended like bleeding wounds. But it is usually a bloodless battle. For several seconds the performing cock birds stand like stone figures. Then, suddenly, they all move about again, their legs hidden under their extended wings, so that like mechanical toys they seem to be rolling over the snow or grass on wheels. Occasionally they leap up and attack each other. Like a bizarre formal dance, the same routine is repeated for several hours.

No other European area is as rich in lakes as the western part of the Continent's conifer forest region. Except for the Caspian, here also are the Continent's greatest inland seas: Ladoga (7100 square miles), Onega, Vanern, and Peipus.

Most of the taiga's lakes have scant vegetation and wildlife, nevertheless they represent a broad variety of inland

The Ural Mountains form a natural boundary between the continents of Europe and Asia. Shown above is Lake Chodata-Jugan-Lor in the northern part of the range. (L. F. Kunitzyn: Institute of Geography, Moscow)

northern Urals thus offer much more variety than the Scandinavian mountain chain. In the central parts of the Urals, south of about latitude 60° N, mixed forests of spruce *(Picea abies* and *Abies sibirica)* and mountain birch *(Betula tortuosa)* climb to a height of about 2600 feet. Above that there is a narrowish belt of birch and larch *(Larix sibirica)* leading onto natural meadows with sporadic birch groves. This type of vegetation is displaced at a still higher level by dwarf spruce, which mark the tree limit between 2950 and 3300 feet. Then the heath takes over with alpine flora, including such plants as the snowy buttercup *(Ranunculus nivalis)*, alpine meadow sue *(Thalictrum alpinum)*, and the arctic diapensia *(Diapensia lapponica)*. Here the dotterel is found on the heath among the meadow pipits and wheatears. All these flowers as well as birds are also found in the Scandinavian mountains to the west, beyond the immense taiga.

In the northern Urals, south of the tundra dominated northernmost parts of the chain, the zones of life are quite different. At the foot of the Urals, where the earth is moist, the lowland taiga gives way to a mossy spruce forest, chiefly *Picea abies,* with patches of mountain birch and Siberian stone pine. These forests climb the slopes to an altitude of 1300 to 1650 feet and, as the taiga fauna follows them, we meet a large number of taiga animals in the Ural spruce forests: for example the capercaillie, hazel hen and willow grouse. There are

also a few species that occur chiefly in the Siberian forests east of the Urals. Among these are the red-flanked bluetail *(Tarsiger cyanurus)* and the black-throated thrush *(Turdus ruficollis)*, both remarkable songsters.

The next stage upward is a vertical zone of about one thousand feet containing meadow birch forests with considerable intrusions of spruce, chiefly *Abies sibirica,* and even larch. This zone of mixed woods marks the forest's highest limit. At about 2300 feet it meets the heath, parts of which support dwarf birch while on all the wet parts grow mosses and grass. In some parts of the northern Urals the mountain birch reigns alone, forming a pure birch belt just as in Scandinavia. In these birch woods as well as in the higher spruce forest we meet the black-throated accentor *(Prunella atrogularis)*— its only occurrence in Europe. The arctic warbler *(Phylloscopus borealis)* is also found in this zone, though its main habitat is the conifer forest. Above the bushy, mossy heath, tundra takes over, the plateau being covered with rocks, lichens and mosses. Mountain anemone grows here and the ptarmigan thrives among the stones and boulders.

Despite the fact that the Urals mark the regional limits of many species, this mountain chain is not a true biogeographic barrier between Europe and Asia, since the overwhelming majority of plant and animal species of the Urals are found both west and east of the mountains.

273

The Frozen Tundra

The Treeless Zone of Northernmost Europe

18

The northernmost parts of the European continent, like those of Asia and North America, consist of treeless moorland and tundra. The polar cap is encircled by these arctic tundras, which are all very much alike.

There is some disagreement as to the meaning of the word "tundra." It is commonly applied to those treeless areas that stretch in a broad, uneven ribbon between the pine forests in the south and the Arctic Ocean in the north. The Scandinavian mountains and the Urals above the tree limit are considered to be southern extensions of the tundra. The term is also used in a more limited sense to refer to areas of permafrost; that is, where the earth just under the surface is permanently frozen. By this definition the extent of the tundra in northern Europe would be somewhat less, and the greater part of the Scandinavian mountain chain and the Urals could not be included in it.

The term tundra is derived from the Finnish *tunturi,* which means an open, flat, and treeless landscape. Such vast expanses, with their sparse vegetation and harsh climate, will seem to many to be an example only of nature at its least inviting—little other than a monotonous, almost sterile world. Indeed such country is harsh and rugged, mile after mile consisting merely of creeping lichen and a succession of stones. There are occasional bogs and stretches of open water, but the flatness and desolation are overpowering. The weather helps to create a feeling of primitive nature's hostility to man. Even during the brief summer it is often cold and cloudy during the day, with frost on the ground at night; and in July winds sometimes blow ice-cold under a gray-black sky, and rain and hail cut into one's face.

Most of the rain on the tundra falls between July and September. The overall precipitation in the tundra area is, however, low, and it decreases in proportion to the distance from the sea—that is, as one goes eastward or southward. The annual average precipitation on the European tundra is estimated to be only from eight to fifteen inches, a very small amount. The moisture is, nevertheless, retained by the earth, because there is little evaporation and high humidity, particularly in the coastal areas. Cloudiness is a conspicuous characteristic of these tracts; the tundra is, in fact, the most overcast region of Europe and Asia.

Although it can be said that light flows freely over the tundra during the summer months, the season is too short to permit high-growing vegetation to take root in the thin layer of earth above the permanently frozen subsoil. In winter, strong winds often blow away the thin blanket of snow and leave the vegetation unprotected from the cold. On the other hand, the snow that does remain tends to melt very slowly during the spring and summer months, and this also shortens the period of growth, hindering bushes and scrub from colonizing the soil.

The rise in the mean temperature that has been observed in many parts of Europe in the last century has also been noted in the tundra. The southern limits of the permafrost area are retreating northward with shrubs and trees following close behind. This northward expansion of the forests represents a reoccupation of former domains, for, during the postglacial period, the forests extended much farther north and also higher up the mountains than they do today. In 1837 the permanently frozen tundra reached as far as Mezen, on the White Sea south of the Arctic Circle. In 1933 no permafrost could be found there. Some isolated permafrost areas could be discovered about twenty-five miles to the north, but the tundra itself lay still farther north. During those hundred years the mean temperature in the area had increased by 7° F. (—14° C.).

Although there is little variation in the tundra itself, certain differences are evident from the southern to the northern areas. There are frequent transitional areas between the forests and the tundra, which the Russians call "forest tundra"; these consist of spruce or birch forests—or sometimes a solitary pine tree—which have followed the valleys northward and which, from these corridors, in some instances spread out over parts of the tundra. But on the tundra the trees, tormented by the wind, become dwarfed and are thinly scattered. A similar feature of isolated forest areas and lone trees north of the forest mass can, in a vertical sense, be found in the Scandinavian mountain chain and in the Urals.

It is north of these partly tree-covered areas that the true expanse of tundra spreads out. It is with this area, irrespective of the bogs (which are more common in the southern parts) that we are concerned; part of it is covered with dwarf birch, willows, and Labrador tea *(Ledum palustre);* and part of it is naked and open, with only a thin blanket of lichen.

Although geologically young, these wastes seem in their awesome austerity to represent what we think of as the original European landscape. This terrain is actually the result of planing by the ice of the last glacial period and of the giant rivers which, as they retreated, deposited the sediment of the ages. Plants and animals then invaded the area. Although the tundra seems static, this process is still going on.

PLANTS AND ANIMALS

During the greater part of the year the tundra lies almost deserted, with few animals in sight. Many mammals do remain in the tundra throughout the winter and somehow find

Young male long-tailed duck, a bird of the tundra lakes and other waters in arctic and subarctic regions. It has no less than four different plumages each year. (Ingmar Holmåsen)

sufficient sustenance to keep alive. But none hibernate there in a torpid state, for it is impossible to dig into the frozen soil, and the blanket of snow is in any event too thin to give protection. A number of mammals therefore go south to the conifer forests, and most of the birds move to more hospitable regions.

Among the mammals remaining on the tundra throughout the winter are reindeer, the arctic fox *(Alopex lagopus)*, wolves and wolverines, ermines, mountain hares, voles *(Clethrionomys rufocanus* and *C. rutilus)* and various lemmings *(Lemmus lemmus, L. sibiricus,* and *Dicrostonyx torquatus)*. The smaller rodents fare quite well and do not appear to suffer unduly from the cold in the surprisingly mild temperature under the snow. Of the birds, only the ptarmigan regularly remains on the tundra throughout the winter—it winters farther north than any other bird—though the snowy owl *(Nyctea scandiaca)* sometimes lingers on.

The contrast is of course considerable when, during June and July, the tundra begins to be crowded with migratory birds from Africa, Asia, and Europe. For a few hectic weeks all the birds in this arctic waste land are concerned with only one function—reproduction. Then it is that the region seems to come alive: leaves burst forth on the dwarf birches and willows, those bizarre trees that seem to cling to the ground instead of growing into the air; mountain avens blossom, causing the fields of lichen to be spotted with white. A majority of the birds keeps to the bogs, marshes and small lakes, but many species, such as the ptarmigan, breed even on the sparse, stone-covered tundra heath. The feathers of this ptarmigan, as well as the willow grouse, change from the protective white of winter to the mottled gray of summer, with a spring and fall plumage in between. These variations seem to be due to gradual changes in light and temperature during the year.

Many waders breed on the tundra nearest the coast of the Arctic Ocean. The little stint *(Calidris minuta)* builds its simple nest there among the crowberry bushes or dwarf birches. Even in its breeding place, this little wader is astonishingly unafraid of man. On several occasions a little stint's eggs and some dried leaves have been arranged in the palm of a man's hand, and, within moments, the male bird has settled in the improvised nest, contented by brooding over its eggs.

The little stint migrates over the whole of the European continent; its routes of flight conjoin in the Mediterranean basin and then continue on through Africa to the Cape. The easternmost populations migrate through Asia or along its east coast to the Indian Ocean, where the birds winter in regions stretching between Arabia and Ceylon.

The surroundings of these little stints on the desolate and frost covered tundra could hardly be more different to those

Left above: The wild reindeer has been exterminated almost everywhere in its former European range. It is essentially an animal of the tundra. Most reindeer in Europe today are domesticated and live in a half-wild state. (Torrey Jackson) Left below: A bar-tailed godwit beside some dwarf birches. It is one of the first waders to reach the tundra in spring. (Per Olof Swanberg)   Right: A marshy treeless heath below Mt. Sautso in Swedish Lapland. Many such areas above the timberline in the Scandinavian mountains resemble tundra. (Per Olof Swanberg)

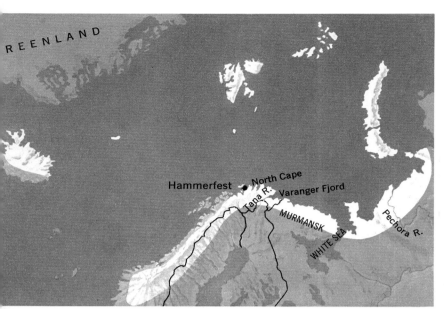

The treeless zone of northern Europe is a tundra in almost everything except permanently frozen soil; it is characterized by open country with low vegetation, large bogs, and many frost phenomena.

A SIXTEEN-THOUSAND-MILE MIGRATION

The common gull will often patrol over the tundra but in the main it keeps to lakes and pools. On such waters one also finds herring gulls and arctic terns. The latter make some of the longest flights on record, flying annually from their arctic breeding places to South Africa and the Antarctic and back again. One arctic tern, marked on the tundra near the Arctic Ocean in July, 1955, was found in May, 1956, on the coast of West Australia. Another, marked in Denmark in May, 1958, was found early the following February in the Antarctic pack-ice near Wilkes Land, roughly eighteen hundred miles south of Australia's westernmost coast and eight thousand miles from Denmark.

The true vagabond of the tundra is the snowy owl. It seems to prefer North America to Europe and Asia, and its spasmodic appearance in Europe always coincides with an abundance of rodents on the tundra. It apparently travels widely in its search for food and it seems to breed first in one part of the world and then in another. The short-eared owl is an occasional visitor to the tundra, common in years when there is a plentiful supply of voles and lemmings; otherwise it prefers the bogs in forests.

Among the smaller birds to be noted on the tundra are the shore lark, found on the drier ridges; the sand martin *(Riparia riparia),* which flies along rivers and digs its nest in banks; the meadow pipit, which ventures everywhere in the region; arctic redpolls *(Carduelis hornemanni),* which nest among the crawling dwarf birch trees; and, among the stones, nests the snow bunting *(Plectrophenax nivalis),* the males decorative in black and white, the females rather more discreetly colored. This bunting, which in Scandinavia is usually found on the highest mountains, is a lowland bird on the tundra; but then the climate and environment are much the same in both areas.

The king eider *(Somateria spectabilis)* nests in or around small pools on the almost naked tundra. The female broods alone, but the colorful male remains nearby during at least a part of the brooding period. The long-tailed duck *(Clangula hyemalis)* and the black-throated diver *(Gavia arctica)* also breed on ground covered with sparse vegetation. In the spring, immediately after the arrival of the loons at the lakes, their mating calls are heard, rising and falling in contrastingly pitched notes—a haunting and primitive serenade. During the courting ritual the male races after the female, calling her as he swims with head stretched forward on the water. Sometimes he seems to be literally running on the water toward her, whereupon, as though taunting him, she will dive and disappear. When she reappears, the hunt resumes. When at long last the female becomes more cooperative, the male approaches her, swimming like a snake, with only his head and

in equatorial Africa, where they live for most of the year. There they live in a world generously—sometimes overgenerously—warmed by the sun and teeming with life.

The gray plover is one of the outstanding birds of the tundra. During the spring it indulges in aerial acrobatics. Playfully it darts here and there, at moments seemingly about to dash itself against the ground. Or it soars with wings stretched upward, now and then making leisurely wing-strokes, and then surprisingly flicks itself over into a series of somersaults.

The bar-tailed godwit *(Limosa lapponica)* prefers drier ground, and generally keeps to the heaths clad in dwarf birch. One of the most beautiful birds of the tundra, it is also among the first of the migratory species to arrive there in the spring. It breeds on high, snow-free ridges and hills.

The ringed plover is generally at home on the tundra, where it appears throughout Eurasia. This astonishes West Europeans, who are accustomed to seeing this little wader on the shores of the North and Baltic seas. It seeks its nourishment partly on the harsh tundra heath, and partly on the shores of the lakes; its display song, a repetitive call, is an integral part of the environment.

Several gulls have adapted themselves to the tundra, where they may be found not only on the lakes but also out on the heaths. This is particularly true of the long-tailed skua *(Stercorarius longicaudus),* which on the Russian tundras is found with two other species, the near-relative arctic and pomarine skuas *(S. parasiticus* and *S. pomarinus).* Elsewhere in Europe, the arctic skua is a coastal bird. During years when lemmings are plentiful the skuas base their diet on these rodents. During such years pairs of the pomarine skua will nest close to each other on the tundra, but in lean years, wherever there is a scarcity of food, they do not breed at all. This is also the case with the long-tailed skua, though both species return each spring to the breeding grounds. Besides living on rodents, these birds eat crowberries as well as a variety of insects.

Right above: Spring arrives in early July on the arctic heaths in the Padjelanta and Sarek National Parks in northern Swedish Lapland. Willow bushes, brownish bogs, snow fields, ice-covered lakes and delta river arms form a black-and-white pattern. (Kai Curry-Lindahl)   Right below: When reindeer are running they produce a clicking sound that comes from a tendon pressing over a small bone in the hind feet. (Wiederøe's Flyveselskap A/S, Oslo)

278

A bog at midnight in July in northernmost Swedish Lapland. In the background the dark-brown earth ridges, created by frost, are called "palsar." (Kai Curry-Lindahl)

of warmth, it may grow no more than 1 to 3 mm, and, even in the conifer forest, to scarcely more than 6 mm. Where lichen has been burned, it takes up to fifty years to recover the area. It is easy to understand its importance to the reindeer's survival. The delicate balance between reindeer and lichen was formerly controlled—unwittingly, of course—by wolves which, preying on the reindeer, prevented their multiplying to the point where they would have exhausted the lichen supply. The food chain—lichen, reindeer, wolves—is important for the tundra's ecology. Nowadays, the decrease in the number of wolves, for which man is responsible, and the subsequent increase of reindeer have resulted in many areas being overgrazed.

Lemmings are periodically the tundra's most common rodents. Having discussed the species found in Scandinavia and on the Kola Peninsula, it will suffice to note that on the Old World tundras east of the White Sea we find the Siberian lemming *(Lemmus sibiricus),* a species resembling the Norwegian lemming, and the arctic lemming *(Dicrostonyx torquatus).* The latter is the only lemming that turns white in winter.

Another mammal that frequents the tundra in summer is the wolverine. During the winter, the majority of the wolverines of the Russian wastes wander down into the conifer forests. In fact, they appear originally to have been forest animals that were driven to the tundra by man.

BOGS

The Dvina and the Petjora are the two largest rivers of the European tundras. They drain vast areas broken by many lakes and bogs. The basin of the Dvina is roughly 140,000 square miles, and that of the Petjora roughly 124,000 square miles. These rivers are frozen for about five months of the year. When the ice breaks up in the spring and the snow melts, the lowland around the rivers, lakes, and bogs, is flooded.

It is at this time that the migratory birds arrive. They change desolate tundra into a panorama of color. During these few weeks life literally seethes in and around the bogs. Ruffs in their carnival colors joust on the frozen peat mounds; red-necked phalaropes *(Phalaropus lobatus)* swim in almost every pool, and all day long sing the tuneful wood sandpipers. High up the little jack snipes *(Lymnocryptes minimus)* utter strange sounds like the hoofbeats of galloping horses; the Temminck's stint *(Calidris temminckii)* flutters around above bog and heath; snipes call from the marshes or from high in the air, and in the background can be heard the golden plover's mournful cry. As pairs of dunlins *(Calidris alpina)* fly past humming, common sandpipers patrol along the rivers, while from the willows, with their throngs of bluethroats, comes the tundra's most beautiful birdsong. Nearby are reed buntings; and where sedge meadows open out among the willow bushes and dwarf birches, the lapland bunting's melancholy call accompanies the willow warbler's soft melody. There too, over the willow bushes, float the mellifluous tones of the red-throated pipit *(Anthus cervinus)* which sings more harmoniously than its European relatives.

In the spring the bog is crisscrossed by open channels and dotted with lakes, sedge-encircled pools and half-flooded beds of willow bushes. In the middle of this labyrinthine network

part of his neck visible. When quite near her, his neck stiffens, his bill points straight up, and for a moment he seems to be swimming in a trance.

The rough-legged buzzard is the most common bird of prey on the tundra. It breeds on the ground or on a boulder. Surprisingly the white-tailed eagle, which breeds for the most part along sea coasts or in the taiga, is also a bird of the tundra. The gyrfalcon *(Falco rusticolus),* the most arctic of all the birds of prey, is seen on the tundra even more often than the white-tailed eagle; it generally hunts the ptarmigan, its favorite food.

The reindeer, the largest animal of the tundra, has shown a remarkable capacity to adjust to the harsh environment. The wild reindeer is almost extinct in Europe; a small population persists in Norway, but there are none at all in Sweden, or Finland, where they were last seen before World War I. They are also very scarce on the Kola peninsula and the other Russian tundras. Everywhere on the European tundra the wild reindeer has been supplanted by the tame reindeer, its descendant.

The reindeer's main food is the tundra's most common lichen—aptly called reindeer lichen *(Cladonia rangiferina).* This plant grows very slowly: during the tundra's brief season

Reindeer in Finnmark, northernmost Norway. Semidomestic reindeer migrate into the mountains in spring and down into the valleys and forests in autumn. (Rougeron: IKO)

stand the *palsar,* dark-brown peat hillocks pushed up by the frost. Throughout, the water-filled hollows and the clusters of sedge and willow are ideal refuges for geese and ducks such as pintails, widgeon, teal, scaups, common and velvet scoters and red-breasted mergansers.

Lesser white-fronted geese graze in the sparse vegetation around the willows, moving dexterously about under bushes. When they lay their eggs under willow bushes, the tundra is still partly snow-covered. After the youngsters are hatched, and the young of the previous year have begun to molt, the birds hide themselves most effectively and it is no longer easy to follow their activities.

The lesser white-fronted geese keep to the southern part of the tundra, where the willow bushes dominate, while their relative, the white-fronted goose, breeds in the northernmost bogs or on islands in rivers and lakes. The tundra bean goose *(Anser fabalis rossicus),* a somewhat smaller edition of the bean goose that breeds in the taiga, is also found here. The cackling cries of the geese as they fly to and fro between their grazing places and the lakes are a familiar characteristic of the bogs. The trumpet-like sounds of whooper swans

are also heard, sometimes carrying across amazing distances. These swans breed mostly around the Petjora and Dvina rivers and on the Kola peninsula; the climate of much of the tundra is unsuitable for them, since the young are not fledged before the ice freezes over. The greater part of the whooper swan population is therefore found in the bogs of the taiga. Bewick's swan *(Cygnus columbianus),* a smaller relative of the whooper, breeds in shallow tundra pools that contain a fertile vegetation.

The spring sojourn of the birds on the tundra is very brief: birdsong and the chorus of calls soon dies out. The majority of waders leave their breeding places in the bogs and on the heaths just as soon as they have fulfilled their tasks of egg-laying and caring for their young. The geese and ducks remain, but hide for the short period when they are molting and cannot fly. Though they stay on for a time, the small songbirds fall silent. Then, when the brief summer is over, the birds begin to make their way south or along the coast of the Arctic Ocean toward the west. Soon the hardy ptarmigan—the only creature that will brave the winter storms and the bitter cold—alone remains.

Polar Bears and Arctic Seas

North Atlantic and Arctic Islands

19

Part of Europe consists of islands far out in the Atlantic and Arctic oceans. Together they comprise an area of about 83,000 square miles, far greater, for instance, than the area of Great Britain. The Faeroe Islands (540 square miles) and Iceland (40,500 square miles) are favored by the Atlantic climate, although the latter is within the Arctic zone and in the neighborhood of the mighty ice fields of Greenland. The other islands—Jan Mayen (147 square miles), Bear Island (69 square miles), Spitsbergen (23,700 square miles), Kolguev (1545 square miles), Vaigach (1430 square miles), Novaya Zemlya (38,600 square miles) and Franz Josef Land (about 7700 square miles)—are in the Arctic Ocean.

The most unfavorable conditions of life are in the Arctic regions, yet these regions provide living space for very many forms of life, both vegetable and animal. One cannot help but wonder how they survive the long, dark, and bitterly cold winter, and how they have time to multiply during the short, cold summer, when the temperature rises only a few degrees above freezing. Even during the warmest months the ground is frozen several inches beneath the surface, just as on the mainland tundra.

Arctic species of plants and animals have solved the problem of life in various ways. The plants are dwarfed and creep along the surface of the ground. Often they find shelter from the wind behind small stones—which is all they require to survive. In the same way, many of the waders inhabiting the naked tundra build their nests in the lee of stones. In this stark environment, exposed to Arctic winds and chilled by the eternal frost, they sit patiently on their eggs, day and night. It is something of a miracle that the tiny chicks, when they leave the eggs, survive at all. The parent birds warm them under their feathers and protect them from icy winds and snowstorms, yet the young must learn to fend for themselves from the very beginning, dashing to and fro among stones and the trickles of water from melting snow. As soon as they can feed themselves, the parent birds leave them.

Birds and mammals living in Arctic regions have become adapted in various ways to the climate. The structure of the fur and plumage of northern species provides better insulation than that of southern species, and a layer of fat built up in summer helps to keep the body temperature constant. Wintering in the Arctic, such birds as ptarmigans and snowy owls have feathers on their legs and feet. The pads of hares, polar bears *(Thalarctos maritimus)* and foxes are covered with fur. Many of the animals turn white in winter—for example, the willow grouse, the arctic fox, the mountain hare, the ermine and the collared lemming. On the other hand, there are several species, such as the musk ox, the reindeer, the wolverine, the Norwegian lemming, and the raven, that do not change into white coats. A third group is white all the year round: for example, the polar bear and snowy owl, and outside Europe the Greenland falcon and the arctic hare *(Lepus arcticus)*. Most of these have been characterized as genuine Arctic species on account of their distribution.

This white coloration of birds and animals has not only a protective value, since the surroundings are white, but also physiological significance. It is supposed that heat radiation is less from warm-blooded animals with white than with dark fur or plumage. This must be especially important for large animals that cannot find shelter under the snow. Nevertheless, most of the large species do not turn white in winter.

Why is it that all warm-blooded Arctic animals do not turn white in winter? This question seems particularly challenging when one learns that, of the two lemmings *(Dicrostonyx* and *Lemmus)* living together on the tundra, only one turns white. The answer may be that these two species represent different degrees of adaptation. Where the environment favors arctic terrestrial animals and birds that are white, evolution tends to provide such a dress. But this process affects various species differently. Apparently the musk ox, for example, does not need the protection of white fur in winter, either to avoid loss of heat or as protection against beasts of prey. And it has thrived in arctic regions for a very long time. It may be that this particular animal is sufficiently protected in another way. The same may be true of the reindeer. Nor do other species such as the arctic fox, the ermine and the mountain hare change color in all parts of their distribution ranges. The arctic fox, the most predominantly arctic species of the three, occurs in two quite separate phases of color. The one that turns white in winter is generally found in the northern parts of its distribution range, but in Iceland, where winters bring little snow, most arctic foxes retain their dark fur.

THE FAEROE ISLANDS

Between Iceland, the British Isles and Scandinavia lies a group of thirty or so islands, the Faeroe Islands, only seventeen of which are inhabited. These islands are the remains of a Tertiary Age volcanic plateau which formed a submarine ridge between Scotland, Iceland, and Greenland. The Faeroes are built up mainly of basalt, usually in horizontal strata alternating here and there with beds of tuff. Tuff erodes rapidly, while basalt is very hard. This has given rise to terraced slopes, providing evidence of the volcanic origin of the islands. Each strata of basalt represents a volcanic eruption, and the bricklike tuff is consolidated volcanic ash, burnt

Terraced slopes of basalt with beds of tuff characterize many of the steep coasts of the Faeroe Islands. (Sixten Jonsson)

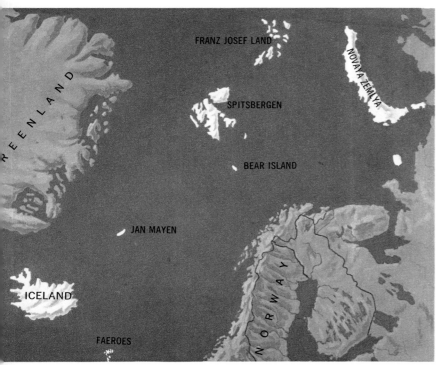

Europe's largest islands in the Atlantic and Arctic oceans vary in climate according to their latitude. The Faeroes and Iceland are much influenced by the Gulf Stream, but to the north the effect of this warm-water current is reduced by polar ice and cold air masses. Thus Jan Mayen, Bear Island, Spitsbergen, Kolguev, Vaigach, Novaya Zemlya and Franz Josef Land are purely arctic. Although often bare or sparse in the interior, the coasts of these islands abound in life.

and pressed hard by beds of lava. The basalt varies in thickness from thirty-five to one hundred feet, while the tuff beds are usually no more than about three feet thick.

There is not much left of the original land of the Faeroes, which once probably formed one continuous stretch of land. In the course of millions of years, erosion by the sea has transformed a large volcanic island into an archipelago; and the work of disintegration is still going on.

When storms rage, the waves of the Atlantic break on the cliffs of the Faeroes with awful violence. No berms or gently sloping beaches exist to diminish the impact; the great waves roll straight up to the steep cliffs. So great is their force that boulders weighing fifteen tons and lying more than ninety feet above high water may be moved. Land ice and weather are other sources of erosion in the Faeroes, which were covered by an isolated sheet of ice during the great glaciations. U-shaped valleys and thin layers of boulder clay are evidence of this.

Grass frequently covers the slopes and plateaus of these treeless islands, but land exposed to the wind is naked. Marine birds dominate the animal life of the islands; cliff ledges, plateaus and grassy slopes are inhabited by kittiwakes, guillemots, gannets, fulmars, puffins and many others typical of the islands of the Atlantic.

Three mammals inhabit the islands: the brown rat *(Rattus norvegicus)*, the house mouse *(Mus musculus)*, and the mountain hare. The latter is not indigenous, but has been introduced by man—as were probably the others. The most re-

markable of the marine mammals visiting the Faeroes is the pilot whale *(Globicephala melaena)*. Growing to a length of thirty feet, it usually appears in schools of about twenty animals, though sometimes these consist of hundreds, and even more than a thousand animals each. An old male leads each school on regular seasonal migrations to various areas. In summer and early autumn, when the whales visit the waters close to the Faeroes, the islanders organize hunting parties to drive them into shallow water and there slaughter them ruthlessly.

ICELAND: ISLAND OF VOLCANOES AND GLACIERS

Iceland is a land of contrasts. The second largest island in Europe, it reaches to the very edge of the Arctic Circle. Although its nearest neighbor is icy Greenland, it has mild winters climate. It is an island of fire and ice: active volcanoes and gigantic glaciers are found everywhere. Although glaciers cover 11.5 per cent of the island's surface, volcanic activity is greater there than in any other territory of comparable size. About one-third of the world's lava formed since the sixteenth century has been produced in Iceland.

Iceland is the most westerly country of Europe, and geologically the youngest. Its oldest formations are only about sixty million years old, and large areas were formed much later, during the past million years or so. It is still developing, and new regions are being created just as were parts of Europe a thousand million years ago. Even today one can see how land is born and consolidated, and how it disintegrates and perhaps disappears under the sea. As such, Iceland is an extremely valuable illustration of geological processes.

As has been said, great areas of the island have been created during the past few million years. Beds of lava less than ten thousand years old cover about ten per cent of the country and, although volcanic activity is declining, during the past twelve thousand years more than 150 volcanoes have erupted. The land was colonized during the ninth century, and since that time nearly thirty volcanoes have proved to be active: on an average there have been volcanic eruptions every fifth year. It has been calculated that if the Icelandic volcanoes continue producing lava at the same rate as at present, they will, in less than a million years, produce an amount of lava equal in volume to Icelandic territory above sea level today.

When Hekla, the most famous volcano in Iceland, erupted in 1947 after being passive for over a hundred years, a cloud of ash and steam rose to a height of 100,000 feet in twenty minutes. On November 14, 1963, the Atlantic began to "boil" off the south coast of Iceland and a pillar of black smoke rose from the water. Explosions then followed each other in rapid succession, and fishermen in the vicinity described tall pillars of fire above the waves. A volcanic eruption was taking place at the bottom of the sea: within a day an island began to rise from the sea in the same way as millions of years ago. The island continued to grow, fed by the endless stream of lava pouring from the crater day after day. Great clouds of steam rose as the molten lava was quenched by the water. After a fortnight the island was about half a mile long and more than three hundred feet high. Above the water this lava island had taken the form of a

The Skaftafell at Vatnajökull in Iceland is a kind of living sample of the ice age. Luxuriant subarctic forests with many plants and animals are surrounded on three sides by permanent ice, the border of which can be seen on the left. (Jens Böcher)

horseshoe-shaped crater. The water in this enormous cauldron was boiling, while hot ash and bombs were being thrown up continuously.

Even when Iceland's land volcanoes are active, they cause movements of water. The volcano of Vatnajökull, 6600 feet high, is also a mighty glacier, the largest in the world outside Greenland and Arctic and Antarctic regions. It covers an area of 3243 square miles, is about 3500 feet thick, and encompasses a large number of craters. When eruptions occur, some of the ice melts and the water dashes down into the lowland plains, at times with such force that everything in its way is carried along to the sea.

In addition to the active volcanoes, there are many other signs of volcanic activity on the island. For example, about seven hundred hot springs, many of which are boiling geysers, are active regularly.

In spite of all its fiery mountains, Iceland has also passed through periods of glaciation, although the volcanoes erupted then, as today, under the ice. Not all of the island was under ice, however, and the greater part of the present flora may have survived on refuges free from ice. The island now has about six hundred species of plants, most of them montane species, and many of them introduced by man. This is a relatively small number. The isolated situation of the island has not helped the colonization of plants; repeated glaciations have, moreover, made immigration impossible for prolonged periods.

Much of the soil of Iceland consists of volcanic ash spread by the wind. Since such mineral soil is not very favorable in such a climate as Iceland's, it takes a long time for plants to colonize a field of lava. This process is more rapid on organic soils, but most of Iceland is still covered with only a thin layer of vegetation or just naked soil.

A thousand years ago forests of birch *(Betula pubescens)* were a feature of Iceland's landscape, but in the period of human occupation man and his domestic animals have destroyed most of them. This same species of birch grows as a dwarf tree in Iceland, and spreads widely, particularly in the mountain regions of the northeast, as a shrub. The regular dwarf birch *(Betula nana)* is also found there.

Only one species of land mammal lived in Iceland before man arrived, and that was the arctic fox. Three small rodents appeared at the time of man's arrival: the house mouse and brown rat—as they also did on the Faeroes—and the long-tailed field mouse. The reindeer was introduced from Norway during the eighteenth century, and a wild population of this animal has established itself in the mountains north of Vatnajökull. The mink *(Mustela vison)* escaped from captivity in 1930, quickly adapted itself to life in the wild, and increased rapidly in number. Some whales and seals are found around the island, most of them visitors from the pack-ice along the coast of Greenland and around Jan Mayen. The only seals breeding on Iceland are the gray seal and the common seal.

But the bird life is rich. Seventy-six species breed in Iceland, and many others are seen regularly during migration and while wintering on the island. The ptarmigan is a characteristic bird of Iceland. Its distribution extends all over the island, although it is far from common everywhere. Its population fluctuates in ten-year cycles, which is curious, for in Scandinavia the variations in population seem to have a different rhythm.

In addition to many marine birds breeding along the coasts, the island shelters a large number of ducks—no fewer than sixteen breeding species. Among these are many not found elsewhere in Europe. One of these is the Barrow's goldeneye *(Bucephala islandica)*. Since it builds in holes in trees, one

Volcanic lava desert on Iceland. Beds of lava less than 10,000 years old cover about ten per cent of the island. (E. Van Moerkerken)

wonders how it can find nesting places in Iceland, so few are the trees. The bird has solved this problem nesting in outbuildings constructed of blocks of lava, or in fissures in basalt cliffs. The harlequin *(Histrionicus histrionicus)* is another duck whose only European occurrence is on Iceland. It lives along streams and swift brooks, a habitat to which few ducks have become adapted. The main distribution of these two species of duck is in North America, though the harlequin is also found in northeastern Asia.

Graylag and pink-footed geese both breed in Iceland. The latter (which is probably a subspecies of the bean goose) is found only in Iceland, Greenland and Spitsbergen. Most of the Icelandic pink-footed geese inhabit the mountains of the interior. The largest colony, consisting of about two thousand pairs, breed in Thjórsárver at the heart of the island. Surrounded by barren fields of lava and sand, this is a fantastic region, a vast oasis of sedge meadows and marshes around the upper part of the Thjórsá River. Thjórsárver is at the foot of one of Iceland's largest glacier volcanoes, Hofsjökull, from which meltwater runs through the oasis down to the river. On the far bank of the river is naked lava, with rare patches of yellowish-green sedge or white cotton grass growing in depressions. About twenty miles beyond the fields of lava and sand is the mighty snow-clad peak of Vatnajökull.

This oasis is an anomaly in the wilderness of barren ground, snow and ice. Many signs of frost action can be seen. Rings of stones and polygons are common there. Low willows *(Salix glauca* and *S. lanata)* grow around brooks and tarns

and, on the undulating heaths, dominated mostly by crowberry *(Empetrum nigrum),* surprisingly large numbers of mountain plants spring up. It is the willow, however, and the brilliant green of dwarf willow *(Salix herbacea),* that give the Thjórsárver oasis its color in summer.

Thirty-one species of birds have been observed in Thjórsárver, of which at least sixteen breed there. The pink-footed goose and the dunlin are the most common species there. When the goslings are hatched in late spring, up to twenty thousand geese may be seen grazing on the meadows—almost half of the world's population of pink-footed geese. The whooper swan breeds in the oasis, too; the most common duck there is the long-tailed duck.

Myvatn in northeastern Iceland is a shallow lake with numerous islands and probably one of the finest bird lakes in northwestern Europe. Approximately 140,000 breeding ducks congregate there. They represent at least fourteen species, among which are such southern species as the gadwall and the shoveler alongside the northern, common scoter. Horned grebes are also found there.

Perhaps the most beautiful and interesting scenery in Iceland is at Skaftafell on the southern slope of Vatnajökull, going down to the ocean. The Skaftafell region is a kind of oasis that provides some clues to what ice-free refuges were like when most of northern Europe was covered with ice. A luxuriant birch wood grows there, close to the largest glacier in Europe; the contrast between the rich vegetation of birches, mountain ashes and shrubs, the many birds and insects, and

Iceland is very rich in hot springs and geysers (such as these at Namaskard), another sign of the volcanic nature of the island. (Helga Fietz: Bavaria Verlag)

the vast expanses of ice on three sides of the woods seems unbelievable and unreal.

Below the wooded slope of Skaftafell a wide sandy plain stretches around the Skeidará River, with a quite different fauna. The arctic fox can be seen there, sometimes being mobbed by great black-backed gulls, arctic skuas and great skuas.

JAN MAYEN

Lying all by itself in the ocean, on latitude 71° N, between Greenland and Scandinavia, is Jan Mayen, 7170 feet above sea level, made up entirely of volcanic rocks. Steam issuing from fissures in the lava and frequent earthquakes demonstrate that Jan Mayen is still alive though the largest volcano, now a mountain of snow and ice, is thought to be extinct. Its crater is full of snow, and several glaciers creep slowly down its slopes to the sea.

Mosses and lichens have colonized parts of the lava and fifty or so flowering plants have reached the island. The arctic fox is the only mammal on the island, which means that it must live on birds, carrion washed ashore, and plants. The bearded seal *(Erignathus barbatus)* and the hooded seal *(Cystophora cristata)* live in the surrounding waters and breed on pack ice. Among the birds on the storm-swept cliffs is the Brünnich's guillemot *(Uria lomvia)*. This species also breeds around Iceland; Jan Mayen and Iceland are its most southerly and westerly habitats in Europe. The little auk

(Plautus alle), the smallest auk in Europe, breeds on Grimsey off the north coast of Iceland and on Jan Mayen; it gathers in large colonies among the boulders on the mountains. Black guillemots and puffins, glaucous gulls *(Larus hyperboreus)* and kittiwakes are other marine birds breeding on Jan Mayen. White wagtails and wheatears are often seen, and snow buntings find good building sites among the blocks of lava.

BEAR ISLAND (BJÖRNÖYA)

Bear Island, or Björnöya, is about halfway between Norway and Spitsbergen, on latitude 74° N, and is nearly always wrapped in mist. In spite of its northerly location, it has a quite mild climate. Thanks to the Gulf Stream, the mean annual temperature there is 24.26° F (-4.3° C). The summer is cold, however, and the mean temperature in July is only 39.5° F (4.2° C).

Steep cliffs with hundreds of birds nesting on them fringe the south coast of Bear Island, where several mountains (the highest is 1758 feet) are concentrated. The island consists of reddish-brown limestone and sandstone, which are being broken down continuously by sea, weather and wind. Wind-eroded cliffs are common on the island. The same phenomenon can thus be seen on a lonely Arctic isle as on the mountains of Greece or Spain, although the cliffs of the Mediterranean region are far older. Bear Island was of course covered with ice during the glaciations, but now it has no glaciers.

287

The northern half of the island is a desolate, Arctic desert of stone, 100 to 135 feet above sea level. It is an undulating plain, naked almost everywhere. At least seven hundred lakes lend variety to the scene, however; and in some of these swim char, along with long-tailed ducks, common scoters and great northern divers *(Gavia immer)*. The most northerly occurrence of the golden plover in the world is on Bear Island, but the great Arctic plateau is more suited to purple sandpipers *(Calidris maritima)* and ringed plovers.

POLAR BEARS AROUND SPITSBERGEN

North Spitsbergen is nearer to the North Pole than to Norway. It is within the maximum boundary of the pack ice, but the ice has changed considerably during the past hundred years. For some decades the waters around Spitsbergen have been open in summer, although many icebergs appear there. In probably no other region has the mean temperature risen so much in so short a time. The most marked change has been in the January temperature. During the years 1912—1916 the mean temperature was -0.4° F (-18° C), but during 1936—1940 it was only 19.6° F (-6.9° Celsius), and during 1947—1950 12.92° F (-10.6° C). These variations in temperature seem to be typical of Spitsbergen, for during the geological history of this group of islands, warm periods with rich vegetation have alternated with glaciations. Although the greater part of Spitsbergen is still covered with ice, the glaciers are melting rapidly.

The prehistory of Spitsbergen seems to have been dramatic, for the islands have formations and rocks representing all geological periods from the Archaean to the Tertiary. Violent foldings have rearranged the original horizontal strata, which now form elongated layers running from south to north. On the north coast the sea is eating its way into the easily eroded sandstone, and the effects of frost erosion can be seen everywhere on the mountains.

It is really astonishing that in spite of their Arctic situation

between latitudes 76° and 81° N, these islands should have such a rich wildlife. Millions of birds live in the coastal cliffs and when they all fly out together, it looks as if a huge segment of the mountain has broken off and shattered into myriads of fragments. It is not only the abundance of good nesting sites on the cliffs that attracts birds to Spitsbergen, but also the fact that in summer the Arctic Ocean teems with food. Besides gulls, terns and auks, whales take advantage of the bountiful food supply—although hunters are rapidly killing off the latter.

The animal life of Spitsbergen is concentrated on the coasts. In addition to the huge colonies of little auks, puffins, Brünnich's guillemots, fulmars and kittiwakes, there are some purely Arctic species that are seldom seen farther south in Europe. One such rare species, the ivory gull *(Pagophila eburnea)*, lives on the pack ice and on glaciers which, on the east coast of Spitsbergen, go right down to the sea. It is also found on Novaya Zemlya and on Franz Josef Land in Europe. Another rare species, the Sabine's gull *(Xema sabini)*, is found in Europe only on East Land in Spitsbergen and on Franz Josef Land.

The mammals of the polar regions also visit the coasts of Spitsbergen. The polar bear is found there regularly, even in summer. The polar bear often wanders over the ice or is carried more or less regularly by the drift ice in a clockwise direction round the Arctic Ocean north of the large islands. Spitsbergen is thus in the periphery of these migrations.

Some polar bears are active all the year round in spite of the six months of winter darkness, while others winter in snow caves from November to April. This difference in behavior is probably related to the supply of food. Pregnant females always dig caves; there the young are born and spend the first months of life. They leave the cave in April. The mother and her young remain together for two or three years.

The polar bear is an expert swimmer and diver, but cannot stay underwater for more than two minutes at a time. Thus it is not so well adapted to water as the seal, which is the bear's main food. Since a polar bear has little chance of outwitting seals in the water, it catches the seals on the ice or when they thrust their heads through their narrow breathing holes.

A polar bear stands patiently beside a breathing hole: when the seal comes up the hole, which may be several yards long, it usually moves rapidly and is often unable to retreat before the bear deals it a death blow. The bear then drags his prey out onto the ice with such violence that the seal's ribs and pelvis are often crushed in the narrow opening. The polar bear is omnivorous, eating practically every variety of organic life found in Arctic regions: whales, foxes, birds, eggs, fish, berries, plants and leaves.

The walrus *(Odobaenus rosmarus)* has beeen almost exterminated around Spitsbergen. It may still be found at Novaya Zemlya, but is otherwise rare in Europe. The ringed seal is the most common seal around Spitsbergen, and sometimes

Left: In winter, domestic reindeer generally migrate from the mountains or are driven down to the conifer forests by the Lapps.   Right: Ivory gull on drift ice at Spitsbergen. A purely arctic bird, it occurs in Europe only on the partly glaciated islands around the North Pole. (Both by Sven Gillsater: Tio)

harp seals *(Phoca groenlandica)* are also seen on the surrounding ice.

Compared with the seething life of the bird colonies on the coasts, the tundra and glaciers of the interior of Spitsbergen seem very desolate. Many species of birds do, however, inhabit the islands and, as on most Arctic heaths, bird life is most abundant around lakes. From the tarns on the tundra the cry of the red-throated diver can be heard. Its nest is usually built on a tussock in the water or close to the shore, so that in case of danger it can immediately take to the water. The king eider frequents all the small lakes on the tundra, and there the eider also breeds. The latter species has several other breeding sites along the coasts.

No fewer than three species of geese breed at Spitsbergen: the barnacle goose, the brant goose and the pink-footed goose. The barnacle goose breeds on mountain slopes, while the brant goose nests on the tundra or in the deltas.

Rare waders that occur in Europe only on the Spitsbergen tundra are the knot and the sanderling. The gray phalarope *(Phalaropus fulicarius)*, a high Arctic wader, is found on the tundra near the coast or by pools of fresh water in the interior. In Europe it breeds only on Bear Island, Spitsbergen and Novaya Zemlya.

All the birds of Spitsbergen except the ptarmigan and a few snow buntings leave the islands in winter. Then, only three other terrestrial vertebrates are found there: the arctic fox, the musk ox, and the reindeer. It is surprising that such large herbivores as the musk ox and the reindeer are able to live on the extremely sparse vegetation of Spitsbergen, particularly when it is borne in mind that the winter lasts for almost nine months. The wild reindeer of Spitsbergen are small, much smaller than those of the mainland. The musk ox was introduced in 1929, and it seems to be thriving, living on the meager grass and willow shrubs of the tundra from which the snow has been blown by strong winds. The vegetation they eat is either withered or frozen, but even on such a poor diet the musk ox can attain a weight of up to eight hundred and eighty pounds. The reindeer subsists mainly on lichens, which it scrapes from beneath the snow with its hoofs.

KOLGUEV, VAIGACH, AND NOVAYA ZEMLYA

The islands of northeasternmost Europe are mostly beyond the influence of the Gulf Stream, and are therefore more Arctic in character than Spitsbergen.

The extensive tundra on the islands of Kolguev and Vaigach, overgrown with lichens, reach a maximum height of about three hundred feet above sea level. The latter island which, like Novaya Zemlya, is a continuation of the Ural Mountains, has been worn down to a lowland by erosion, while Novaya Zemlya is still highland. The highest mountain on Novaya Zemlya is 3543 feet high; although erosion is fairly rapid there, the land itself is rising.

The twin islands of Novaya Zemlya, separated by a narrow sound, are together almost as large as Iceland. Like Spitsbergen, the northern part of Novaya Zemlya, in spite of its more

southerly situation, is largely covered with glaciers. During a five-year period in the 1930's the mean temperature in January was much lower than on Spitsbergen. Nevertheless, the flora and fauna of the two groups of islands are very similar. Characteristic plants are such creeping species as polar willow *(Salix polaris)*, twinleaf saxifrage *(Saxifraga oppositifolia)*, mountain avens *(Geum montanum)*, and mountain lichens *(Erastium arvense)*. Among the exceptions is a species of tundra sweetgrass *(Hierochloë pauciflora)*.

Except for the great black-backed gull, the same species of birds inhabit the cliffs of Novaya Zemlya as are found on Spitsbergen. This is also generally true of the birds on the tundra—among which are the purple sandpiper and the ringed plover, the arctic skua and the long-tailed skua. Among the several species that are not found on Spitsbergen, but that occur on Novaya Zemlya, are the Pomarine skua, the little stint, the black-throated diver, the white-billed diver *(Gavia adamsii)*, the white-fronted goose, the Bewick's swan, the red-breasted merganser, the peregrine, the arctic redpoll,

the Lapland bunting, the white wagtail and the snowy owl.

The reindeer and the arctic fox are common on Novaya Zemlya, and the same marine animals are found there as around Spitsbergen; the walrus is, however, more numerous. Of freshwater fish, the char is distributed on Novaya Zemlya.

FRANZ JOSEF LAND

An Arctic archipelago of about eight hundred islands, Franz Josef Land is the most northerly territory of Europe, lying between latitudes 80° and 82° N, and about six hundred miles from the North Pole. Almost every part of the archipelago, land as well as water, is covered by ice. The islands consist mostly of low plateaus with a few mountains, the highest of which is more than three thousand feet high. About ninety-seven per cent of the land area is hidden by glaciers. Geologically, the islands consist of marine sediment (from Jurassic times, more than 130 million years ago), above which

a layer of basalt about sixty feet thick was deposited by volcanic action after the sea had receded. The area seems then to have been a continuous expanse of land, that was later broken by faults into numerous islands.

In spite of its location in the extreme north, the mean temperature of Franz Josef Land is not particularly low. The coldest month is March, with a mean temperature of -8° F (-22.2° C), while July is the warmest, with a mean temperature of 2.34° F (-16.5° C). The vegetation consists mainly of lichens which, on latitude 76° N on the west coast, are represented by more than two hundred species. About seventy flowering plants have succeeded in colonizing the ice-free zones in the same region. The polar bear is always found in this northern archipelago, and in summer, after a long trek over the ice, the arctic fox visits the islands where it helps itself to the abundance of eggs and young birds.

Birds occupy nearly every habitable corner of the region. The black guillemot breeds among the boulders on the shore; the silver tern on the beach; the Brünnich's guillemot, fulmar

Herd of musk ox on the barren ground in the interior of Spitsbergen. The species was long extinct in Europe but has now been successfully introduced on Spitsbergen and in Norway. (Sven Gillsater: Tio)

and glaucous gull in the fissures in the cliffs; the little auk on the mountain slopes; the red-throated diver, brant goose, purple sandpiper, Sabine's gull and Arctic skua on the coastal tundra; the eider by the sea and lakes on the tundra; the snow bunting in the screes near the beach; and the ivory gull near a calving glacier.

For a short period each year, during which the sun never sets, there is seething life on these desolate islands of the Arctic Ocean. Birds fly back and forth between the sea and their nests, and the hubbub of hundreds of thousands of their voices is heard all through the long Arctic day. For some ten months of the year, however, silence reigns supreme and everything seems lifeless. It is almost impossible to imagine an Arctic winter on latitude 82° N. The continuous night is lighted only now and again by the pale light of the moon or the rays of the aurora borealis reflected by the white snow and ice. The Arctic silence is broken only by the whining of the wind and the muffled thunder of the pack ice.

Bibliography

Listed here are only those works that have been of particular value in the preparation of this book and should therefore be of interest to readers who want further information.

2 MEDITERRANEAN LANDS

Couturier, M. A. J. (1959). Statut actuel des représentants du genre *Capra* dans le bassin Méditerranéen. In Animaux et végétaux rares de la région Méditerranéenne. *La Terre et la Vie,* Supplément, pp. 12—19.

Moreau, R. E. (1961). Problems of Mediterranean-Saharan migration. *Ibis,* 103A:373—427, 580—623.

Zeuner, F. E. (1963). *A history of domesticated animals.* London.

3 SPAIN

Bernis, F. (1955). An ecological view of Spanish avifauna. Acta XI, Congressus Internationalis Ornithologici. *Experientia,* Supplementum III:417—423.

Mountfort, G. (1958). *Portrait of a wilderness.* London.
   (1961). The birds of the Coto Doñana. Ibis, 103A:86—109.

Nicholson, E. M., Ferguson-Lees, I. J. and Hollom, P. A. D. (1957). The Camargue and the Coto Doñana. *British Birds,* 50:497—519.

Valverde, J. A. (1957). Notes écologiques sur le lynx d'Espagne, *Felis lynx pardina* Temminck. *La Terre et la Vie,* pp. 51—67.

Valverde, J. A. (1958). An ecological sketch of the Coto Doñana. *British Birds,* 51:1—23.

4 THE CAMARGUE

Bigot, L. (1957). Un micromilieu important de Camargue. *La Terre et la Vie,* pp. 211—230.

Gallet, E. (1949). *Les flamants roses de Camargue.* Lausanne.

Hoffmann, L. (1958). An ecological sketch of the Camargue. *British Birds,* 51:321—350.

Lévêque, R. (1957). L'avifaune nidificatrice des eaux saumâtres camarguaises en 1956. *La Terre et la Vie,* pp. 150—178.

Nicholson, E. M., Ferguson-Lees, I. J. and Hollom, P. A. D. (1957). The Camargue and the Coto Doñana. *British Birds,* 50:497—519.

Schloeth, R. (1961). Das Sozialleben des Camargue-Rindes. *Zeitschrift für Tierpsychologie,* 18:574—627.

Tallon, G. (1959). Les sols alcalins de Camargue et leur végétation. *La Terre et la Vie,* pp. 1—17.

Yeates, G. K. (1946). *Bird life in two deltas.* London.
   (1950). *Flamingo city.* London.

6 THE BALKAN PENINSULA

Fries, C. (1959). The fate of Arcadia. In *Erosion and Civilizations.* Seventh Technical Meeting of the International Union for Conservation of Nature and Natural Resources. Vol. I. Brussels.

Goulimis, C. (1959). Report on species of plants requiring protection in Greece. In Animaux et végétaux rares de la région Méditerranéenne. *La Terre et la Vie,* Supplément, pp. 168—188.

Hyams, E. (1952). Soil and civilization. 312 pp. London.

Janssens, E. (1959). Fluctuations historiques et géographiques en Grèce. In *Erosion and Civilizations.* Seventh Technical Meeting of the International Union for Conservation of Nature and Natural Resources. Vol. I. Brussels.

Mistardis, G. G. (1959). Effets de l'érosion sur le déclin de la civilisation mycénienne. *Ibid.*

Monod, T. (1959). Parts respectives de l'homme et des phénomènes naturels dans la dégradation du paysage et le déclin des civilisations à travers le monde méditerranéen *Lato sensu. Ibid.*

Stanković, S. (1960). The Balkan lake Ohrid and its living world. *Monographiae Biologicae,* 9:1—367.

7 BLACK AND CASPIAN SEAS AND THE CAUCASUS

Berg, L. S. (1950). *Natural regions of the U.S.S.R.* New York.

Bodea, M. et al. (1958). *Din viata Deltei Dunarii.* Bucharest.

Caspers, H. (1951). Die bulgarische Fischerei im Schwarzen Meer. *Abhandlungen aus der Fischerei und deren Hilfswissenschaften,* 4:719—786.

Ekman, S. (1953). *Zoogeography of the sea.* London.

Fuhn, I. E. (1960). Amphibia. *Fauna Republicii Populare Romine.* XIV. Fasc. 1:1—289.

Fuhn, I. E. & Vancea, S. (1961). Reptilia. *Fauna Republicii Populare Romine.* XIV. Fasc. 2:1—353.

Vasiliu, G. D. (1959). *Pestii apelor noastre.* Bucharest.

Zenkevitch, L. (1963). *Biology of the seas of the U.S.S.R.* London.

8 STEPPES OF THE U.S.S.R.

Bannikow, A. G. (1961). The biology of the saiga antelope. Moscow. (In Russian.)
   (1963). *Die Saiga-Antilope.* Wittenberg Lutherstadt.

Berg, L. S. (1950). *Natural regions of the U.S.S.R.* New York.

Formozov, A. N. & Kodachova, K. S. (1961). Les rongeurs vivant en colonies dans la steppe eurasienne. *La Terre et la Vie,* pp. 116—129.

Haviland, M. D. (1926). *Forest, steppe and tundra.* Cambridge.

Mohr, E. (1959). Das Urwildpferd. Wittenberg Lutherstadt.
   Proceedings of the Central Governmental District of the Black Earth. Kursk. (In Russian.)

9 THE CARPATHIANS

Beldie, A. (1956). Rezervatia Naturala "Bucegi." *Ocrotirea Naturii,* 2:31—63.

George, P. & Tricart, J. (1954). *L'Europe Centrale.* Vol. I. Paris.

Marchlewski, M. (1960). The Tatra National Park. *State Council for Conservation of Nature,* 4:1—19. Warsaw.

Smolski, S. (1960). Pieninsky Park Narodowy. *Polska Akademia Nauk,* 18:1—272.

10 THE HUNGARIAN PUSZTA

Mountfort, G. (1962). *Portrait of a river.* London.

Scott, P. (1946). *Wild chorus.* 119 pp. Glasgow.

Zimmermann, R. (1944). *Beiträge zur Kenntnis der Vogelwelt des Neusiedler Seegebiets.* Vienna.

11 THE ALPS

Dottrens, E. (1950). Le Corégone actuel de Léman. *Revue Suisse de Zoologie,* 57:789—813.
   (1959). Systématique des Corégones de l'Europe occidentale. *Ibid.* 66:1—66.

Richard, J.-L. (1961). Les forêts acidophiles du Jura. *Beiträge zur geobotanischen Landesaufnahme der Schweiz,* 38:1—164.

Vaucher, C. (1946). *La vie sauvage en montagne.* Geneva.

13 THE BRITISH ISLES AND IRELAND

Atkinson-Willes, G. L. (ed.) (1963). Wildfowl in Britain. *Monographs of the Nature Conservancy*, 3:1–368.
Boyd, H. and Scott, P. (1955). The British population of the pink-footed goose. *Annual Report of the Wildfowl Trust*, 7:99–106.
Darling, F. F. (1937). *A herd of red deer*. London.
        (1939). *A naturalist on Rona*. Oxford.
        (1947). *Natural history in the highlands and islands*. London.
Fisher J. (1952). *The fulmar*. London.
Fisher, J. and Lockley, R. M. (1954). *Sea-birds*. London.
Gordon, S. (1955). *The golden eagle*. London.
Jenkins, D., Watson, A. and Miller, G. R. (1963). Population studies on red grouse, *Lagopus lagopus scoticus* (Lath.), in northeast Scotland. *Journal of Animal Ecology*, 32:317–376.
Lack, D. (1942). Ecological features of the bird faunas of British small islands. *Ibid.*, 10:9–36.
Lockley, R. M. (1953). *Puffins*. London.
Matthews, L. H. (1952). *British mammals*. London.
Praeger, R. L. (1950). *Natural history of Ireland*. London.
Shorten, M. (1954). *Squirrels*. London.
Smith, M. (1951). *The British amphibians and reptiles*. London.
Stamp, L. D. (1948). *The land of Britain*. London.

14 DECIDUOUS FORESTS

Berg, L. S. (1950). *Natural regions of the U.S.S.R.* New York.
Garnett, A. (1945). The loess region in Central Europe in prehistoric times. *Geographical Journal*, CVI:132–143.
George, P. & Tricart, J. (1954). *L'Europe Centrale*. Vol. I. Paris.
Gut, S. (1960). Le Parc National d'Ojców. *Conseil National pour la Protection de la Nature, Pologne*. 15:1–16.
Hoffmann, G. W. (1953). *A geography of Europe*. London.
Jentys-Szaferowa, J. (1953). Studia nad brzoza ojcowska *(Betula oycoviensis Bess.)*. *Ochrona Przyrody*, 21:34–57.
Pachlewski, R. (1960). The Bialowieza National Park. *State Council for Conservation of Nature*, 14:1–25. Poland.
Schou, A. & Antonsen, K. (1960). Denmark. In A. Sømme, *A geography of Norden*, pp. 87–136. Oslo.
Turěk, F. J. (1955). Bird populations of some Lowland forests near the Danube in southern Slovakia. Acta XI, Congressus Internationalis Ornithologici. *Experientia*, Supplementum III:532–536.
Vaucher, C. (1954–1955). Contribution à l'étude ornithologique de Dombes. *Alauda*, 22:81–271; 23:108–136, 182–211.

15 THE BALTIC SEA

Albertson, N. (1950). Das grosse südliche Alvar der Insel Öland. *Svensk Botanisk Tidskrift*, 44:269–331.
Hausen, H. (ed.) (1946). Ålands natur. 243 pp. Åbo.
Hörstadius, S. & Curry-Lindahl, K. (ed.) (1948). *Natur i Uppland*. Göteborg.
Paludan, K. (1962). Ederfuglene i de danske farvande. *Danske Vildtundersøgelser*, 10:1–87.
Pettersson, B. & Curry-Lindahl, K. (ed.) (1946). *Natur på Gotland*. Göteborg.
Sterner, R. & Curry-Lindahl, K. (ed.) (1955). *Natur på Öland*. Uppsala.
Sømme, A. (ed.) (1960). *A geography of Norden*. Bergen.

16 THE SCANDINAVIAN MOUNTAIN CHAIN

Curry-Lindahl, K. (ed.) (1963). *Natur i Lappland*. I–II. Uppsala.
        (ed.) (1959–1963). *Våra Fåglar i Norden*. I–IV.
Dahl, E. (1955). Biogeographic and geologic indications of unglaciated areas in Scandinavia. *Bulletin of the Geological Society of America*, 66:1499–1520.

Du Rietz, G. E. (1942). De svenska fjällens växtvärld. *Ymer*. 62:169–190.
Ekman, S. (1922). *Djurvärldens utbredningshistoria på Skandinaviska halvön*. Stockholm.
Faegri, K. (1949). Studies on the Pleistocene of western Norway. IV. Universitetet i Bergen Årbok. Nat. rekke. I–1–53.
Faegri, K., Gjaerevoll, O., Lid, J. & Nordhagen, R. (ed.) (1960). *Maps of distribution of Norwegian vascular plants*. I (Coast Plants). Oslo.
Hoppe, G. (1957). Problems of glacial morphology and the Ice Age. *Geografiska Annaler*, 39:1–18.
Hultén, E. (1950). *Atlas över växternas utbredning i Norden*. Stockholm.
Lundqvist, G. (1948). *De svenska fjällens natur*. 2nd ed. Stockholm.
Magnusson, N. H., Lundvist, G. & Granlund, E. (1957). *Sveriges geologi*. 3rd ed. Stockholm.
Sjörs, H. (1956). *Nordisk växtgeografi*. Stockholm.
Sømme, A. (ed.) (1960). *A geography of Norden*. Oslo.
Ångström, A. (1946). *Sveriges klimat*. Stockholm.

17 NORTHERN EUROPE

Berg, L. S. (1950). *Natural regions of the U.S.S.R.* New York.
Couturier, M. A. J. (1954). *L'ours brun*. Grenoble.
Curry-Lindahl, K. (ed.) (1963). *Natur i Lappland*. I–II. Uppsala.
Kalliola, R. (1959). *Finlandia*. Helsinki.
Novikov, G. A. (1962). *Carnivorous mammals of the fauna of the U.S.S.R.* Jerusalem.
Ognev, S. I. (1962). *Mammals of eastern Europe and northern Asia*. Vol. I. Jerusalem.
        (1963). *Mammals of the U.S.S.R. and adjacent countries*. Vol. V. Jerusalem.
Sjörs, H. (1956). *Nordisk växtgeografi*. Stockholm.
Sømme, A. (ed.) (1960). *A geography of Norden*. Bergen.

18 THE TUNDRA

Berg, L. S. (1950). *Natural regions of the U.S.S.R.* New York.

19 ATLANTIC AND ARCTIC ISLANDS

Ahlmann, H. W. & Thorarinsson, S. (1937–1943). Vatnajökull. *Geografiska Annaler*, 19:146–231; 20:171–233; 21:39–65, 171–242; 22:188–205; 25:1–54.
Berg, L. S. (1950). *Natural regions of the U.S.S.R.* New York.
Degerbøl, M. (1940). Mammalia. In *Zoology of the Faroes*, 65:1–132.
Freuchen, P. and Salomonsen, F. (1958). *The arctic year*. New York.
Gudmundsson, F. (1960). Some reflections on ptarmigan cycles in Iceland. XII. *International Ornithological Congress*, pp. 259–265. Helsinki.
Lundgren, S. (1958). *Björnöya*. Stockholm.
Pedersen, A. (1945). Der Eisbär *(Thalarctos maritimus Phipps)*. Copenhagen.
Salomonsen, F. (1935). Aves. In *Zoology of the Faroes*, 64:1–269.
Scott, P., Boyd, H. and Sladen, W.J.L. (1955). The Wildfowl Trust's second expedition to central Iceland, 1953. *Seventh Annual Report of the Wildfowl Trust*, 1953–1954, pp. 63–98.
Scott, P. and Fisher, J. (1954). *A thousand geese*. 2nd ed. London.
Scott, P., Fisher, J. and Gudmundsson, F. (1952). The Severn Wildfowl Trust expedition to central Iceland, 1951. *Fifth Annual Report of the Severn Wildfowl Trust*, 1951–1952, pp. 79–115.
Sømme, A. (ed.) (1960). *A geography of Norden*. Bergen.
Tolmachev, A. J. (1936). Obzor flory Novoy Zemli. *Artica*, 4:143–174.
Voous, K. H. (1960). *Atlas of European birds*. Amsterdam.
Yeates, G. K. (1951). *The land of the loon*. London.
Zubkov, L. I. (1935). Dikie oleni Novoy Zemli. *Trudy Arkt. Inst.*, 12:55–60.

THE AUTHOR

Kai Curry-Lindahl, a leading European zoologist, ecologist and conservation expert, is Director of Natural History at the Nordiska Museum in Stockholm. An advisor to many governments on the preservation of wildlife, he has lived, studied or traveled in every part of Europe from northernmost Lapland (where he is currently carrying out wildlife research) to Spain's rich Coto Doñana, the steppes of the Ukraine and the high Caucasus. He is the author of many books and scientific papers, the latest being *Nordens Djurvärld,* a comprehensive volume on the animal life of Scandinavia.

ENGRAVED AND PRINTED BY CONZETT AND HUBER OF ZURICH — DESIGNED BY ULRICH RUCHTI

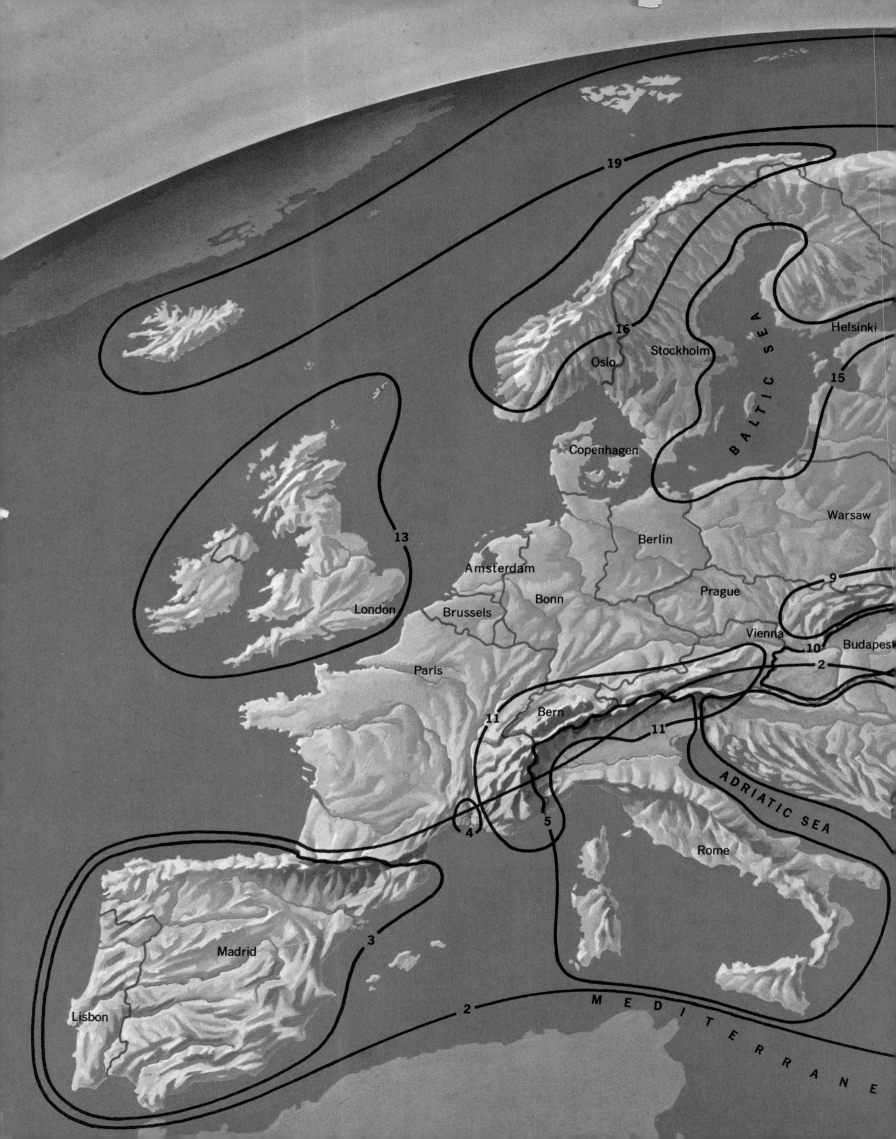